# Crime and the Media

# Crime and the Media

By Sarah E.H. Moore

First published 2014 by
PALGRAVE MACMILLAN

Palgrave Macmillan in the UK is an imprint of Macmillan Publishers Limited, registered in England, company number 785998, of Houndmills, Basingstoke, Hampshire RG21 6XS.

Palgrave Macmillan in the US is a division of St Martin's Press LLC, 175 Fifth Avenue, New York, NY 10010.

Palgrave Macmillan is the global academic imprint of the above companies and has companies and representatives throughout the world.

Palgrave® and Macmillan® are registered trademarks in the United States, the United Kingdom, Europe and other countries.

ISBN: 978–0–230–30288–4 hardback
ISBN: 978–0–230–30289–1 paperback

This book is printed on paper suitable for recycling and made from fully managed and sustained forest sources. Logging, pulping and manufacturing processes are expected to conform to the environmental regulations of the country of origin.

A catalogue record for this book is available from the British Library.

A catalog record for this book is available from the Library of Congress.

Typeset by Cambrian Typesetters, Camberley, Surrey.

Printed in China.

*For Alex, Sylvie, and Fraser*

# Contents

List of figures and tables                                                xii

Acknowledgements                                                          xiii

**Introduction**                                                            **1**

—Crime categories in the news: creating new words in the 'dictionary
   of fear'                                                                 3

—'Knife crime' in the news: or, five golden rules for studying crime news   4

—The Madeleine McCann case: the mass media as 'institutionalised
   story-teller' and 'moral guardian'                                       8

—Overview of the book                                                     10

## PART I: Crime in the news

**Introduction**                                                           **15**

**Chapter 1: How does crime become news?**                                 **17**

—Sourcing crime news                                                      21

—Selecting crime news                                                     25

—Online news: who selects the news now?                                   34

—Questions for discussion                                                 35

—Chapter summary                                                          36

—Recommended reading                                                      37

**Chapter 2: Terrorism in the news**                                       **39**

—Why does terrorism top the global news agenda?                           40

—Rhetorical devices in the 'semantics of terror'                          42

—The Northern Irish Troubles in the British news                          44

—The Israel–Arab conflict in the UK and US news                           49

—Explaining the pro-state line in news reporting on terrorism             53

—The political uses of terrorism                                          55

—Questions for discussion                                                 59

—Chapter summary                                                    59
—Recommended reading                                                61

**Chapter 3: Victims of sexual violence in the news**               **62**
—How newsworthy is sexual violence?                                 63
—Rape in the news                                                   64
—Child sex abuse in the news                                        73
—Questions for discussion                                           80
—Chapter summary                                                    80
—Recommended reading                                                82

**Chapter 4: Crime news effects**                                   **84**
—The effect of crime news on government policy and legislation      85
—Registering crime news on our emotional radars                     87
—A word (or two) of warning                                         87
—Crime news as a shaper of public attitudes                         89
—Does crime news increase our fear of crime?                        91
—Media effects as diffuse                                           93
—Questions for discussion                                           94
—Chapter summary                                                    94
—Recommended reading                                                95

## PART II: Conceptualising media coverage of crime

**Introduction**                                                    **99**

**Chapter 5: Moral panic**                                          **103**
—The pioneers of moral panic theory                                 104
—Moral panic studies in the USA                                     111
—Are moral panics a thing of the past?                              114
—Moral panics as moral regulation                                   117
—Chapter summary                                                    119
—Recommended reading                                                121

**Chapter 6: Cautionary tales**                                     **123**
—The cautionary tale: key features                                  123
—Identifying cautionary tales                                       126
—The social origins of cautionary tales                             128
—Questions for discussion                                           130
—Chapter summary                                                    130
—Recommended reading                                                131

**Chapter 7: Crime legends**    **133**
—Conveying crime legends: from word-of-mouth to e-mail forwards    134
—Core themes    137
—Why have we seen the proliferation of crime legends?    138
—Questions for discussion    140
—Chapter summary    141
—Recommended reading    142

**Chapter 8: Cultural trauma**    **143**
—Defining cultural trauma    144
—Representing cultural trauma: the role of the mass media    145
—Crime as the precipitating event in cultural trauma    147
—Questions for discussion    150
—Chapter summary    151
—Recommended reading    152

## PART III: Analysing the media

**Introduction**    **155**
—A preliminary observation    156
—Developing a research question    157
—Accessing data    158
—Sampling    161

**Chapter 9: Content analysis**    **163**
—Quantifying media content and examining use of language    164
—Thinking through content analysis: studying homicide in the British
 news and references to violence in rap lyrics    168
—Chapter summary    174
—Recommended reading    174
—Workshop session    175

**Chapter 10: Narrative analysis**    **177**
—Structuralism as a forerunner to narrative analysis    178
—Analysing narratives    179
—Visual narrative analysis: studying *Superman*    183
—Thinking through narrative analysis: studying female criminals in the
 news    186
—Chapter summary    190
—Recommended reading    191
—Workshop session    191

**Chapter 11: Discourse analysis**     **193**
—Approaches to discourse analysis: Foucault and Fairclough     195
—Analysing texts using discourse analysis     197
—Thinking through discourse analysis: studying mass media depictions
    of incarceration, domestic violence, and gang violence     201
—Chapter summary     208
—Recommended reading     208
—Workshop session     209

## PART IV: Fictional worlds of crime, justice, and order

**Introduction**     **213**

**Chapter 12: Revenge and retribution in *Deadwood***     **215**
—Morality, law, and order in the Western     216
—The West and the Western     219
—Introducing *Deadwood*     220
—Unruly and rule-based justice in *Deadwood*     221
—Concluding discussion     226
—Questions for discussion     227
—Recommended viewing     227
—Recommended reading     227

**Chapter 13: Prison and rehabilitation in *A Clockwork Orange*:**
**thinking afresh about 'what works'**     **229**
—Prison drama and penal populism     230
—How and why do we punish?     232
—Punishment in *A Clockwork Orange*     233
—Concluding discussion     239
—Questions for discussion     239
—Recommended reading     240

**Chapter 14: Stories of criminal detection from Christie to *CSI***     **241**
—Early detective fiction     241
—Styles of detection and characterisation     242
—Detective-work in Christie's novels: rooting out the bad apples     244
—Detective-work in hard-boiled fiction: stepping inside the underworld     249
—Detective-work in *CSI*: routine investigations     252
—Concluding discussion     254
—Questions for discussion     257
—Recommended fiction     258
—Recommended reading     258

**Chapter 15: Passing judgement: the 'double trial structure' of four Hollywood legal dramas**      **259**
—Places of performance, spectatorship, and judgement: the courtroom
   in legal drama      261
—Golden Age legal drama: law on trial      263
—Legal drama of the mid-1990s: corporate greed and political
   self-interest on trial      267
—Concluding discussion      271
—Questions for discussion      273
—Recommended reading      273

**Chapter 16: 'Real-life' crime and police-work in *Cops***      **275**
—The rise of 'real-life' crime television      276
—The camera as a neutral spectator in *Cops*      277
—The selective view of police-work and crime in *Cops*      284
—*Cops* and the pro-police line      285
—Concluding discussion      286
—Questions for discussion      287
—Recommended reading      287

**Conclusion**      **289**
—Recurring narrative features in contemporary crime stories      291

*Bibliography*      297
*Index*      315

# List of figures and tables

## Figures

0.1 The number of mentions of 'knife crime' in UK national newspapers 1998—2008   5

0.2 Total homicides and homicides by sharp instrument, 1998—2008   6

9.1 Comparing the number of articles about 'gun crime' in three US national newspapers, 2001—2011   165

9.2 Bar chart comparing the average word count of newspaper articles about 'gun crime' in three US national newspapers   166

12.1 The mob confronts the law   222

12.2 'I'll help you with the fall': formal justice by any means   224

13.1 Being made to toe the line: Alex is admitted to prison   234

13.2 Rehabilitative treatment as corporal punishment   238

16.1 The camera comes along for the ride ...   279

16.2 ... but is too slow to keep up with the police   279

16.3 The chase, unedited ...   281

16.4 ... and the subsequent police framing   281

## Tables

4.1 Triggers for fear in crime news   92

5.1 Comparing moral panics, crime legends, cautionary tales, and media representations of cultural trauma   101

5.2 Comparing newspapers/television news and the Internet as sources of news   115

6.1 Two poles of moral regulation in media reporting on crime   125

9.1 Example of a preliminary analysis schedule   164

# Acknowledgements

This book was written during an especially full and changeful period of my life: I started writing it shortly after giving birth to my first child and finished it not long after having had my second. My first thanks, then, go to Sylvie and Fraser for affording me the time to write and giving me something worth writing for. My deepest gratitude goes also to Alex Clayton for his support and all-round cleverness. The anonymous reviewers of the book need special mention too – their suggestions were always useful, considered, and helped me see the proverbial wood for the trees. I've enjoyed an excellent relationship with my editors – particularly Anna Reeve – and am hugely grateful for their support, advice, and patience during the writing of this book. Finally, my thanks to the undergraduate students at Queen's University, Belfast, and Royal Holloway, University of London, who took my 'Crime and the Media' course over the past six years. Amongst other things, they've helped me understand what it means to be coming to these issues for the very first time.

The author and publisher would like to acknowledge the inclusion of screen captures from:

*Deadwood*, Season 1, Episode 1 (2004), directed by Walter Hill and produced by David Milch (executive producer), Gregg Fienberg (co-executive producer), Davis Guggenheim, Scott Stephens, Steve Turner, Walter Hill, Jody Worth, Hilton Smith, Kathryn Lekan and Bernadette McNamara, HBO, Paramount Television and Red Board Productions;

*A Clockwork Orange* (1971 USA, 1972 UK), directed and produced by Stanley Kubrick, Warner Bros;

*Cops*, Season 20, Episodes 1 & 7 (2007), produced by John Langley (executive producer), Douglas Waterman, Jimmy Langley, Morgan Langley, John La Court, Hank Barr, Steve Kiger and Bryan Jerel Collins, Langley Productions, Fox Television Stations and 20th Century Fox Television.

# Introduction

Try this experiment: go online and check today's newspaper headlines, best-seller novel lists, video games reviews, and 'top 20' movie chart. Now go and have a look through a television guide for the coming week. The test should confirm something that you might have long had a hunch about: a very significant proportion of mass media output is devoted in some way to crime – more than is given over to romance, war, or comedy. From video games that allow us to participate in Mafia-style violence to newspaper reports about the latest terrorist atrocity, from the Wallander mysteries that fill our bedside cabinets (and television schedules) to the legal dramas that are so beloved of Hollywood – the mass media are saturated with images of crime, justice, and disorder. Together, they create a cultural landscape of crime, one that is distinctly at odds with reality, as criminologists are apt to complain. The mass media tend to portray crime as widespread, out of control, and mainly violent. None of this is true – for most of us, at least. In most economically advanced countries, the overall crime rate has been on a steady decrease since the mid-1990s and the vast majority of recorded crime (roughly three-quarters) consists of property offences. In fact, for most of us, the only experience we have of serious crime, courts, and prison is vicarious and mediated by television, films, and news reports.

This book attempts to make sense of the cultural landscape of crime and its relationship to broader social trends and public attitudes. The discussion ranges across media formats and texts – from *CSI* to *Superman*, e-mailed crime legends to detective novels, Westerns to trial movies. We consider crime news as well as fictional representations of cops, courts, and corrections. The discussion draws particularly on British cases and media, but includes numerous examples and studies from around the world, with media output from the USA, Australia, and New Zealand especially well represented. The book has three main aims. First, to provide a critical discussion of crime and the media that is informed by scholarly work from a range of disciplines, principally sociology and criminology, but also cultural studies, social psychology, film studies, and media studies. Parts I and IV of this book contain chapters that make use of this interdisciplinary approach to critically examine the depiction of criminals and victims in the news and fictional worlds of crime, justice, and order. The book's second aim is to equip students with a better understanding of key theoretical concepts and methodological tools to undertake analysis of media texts. Parts II and III are directed towards achieving this aim. Here you'll find chapters introducing key concepts for studying crime in the media and methods for analysing a range of media texts, including news, songs, television programmes, comic-books, and films. The book's final aim is to identify recurring narrative features in contemporary crime stories. To this end, the Conclusion draws together our discussion of various media texts and formats to consider what they have in common as crime stories.

The book is also structured around a set of core concerns to which we frequently return. These include the selective media representation of violence, victimhood, and crime control; the participation of mass media depictions of crime, justice, and order in broader cultural currents; the contribution of media texts to criminological understanding; the role of multimedia platforms and social media in changing media consumption; and the problems in presuming that specific elements of the media cause us to think, act, and feel a certain way. The latter might seem like an obvious point, but a good number of studies on crime in the media imply that whatever item or format is being looked at has a monolithic influence over public opinion – and that, I think, is a great mistake. Take, for example, the popular suggestion that the TV show *CSI* is responsible for raising the US public's expectations of scientific evidence in serious trials – the so-called '*CSI* Effect'. To draw a connection between one programme and public attitudes is to imagine the various elements of our culture as operating unilaterally, and that is a view this book actively works against. In Chapter 4 I consider this argument in relation to the 'Media Effects' debate (and we return, here, to the argument about the '*CSI* Effect'). For now it's enough to say that this book generally approaches the mass media as *elements* of a culture and society, as part of a *cultural landscape*, as I put it above. Looked at from this perspective, the *overall* picture of crime, justice, and order in mass media representations becomes something of real interest – hence the fact that this book ranges across media texts and formats.

Before any of this, and by way of introduction, we turn to something really foundational: the mass media's role in transforming raw events into stories. Below we look at the construction of crime categories, first in general terms and then by considering the example of 'knife crime' – and along the way we start to think about how to go about studying crime news. We turn then to a discussion of the global media coverage of the Madeleine McCann case to consider further the mass media's role as a story-teller. The Introduction ends with an overview of the book.

## Crime categories in the news: creating new words in the 'dictionary of fear'

The US sociologist Joel Best has devoted considerable attention to how social problems are produced by claims-making groups, the media, and other social institutions. In his book *Random Violence* he makes a useful distinction between an *incident* and an *instance*: crime news often works towards transforming the former into the latter by suggesting that a single event is an example of a broader crime problem (an instance *of something*, in other words). We're all familiar with the news vernacular that marks this transition, the labelling of a given event as part of an 'epidemic', 'crime wave', 'spate', or 'outbreak'. Categorising a crime using a popular tag – 'knife crime' or 'mugging', say – is an integral part of this labelling process, and is often a stage in the production of a full-blown moral panic (see Chapter 5 for more on this). Let's leave aside the role of crime categories in producing moral panics for now, suffice it to say that the construction of such a label is a sufficient though not necessary condition for the emergence of a moral panic. Best, for one, is more interested in the use of such crime categories as a journalistic convention, that is, as a typical step in the production of crime news. He takes the cases of 'freeway shooting' and 'wilding' as examples. In the spring of 1989 a young woman was viciously attacked and gang-raped in Manhattan's Central Park. Within days news stories started to report that the incident was a case of 'wilding' – a term that the youths arrested for the attack had apparently used to describe the crime. As Best (1999: 29) comments,

> Wilding seized the media's imagination. What had been a local crime story now received coverage on all three network news broadcasts ... on ABC's Nightline ... and in newspapers nationwide (the *Los Angeles Times* called wilding 'a chilling new word ... in the dictionary of fear') ... Nevermind that no one seemed sure whether 'wilding' was actually a term from the youths' vernacular or just a product of a misunderstanding.

At their most successful, crime categories do indeed become 'chilling' new words in the 'dictionary of fear'. They sometimes emerge in the manner 'wilding' did: with one particularly newsworthy and horrific event. More often, though, they are the product of a more drawn-out process of journalistic invention. Journalists, Best observes, are always looking out for crime trends:

they have, he comments, 'a rule of thumb: the third time something happens, you have a trend' (p. 31). In practice this means that, after one or two incidents of a given crime, journalists are looking out for a third case that will warrant the creation of a category to describe a new crime wave. The case of 'freeway shooting' serves as a useful example here. Two unrelated shootings on freeways in 1987 meant that journalists were poised to pronounce a new crime problem. At the *Los Angeles Times* a reporter was even assigned to write an item on the issue in preparation for a third – and, in journalistic terms, conclusive – incident that remotely resembled the first and second. It is, of course, easy to find something if you actively go looking for it: after another vaguely similar incident occurred, newspapers started to report on the 'freeway shooting' crime wave. 'As the story received more attention', Best observes, 'the freeway shootings category began showing elasticity: not all reported incidents occurred on freeways, and not all involved shooting' (p. 32). Thus, once the crime category had caught on it came to be applied liberally – this had the double benefit of reinforcing the popularity of the label and transforming otherwise singular and un-newsworthy 'incidents' into 'instances' of a bigger problem.

Crime categories such as 'wilding' and 'freeway shooting' serve various functions: They condense a crime problem, providing a useful shorthand for headlines and stand-firsts. They also seem to suggest that a genuinely new social problem has emerged (one that even has a name!), thus ensuring public interest in the story. What should be abundantly clear from the above discussion is that the act of categorising a set of incidents as instances of a crime wave has more to do with journalistic enterprise than anything else. Let's have a look at an example of our own – and, along the way, I want to introduce you to five rules for studying crime news.

## 'Knife crime' in the news: or, five golden rules for studying crime news

In 2007 the British press started reporting on a new crime category – 'knife crime'. Figure 0.1 shows the number of mentions of 'knife crime' in national UK newspapers from 1998 to 2008.

We can clearly see the ascendancy of the crime category 'knife crime' in the British news here. The tempting conclusion to draw from all this is that there was an outbreak of 'knife crime' incidents during this period. Instead, as a rule:

> Never presume that a sharp increase in news coverage equates to more crime.

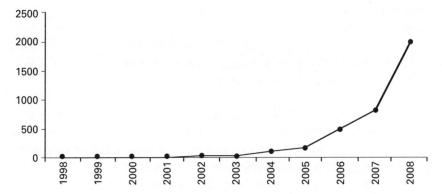

**Figure 0.1**    The number of mentions of 'knife crime' in UK national newspapers 1998–2008

*Source*: Nexis®. Figures are for the number of UK national newspaper articles that made 'major mention' of 'knife crime' 1998–2008. Reproduced by permission of Reed Elsevier (UK) Limited trading as LexisNexis.

In fact, if we dig a bit deeper, we find that the media emphasis on 'knife crime' is not commensurate with the official, statistical picture of 'knife crime'. The first thing we might notice when looking for statistical data to back up the media picture above is that 'knife crime' is not an official offence category at all (Eades *et al.* 2007: 10). This gives us our next golden rule for studying crime news:

> Ascertain whether the crime category used in media reports has an equivalence in legal or policing terms. If not, try to work out which institution created and originally promoted the category.

Hall *et al.* (2013), in their study of the mugging moral panic that beset the UK in the 1970s, trace the origin of the term 'mugging' and argue that the police were the 'primary definers' of the category – despite the fact that it had limited official application in terms of actual police-work. Best's work attests to the possibility of the media themselves being primary definers of a crime category, and this appears to be the case with the term 'knife crime'. During the period of media coverage we're looking at, the nearest concept in official Home Office terms was the offence category of 'knife-enabled crime'. It isn't as catchy as 'knife crime' and, more importantly, the Home Office only created this offence category in 2007, so there is no official statistical data on 'knife-enabled crime' prior to this (Silvestri *et al.* 2009: 10) . Yet, when we look closely at newspaper reports on 'knife crime' during this period many of them point to a sudden increase in incidents. The absence of long-term police records on this crime undermines such suggestions. Herein lies our third rule for studying crime news:

> Any statistics cited in the news and allusions to trends or changes in incident rates need to be carefully scrutinised.

Just because the official police data is lacking, of course, doesn't mean that 'knife crime' hasn't been on the increase. Eades *et al.* (2007) do a brilliant job of reviewing the available evidence – and there's a striking lack of supporting data for a significant increase in 'knife crime' during this period. Take, for example, the statistics for deaths caused by stabbings. The Homicide Index provides us with the relevant information. Again, we're rather stymied by the disjuncture between official measures and the popular conception of 'knife crime': the closest approximation to deaths caused by 'knife crime' is the category 'homicides by sharp instrument', and these can involve screwdrivers, broken bottles, as well as knives (Eades *et al.* 2007: 18). We might nonetheless reason that a really significant increase in 'knife crime' would involve an increase in this category of homicide. Figure 0.2 is based on Eades *et al.*'s (2007: 19) assimilation of data for 1998–2006 and Home Office data for 2006–2008.

As Eades *et al.* (2007: 19) note, what's immediately striking here is that the number of 'homicides by sharp instrument' is relatively unchanging across

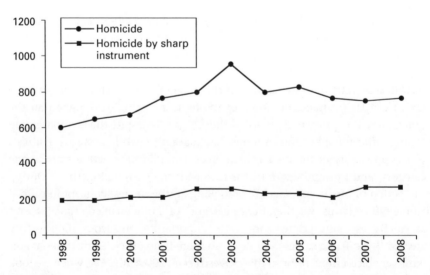

**Figure 0.2**   Total homicides and homicides by sharp instrument, 1998—2008
*Source*: Author's own graph based on Eades *et al.* (2007) and Home Office (2009).

the period. It's starting to look like the sharp increase in newspaper reporting on 'knife crime' doesn't reflect an increase in incident rates – the latter, in other words, does not adequately explain the former. Yet, and as most British readers of this book will recall, there has been real public and governmental concern about 'knife crime' during the last few years. We've even seen new, more punitive, legislation passed to punish those caught carrying knives (Eades *et al.* 2007: 8). All this should alert us to the fact that news coverage can construct a crime problem where none exists in official terms, and that the promotion of crime categories is central to this process.

As we found above in our discussion of 'freeway shootings', over time crime categories can be stretched and used to describe a whole range of incidents – and here we get our fourth rule:

> A crime category does not have a fixed meaning. We need to be alert to changes in the meaning of a category.

Take, for example, the crime category 'stalking'. In analysing the media's use of the term, Lowney and Best (1995) observe that the term (or 'typification', as they prefer) was originally used by US women's groups to refer to men following and harassing their female partners (so, again, it's not an official offence category). The term was only taken up by the US media once a female celebrity became a victim – and they co-opted the phrase to refer primarily to celebrities being followed by besotted, crazed male fans. As we'll see in Chapter 3, this is entirely in keeping with a focus on stranger-perpetrated crime in the news and a lack of media interest in acquaintance-perpetrated crime. The changing meaning of stalking is a striking example of this media bias, and it's by no means the only one. Elsewhere I've written about the shifting uses of the phrase 'date rape' in the US news (Moore 2011). Analysing US newspaper articles from the mid-1980s to the late-1990s I found that the original meaning of 'date rape' – a sexual assault by an intimate (literally, a date) – is now more generally used to refer to drug-facilitated sexual assault, a form of stranger rape. As with 'stalking', 'date rape' is a crime category that the media has co-opted from feminist groups and in both cases the original radical meaning of the term has been effaced.

All this alerts us to the importance of looking at the changing meaning and application of crime categories. It should also prompt us to think about the sort of social forces that are at work in the construction of the news. It's not just journalistic conventions that shape the creation of crime categories; more complex social factors, like norms and values, are at work too. Crime categories tend to support an overall picture of crime as random, inexplicable, and out of control: this, as we'll find at various points in this book, is a politically expedient story to tell about the problem of crime. If crime is centrally an issue of crazed people lashing out at whoever happens to be nearest, we don't have to confront the idea that social conditions give rise to violence and that some people, simply by virtue of their social position, are more likely to be victimised. If we're really interested in studying the media we need to be alive to these sorts of biases, and so we get our last golden rule:

> Approach the news critically, and always with a sense of its role in reinforcing social norms and perpetuating convenient myths about human behaviour.

If crime problems don't arise naturally, as it were, but are selected and subject to media invention, then this should prick our curiosity about the social and cultural conditions that have allowed for the ascendancy of a particular crime category – we should think 'Why *this* category, why *this* meaning, and why has it hit headlines *now*?' News reporting on crime, rather than being subject to some sort of ahistorical, primal desire for blood, guts, and titillation, is a product of a particular historical and cultural moment. We therefore need to be sensitive to socio-cultural shifts when attempting to understand media coverage of crime.

## The Madeleine McCann case: the mass media as 'institutionalised story-teller' and 'moral guardian'

Let's think a bit more deeply about the role of crime news in reinforcing social norms and values – in constructing convenient stories. We're going to focus here on the global media coverage of the kidnap of the British girl Madeleine McCann. I'd hazard a guess that this is a story all readers of this book are basically familiar with. In 2007 the McCann family were enjoying a holiday in Portugal. One evening, having put their children to bed, the McCanns decided to have dinner at a restaurant a little way from the holiday apartment. At some point during the evening, their eldest daughter Madeleine was taken from the bedroom, and hasn't been seen since. The global media response to this crime was extraordinary: rolling news was focused on the story for weeks and newspapers around the world ran headline stories day after day. A central feature of reports was the use of images. Pictures of the middle-class, professional McCanns filled the newspapers, and Madeleine's image was *everywhere* – front pages and news bulletins relied heavily on pictures of the blond-haired, blue-eyed three-year-old. As the search went on, and in response to police and media appeals that Madeleine could have been transported across national borders, people around the world began cutting out her picture and putting it in their front windows, shop fronts, and on lamp posts. I remember, several years later, seeing a faded picture of her on a public notice board in a tiny Sicilian village.

The first, and most obvious, observation to make about the mass media treatment of this crime is that it testifies to the possibility for crime to spark a tide of mutual outrage and grief on a global scale. Benedict Anderson (1991) suggests that the emergence of national news industries in the nineteenth century allowed for the emergence of 'imagined communities' in Western European countries, and this, in turn, helped foster a sense of nationalism. Today, we might make a similar claim about global news media producing a sense of international solidarity and collective identity – and the Madeleine McCann case is a fascinating example of this. Of course, none of this explains why the case received such extensive and enduring mass media coverage – and this should be something about which we're deeply curious. After all, the crime wasn't completely novel, and Madeleine wasn't the only little girl who went missing in 2007. What made this story particularly appealing to news outlets? (What made it so newsworthy, in other words? – but more on that in Chapter 1.) Madeleine's physical appearance was clearly one important factor: her picture quickly became iconic, and this was surely factored into media organisations' decisions to give the story a high profile. Gender, age, and social class were also important: consider the fact that we rarely hear about young boys, teenagers, or those from socially deprived backgrounds being kidnapped (even though people from these social groups are *more likely* to go missing than young middle-class girls). In short, Madeleine fitted dominant social norms concerning the innocent victim – again, social factors help determine what makes the headlines.

The other thing that the media treatment of the Madeleine McCann case highlighted was the news media's eagerness to transform an event into a *story*. This was a situation that never quite evolved into a discrete and easily digestible narrative of events. For one thing, it was a story without a conclusion (*is* a story without a conclusion: the British Prime Minister announced in 2012 that the case was to be reopened). Madeleine is still missing and suspects have been in turn dismissed. This indeterminacy shines a light on the mass media's attempts to gain control and frame a situation. One thing that initially piqued mass media interest in the case was the possibility of fitting the situation into what was by then a well-established narrative of stranger-perpetrated child sex abuse. A local man with a shady past was quickly lined up as a likely suspect – but this came to nothing. After several weeks of waiting to develop the story in this direction, the worldwide press's focus turned to the issue of parental negligence, and particularly the behaviour of Madeleine's mother. The McCanns' middle-class respectability made this narrative difficult to sustain and the couple were articulate in dealing with the accusations. The mass media turned their attention to errors made by the local police, but they too were efficient at establishing a counter-discourse based on the idea that what looked like negligence could easily be explained by the fact that the Portuguese criminal justice system simply did things differently.

This reaching around for a standard narrative on which to hang the case illuminates something fundamental about how crime news works: it centrally involves fashioning a situation into a familiar story. There is another important observation to be made here. Each of the narratives the media attempted to establish was very centrally about allocating blame. As Wardle (2008: 139) suggests, the news media not only serve as an 'institutionalised story-teller', providing us with official stories of what happens in the world; they also fulfil the role of 'moral guardian', instructing us on how to morally judge a case and, in particular, where blame lies. In doing so they draw upon well-established ideas about, for example, maternal responsibility, youthful transgression, the sources of aggression, childhood innocence, predatory males, and female sin.

## Overview of the book

This book is split into four parts, each of which starts with a brief introduction to draw out themes and common strands of argument across the chapters. Part I focuses on crime in the news. We start, in Chapter 1, by examining how crime makes the news. Here we consider the meaning of the term newsworthiness and the nature of news production. There are a wide range of variables that influence the selection and production of a news story, many of them indivisible from one another; so we find that a range of factors – socio-cultural, ideological, institutional, and practical – exert an influence. As a consequence the prioritisation of certain news stories needs to be carefully examined and we should resist the idea that there's an absolutely inexorable logic to what makes it onto the front page. Nonetheless, it is clear that certain stories are very *unlikely* to make it onto the front page, or, indeed, into a newspaper at all. The selectiveness of news reports on violence is the subject of Chapters 2 and 3. Here we discuss two specific types of violent crime in news reports: terrorism and sexual violence respectively. Studying terrorism in the news gives us a really good insight into the media's role in defining what is criminal and what is acceptable (indeed, morally necessary) violence. To put it differently, the news can urge us to see certain political groups' actions as legitimate, reasonable, and necessary – or, in contrast, it can urge us to see such actions as criminal. From terrorism we move on to consider an altogether different category of violence – sex crime. If an important aim of the chapter on terrorism is to establish that perpetrators of violence are treated variously in news reporting, a central aim of Chapter 3 is to establish the differential treatment of victims of violence. The media helps reinforce the idea that certain victims of crime are less deserving of victim-status than others – not everyone, to paraphrase Christie, is an 'ideal victim', and this is amply evident in reporting on sexual offences. The implicit suggestion here is that news reporting on crime influences people's perceptions of victims and offenders of crime. It's unlikely that there is a direct relationship, however, between these two things: instead, and as argued above, the media should be seen as participating in general cultural currents. This point of argument is of direct relevance to the material covered in Chapter 4. Here we consider, amongst other things, the 'CSI Effect', the relationship between fear of crime and crime news consumption, and methodological difficulties in studying media effects.

Part II of the book is concerned with concepts that help describe and explain sustained media coverage of crime. The aim here is to equip students with a conceptual toolkit for studying crime in the media – and to encourage them to see beyond the concept of 'moral panic' when thinking about intensive media coverage of crime. This enduringly popular concept is the subject of Chapter 5. From there we go on to consider the cautionary tale in Chapter 6 – that is, a media story that focuses on the negligence of (generally female) victims and would-be victims in failing to guard against crime. Chapter 7 introduces students to crime legends – salacious, empirically unverified crime stories generally spread via e-mail forwards and Internet news groups. The final chapter in this section, Chapter 8, focuses on the media as a representational arena for cultural trauma, and we look at studies of the media coverage of 9/11 and the assassination of Theo van Gogh. The introduction to Part II compares the four concepts and draws out their core differences.

Part III of the book focuses on methods for analysing media content. We look at a wide range of media here, and consider how techniques of analysis can be used to study written texts, images, and audiovisual media. Chapter 9 introduces students to content analysis, both as a quantitative and qualitative technique of analysis. Chapter 10 outlines narrative analysis as an approach to analysis, and Chapter 11 focuses on discourse analysis. Each chapter in this section starts by outlining analytical techniques and working through practical examples. The second half of each chapter describes and evaluates studies that make use of the given method to analyse crime in the media, and draws attention to good practice and problems. Each chapter ends with a suggested workshop session so that students can further develop their skills of analysis.

Part IV of the book takes a focused look at fictional worlds of crime, justice, and order. We look carefully at television programmes, films, and novels here and discuss the representation of lawlessness, revenge and retribution, prison and rehabilitation, detective-work, trials and the courtroom, and police-work. This final set of chapters is based upon focused readings of texts and deeper engagement with theory. As the discussion is more nuanced, these chapters have concluding discussions rather than the bullet-point summaries that are provided for the other chapters in this book. These chapters are much more akin to the traditional coursework essays that students taking 'Crime and the Media' courses are often asked to write, and in this sense they provide models for student writing. Beyond this pedagogical value, the chapters in this part of the book seek to extend our thinking about the cultural landscape of crime and consider how specific media texts can spark our criminological imagination. In Chapter 12 we carry out a close reading of the pilot episode of the television Western *Deadwood* (2004, dir. Walter Hill) and consider what it can tell us about the nature of the shift from revenge-based justice to more official, retributive forms of justice. The underlying idea here is that certain media texts can contribute to and deepen criminological understanding. This approach is also used in Chapter 13 where we consider what the film *A Clockwork Orange* (1971 USA, 1972 UK, dir. Stanley Kubrick) tells us about the ethical problems in trying to change someone – more specifically, we're interested in the representation of prison and rehabilitation here. An alternative approach is taken in Chapters 14 and 15. Here media texts are treated as indicative of broader cultural currents and social trends – as cultural products rather than works of art, in other words. These chapters focus on detective fiction and Hollywood legal dramas respectively and compare media texts from different historical periods, thus allowing us to think about crime stories in the context of broader cultural-historical shifts. From the representation of detective-work and the courtroom we move on to consider the media depiction of police-work. Chapter 16 considers what the US documentary series *Cops* suggests about the nature of police-work and crime. We give particular attention to camera work here, and in doing so try to demonstrate that even 'real-life' depictions of crime are constructed.

The book's Conclusion considers the overall impression of crime and criminal justice in the mass media. Here we identify recurring narrative features in contemporary crime stories by ranging across the different media texts and formats discussed in the book.

## PART I

# Crime in the news

# Introduction

This part of the book examines crime in the news. The chapters look, in turn, at where crime news comes from, terrorism in the news, sexual violence in the news, and the idea that crime news shapes our behaviour and attitudes. Before any of this, though, let's consider a few preliminary questions: How much news is about crime? Have there been any notable changes in crime news reporting over the last few decades? And are all crimes just as likely to make the front page?

Despite an intuition we might have that crime is an especially popular news topic there is actually little consensus amongst academics about the proportion of news that is given over to reporting crime. Sacco (1995: 142) notes that estimates of the proportion of US newspaper coverage focused on crime vary dramatically from 5 to 25 per cent. In an early and influential study of US crime news, Graber (1980: 26) found that *at least* 25 per cent of news reporting is focused on crime. This is all rather confusing. One thing we can be confident about, though, is that the amount of space devoted to crime in newspapers has risen over the past 25 years – in the economically developed world, at least. Take the UK as a case in point. Ditton and Duffy's (1983) study showed 6.5 per cent of British newspapers was given over to crime reporting in the early 1980s. Williams and Dickinson's (1993) subsequent study of ten British national newspapers in the late 1980s demonstrated a rise to 12.7 per cent – that's a near doubling of content. Reiner, Livingstone, and Allen's (2003) study of crime coverage in *The Times* and the *Mirror* from 1945 to 1991 reinforced the idea that there had been a growth during this period and reported that, by the early 1990s, crime coverage had come to account for 21 per cent of newspaper content. Schlesinger and Tumber (1994) make a similar observation: their study is based on interviews with British journalists and editors and concludes that, since the 1970s, crime has become an ever more popular news topic. As one of their interviewees, an experienced crime reporter for a British tabloid newspaper, put it: 'You have gone from smash-and-grabs and the odd murder story into this vast field of crime that's developed in the last twenty years ... you find that there is more and more crime to cover and many offices are increasing their coverage and their crime teams' (p. 144). A similar trend is evident in the USA. Robert McChesney (1999: 54), for example, has found an even more marked increase in US news television broadcasting on crime: he indicates that between 1990 and 1996 the number of crime stories on network news shows *tripled*. The Center for Media and Public Affairs (CMPA), an organisation that carries out research on US media coverage, found that during the 1990s crime was 'the biggest topic of the decade', with economic news a distant second (CMPA July/August 1997).

Of course, not all crimes make the front page. In fact, we know that certain types of crime are much more likely than others to make the news. Studies demonstrate that roughly 50 per cent of crime news focuses on violence, despite the fact that violent crime accounts for less than 10 per cent of police-recorded crime. Graber (1980), in what remains a fascinating study of four US newspapers in the mid-1970s, found that whilst murder was the focus for a massive 26 per cent of crimes reported in the *Chicago Tribune* during 1976 it only represented 0.2 per cent of crimes in the police statistics for that year. The opposite pattern is evident with other crimes. Property crime, for example, is highly unlikely to make the news, even though it accounts for roughly three-quarters of police-recorded crime (see, for example, Sherizen 1978; Ditton and Duffy 1983; Reiner *et al.* 2003). Interestingly, these patterns in reporting are evident across economically advanced countries (see 'Crime news around the world').

All this helps confirm a widely held view amongst scholars in this field: news reporting on crime runs directly counter to what we know about the 'reality' of crime from official statistics. The media analyst Jack Katz (1987: 57) noted this some two decades ago: 'the picture one obtains about crime from reading the newspapers', he commented, 'inverts the picture about crime one gets from reading police statistics'. Ray Surette (2010: 47) refers to this phenomenon as the 'law of opposites'. News outlets, he argues, suggest that crime is predominantly violent, that the usual victim is middle class, and that crime is spiralling out of control, whilst crime statistics show that violent crime is rare, victims generally belong to socially disadvantaged groups, and crime is decreasing (from a historic high in the mid-1990s, at least). All this raises a really important question, one that we attend to further in Chapter 4: Is it the media-spun image of crime or the 'reality' of crime that influences public attitudes?

---

### Crime news around the world

Marsh (1991) looked at crime news in fifteen countries from 1965 to 1988. His aim was to ascertain whether the trends in crime reporting in the USA held across different countries, including the UK, Canada, Australia, Israel, India, and Norway. Interestingly, his results suggest a striking similarity in newspaper coverage of crime between the USA and other countries in terms of the over-emphasis of violent crime (relative to official statistics), the understating of property crime, the exaggeration of the crime rate, and a lack of information concerning the social causes of crime.

Discussion Question: How might we explain the international nature of these trends?

## CHAPTER 1

# How does crime become news?

This chapter is concerned with how journalists find out about crime and select stories for coverage – and how the increasing importance of the Internet as a news provider might be altering things. These matters are intimately linked to the question of why so much news is devoted to crime. As we'll find below, the commercial constraints on journalists, the appeal of official sources, and news values all contribute to making crime an ideal topic for news reporting. Before any of this, and by way of introduction, we need to briefly consider the press's historical role in reporting events of public interest as well as the ownership of news outlets.

It has become commonplace to express open cynicism concerning news organisations. Many believe that newspaper articles are heavily biased and journalists are shady characters using underhand (and sometimes outright illegal) tactics. Even media commentators are quick to point out that the quality of journalism has deteriorated and the influence of big media conglomerations has increased. Despite the apocalyptic tone of such accounts, concerns about the press's integrity have been around for a long time. In the late nineteenth century, the British playwright Oscar Wilde had cause to complain about the dominance of the press – good cause, in fact: his arrest and eventual imprisonment for taking part in homosexual acts were in no small part due to the salacious newspaper reporting on the matter. What I want us to focus on here, though, is how familiar his tone and argument are in the following diatribe against the press, published in his extended essay *The Soul of Man under Socialism*:

In old days men had the rack. Now they have the press. That is an improvement certainly. But still it is very bad, and wrong, and demoralizing. Somebody – was it Burke? – called journalism the fourth estate. That was true at the time no doubt. But at the present moment it is the only estate … We are dominated by Journalism. (Wilde 2008 [originally 1891]: 26)

Wilde refers here to the popular idea that the press represents the 'fourth estate' (or seat of power) alongside the English House of Commons and the two sections of the House of Lords. As far as Wilde is concerned the press has 'eaten up' the political elite to become the dominant power broker in our society. His argument, made well over a century ago, may well strike you as deeply familiar. It seems, then, that the press's power has long been a source of consternation and complaint.

What *is* distinctive to the current period, though, is the concentration of power within the media, so that, increasingly, media outlets are owned by a small number of conglomerations – in this sense, at least, the press has become potentially more powerful than even Wilde could have dreamed. Trevor Barr, in his excellent review of the growth of new media in Australia, gives a succinct example: 'In 1903 the twenty-one capital city newspapers were owned by seventeen independent owners; by 1960 the fourteen daily newspapers had seven owners; and by 1999, two groups owned ten of the twelve dailies in Australia' (Barr 2000: 2–3). Of course, the concentration of media ownership is a global phenomenon affecting all media, not just news organisations. The media analyst Robert McChesney (1999) estimates that most of the world's media are owned by just nine big media conglomerations, and, importantly, the trend is for ownership to concentrate still further into the hands of an even smaller number of organisations. In the news industry, the process of centralisation started over one hundred years ago, and was aided by the creation, in the mid-nineteenth century, of press agencies, organisations that produce and sell news stories en masse (see 'Press agencies – the kings of the newspaper industry?', p. 25). Early news-holding companies tended towards expansion, possibly because they were often family-ran, and the cultivation of a family trade requires, we might surmise, the development of a portfolio of related companies.

In the early twenty-first century many of the really powerful media conglomerations remain family-run (if not family-owned). The most famous of these is perhaps News Corporation, headed by the Australian-born Rupert Murdoch. The company owns a set of prestigious and widely read newspapers, including the *Wall Street Journal*, and the British newspapers the *Sun* and *The Times* – the former has the highest circulation figures in the country. News Corporation also owns the influential news channels Fox News and the British-based Sky News. To return to our more general point here, such conglomerations have, increasingly, come to dominate the news industry so that a small number of companies own a large number of titles and news channels. Take Canada's CanWest Global, owned by the Asper family. This group controls a very significant proportion of the nation's newspapers – in fact their publications account for 35 per cent of the country's newspaper circulation (Pitts 2002: 3).

Why does any of this matter? One common argument is that the news industry is dominated not just by a small number of corporations but also by a narrow range of viewpoints. Proprietorial bias is often seen in simplistic terms – as a big bad media tycoon barking out a byline down the phone! Nonetheless, there is reason for concern. Take the fact that, on buying the *Wall Street Journal*, News Corporation was forced by the previous owners to sign a clause that said the new owners wouldn't interfere with the writing of the paper's editorial, such was the concern for journalists' autonomy (Scribner and Chapman 2010: 587). In most cases, though, proprietorial influence is expressed indirectly. In a book that explores journalistic practice in Canada, Hackett *et al.* (2000: 206–210) describe the often subtle processes of control and coercion in the newsroom, how these contribute to bias, and their relationship to the concentration of media ownership. The journalists and editors they interviewed found it difficult to maintain professional integrity: they were fully aware of who fires and hires, of the hiring and promotion of journalists (particularly editors) with certain sympathies, and pointed out that finding a job on a different newspaper is increasingly difficult when a small number of companies own a large number of titles. More than this, they found that critical reporting on certain matters – specifically those related to business – was frowned upon. For large conglomerations, some of which have stakes in commercial areas outside the news industry and all of which depend upon economic buoyancy, there is a tendency to protect the status quo, and this may manifest itself as a pro-business slant in reporting.

There are other problems related to the concentration of media ownership. For the corporation, the bottom line is all that really matters – achieving greater efficiency and saving money, come what may, tends, after all, to be central to the corporate logic. Certainly, both McChesney (1999) and Davies (2009) have pointed to the increased reliance on easy-to-access (and therefore cheap) news in the USA and UK – 'soft news', as McChesney describes it. Both see this as a consequence of the institutional constraints on news outlets: the fact that newspaper circulations are falling exponentially and that corporate bosses expect ever quicker and cheaper news production. McChesney (1999) argues that in this environment crime news, and stories about shootings in particular, have become increasingly popular – the related press releases are easy to come by and the police are treated as a highly reliable, single source. Could it be that this explains the trends identified by Reiner *et al.* (2003) and Marsh (1991) that we discussed in the introduction to this part of the book? Certainly, the commercial pressures on newspapers to produce salacious stories at speed and low cost are likely to improve the chances of violent crime making it into the headlines (see 'Are newspapers dying out?').

### Are newspapers dying out?

It might be difficult to imagine, but your children could well see newspapers as a thing of the past! Declining revenues from advertising have had an impact, as has the rise of the Internet, and the increased prominence of free papers. All have contributed to a secular decline in circulation numbers over the past decade, particularly marked in the USA and UK. In 2007 the week-day circulation figure for US newspapers fell to 50.7 million — its lowest recorded level since 1945 (Meyer 2009: 1). In 2010 the Organisation for Economic Co-operation and Development (OECD) published a report on the future of the news industry worldwide and found a marked decline in paid-for newspaper titles as well as circulation numbers across member countries (OECD 2010: 22—26). In France, for example, from 1945 to 2004 national titles decreased from 26 to 10. Looking just at the last decade they found that the UK had seen an extraordinary 19 per cent decline in paid-for circu-lation numbers between 2002 and 2008. Australia's two top daily newspa-pers — the *Herald Sun* and *Daily Telegraph* — experienced declines in circulation of 2.8 per cent and 6.3 per cent respectively between 2001 and 2008. In the USA, decreases in circulation have been much more marked, with the *Los Angeles Times* and the *Washington Post* experiencing a 22 per cent and 18 per cent decline respectively between 2001 and 2008. Nonetheless, the picture wasn't entirely bleak: certain publications have increased their circulation, including *USA Today* and the *Wall Street Journal.* Newspapers that foreground news about celebrities and serve a specialist readership are still going strong — this alone tells us an awful lot about the future of the news industry.

Discussion Question: How might the decline in newspaper circulation affect the reporting of crime news?

With all this doom and gloom about the future and value of the press, we are often apt to forget about the *potential* of news organisations, and specifi-cally their role in safeguarding important freedoms and liberties. It's worth reminding ourselves that free and public-minded news groups are absolutely key to maintaining democracy. As Habermas (1991) notes, in his analysis of the rise of a public sphere in European societies, the press has played a key role in holding the political elite to account, urging greater transparency, and informing the public about what goes on within public courts and sessions of Parliament. Though we might take it for granted, the press's ability to inform us in this manner often involved very hard-fought battles. In his fascinating study of the freedom of the British press, Ben Wilson (2010) draws attention to two really important historical developments. First, in 1788, the requirement that writers have their work officially vetted before publication was removed. Secondly, from 1787, news journalists were permitted to sit in on and report sessions in the House of Commons. Achieving the latter, as Foster points out, involved a very significant political struggle and contravening the former meant risking a prison sentence. How incredible it sounds, to modern ears, that the political elite could vet articles ahead of publication and carry on all debates in secret! Without legal protections journalists wouldn't be able to tell us about decisions made in Senate or Parliament concerning detention, sentencing, policies about punishment, and new criminal laws. In fact, the relationship between journalists and government institutions is symbiotic. Journalists hold the government to account, but they also rely heavily upon state agencies for information – this is particularly true of crime reporting. We examine this reliance in the next section.

## Sourcing crime news

How do journalists find out about crime? Just as very few crimes are independently detected by the police, it is relatively – and increasingly – rare for news journalists to personally uncover a story. In fact there is evidence that newspaper journalists rarely write the news themselves; instead, much of it is cobbled together from other sources – but more on this below. For now let's just say that journalists rely heavily on press releases, wire copy (that is, articles from press agencies), inside tips from officials (particularly the police), and information they pick up from lay people (witnesses, family members, etc.). Television news is particularly unlikely to involve journalistic enterprise. Journalists who work in this sector are much less likely than newspaper reporters to carry out routine information-finding missions of key public buildings and officials – 'newsbeats' or simply 'beats', as they are referred to in the trade (Weaver and Wilhoit 1991: 69). Edward Jay Epstein (2000), in his classic book on network television news, *News from Nowhere*, explores how television news organisations source and produce the news, and concludes that they receive an awful lot of their leads from newspapers.

Newspapers tend still to use some form of the 'beat system', whereby certain journalists are given responsibility for picking up and covering news from the courthouse, parliament, police stations, mayor's office, etc. These are what Gans (1979) calls 'locational beats'. Some newsrooms operate a different type of beat system where journalists are responsible for specific topics (crime, celebrities, etc.). Lee Becker *et al.* (2000) studied the organisation of the newsroom for three newspapers distributed in the USA's South-East in order to assess the use of the beat system. Each of the newspapers had a range of locational beats organised to provide five main points of coverage: courts, crime, education, government, and hospitals. Interestingly, 'an editor ... termed the first four of these the basic beats of American newspapers' (p. 4) – and, we might add, crime and criminal justice account for two of these. This helps explain the popularity of crime as a news topic: it may be that crime dominates the news simply because journalists routinely scout criminal justice agencies for stories.

Some criminal justice sources are more useful and approachable than others. As the British journalist Martin Brunt puts it, 'success as a crime reporter still comes down to one thing, personal contacts', and he means, predominantly, *police* contacts (Brunt 2007: 38). The police are often particularly keen to provide press releases, statements, and inside information, and they are frequently journalists' main source of information for a criminal case. Over time the police have developed strategies and procedures for dealing with media interest: they are, for example, well used to holding press conferences and have staff whose specific job is to manage media relations. Steven Chermak has written widely on the relationship between the police and journalists in the USA. His research demonstrates that the police are by far the most frequently cited sources in crime stories in US newspapers (Chermak 1995; Chermak 1997). This, he reasons, is due to the symbiotic relationship between the media and police – the former need the latter for information, but, as the most visible representative of the criminal justice system, the police need to maintain a good standing in the public consciousness, and they do that via news outlets (Chermak and Weiss 2005: 502). Given this, it is perhaps unsurprising that the police are very media friendly, even providing dedicated working spaces for journalists and training new recruits in media communication. Mawby (2010) draws similar conclusions about the relationship between the police and news organisations in the UK, noting the increase in resources deployed by the former to manage their media image; this, combined with the financial difficulties faced by many news organisations and the drive to cut specialist reporters (including crime reporters) may lead, Mawby suggests, to an increasingly unequal relationship that benefits the police (see 'Journalists and the police – an over-friendly relationship?').

The closeness of the relationship between news organisations and the police has, quite understandably, provoked criticism. Hall *et al.* (2013: 71), in their famous study of the 1970s mugging moral panics in Britain, argue that, along with the Home Office and courts, the police control the media portrayal of crime – official crime control institutions are inevitably, they argue, the 'primary definers' of crime, setting up the parameters for subsequent media debate. Not everyone agrees with this view.

Schlesinger and Tumber (1994), for example, in a highly influential account of the media's treatment of crime, argue that the process whereby a

---

**Journalists and the police – an over-friendly relationship?**

The friendly — perhaps *too* friendly — relationship between the police and journalists has become a subject of heated debate over the last few years. The furore in the UK concerning some journalists' use of phone-hacking and other illegal tactics, and the ensuing Levenson Inquiry, has shed light on some really troubling practices, including the police seemingly turning a blind-eye to journalists' criminal activities and journalists' bribery of the police for information. Accusations have been made that the original police investigation into the journalists' use of illegal practices was wholly inadequate. This, along with the fact that a former editor of Britain's most widely circulating daily, the *Sun*, told the UK's House of Commons Media and Culture Select Committee that the newspaper customarily paid police officers for information has stirred up real concern. The level of public anger and government concern about such things means that the special relationship between the police and journalists might just be set to change.

Discussion Question: Why might it be a problem that crime reporters depend so heavily on the police as a source of information?

---

newspaper takes up a source's story is more complex. For one thing, they argue, official sources of crime news are rarely as organised and coherent as the label 'primary definer' implies. They suggest that certain conditions need to exist for a source's story to be taken up: the story needs to be sufficiently succinct and of obvious newsworthiness (see the next section for more on this); the story has to be well communicated; and it helps if the contact is an insider and can time a leak (p. 39).

The relationship between a source and journalist isn't, then, as straightforward as we might imagine. The fact remains, though, that official sources – the police included – are better placed and resourced to promote their take on events than members of the public and non-governmental groups. We need simply look at the proportion of crime news stories that rely upon official sources to recognise this to be the case. Welch, Weber, and Edwards (2000) looked at the sources used in articles about prison in the *New York Times*, a liberal US daily newspaper, and found that there was a very heavy reliance on government sources. Similarly, in an analysis of Rhode Island newspaper coverage of child sex abuse stories, Cheit (2003: 616) found that the prosecutor's office regularly featured as a source in stories. He also found that newspaper stories on this offence category tended to be about offenders who received harsh sentences, thus obscuring the fact that most convicted child sex offenders spend no time in prison. He argues that these two details are related: the prosecutor's office has a vested interest in promoting the idea that harsh sentences are usual.

The lesson we can take from this is that the official line on crime is likely to be self-affirming. This means, amongst other things, that newspaper reports based on official sources are unlikely to raise critical questions about the criminal justice system. Nick Davies' (2009) book, *Flat Earth News*, makes similar points about newspaper reporting in general. Davies, a former journalist at the British newspaper the *Guardian*, demonstrates that much of what appears in British newspapers derives directly from official organisations' press releases. He starts with an observation: despite really substantial media interest in the 'Millennium Bug' the new millennium was ushered in with very little trouble. How, Davies wonders, could so many news outlets have been fooled into promoting a story that, in retrospect, seemed so completely unlikely to come to anything? The answer, he argues, lies in lazy journalism, or what he calls 'churnalism'. A story is propagated by one news outlet and others follow suit (or 'churn out' the same sort of material). Soon the story becomes self-perpetuating and is presumed to be true or accurate – hence the phrase 'flat earth news'. Davies' main concern here is with the lack of fact-checking. Validating a source is a golden rule of journalism. You don't simply take one person's word for it: you seek out other opinions on the matter. Why has this fact-checking process fallen by the wayside? According to Davies a key reason is newspapers' increased reliance on press releases and articles produced by press agencies, so-called wire copy (see 'Press agencies – the kings of the newspaper industry?'). Davies enlisted the help of academics at Cardiff University to analyse 2207 articles in British newspapers. Their findings showed that, extraordinarily, very little of what appears as news in British publications is original writing:

> They found that a massive 60 per cent of these quality-print stories consisted wholly or mainly of wire copy and/or PR material, and a further 20 per cent contained clear elements of wire copy and/or PR material to which more or less material had been added. With 8 per cent of the stories, they were unable to be sure about their source. That left only 12 per cent of stories where the researchers could say that all the material was generated by the reporters themselves. (Davies 2009: 52)

It was, the researchers found, one particular press agency – the Press Association – that produced many of the news stories recounted in British newspapers.

Why might newspapers' reliance on wire copy be a problem? For one thing, journalists and editors often take press agency articles to be a single

---

**Press agencies – the kings of the newspaper industry?**

Press agencies produce articles (sometimes referred to as wire copy) en masse. Newspapers can then buy these items to pad out a journalist's story, or — as is more often the case — publish in full alongside articles produced by their own writers. There's an obvious efficiency to this system: press agencies provide a surplus of articles from which an editor can choose to 'fill up' his newspaper. Press agencies come in all shapes and sizes: there are, for example, government-sponsored agencies (such as the BBC and China News Agency) and religiously oriented agencies (Catholic World News). Nonetheless, as Jeremy Tunstall (1999) notes, the industry is dominated by two giants of wire copy production: Reuters and the Press Association. Tunstall argues that these kings of the news industry are so powerful as to constitute a 'duopoly'.

Discussion Question: How might the articles written by press agencies give a biased view of events?

---

source. This means that the information is held to be highly reliable and it is presumed that the story doesn't need checking. Wire copy, then, often passes into print without being verified. Moreover, Davies notes that press agency articles tend to be simple regurgitations of official organisations' press releases. In this sense they are conduits of information for official sources, more akin to public relations offices than newspaper outlets. Hence the fact that those who work in public relations will commonly send a press release or statement to the Press Association first because, as one of Davies' interviewees put it, 'we are rarely subjected to the sort of cross-examination that, say, the *Sun* or *The Times* would give us'. All this should give us pause for thought because it means that a large amount of the news originates, often word-for-word, from official sources and organisations. Think, for a moment, about what this means about crime news.

## Selecting crime news

As Schlesinger and Tumber (1994) point out, not all sources' stories make the news: what, then, prompts a journalist to run one story and ignore another? Press agencies produce many articles every day: what makes a newspaper editor pick out particular items from the range on offer? Here we consider two sets of explanations for crime news selection: first the idea that potential news items are measured against set criteria of newsworthiness and secondly the idea that crime news selection is a largely passive, intuitive process, to do with journalists' and editors' sense that an item reinforces a collective identity, certain shared values, or contributes to a consensual view of crime and justice.

### Newsworthiness and news values

It has long been said that it's unexpected events that make the news. As the sociologist Robert Park had it, '"Dog bites man" – that is not news. But "Man bites dog" – that is' (Park 1940 in Tumber 1999: 13). This, as Park himself notes, isn't entirely true; rather it's the 'not *wholly* unexpected' that makes it into the news. Fundamentally, in reading or hearing a crime news story we need to believe that we live in a world where this particular bad thing can and does happen.

The other truism concerning what makes it into the news is that violence is of exceptional value. As Hall *et al.* (2013: 70) put it:

> One special point about crime is the special status of violence as a news value. Any crime can be lifted into news visibility if violence becomes associated with it … Violence represents a basic violation of the person … Violence is also the ultimate crime against property, and against the State. It thus represents a fundamental rupture in the social order.

Whilst we might agree with the main thrust of Hall *et al.*'s argument here, we need to recognise that certain forms of violence are more likely to make it into the news than others. It's important to recognise, then, that the process whereby news is selected isn't a simple matter of choosing the most violent – or, for that matter, unusual – stories. There have been many attempts within media studies to schematise the process whereby the news is selected and to conceptualise newsworthiness, as it's often described. Newsworthiness is a much-misused term so it's important to be clear about its meaning here: to say that something is newsworthy means that it is *of public interest*. It might be *in* the public's interest to find out about all sorts of things – the state of the Nepalese economy, the five-year survival rate for stomach cancer sufferers, an increase in pension mis-selling – but that does not mean that these things are *of* public interest. We are not, in other words, making a value judgement when we say that something is newsworthy; rather, we are involved in the assessment of what entertains and chimes with a given audience.

There is a sizeable body of literature on newsworthiness, much of it directed towards listing the attributes that make something of public interest, 'news values' or 'news factors' as they're commonly known. The assumption is that the extent to which a story has certain news values dictates not just whether it will get included in the newspaper or bulletin but also its placement (on the front page, for example). Even the organisation of story elements within an article is shaped by a journalist's and editor's perception of an event's news value. Crime happens to have many of the ingredients that researchers see as essential to newsworthiness – helping to account, we might add, for the priority given to these sorts of stories in the news. More on this later: let's turn now to academic work on newsworthiness.

Galtung and Ruge (1965) are widely credited with coming up with the first list of news values. They studied articles about foreign political crises in four Norwegian newspapers and created a list of common attributes which, they reason, help explain why particular events make the news. In producing an explanatory framework they use the metaphor of a radio set being tuned. They ask the reader to imagine that world events are all captured on an old-fashioned radio set – it's a stretch, but stick with the analogy! Now imagine that you're tuning into a station, whizzing through the various channels, hearing snippets of broadcast as you find the right place. What makes you settle on a signal? You might hear a sound that is unambiguously a radio station (a human voice, say), has meaning (a voice speaking English rather than German), offers up something unexpected ('the President has died …'), or is in keeping with what you expect (a jingle on a favourite programme, perhaps) – and, beyond all this, your choice will be limited to what is included in the radio's frequency. The same sort of conditions, Galtung and Ruge argue, influence our reading of newspapers and, in turn, journalists' selection of the news. They conclude that the following twelve criteria influence whether a story gets picked up by a newspaper – they see the first eight as general, universal principles and the last four as specific to the economically developed world.

- Frequency: By this they mean something quite fundamental: a news item must be suited to the news medium (be 'on the right frequency') to be picked up by a newspaper. They're referring here to something known within media studies as 'medium specificity'. Certain events are particularly suited to certain media, so we wouldn't expect a film about this month's newest fashion trend or a glossy women's magazine article about a Roman chariot race! In the case of newspaper reporting, time-span is, in Galtung and Ruge's estimation, crucial: an event that takes place over a long period and has no discernible climax is unlikely to make it into the news – it simply isn't the sort of event that newspapers deal with. Or, as they put it, 'the building of a dam goes unnoticed, but not its inauguration' (p. 66). An event that is short in terms of its entire length – murder is the example they use – is absolutely in the right register for newspapers. The social theorist Roland Barthes (1972: 151) saw this in rather more critical terms, arguing that news involves the 'miraculous evaporation of history' from events. Certainly, we should recognise that news items don't deal with historical context in a particularly full manner.

- Threshold: Galtung and Ruge continue the radio metaphor and argue that 'there is something corresponding to amplitude' (p. 66) in newspaper reporting. The 'bigger' the event the more likely it is to get reported. As the authors point out, this doesn't tell us anything about why one event is prioritised over another, but simply why certain events that are the same in kind but different in degree receive differential reporting.

- Unambiguity: Readers must be able to distinguish between 'signal' and 'noise', Galtung and Ruge reason: 'an event with a clear interpretation, free from ambiguities in meaning, is preferred to the highly ambiguous event from which many and inconsistent implications can and will be made' (ibid.).

- Meaningfulness: There must be a sense of the story in question springing from or relating to a society the reader recognises as his own – a sense of geographical and 'cultural proximity'. Otherwise, there should be a sense of relevance: that is, the event in question should touch upon the reader's life or values (p. 67).

- Consonance: The story should fit the reader's 'mental pre-image' of what would happen under certain circumstances. As the authors put it, in this sense 'news are actually "olds", because they correspond to what one expects to happen' (ibid.).

- Unexpectedness: This news value, Galtung and Ruge note, qualifies the former two prerequisites. 'It is', they add, 'the unexpected *within the meaningful and consonant* that is brought to one's attention, and by "unexpected" we simply mean essentially two things: unexpected or rare' (ibid.). A murder carried out by a much-respected celebrity is an example of this.

- Continuity: Once we've tuned into a station and the broadcasters have got our attention, the authors reason, we carry on listening. Similarly, once a news story has broken, it remains the subject of coverage. A story might be covered, then, simply because it is part of an ongoing news narrative.

- Composition: Matters of overall composition are important too. A story may be deemed valuable in relation to the existing stock of stories for a given day or broadcast. If all the stories that have come to an editor's attention during a particular day focus on matters abroad, a story dealing with a problem at home, however lacking in news value it may be as a stand-alone item, is likely to be given space in the newspaper.

- Reference to elite nations: This, along with the next three values, relates specifically to newspaper coverage in the developed world. Stories that concern nations with economic and political clout, Galtung and Ruge argue, are particularly likely to receive coverage in this part of the world.

- Reference to elite persons: Stories about royalty, MPs, and celebrities have particular value.
- Reference to persons: If a personal angle can be brought to bear, the authors argue, a story is more likely to be covered. As Galtung and Ruge put it, 'the thesis is that news has a tendency to present events as sentences where there is a subject ... and the event is then seen as a consequence of the actions of this person or those persons' (p. 68).
- Reference to something negative: If an event is negative it's more likely to be covered.

It's worth noting that Galtung and Ruge weren't acritical of news values and argued that journalists should attempt to pay more attention to long-term trends, deal with ambiguous issues, and include more coverage of non-elite people and nations (pp. 84–85).

In the UK, work on newsworthiness has tended to be of a more obviously critical nature, treating news values as manifestations of political structures. Chibnall's (2005 [originally 1977]) work is noteworthy here. In *Law and Order News* he looks at crime news published from 1945 to 1975 and considers the ideological underpinnings to news selection. His remains one of the most influential conceptions of the professional structures and news values that influence crime reporting. There are, he argues, 'two basic components in the system by which the press identifies and interprets the news' (p. 12). First, there is the framework that categorises news into certain types of event (sport, crime, celebrity news, etc.) and determines the meaning of that event ('as legitimate or illegitimate, as the result of certain processes, as similar to other events or unique ...' p. 13). Secondly there is 'the professional imperatives of journalism', or what are generally referred to as news values (p. 13). Despite their general applicability, Chibnall suggests, these are likely to be somewhat specific to the news organisation; certain outlets, in other words, will require their journalists to give weight to certain values over others. Nonetheless journalists are beholden to eight professional imperatives:

- Immediacy: Events, rather than historical narrative, are chosen for news. Chibnall argues that neglecting the 'historical dimension' of a story means that political interpretations of an event are easily obscured (p. 24).
- Dramatisation: Actions, rather than thoughts or beliefs, make the news. A focus on *what* happened, Chibnall observes, means that the question of *why* something happened is often sidelined. News, he argues, is becoming increasingly like entertainment (p. 26).

- Personalisation: See 'Reference to Elite Persons' in Galtung and Ruge's schema. Chibnall adds that the involvement of celebrities increases the newsworthiness of an item.
- Simplification: See 'Unambiguity' in Galtung and Ruge's schema, though Chibnall's preference for the term 'simplification' indicates that he understands the news to actively work towards eliminating complexity.
- Titillation: Scandal and sex, Chibnall notes, secure a story a place in a newspaper, even whilst the publication retains a morally self-righteous mode of address (p. 32).
- Conventionalism: Stories that conform to the prevailing ideology (that are therefore conventional) are likely to be deemed relevant and newsworthy.
- Structured access: Events as dictated by official sources – those who have structured access to news organisations – are particularly likely to make it into print.
- Novelty: A twist or new angle increases an item's newsworthiness.

Chibnall noted further factors that apply specifically to reports of violence and make these items particularly newsworthy. Those stories that involve visible and spectacular acts, have a sexual or political dimension, use graphic presentation, point to an individual pathology, and seem like they'll deter others, he argues, are deemed particularly newsworthy (p. 77).

Chibnall's work has been highly influential and was recently adapted by the British criminologist Yvonne Jewkes (2011), who suggested the need to update his list to understand the news values that influence crime reporting in the twenty-first century. Jewkes (p. 45) draws upon Chibnall's and Galtung and Ruge's work to create a list of twelve news values and structures. She agrees that threshold, simplification, reference to high-status persons, spectacle and graphic imagery, violence, proximity (roughly equivalent to Galtung and Ruge's 'meaningfulness'), and sex (roughly equivalent to Chibnall's 'titillation') are all important news values. She then suggests the following additions to the list of news values that inform crime reporting:

- Predictability: This is *not* the same as 'consonance' in Galtung and Ruge's schema and 'conventionalism' in Chibnall's schema. Jewkes refers here to the idea that stories that follow (or can be made to follow) a predictable *structure* allow for news organisations to plan their coverage and resources in advance and this increases an item's newsworthiness. Jewkes notes that news coverage of London's Notting Hill Carnival typically emphasises criminal wrong-doing simply because this is the angle or slant that journalists have historically taken.

- Individualism: This is a very useful addition from Jewkes, who argues that 'individual definitions of crime, and rationalizations which highlight individual responses to crime, are preferred to more complex cultural and political explanations' (p. 49). Offenders are portrayed as sick individuals and victims as isolated – in both instances the 'normative ties' that link either to society are obscured.
- Risk: Irrespective of the fact that crime is carried out and experienced by people in specific social groups, the media 'persist in presenting a picture of serious crime as random, meaningless, unpredictable, and ready to strike anyone at any time' (p. 51). The structure of the random violent crime – stranger-perpetrated crime, in other words – is one that is deemed highly newsworthy, perhaps because it allows for simplicity in story-telling and emphasises the individual experience of crime.
- Children: Another useful new addition from Jewkes. Crimes that involve a child-victim or perpetrator became particularly newsworthy in the late twentieth century (see Chapter 3 for more on this).
- Conservative ideology and political diversion: Jewkes observes that since the mid-1990s we have seen a 'right-wing consensus' on crime, justice, and punishment emerge and news reporting reinforces this set of views. This manifests itself, to Jewkes' mind, in a focus on crimes of the working classes and ethnic minorities, support of punitive sanctions, and a moralising discourse. Events that fit this agenda, she argues, have greater value as news stories.

News values are, as Jewkes remarks, socially contingent – some may have a more universal and lasting appeal (such as threshold and frequency) but others, like the news value of child-victims and perpetrators, are culturally and historically specific. We'll return to discuss news values in the following chapters where we attempt to explain core themes in news reporting on terrorism and sexual violence. For now, let's consider some other factors that affect the selection of crime news.

## The emotional and moral value of crime news

Galtung and Ruge, Chibnall, and Jewkes conceive of crime news selection as a relatively transparent process that can be understood in terms of discrete criteria. The US sociologist scholar Jack Katz offers an alternative conception of news values in his 1987 article 'What Makes Crime "News"?' Katz's argument isn't really given much attention in current debates about news values but he offers up some really important insights about why crime makes the news. Katz's point of departure is that 'crimes do not become newsworthy because of what they tell us about crime, but because crimes may be especially telling about other things of interest to readers' (p. 50). It's a deceptively simple idea, one that urges us to reject the commonsensical idea that crime makes the news because, well, because it's *crime*. People do not, Katz argues, read about crime as a fact-finding enterprise, nor because of the unexpected nature of the events in question: in fact, people seem to particularly enjoy reading about crimes that *confirm* their view of the world. In other words, journalists and editors select stories on the basis that they'll get readers shaking their heads and pursing their lips in grim recognition that this particular evil exists to threaten what all right-minded people hold dear.

Katz's study is based on an analysis of around 2000 articles in US national newspapers. From this he concludes that crime stories are particularly newsworthy when they allow for the rehearsal of mainstream social values, a collective identity, or a moral lesson. He found that crime news stories are often moral vignettes, marking out right and wrong, employing a moral register, and enjoining the reader to share feelings of anger, hatred, disapproval, or empathy. It's also common, he suggests, for crime news to reinforce a sense of shared belonging and identity by warning of moral collapse and threats to a collective way of life. Crimes involving major fraud, he notes, are commonly represented in the news as a threat to national security and 'virtually all thefts deemed newsworthy are depicted as events endangering one or another foundation of collective identity'. Crimes in which the American 'Good Life' has been put at risk – a well-known American company or institution, an aspect of American life (baseball, entrepreneurialism, etc.) – are especially newsworthy, as are crimes without alleged perpetrators if they 'document the existence of other forms of vast, uncontrolled, anti-social forces' (p. 53).

For Katz, crimes are selected for reporting on the basis that they allow for this type of moralistic, consensus-affirming story-telling. Katz goes on to consider the possibility that the moral register used in crime reporting is socially functional, allowing for a sense of 'effervescence', as the sociologist Émile Durkheim put it. Effervescence refers to a collective sense of emotional togetherness that binds members of a society: we experience it, Durkheim suggested, when we attend religious ceremonies. Katz discards this explanation for the tone and content of crime news: the 'contemporary reading of crime disconcerts rather than reassures', he points out (p. 64). We don't experience a sense of togetherness by reading crime news, he continues; rather, it makes us feel collective outrage, anger, and fear – very far, in his estimation, from the social glue quality of effervescence. Instead he decides that crime reports are functional because they offer us the opportunity to work through moral dilemmas in our own lives: thus, crime news provides us with a 'daily moral workout' (p. 70).

I think that Katz is too quick to reject the Durkheimian interpretation – or it might simply be that effervescence has become more relevant an explanation for what makes crime news today. News outlets have come to play a really central role as moral campaigners in today's society, calling for law changes and collective action. More importantly, though, Katz's suggestion that creating a negative feeling of uncertainty or unease cannot feed into a feeling of effervescence seems to me to be incorrect. After all, and as he himself remarks, this is done in the service of the idea that certain aspects of collective life should be prized and protected. As we'll find in Chapters 2 and 3, reporting on terrorism and child sex abuse seems to do this: newspaper reports denounce a common enemy, and in doing so they ask us to recognise that there are things that we collectively hold to be sacred. This in itself says an awful lot about our society – that we are united in outrage rather than through declamatory expressions of common purpose – but that's a different discussion! To return to my main point: it's entirely plausible, I think, that newspaper articles are selected on the basis that they will stir up public sentiments of mutual outrage and reinforce (by counter-distinction) collective values.

Such a suggestion implies that there are deep cultural structures at work in the selection and placement of crime news – factors that can't necessarily be listed. Golding and Elliott (1979 in Tumber 1999: 118) provide a useful journalistic perspective on newsworthiness, and point out that 'news production is rarely the active application of decisions of rejection or promotion to highly varied and extensive material'. It is, they continue, 'the passive exercise of routine' that governs news selection. As Stuart Hall (1973: 181) argues, too frequently we speak of news as if there are set and clearly identifiable criteria for selection. In fact, he argues, news selection is often 'un-transparent' and reflects seemingly intuitive journalistic decisions about what *feels right* as news. In this context David Manning White's (1950) early study of newsworthiness is really instructive. His is one of very few studies that looks at what *doesn't* make it into the news. Describing journalists and editors as 'gatekeepers', White looked at the process whereby the latter filter the news. He asked a US wire editor – that is, an editor whose job it is to scan and select press agency articles for inclusion in a newspaper – to note the reasons for selecting or rejecting all the articles he surveyed during a single week in 1949. Most items were rejected on the basis of a vague feeling that they weren't quite right: there was no formal assessment process of items' news value, in other words. Moreover, in many cases the editor had simply written something to the effect of 'would use if space' on a potential news item, suggesting that there is a lot of 'grey' news material that doesn't make the news for indeterminate, complex reasons.

In our discussion of how news is selected we've found that this process might be thought of in terms of conscious and unconscious decisions about the value of crime stories. The presumption here – and, in fact, throughout this section – is that editors and journalists select the news for consumers. The increased popularity of the Internet as a means of accessing the news may well be changing this relationship – we turn to this in our final section.

## Online news: who selects the news now?

Whilst the newspaper industry might be struggling, there has been a significant growth in the users of online news. Take the fact that ComScore, one of the leading analysts of worldwide Internet use, announced an 11 per cent increase in traffic to European online news sites from 2010 to 2011 ('Newspaper Sites Across Europe Demonstrate Growth in the Past Year', 2011). According to their report, the *Daily Mail*'s website was the tenth most popular in Europe in 2011. If we look just at web use in the UK, we find that BBC Online was the fifth most visited website in the UK in 2012, with only Google UK, Google, YouTube, and Facebook preceding it in the rankings (Alexa UK Traffic Rank, August 2012). In fact, four of the 20 most visited websites in the UK in 2012 were news sites, namely BBC Online, dailymail.co.uk, guardian.co.uk, and telegraph.co.uk (ibid.). Many of the news items published on these sites originate from the newspapers' print versions, and in that sense the news we consume online isn't different in content to the items we read in print. In other respects, though, the type of news we access online is dramatically different to reports found in more traditional sources. Take the items published in the *Huffington Post*, an entirely online news publication. Launched in 2005 in the USA, the *HuffPost* is an online news hub – it publishes in-house work from a dedicated team of columnists, but mainly consists of republished news items from international news outlets and, importantly, selected posts from an army of bloggers. Here, traditional sources of news sit alongside blogs from celebrities, policy-makers, scientists, and stay-at-home mums – and this mix does signal a change in news content. The extraordinary success of the *HuffPost* suggests that this is a format that works. At the time of writing, the original US version of the site is the third most visited news website in the world (Alexa Global News Traffic Rank, August 2012).

There are some obvious reasons for the popularity of online news: it's often free, easy to access, and constantly updated. Beyond that, it allows us to take a more active role as news consumers, clicking on links that catch our eye, bypassing sections of news that don't seem relevant to us, and commenting on news items. The Internet also allows us to check a news story, comparing the BBC's version to reports in, say, the online *Daily Mail* and *New York Times* – and perhaps looking at a couple of relevant blog posts too. In this sense we can assimilate a range of reports from different vantage points. The Internet is unique in providing us with the capacity to customise, contribute to, and easily cross-reference the news. It's not just that the Internet is a *convenient* news provider; it meets our desire to choose the news we read or watch and to take part in news creation and selection. There's something really culturally resonant about all this. Social theorists have long suggested that the postmodern citizen is fundamentally a consumer, interested in personally choosing from a range of products, and cynical about the veracity of official accounts. We should see the popularity of online news in this context.

Before we rejoice about the possibilities afforded by online news, it's important to realise that it's not quite the revolution that it seems. We might be able to select which items to read online, but the range of articles from which we choose is not determined by us. Moreover, online news organisations still prioritise certain items over others, their main page tending to mimic that of a newspaper's front page. Remember also that most online news derives from print news – and so the same problems of dependency on official sources and press agency material apply. As for the possibility that blogs offer up a more informal source of news, free from institutional bias, there's much to suggest otherwise. The important question here is: how do bloggers source their news? With the exception of a handful of bloggers, the answer is, mainly from online newspapers! Bloggers frequently quote formal news items at length, sometimes even integrating whole sections of text into the blog. In 2008 the Associated Press decided to create clear rules concerning bloggers' use of their articles, such was their concern about the level of copyright infringement. All this suggests that traditional sources of news are simply being delivered through different platforms, not disappearing altogether.

## Questions for discussion

Q1) What are the problems with newspapers' reliance on press agency material when it comes to crime news?

Q2) What does Roland Barthes (1972: 151) mean by the suggestion that news involves the 'miraculous evaporation of history' from events? Why might this be a particular problem for crime news?

Q3) What would you include in a list of news values for twenty-first-century crime reporting?

Q4) To what extent has the Internet transformed the way in which we consume crime news?

## Chapter summary

This chapter has considered how journalists source and select crime news. In summary, we've considered the following points:

- Many newspapers in the economically advanced world are experiencing a sharp decline in circulation figures as a result of the rise of free news on the Internet, amongst other things. This means that journalists and editors are under increased pressure to produce news cheaply. One consequence of this has been a new emphasis on 'soft news' stories – items that require little journalistic investigation and have an obvious hook. Violent crime often constitutes 'soft news' and research suggests that coverage of such incidents has increased significantly over the past few decades.
- Few crime stories are uncovered by journalists' independent investigations. Instead, journalists rely upon information from criminal justice agencies (particularly the police) and material produced by press agencies.
- The official, government version of events is particularly likely to feature in crime news: press agency articles are often based on press releases from state-run organisations, and journalists often prioritise quotations from criminal justice personnel.
- Journalists and editors often judge potential news items on the basis of their newsworthiness, that is, their possession of such news values as a negative outcome, personalisation, and simplicity. Incidents that possess these values are particularly likely to make the news, with the most newsworthy items making front page news. Violent crime possesses many of these news values, and this might explain why this sort of incident receives disproportionate media attention.
- Some news values are of enduring importance – such as immediacy and novelty. Others are context-specific. For example, Jewkes (2011) points out that child-victims and offenders, random violence, and individual explanations for crime have become especially newsworthy in the last few decades.
- Incidents that might prompt a collective outpouring of grief, outrage, and anger are also particularly likely to make the news – terrorism, child sex abuse, and murder are all good examples.
- The Internet seems to have radically transformed the way in which we consume crime news by allowing readers to select news items and seek out multiple stories on the same event, even informal, personal versions in the form of blog posts. However, online news websites tend to be based on the print version of the newspaper and most bloggers report news stories

covered by online newspapers. In this sense traditional forms of news are simply being delivered differently, rather than disappearing altogether.

## Recommended reading

Becker, Lee, Lowrey, Wilson, Claussen, Dane, and Anderson, William (2000) 'Why Does the Beat Go On? An Examination of the Role of Beat Structure in the Newsroom', *Newspaper Research Journal*, 21(4): 2—16.
This article gives an insight into the practical, day-to-day workings of three local US newspapers. The authors focus on how these newspapers' newsrooms use the beat system to organise news production. The study demonstrates the continued importance of the 'crime beat'.

Chermak, Steven and Weiss, Alexander (2005) 'Maintaining Legitimacy using External Communication Strategies: An Analysis of Police—Media Relations', *Journal of Criminal Justice*, 33(5): 501—512.
This article provides a fascinating insight into the relationship between the police and news organisations in the USA. Based on a survey of police public information officers, Chermak and Weiss highlight the symbiotic nature of this relationship: the police use the news to promote a positive image of themselves and news organisations enjoy privileged access to official information about crime.

Chibnall, Steve (2005) *Law and Order News*. London: Routledge.
A classic study that looks at news production from a Marxist perspective. Chibnall looks at crime news from 1945 to 1975 and considers the ideological underpinnings to news selection. His remains one of the most influential conceptions of the professional structures and news values that influence crime reporting.

Galtung, Johan and Ruge, Mari H. (1965) 'The Structure of Foreign News', *Journal of Peace Research*, 2(1): 64—91.
Often seen as the first major contribution to the literature on news values, Galtung and Ruge's article is based on a study of foreign political crises in four Norwegian newspapers. Based on this analysis they created a list of common attributes which, they reasoned, helped explain why particular events make the news.

Jewkes, Yvonne (2011) *Media and Crime*. 2nd edition. London: Sage.
Jewkes sets about producing a list of news values for the twenty-first century, thus updating the work done by Galtung and Ruge and Chibnall. She suggests that contemporary news values include child-victims and risk, amongst other things.

Katz, Jack (1987) 'What Makes Crime "News"?', *Media Culture and Society*, 9.
An under-rated but brilliant essay from the US sociologist, Jack Katz. His study is based on an analysis of newspaper articles about crime in the *New York*

*Times*, *Newsday*, and the *Los Angeles Times*. He argues that it is generally the moral features of crime stories that attract journalists, editors, and readers alike. Crime news stories are, almost without exception, moral vignettes, marking out right and wrong, employing a moral register, and enjoining the reader to feel the force of anger, hatred, disapproval, or empathy.

## CHAPTER 2

# *Terrorism in the news*

A terrorist is someone who performs acts of violence to challenge the current social and political structure. We should recognise from the outset that terrorist acts are subject to redefinition over time. There are numerous historical examples where a wholesale shift in the social order or social values means that a group that was once described as 'terrorists' come to be seen retrospectively as 'freedom fighters'. Take the fact that the parliament for the newly formed Irish state in 1922 was made up of people who had been in prison on charges of political violence just a year before. Or consider the fact that Nelson Mandela, Martin McGuinness, and George Washington were all judged at one time to be part of terrorist groups. We tend to see the violence they engaged in rather differently now, as, for example, legitimate resistance to state repression. The fact that public perception of political violence can change so radically highlights that our ideas about who is 'in the right' and who is 'in the wrong' are culturally constructed when it comes to this set of offences. As we'll see, the mass media play a key role in persuading us one way or the other.

This chapter starts with a consideration of the centrality of terrorism in the news since 2001, proceeds by considering the rhetorical devices commonly used in news reporting on terrorism, and then looks at a couple of case studies. We examine the treatment of the Northern Irish 'Troubles' in the British news and the Israel–Arab conflict in the US and UK news. In both cases we can see a pro-state line in news reporting. In the case of reporting on the Troubles this was mainly a consequence of state censorship and control of media content. The reasons for one-sided reporting on the Israel–Arab conflict are less immediately evident. In sum, we'll be looking at a number of different ways in which media bias can manifest itself and operate. We end the chapter with a consideration of why news reporting on terrorism tends to support the role of the nation-state and the political uses of terrorism.

## Why does terrorism top the global news agenda?

Very few crimes today are as newsworthy as a terrorist attack. This is the sort of crime that tops the news agenda and stays there for weeks, sometimes even months. Just think of the coverage of the attacks on Manhattan's World Trade Center in 2001, the London underground in 2005, and a Norwegian youth summer camp in 2011. Why is so much news devoted to terrorism? If we think back to the material we covered on news values in Chapter 1, we might point out that it's violent, easily passes the threshold for news, and allows for a moral register in reporting. As important as these features are in propelling a story about a terrorist atrocity to the front page, we should recognise that there is something historically specific about contemporary news coverage of terrorism. For one thing, there's *so much more* news today about the threat of terrorism than there was 20 or 30 years ago.

One popular idea is that terrorists today have become more adept at using the mass media for the purposes of publicity – indeed, modern forms of terrorism are partly distinguished by their reliance on global media. In turn, terrorist atrocities today are *designed* to attract international media attention so that, as Nacos (2002: 3) suggests, media impact has become part of the 'calculus' of terrorism. There's certainly much to suggest that terrorist groups have become more concerned with how an act can be translated into an iconic media image. Think, for one moment, about the attack on the Twin Towers in Manhattan in September 2001. Hijacking and then crashing airplanes into a symbol of US financial prowess in a city that is itself an icon of Western consumerism was meant as a message of disgust with the very tenets of Western society. The hallmarks of US society – skyscrapers, financial success, consumerism, and high technology – were transformed into tools for causing great harm and suffering. The images of events that day *by themselves* succinctly conveyed the terrorists' message. There was no need for translation, voiceover, or soundtrack: the pictures were perfectly suited to instantaneous global news broadcasting. The act was clearly designed with the mass media in mind.

We could say, then, that the free and mass media were another of the foundational elements of Western society implicated in the terrorists' act. The perpetrators of 9/11 intended for the event to attract global media coverage, but they didn't distribute the iconic images from that day – news organisations did. If the former produced the bare content of the publicity message, the latter were responsible for its packaging and delivery. After all, it was the mass media that succinctly branded the terrorist attacks in Manhattan as '9/11' and the London attacks in 2005 as '7/7'.

All this is deeply suggestive of the fact that news outlets benefit from modern terrorism as much as modern terrorism benefits from the media. The symbiotic relationship between news outlets and modern terrorist groups goes some way towards explaining why terrorism has come to top the global news agenda. Another, more obvious explanation, for the increase in news reporting is that the events of 9/11 made terrorism the global political issue of the twenty-first century and provided a means of framing subsequent terrorist threats and attacks. Most obviously, perhaps, post-9/11, terrorism has become synonymous with radical Islam. Commenting on global television networks' handling of terrorism, Thussu (2006: 9) notes that Islamic Fundamentalism receives a 'disproportionate amount of airtime … in comparison with Christian, Jewish, or Hindu varieties of religious fundamentalisms'. Dreher (2007) draws a similar conclusion about reporting on domestic terrorism in Australian newspapers. Focusing on how newspapers framed the detention of Dr Haneef, an Indian doctor held without charge in Australia under counter-terrorism laws, Dreher shows that reporting drew upon a stock of familiar ideas concerning the distinctive threat of Islamic Fundamentalism to national security. Taking a rather different approach, Richardson (2004) finds that British newspapers have come to associate Islam with terrorism. In a content analysis of 276 British newspaper articles he found that terrorism was mentioned in 16 per cent of the articles that contained substantial reference to Islam. He concludes that 'the topic of terrorism is a perpetual feature of reporting on this subject' (p. 130).

The objection that many, including Richardson, make is that, in terms of terrorist attacks in economically advanced countries, Islamic Fundamentalists are far from being the most likely perpetrators. The European Union (EU) publishes a special report on terrorist attacks within its member states, entitled the 'EU Terrorism Situation and Trend Report' (TE-SAT). In 2011, the report identified three groups of organisations which had committed terrorist attacks during 2010: Islamic Fundamentalist groups, separatist groups, and left-wing/anarchist groups. Islamic Fundamentalist groups had been responsible for three attacks with no fatalities during the year. However, this figure is dwarfed by the number of attacks carried out by the other two groups during 2010: left-wing/anarchist groups had been responsible for 45 attacks with six fatalities and separatist groups for 160 attacks and one fatality (TE-SAT 2011: 20–25). When it comes to the type of organisation that carries out terrorist attacks in the USA, as in Europe, they are very rarely of an Islamic orientation. The Federal Bureau of Investigation's (FBI) report on the threat of terrorism in the USA between 2002 and 2005 showed that, of the 27 recorded attacks on home soil since 9/11, the vast majority (24) had been carried out by radical environmental/animal activist groups, one by a white supremacist, one by an unknown organisation or person, and one by an individual whose motivation was unclear, but appeared to be related to religious and political beliefs (FBI 'Terrorism 2002–2005': 65–66).

Yet, across the US and Europe, the threat of domestic terrorism remains firmly associated with Islamic Fundamentalism. Take the fact that when a Norwegian youth summer camp was attacked in the summer of 2011, the media immediately – and erroneously – presumed it was a radical Islamic group that was responsible. The perpetrator was in fact a deeply patriotic Norwegian citizen. That the global news media had problems in integrating this perpetrator profile into reporting demonstrates our expectation that terrorism is the work of social outsiders.

Indeed, it's reasonable to suggest that one reason why news reports on terrorism focus disproportionately on Islamic Fundamentalism is that it is easy to frame this as an alien ideology and a threat to mainstream social norms and values. Environmental extremists and conservative patriots just don't fit the conventional media image of the terrorist: both are just too close to home, in both senses of the phrase. This should draw our attention to a central news frame in reporting on terrorism – the idea of 'them versus us' (see 'News frames'). We turn again to this idea in Chapter 8 when we discuss the theory of cultural trauma; for now it's enough to point out that an important feature of news reporting on terrorism is the emphasis on the distance between 'our' values and way of life, and that of the terrorist group.

---

**News frames**

The news interprets events for us, encouraging us to mentally place or frame an incident in a certain way. These so-called news frames are 'persistent patterns of selection, emphasis, and exclusion that furnish a coherent inter-pretation and evaluation of events' (Norris, Kern, and Just 2003: 4). Take the frequent suggestion that there is a 'war on terror'. This encourages the reader or viewer to frame terrorism as a particular kind of threat, requiring a particular kind of response.

Discussion Question: An official response to a serious crime problem or criminal incident is often framed by politicians and news reporters as a 'war' (think, for example, of the 'war on drugs'). What does this news frame encourage us to think about crime?

---

## Rhetorical devices in the 'semantics of terror'

The idea of 'them versus us' is just one of the rhetorical devices used to persuade us of the legitimacy of state violence and the illegitimacy of terror-ist violence. Another important tactic is to frequently suggest to the public that 'they' struck the first blow – we can see this very clearly in the section below on reporting of the Northern Irish Troubles. The presumption is that the public will see whoever 'started it' as the guilty party and any violent state action as retaliation and just. In his speech following the death of Osama bin Laden, President Obama repeatedly asserted the idea that the USA's 'war on terror' was not of their choosing, that they were not the initiators of violence. The intended effect of such a statement was to render state violence legitimate and legal – fair punishment, even.

This structure of initiator–retaliator is part of what Chomsky and Herman (1979: 85–95) famously described as the 'semantics of terror'. They point out that the word 'terrorism' is popularly used to denote not simply political violence, but political violence used specifically against the established order, or 'terrorism from below'. This is in strict contrast to the original use of the term 'terrorism'. The term was first used to refer to the killing of civilians during the French Revolution in the late eighteenth century – 'Le Terreur' referred, in other words, to violence carried out *by* the state (Eagleton 2005: 1). The popularisation of the idea that 'terrorism' refers specifically to violence carried out against the state is, in Chomsky and Herman's view, a 'device to facilitate an exclusive preoccupation with the lesser terror of the alienated and the dispossessed, serving virtually as an apologetics for state terror' (p. 87). Note the phrase 'lesser terror': Chomsky and Herman's point is that economically advanced nation-states are much more able and likely to inflict suffering than groups of political radicals. They point out that during the period of the Vietnam War in the USA 'students, war protesters, Black Panthers, and assorted other dissidents were effectively branded as violent and terroristic by a government that dropped more than five million tons of bombs over a dozen year period on a small peasant country with no means of defence' (pp. 86–87).

Chomsky and Herman suggest that public debates about terrorism cast our attention away from gross acts of violence perpetrated by the state. A rhetorical device that helps in this construction is the persistent suggestion that the terrorists' behaviour is absolutely inexplicable, the expression of some sort of misplaced bloodlust, or born out of anarchic sentiments. At the same time, the history and politics of a situation tend to be neglected. These features work together: obscuring the context for terrorism works towards the impression that there is no real or good reason for the violence.

A further, distinctive rhetorical device has emerged in twenty-first-century news reporting on terrorism, and that is the assertion that the state is engaged in a 'war on terror'. Levenson (2004) notes that this military frame quickly became predominant in news reporting on 9/11, something that is supported by Dreher's (2007) analysis of Australian news reporting. The military framing urged readers and audiences to believe that the state response should be combative (rather than, say, diplomatic), and violent retaliation was just and necessary. It also helped legitimate the USA's subsequent attack on Afghanistan; the idea of fighting a 'war on terror' was easily conflated – in political as well as media rhetoric – with the idea that it was necessary to launch military attacks on a country with which the terrorists were associated in various ways.

The final rhetorical device I want to mention here is the insistence that terrorism is a criminal rather than political act. As we'll see below, this was a device that was regularly used in British reporting on the Northern Irish Troubles. What is the intended effect of this? Unpacking what it means to describe someone's behaviour as criminal should help us answer this question. When we use this label we're insisting that:

- The person or group is individually responsible and culpable for an act
- There are no convincing mitigating factors that explain why someone/a group acted a certain way
- An act is a rejection of mainstream social values and rules
- An act requires state-administered punishment.

To insist that terrorists are criminals, then, is to deny the legitimacy of any political or religious motivation for the act and to accept state violence as just punishment. We return to this point in the concluding section of this chapter – now, let's consider more closely news reporting on two specific terrorist groups.

## The Northern Irish Troubles in the British news

The euphemistically named 'Troubles' began in the late 1960s with an escalation in political protests across Northern Ireland – like, it should be said, much of Western Europe and North America during this counter-cultural period. The situation in Northern Ireland worsened significantly in 1972 when a march in the Northern Irish city of Derry erupted into violence. The marchers, many of them members of the Northern Ireland Civil Rights Association, had turned out to protest against the ongoing infringement of Catholics' civil and human rights by the British government, particularly the practice of internment without trial. Brought in to control a fractious group of protesters, British military personnel opened fire on the crowd, killing 14 and injuring 30 – hence the fact that the march quickly became known as 'Bloody Sunday'. The British military and protestors told very different stories about what happened on that day: the former claimed that they were responding to shots fired by an increasingly aggressive crowd whilst the marchers claimed the military attacked an unarmed, peaceful group of protestors. The key issue, in other words, was who started things, and that remained a highly contentious matter until 2010, when the government-funded Saville Inquiry into Bloody Sunday published its findings. The Inquiry fully supported the marchers' version of events. Discussing the report in the House of Commons, the British Prime Minister David Cameron condemned the British military's actions as 'unjustified and unjustifiable' (BBC News Online, 2010).

Back, though, to 1972. In the tumult that followed Bloody Sunday, the British government decided to take 'direct rule' of Northern Ireland, transferring power for the running of the province from Stormont to Westminster. So began several decades of stalled negotiations and violence to wrest back political control of the region. Of course, like most seminal historical events, the backdrop to the Troubles is centuries of turmoil and antagonism, in this case between those loyal to the Irish state, dominated by Catholicism and left-leaning politics, and those loyal to the British state, the home of Protestant Anglicanism. Whilst much of Ireland had gained independence from the UK in 1922, six of the Northern provinces had, at the last minute, been retained as part of the UK. Yet the partitioning of North and South was far from straightforward: many in the Northern provinces still wanted to be part of a united, Catholic Ireland – they were Irish Republicans. The fractious relationship between Protestants and Catholics in Northern Ireland is well known, and there's no need to dwell on the history too much here. Suffice it to say that at the time of the march in 1972 the tension between the two groups had become particularly marked and increasing numbers of Catholic Northerners were becoming affiliates of the anti-British Provisional Irish Republican Army (PIRA).

The situation in Northern Ireland quickly progressed into something approaching a civil war, with the military and police enforcing curfews and 'no go' areas, and dissident Republicans embarking upon a series of attacks on police, politicians, and public buildings. It would take some three decades, and over three thousand deaths, before there was anything like reconciliation in Northern Ireland. In that time the British media would play a central role in defining the conflict for a British audience (and, of course, Protestants in Northern Ireland).

One thing that's immediately striking about the British media coverage of the Troubles during the 1970s and 1980s is the consistency in reporting. As we'll see below, this was principally because the British media were strongly encouraged – and in some senses forced – to support the government line on events. For now let's concentrate on sketching out the portrayal of the Troubles in the British press. The civil strife was framed as the work of a small number of anarchic Catholic dissidents. The British government, along with various agencies of state control, were depicted as working to restore peace and get rid of a fractious element of Northern Irish society. Violence, it was insisted, was essentially one-sided – where the police and military did use violence it was in keeping with their role as defenders of the peace. Above all else, there was an insistence that the Republican agitators were criminals and the agents of the state law-enforcers. In the case of Bloody Sunday, for example, the military's assault on the protestors was immediately presented by the British government and media as a *defensive* act. The protesters, the British military claimed, had opened fire first, making this an act of terrorism against the state.

It is just such neat categorisations that Liz Curtis (1984: 1) has in mind when she describes the British media's depiction of the Troubles as a 'propaganda war ... for the hearts and minds of the British people on the question of Ireland'. In what is often seen as the seminal work on this subject, Curtis describes the extraordinary steps the British government took to control media coverage of the conflict. Indeed, not since the Second World War had the British state waged such a consistent and unswerving war of propaganda: and this war, Taylor argues, was fought 'chiefly through the mass media' (1999: 249). So it was that reporting on the Troubles was subject to a very significant level of state control and censorship. As Bill Rolston (1996) points out, we should acknowledge also that various indirect and non-legislative controls were set in place to encourage pro-British news reporting. For example, in 1971, and to avoid political flak from Westminster and conservative strands of the press, the British Broadcasting Corporation (BBC) instituted a form of self-censorship, commonly referred to as the reference upwards system (Curtis 1984: chapter 8). Though not direct censorship, this set up a system of internal checks so that handling of the Troubles met professional standards: in practice it meant that BBC managers had an extraordinary degree of control over programming decisions (pp. 10–14). In particularly sensitive cases, where, for example, a member of the PIRA was to be interviewed, the Director General of the BBC was to be consulted. Curtis suggests that 'referencing up' had two key benefits for the British state: first, in creating an atmosphere of suspicion and anxiety it was just as effective as state censorship in making sure the 'right message' got across and, secondly, as the state officially had no hand in policing journalistic output, it could not be subject to charges of censorship.

News reporting was also affected by the swathe of legislation brought in to tackle the Troubles, and this is where there was direct state control over news broadcasting and reporting. The 1974 Prevention of Terrorism Act (PTA), for example, officially declared the PIRA an illegal organisation, and this all but ended journalists' interviews with its spokesmen. Perhaps the most famous legislation to affect media coverage, though, was the 1988 broadcasting ban on certain pro-Republican organisations (see Curtis and Jempson 1993 for a full discussion of the ban). The ban prevented the broadcasting of any word spoken by representatives of eleven listed organisations and any word spoken in support of these organisations. The ban was extraordinary, not least of all because three of the eleven affected organisations (including Sinn Fein) were in fact legal political parties at the time. Nonetheless, as Rolston (1996) points out, it had a solid legislative foundation: the ban was an amendment to stipulations already in place in the Broadcasting Act 1981 and the BBC Licence and Agreement, both of which give the government power to restrict media content. Indeed, the state's censorship of media reporting on the Troubles was, as Rolston puts it, 'a peculiarly democratic form of censorship' (p. 243), achieved by extending legislation that had been fully discussed at Westminster and by urging media organisations to self-police.

It was through such means that the British government attempted, with great success, to make itself the sole and primary definer of the Troubles. There was, nonetheless, some media ingenuity when it came to interpreting and getting round the various government diktats. For example, broadcasters came up with the canny solution of using actors to provide voiceovers for interviews with members of the organisations affected by the broadcasting ban. An entire generation grew up watching lip-synched interviews with, amongst others, Gerry Adams, his Irish accent replaced with a clipped English intonation. The innovation showed up the ridiculousness of the broadcasting ban, and its failure to deny terrorists the 'oxygen of publicity', as Thatcher had described its purpose in a speech to the American Bar Association in 1985.

Nonetheless, the ban did mean that media coverage focused more on the views of those taking the official, government line than those representing Republican dissident organisations. One consequence of this was a need for an expanded government personnel and funding to provide press releases and official commentaries on the Troubles. In 1969/70 the Northern Ireland Office (NIO) spent £184,100 on press, public relations, and advertising. A decade later they were spending around £2.5 million a year (Miller 1994: 292). In his fascinating study of the Northern Ireland Information Service (NIIS), the branch of the NIO responsible for media relations, Miller (ibid.) observes two main lines taken in press releases from the NIIS: that Republican violence was an 'assault on democracy' and that Northern Ireland was a 'community on the move'. The use of crime metaphors to describe the threat to a nation's values – exemplified in that phrase 'assault on democracy' – is commonplace in media reporting on terrorism. That such rhetorical flour-ishes are used in cases of political violence is deeply suggestive of the impor-tance social authorities attach to the allocation of criminal responsibility to terrorist groups.

In fact, the criminality of the PIRA was a central theme in official pronouncements relayed in news reports. Take, for example, Margaret Thatcher's much-publicised speech at Stormont in 1981. The speech was prin-cipally a response to a hunger strike organised by members of the PIRA held at HM Prison Maze. The strike – in which ten prisoners died, including Bobby Sands – was to protest the government's refusal to grant special category status to prisoners belonging to the PIRA. That is, they were being denied the status of 'political prisoner' and were instead being treated as rank and file criminals. The protest illuminates the ideological importance of the label 'criminal' – the fact that, in cases of terrorism in particular, the use of the rhet-oric of crime and punishment can become the very heart of the matter. Just as the hunger strikers and the wider PIRA were battling for their acts *not* to be described as criminal, the British government sought to make this the frame of reference for Republican violence. Thatcher's 1981 speech is a case in point. Here she introduced a turn of phrase that would prove to be deeply resonant – the Republican dissidents were, she said, nothing more than 'men of violence'. 'I recognise', she went on, 'that the present violence has its roots deep in the past'. 'But', she added, 'past failure cannot justify crime and violence today' and the government should 'staunchly uphold the law and ensure that it is applied equally and fairly' (Thatcher 1981). Here Thatcher urged a view of Republican dissidents as driven by bloodlust and the state as the neutral (staunch and fair) defender of law and order.

We see this representation of the state as protector elsewhere in news reporting on the Troubles. Take, for example, the coverage of the 1984 PIRA bombing of the Brighton hotel at which the Conservative Party conference was taking place. Ten people died, including the Queen's cousin Lord Mountbatten. The British newspaper coverage of the incident was unanimous in decrying the act and also, more importantly, in promoting mainstream social values and the state's plight in protecting them. 'Thus', Taylor writes, 'in the aftermath of Brighton, Fleet Street declared that Britain would not be bombed out of Ulster, and would emerge with renewed determination to defend democracy against the men of violence' (1996: 329). Taylor fittingly describes the news coverage as an 'affirmative media ritual'. Certainly, the moral register employed in such accounts urged collective and unifying outrage and promoted the state's role as moral arbiter.

To many scholars, this rendering of the conflict contributed to a gross public misconception of the Troubles. The uncompromising, moral tone of reporting meant that the political and historical context for events was often obscured. Hayes (2003: 150), for example, points to a decontextualisation of the Troubles in the news and the continual suggestion, in the British media, that the situation was simply the work of 'immoral alchemists of anarchy'. Curtis, too, emphasises that news reporting tended to present the Troubles in an ahistorical and apolitical manner, concentrating on 'violence to the exclusion of politics' (1984: 107). This meant that during the early 1980s, when there was an escalation in British media propaganda as a response to the Irish Republican prisoners on hunger strike, it was possible for the British media to assert that Republican dissidents had been responsible for practically all of the deaths during the Troubles without much concern about public backlash (ibid.). The British media suggestion that violence was one-sided and inexplicable had won out. Take the fact that on the day of the funeral for the hunger striker Bobby Sands *The Times* ran a front page story that began: 'The Roman Catholics buried Bobby Sands today as Protestants lamented their 2,000 dead from 12 years of terrorism' (in Curtis 1984: 108). In fact, by 1981 the police and British military had been responsible for the death of over 200 people, Protestant loyalists for the death of over 600 people, most of whom had been civilians (p. 109). The idea that the news is focused on the present to the neglect of historical background is something we came across in the previous chapter when we considered 'news values'. What Barthes (1972: 151) called the 'miraculous evaporation of history' in the news is, we find here, a key lever for protecting the status quo and obscuring dissenting voices.

## The Israel—Arab conflict in the UK and US news

Like the Northern Irish Troubles, the Israel–Arab conflict has a long history. The modern state of Israel was formed in 1948 on an area of land known then as the Palestinian Mandate. The date is not incidental: the new state provided a home for the millions of Jewish people fleeing persecution in the aftermath of the Second World War. In fact, finding a new home had long been a central concern for Jewish Europeans, and the quest was a spiritual one, a central plank of the Zionist faith. The area known as the Palestinian Mandate was, Jewish religious leaders argued, their people's ancient and rightful homeland. This view received something like international validation in 1947 when the newly formed United Nations (UN) passed a motion to partition this strip of land into an Arab state (Palestine) and a Jewish state (Israel), with an international enclave surrounding the important religious sites of Jerusalem and Bethlehem (Bickerton 2009: 66). The decision met fierce resistance from the residents of the Palestinian Mandate. The ensuing war is known to Israelis as the War of Independence and to the Palestinians as The Catastrophe, which gives some indication of how the conflict went (ibid.). It ended with Israel announcing statehood, with a far more significant portion of land than that recommended by the UN, and the Palestinians becoming a dispossessed people.

The Palestinians, and many others besides, saw the founding of Israel as an illegal act. Nonetheless, within hours of announcing the formation of the new state, Israel's status had been recognised by the USA: this seemed to signal their legitimacy as a nation-state. Over the years, and much to the anger of Palestinians, Israel has managed to extend its borders and absorb more and more territory through war, most famously in the six-day war of 1967, initiated by Palestine's neighbours Jordan, Syria, and Egypt. Refusing to rescind their control of the areas gained through this war – in direct contravention of international law – Israel has approved the building of thousands of Jewish settlements on this land. In a conflict that is essentially about territory and belonging, the issue of Israeli settlement-building is deeply sensitive. It is also of great significance that, irrespective of the original UN recommendation, there is, at time of writing, no official state of Palestine. From the Israeli point of view this is because the Palestinians resisted the formation of the Israeli state and in that struggle came out as the losing side, failing to take control of the territory. From the Palestinian point of view the Israelis have no claim over the land other than that based on military might. Today, the paramilitary wings of Hamas and Hezbollah are central in fighting what they see as Israel's illegal occupation of Arab land. Both have been involved in violent attacks on Israel, most notably rocket attacks and two intifada (violent uprisings), and both are seen by the USA and EU as terrorist organisations.

The Israel–Arab conflict is a bitter one, the problem seemingly intractable. Bickerton sums it up as follows: 'The Palestinian Arabs ... regarded the Israelis as foreign intruders who had invaded their land, and from their point of view they were in the right ... Equally, the Zionists could not have accepted anything less than a Jewish state in Palestine' (2009: 66). Certainly, in many senses this conflict appears less 'black and white' than the case of the Northern Irish Troubles. What's interesting, when we look at the UK media depiction of the Israel–Arab conflict, is that, again, political complexity is obscured in news reporting and there is a marked bias that favours one side over the other. Of particular note are the findings from a study by the Glasgow University Media Group (GUMG) (Philo and Berry 2004). The study made use of content analysis to analyse ITV and BBC television news programmes during select periods from 2000 to 2002. By complete coincidence, this overlapped with the period of the second intifada. An incident that precipitated an escalation in the violence was Ariel Sharon's visit to the Temple Mount complex, a site of great religious significance for both Jews and

Muslims. The Israeli politician was campaigning to become prime minister and used the visit as an opportunity to declare that the important religious site would remain under Israeli control.

When the GUMG looked at UK news coverage of the intifada, however, they found that contextual details such as these were given little coverage and, instead, there was a significant and consistent pro-Israeli bias. They discovered that the Israeli perspective was over-represented in the news, with this side's view of things receiving more than twice as much news coverage. The Israelis were often represented as responding to Palestinian violence, as opposed to initiating violence; moreover, the Palestinians were frequently described as terrorists. The history of the conflict was very infrequently covered, allowing for the current state of things – Israel's status as a nation-state and Palestine's status as a group of terrorists – to dominate the public perception of events. Moreover, Israeli casualties were more likely to be reported, even though Palestinian casualties were two times higher during the period in question.

The following television news bulletin headlines, taken from the GUMG study (Philo and Berry 2004: 140–142), reveal further the one-sided nature of media coverage:

Israel gives Arafat an ultimatum: stop the violence or no more peace talks (BBC One Main News, 7 October 2000)

Israel threatens to go in harder if Palestinian attacks don't stop. Palestinians are told they've seen nothing yet, but won't back down (BBC One Early Evening News, 8 October 2000)

A peace process on a knife-edge as Israel's ultimatum to Arafat runs out (BBC One Main News, 9 October, 2000)

More killings as ceasefire fails (ITV Late News, 3 October 2000)

At least a dozen dead as Palestinian protests continue (ITV Late News, 20 September 2000)

Notice how Israel is consistently depicted as the authority figure here – issuing ultimatums and threats – and the Palestinians are represented as childishly ignoring the orders and continuing with the violence. There is a clear sense, in other words, of which side represents social order and which side is precipitating chaos.

We find a similar bias when we look more closely at television news reports in the GUMG study (see, for example, p. 101). Here we find that live action is given priority and political context is generally left uncovered. We're frequently informed that diplomatic efforts, aimed at restoring peace, have been up-ended by a seemingly spontaneous eruption of violence from the Palestinians and that apparently sporadic Palestinian riots have escalated, 'causing' violence on the West Bank. What's particularly striking, though, is the frequent juxtaposition of the two sides in television news reports. The Palestinians are often depicted as setting fire to things and throwing rocks in acts of provocation. The Israeli side is represented by soldiers and police officers who retaliate with rounds of fire. To a British viewer the Israelis possess the familiar paraphernalia of statehood – police stations, a military, weapons, the mechanisms and desire for law and order – whilst the Palestinians employ primitive weapons and tactics – rocks and fire. The effect is to give a clear sense of where proper authority and legitimacy lie, and, interestingly, this is achieved by associating Israel firmly with the iconography of the nation-state and the Palestinians with savagery.

The GUMG study isn't, of course, the only piece of research on the news coverage of the Israel–Arab conflict, and other studies suggest a pro-Palestine bias in the news. In fact, both sides have established media watchdogs to chart biases in media representation, so strong are the concerns amongst both Israeli and Palestinian commentators. Academics, too, have drawn attention to pro-Palestine biases in the US news. Joshua Muravchik (2003), for example, looked at news reporting on ten episodes in the conflict post-2000. He found that the television news channel ABC was particularly anti-Israel, and that this was mainly due to editorial slant and omissions in reporting. Muravchik argues that this news outlet consistently represents Palestine as an 'underdog' and Israel as a bully. Liebes and First (2003) make similar claims about ABC in their fascinating analysis of news coverage of the death of Muhammad Dura, a Palestinian boy who died in his father's arms in front of a news camera. This image, the authors note, became iconographic, and its seemingly direct portrayal of the suffering of an innocent child was central to its effect (p. 67). On closer inspection, though, they found that the image was framed in a certain way, particularly by oral commentary. When it was shown on ABC World News, for example, the news anchor effaced any historical or political context to the incident, opening with the line, 'It happened yesterday in Gaza. A man and his injured son are trapped under Israeli fire ...' (ibid.). The authors argue that the reference to innocent bystanders being 'trapped' by 'Israeli fire' clearly frames Israel as an aggressor and Palestine as an embattled victim. The broadcast went on to refer to Palestinian suicide bombers as 'martyrs', suggesting the rightfulness of their cause.

The bulk of academic writing, however, suggests a pro-Israel slant in the US news and, in turn, an anti-Islamic tone. Friel and Falk (2007), for example, studied coverage of the conflict in a single publication, the *New York Times*, from 2000 to 2006. They suggest that the newspaper ignored Palestinian deaths and Israeli lawlessness, despite the evidence that Israel has contravened international law. They argue that the choice of predominantly pro-Israel experts in newspaper coverage is particularly important in achieving this effect. The US journalist Bruce J. Evenson (2007: 15) has also written about Israel's hold over the US media coverage of the conflict, drawing attention to alterations CNN have allegedly made to broadcasts to appease Israeli lobby groups.

## Explaining the pro-state line in news reporting on terrorism

Traditionally, news reporting on political violence has depicted the nation-state as the 'innocent party', as peace-makers using legitimate force for the sake of a rightful cause. Yet, as we've found above, the state's involvement is rarely unambiguously positive and legal. This begs the question: how can we explain the pro-state bias in news reporting? Let's attend first of all to the two obvious explanations: the fact that the state owns certain news outlets, most notably the BBC, and this logically increases its control over output; and, secondly, the state has the ability to censor the media, thereby obscuring dissident voices. In the case of British reporting on the Northern Irish Troubles these two factors were clearly important: media outlets were clearly coerced into taking a pro-state stance. Whilst it's tempting to see these factors as decisive, though, we should recognise the body of evidence that demonstrates that commercially run news outlets also favour the official, state line on events and in the absence of direct state interference. This was precisely the argument of Herman and Chomsky (1988), in their classic work *Manufacturing Consent: The Political Economy of the Mass Media*. Here they argue that media bias is a consequence of the particular political and economic structure of US society, and, more specifically, the fact that media organisations are driven by capitalist interests. Even in countries where the media are not state-owned or -controlled, in other words, a pro-state line, or 'establishment orientation' is evident. They identify five main 'filters' of news output in the US, all of which provide the conditions for this bias:

1) Ownership: As in other industries, there is a tendency for media organisations to be owned by companies capable of capital investments in the technology needed for large-scale production and distribution. Herman and Chomsky argue that precisely the sort of companies that can make this investment tend also to hold conservative values, presumably because, as highly successful businesspeople, those who head such

organisations have a vested interest in preserving the status quo. Herman and Chomsky draw attention to the gradual disappearance of the radical left-wing press in the UK during the nineteenth century, and argue that this was primarily due to market pressures towards the concentration of ownership (see Chapter 1 for more on this). They suggest that this is evidence that large media corporations are unlikely to support politically radical views.

2) Advertising revenue: Herman and Chomsky point out the central income source for a newspaper is advertising. A newspaper's main product is not the news, then, but a readership or audience (or, put differently, us!). The central commercial interest of a newspaper, therefore, is keeping advertisers happy, and this may mean shelving articles that jeopardise their sponsors' commercial interests.

3) Sources: As we saw in Chapter 1, state officials constitute really important sources of information for journalists. There may well be reluctance to alienate such sources by publishing items that call into question the state's legitimacy. The mass media, they argue, 'are drawn into a symbiotic relationship with powerful sources of information by economic necessity and reciprocity of interest' (p. 14).

4) Flak: News organisations aren't the only conduit for mass communication in our societies. Religious groups, major charities, non-governmental organisations (like Friends of the Earth and Oxfam), and government bodies can all influence public opinion. News outlets therefore tend to avoid making enemies of other major power brokers, lest they provoke their criticism, or 'flak'. This, Herman and Chomsky note, is a key means of 'disciplining' the media (p. 2).

5) An anti-communist ideology: Herman and Chomsky point out that many US journalists held and expressed anti-communist views in the second half of the twentieth century. Whilst most US journalists no longer see communism as a particularly salient threat today, Herman and Chomsky's more general point is still relevant: journalists tend to belong to social groups that hold conservative views and refute any threat to state power.

Herman and Chomsky refer to this as the 'propaganda model', arguing that, along with business leaders and politicians, media owners are members of a political elite that has a vested interest in sustaining the status quo. Overall, and as they put it, 'money and power are able to filter out the news fit to print, marginalise dissent and allow the government and dominant private interests to get their message across to the public' (ibid.). If we see the mainstream media as Herman and Chomsky do, as in various ways beholden to the state and as possessing an inherent tendency to support the status quo, then a pro-state bias in news reporting on terrorism might appear inevitable.

As compelling as this Marxist explanation for bias in reporting might be, we need to beware boiling the propaganda model down to the idea that media owners, editors, and journalists are by nature greedy, self-seeking, and prejudiced. After all, Herman and Chomsky are drawing attention to the effect of abstract social structures – namely capitalism and its relationship to the state – on media production. We should also recognise that there are other important factors that encourage a pro-state bias in news reporting. The pro-Israel slant of news reporting on the Israel–Arab conflict, for example, requires us to develop a more fine-graded argument. To return to Philo and Berry's (2004) study of the British news reporting on the second intifadas, they point to the following reasons for the pro-Israel bias:

- Israel has a superior public relations office and, in turn, is able to better publicise stories that represent their view of things (this view is supported by Liebes and First 2003: 61; Evenson 2007).
- British news programmes favour US experts, many of whom take a pro-Israel line.
- There is a practical difficulty in covering political context in a news programme containing short and succinct bulletins.
- It was easy to use the already available interpretive framework of 'Islam versus Western civilisation' in news reports on the second intifada given that it coincided with 9/11. Israel, in this sense, was associated with 'us', the Palestinians with 'them' (supported by Liebes and First 2003: 61).

If we recall what we learned about 'news values' in Chapter 1 we might say that the pro-Israeli bias is due to the fact that this sort of story is supported by official sources, lends itself to simplification, and is culturally consonant.

## The political uses of terrorism

Governments' interest in controlling media coverage of terrorism and encouraging a pro-state line is in one sense completely understandable. It means that the state's course of action can be defined as right, just, and necessary. However, the value of pro-state news reporting on terrorism goes beyond promoting a certain view of a specific terrorist incident or group. At various points above we've found that terrorism can be used by governments and news outlets to bombastically promote a particular way of life. This serves a double function: it punctures a terrorist group's ideological formulations and reinforces a sense of national pride and unity. In other words, it bolsters *both* a sense of who 'they' are and who 'we' are. In this sense, terrorism has its political uses, and it is this deeper ideological function that I want to explore in this final section of the chapter.

There is, after all, much at stake for a government when it comes to public discussions about terrorism. Just as the Northern Irish hunger strikers perceived the removal of their status as political prisoners to be a threat to their legitimacy, so the political elite resists any challenge to the state's authority – because such a challenge, successfully wrought, delegitimises not just the government in question but also *the very idea* of the state as ultimate law-maker and peace-keeper. The Marxist thinker Jürgen Habermas made a parallel argument some 40 years ago in his book *Legitimation Crisis* when he argued that the trend towards low voting turnouts in economically advanced countries signals an imminent crisis of confidence in the political system. His argument rested on the premise that one of the founding principles of liberal democracies is equal and unhindered political participation. If the public stops contributing to the political process by, for example, not turning out to vote, then surely the very basis for this form of governance is called into question. As it turns out Habermas seems to have been wrong in this particular assumption, but, nonetheless, his work draws attention to something that we often forget: a nation-state and its system of governance are not naturally occurring entities, but *ideas*, and their existence is dependent upon the public investing in these ideas.

The modern nation-state's legitimacy is partly founded on us recognising it as a neutral and rightful rule-maker. Any narrative that challenges this is highly damaging. During periods when the state's legitimacy is in crisis or weakened it is particularly likely to attempt to quash such stories: not only do they weaken further the state's power, but a counter-assertion of shared values can help provide much-needed support for the status quo. This means that the state is particularly likely to censor news reporting on political violence when it is experiencing a broader problem of legitimacy, not, as might be reasonably believed, when the violence in question is especially contentious or the media particularly sympathetic towards the terrorist group in question (for a similar argument see Carruthers 2000). This is borne out by looking again at our two case studies.

Taylor points out that the British government took particularly significant steps in controlling the media during the Second World War and the Northern Irish Troubles – which begs the question: Why did the government seek to control the depiction of *these* conflicts in particular? In the case of the news reporting on the Troubles, it's possible to see the British state's behaviour as linked to a concern amongst the political elite about the loosening of the state's legitimacy. The late 1960s – the point at which the Troubles escalated – was a period of tension across the economically advanced world. The 1960s had been a period of great unrest as large swathes of the population in industrialised countries took to the streets to protest inequalities and discrimination: this was the era of counter-cultural movements such as second-wave feminism, the gay rights movement, the modern environmental movement, and the civil rights movement. Across Europe and North America the role of social authorities was being debated and challenged. Nothing encapsulated this mood quite like the protests concerning military involvement in the Vietnam War. This had become a deeply unpopular conflict in the US in particular, partly because of an entrenched public cynicism about the state's involvement. Debates focused, in other words, on the legitimacy of the state. Curtis (1984) comments that, in the case of British news reporting on the Troubles, the desire to promote a pro-British narrative was accentuated by politicians' fears that this conflict would become the UK's 'Vietnam'. Add to this the fact that the British state was in the process of undergoing a very significant shift in its power, and the motivation for media control becomes clearer. During the mid-twentieth century the UK had been forced to dismantle its Empire. By the late 1940s it had lost its hold over the Indian sub-continent and by the late 1960s most of its African colonies had gained independence – and it had, of course, lost control over most of Ireland several decades before. The protests in Northern Ireland and the spectre of a united Ireland threatened to further diminish their status as a world power. Both – the concern that the Troubles could prove as unpopular as the conflict in Vietnam and the diminished power of the UK – contributed to a sense of real unease about the difficulties in sustaining authority, nationally and internationally. The British state's attempt to control the media image of the Troubles should be seen in this context.

The historical context for the reporting on the Israel–Arab conflict is equally important for understanding the pronounced pro-Israel bias in the US news. The prominent cultural theorist Edward Said (1997), for example, has described the US media as Islamophobic, and explains the pro-Israel bias in this context. Said notes that, according to the US State Department, terrorist attacks originating from the Middle East are sixth in order of frequency, yet the US media associates the region with out-of-control Islamic extremism (1997: xiv). In the US media, Said argues, 'fundamentalist equals Islam equals everything-we-must-fight-against' (ibid.). We devoted considerable space to this argument in the opening section of this chapter, so we won't dwell on the details again here. What is important to emphasise, though, is that in presenting Israel's actions as legitimate the US media reiterates the severity of the threat of Islamic Fundamentalism – thus contributing to the dominant news frame used for reporting on the threat of domestic terrorism. Here news reporting on terrorism is useful in sustaining a narrative about the nature of modern terrorism and its threat to Western civilisation.

We might also see the marked media interest in Islamic Fundamentalism as part of an attempt to reiterate the state's legitimacy, an ideological prop that has been particularly useful for the US during the last decade. Just consider, for a moment, the difficulties facing the USA over the past decade or so, and particularly how tough it has been to consolidate a sense of national identity and state legitimacy: during this period its superpower status has come under threat and it has experienced an economic downturn. Again, we might see media interest in terrorism as a reflection of a broader problem of state legitimation.

Looked at from this perspective, the prominence given to terrorism in newspapers and political debate today is evidence of a crisis of political confidence. Terrorism allows for declamatory assertions of a particular social and political system – of *our* way of life. Waging an ideological war against terrorism is an easy way of shoring up support for a particular social and political system, and an especially attractive ideological prop when other arguments in favour of 'our way of life' are difficult to make or appear redundant. Given this, it is interesting to note that certain sections of the mainstream press have started to become more critical of state involvement in political violence. Take international news outlets' reaction to an Israeli attack on a ship bringing aid to Palestinian refugees in the Gaza strip in 2010: most news organisations framed the event as exemplary of Israel's belligerence. Contributing to this wave of anti-state reporting is the emergence of unofficial news reporting on the Internet. Blogs that reveal the personal costs of conflict and political crisis – so-called 'citizen journalism' – have become especially popular in the last few years, and they allow for a non-state-sanctioned view of a situation to be circulated. Also important is the launch and influence of WikiLeaks, an online news organisation specifically aimed at revealing secret state practices of coercion, negotiation, and warfare – so sensitive is the material reported that the organisation's activities are deemed illegal by many nation-states. All of these developments – the emergence of an anti-state slant in official news reporting, the rise of citizen journalism, and the emergence of WikiLeaks – reflect and contribute to the loosening of state legitimacy. They may signal an important shift in news reporting on political violence, but they may also prompt the state to use more controlling measures to ensure a pro-state line remains the dominant interpretation of events – by, for example, labelling those who pass on information to WikiLeaks as criminals and punishing them accordingly.

## Questions for discussion

Q1) Why is terrorism given such prominence in the news?

Q2) Do you agree with Herman and Chomsky that 'money and power are able to filter out the news fit to print'? How does their propaganda model help explain the pro-state bias in news reporting on terrorism? Can you think of other, more convincing explanations?

Q3) Is there evidence that the pro-state bias in reporting on terrorism is weakening? Why might this be the case?

## Chapter summary

This chapter has explored news reporting on terrorism, giving particular attention to British news reporting on the Northern Irish Troubles and UK and US news reporting on the Israel–Arab conflict. In summary, we've considered the following points:

- Modern terrorist organisations have a symbiotic relationship with news organisations: the former need the latter to spread their ideological message (their access to formal political outlets for communication being blocked) and, in turn, modern terrorist acts provide the basis for front page news stories and intense media coverage.
- Modern terrorist attacks are often designed with the mass media in mind. The attacks on the World Trade Center in September 2001, for example, were easily transformed into a set of iconic images that could be broadcast instantaneously round the world.
- Post-9/11, terrorism has come to be associated with Islamic Fundamentalism despite the fact that most domestic terrorist attacks are carried out by radical environmental groups in the USA and separatist groups in Europe. The threat of Islamic Fundamentalism seems more salient, though, and this is partly because it's easier to frame terrorism as the work of social outsiders. Constructing a 'them versus us' narrative is key to news reporting on terrorism.
- A range of rhetorical devices is used in news reports to focus our attention on a terrorist group's guilt. Stories emphasise that the terrorists struck the first blow and the state is simply retaliating. The word 'terrorism' is used to refer exclusively to violence carried out against the state. The terrorists' violence is described as anarchic and criminal, rather than political.

Historical context is neglected. Post-9/11 a rhetorical device that has become particularly popular is the idea that the state is engaged in a 'war on terror'.

- In some cases news reporting on terrorism can be subject to censorship. For example, British journalists reporting on the Northern Irish Troubles were subject to a range of direct and indirect measures that encouraged them to support the government line. These included making it illegal to broadcast interviews with certain Republican groups. Journalists and editors also adopted systems of self-censorship to avoid flak from mainstream political parties. The consequence of these various measures was uniformity in British news reporting: the British state was consistently represented as a disinterested peace-keeper and Republican groups as 'men of violence'.

- In US and UK news reporting of the Israel–Arab conflict, too, we can detect a dominant pro-state line in reporting, this time in the absence of direct state censorship. The Glasgow University Media Group's study of UK news reporting of the second intifada (2000–2002) indicates that Israelis were often represented as responding to Palestinian violence, as opposed to initiating violence.

- Herman and Chomsky's (1988) propaganda model helps explain the dominance of a pro-state line in news reports about terrorism. They point out that the state controls official sources of news, journalists are often politically conservative, and news providers have a vested interest in protecting the status quo – all of these factors, they argue, work towards dampening critical commentary and encouraging an 'establishment orientation' in news reports.

- Philo and Berry (2004) point to a range of institutional, ideological, and practical factors that have led to a pro-Israel line in news reporting on the Israel–Arab conflict, including the fact that established nation-states have superior public relations offices to radical groups and the practical difficulties in covering the complex historical background to a terrorist group's actions in a news report.

- The final section of this chapter considered the broad political uses of news reporting on terrorism. A government is particularly likely to seek to promote a pro-state line in news reporting on terrorism during periods when public confidence in the government and shared values are low. This is when suggestions that the state has acted illegally or immorally are particularly threatening and stories that reinforce the rightfulness of 'our' way of life are particularly valuable to the political elite.

## Recommended reading

Curtis, Liz (1984) *Nothing But The Same Old Story: The Roots of Anti-Irish Racism*. Belfast: Information on Ireland.
Curtis' book about the media representation of the Northern Irish Troubles is a compelling read, particularly for its discussion of the roots of media bias.

Hayes, Mark (2003) 'Political Violence, Irish Republicanism and the British Media: Semantics, Symbiosis and the State', in P. Mason (ed.) *Criminal Visions: Media Representations of Crime and Justice*. London: Routledge, pp. 133—155.
A thorough and well-written review of the British media's framing of the Troubles. Highly recommended.

Herman, Edward S. and Chomsky, Noam (1988) *Manufacturing Consent: The Political Economy of the Mass Media*. New York: Pantheon Books.
A classic text, *Manufacturing Consent* takes a political economy approach to the mass media and sets out to explain why we commonly find a pro-establishment line in news reporting.

Philo, Greg and Berry, Mike (2004) *Bad News From Israel*. London: Pluto Press.
Philo and Berry's thoughtful content analysis of British television news coverage of the Israel–Arab conflict is worth reading in full. An incisive and accessible history of the conflict precedes the analysis.

## CHAPTER 3

# Victims of sexual violence in the news

The first part of this chapter looks at deficiencies in news reporting on rape, and considers how and why the news perpetuates certain myths about sexual violence. The second half of the chapter looks at how and why the news misrepresents child sex abuse, paying particular attention to the question of why this crime has received so much news coverage in recent decades. These are the main topics covered in this chapter, but we have other, perhaps bigger concerns here too, not least of all the relationship between gender and the representation of victimhood. With that in mind, let's briefly consider a recent report from the Global Media Monitoring Project (GMMP). The group studies the representation of women in national newspapers and news bulletins around the world. One recent study found that a mere quarter (24%) of people who feature in the news (as presenters, experts, interviewees, etc.) are female (GMMP 2010: 7). The group also found that an extraordinary 46 per cent of news stories reinforced gender stereotypes – and, interestingly, crime news was the worst offender, with 50 per cent of stories promoting traditional ideas about femininity and masculinity (p. 9). By far the most significant revelation – and here we return to the main point, above – concerns the association of women with victimhood in the news. In 2009, 18 per cent of women in the news were depicted as victims, in contrast to just 8 per cent of men; 6 per cent of women, as opposed to 3 per cent of men, were represented as survivors (p. 8). Just think about what that means for a moment: roughly *a quarter* of *all* the women that appear in the news world-wide are depicted as experiencing or recovering from some sort of victimisation. When the figures are broken down into different victim categories (victims of natural disaster, war, murder, etc.) we see that around 40 per cent of the female victims and survivors in the news are victims of violent crime of one sort or another, particularly interpersonal violence (GMMP 2010: 15).

The GMMP study raises a set of really interesting questions relevant to the discussion below about crime victims in the news. Why is it that such a high proportion of women in the news are represented as victims? After all, it's *men* who are more likely to be victims of violent crime. Does the association of women with victimhood mean that the label 'victim' has a gendered meaning? And what's involved in the attribution of victim status to women in the news? For example, is there what Chris Greer (2007: 22) calls a 'hierarchy of victimization'?

This chapter considers these issues and questions more deeply. We think about what it means for female victims of sexual violence to be given (or denied) the description of 'victim'. This line of argument mirrors that developed in the previous chapter. There, we were partly concerned with the meaning of the label of 'criminal' as it is applied to cases of terrorism. We were interested in the way in which the language of crime is used in such cases to indicate that responsibility for an act lies squarely with the individual, that there is no need for historical or political contextualisation, and, overall, that an act is to be understood as straightforwardly immoral and worthy of censure. This is why radical terrorist groups often fight being labelled 'criminals': the description denies that an act has a meaning beyond individual pathology or sociopathy.

What does it mean, then, to assert that someone is a 'victim'? As we'll see below, it is to suggest that we see the person as absolutely blameless and having no role to play in his or her victimisation. Just as it's the case that not every group or person who intentionally causes harm is labelled a criminal, not everyone who suffers harm is labelled a victim; one must first meet certain culturally accepted criteria to be granted the label. We consider this more fully below, in the section on rape in the news. Before we turn to these matters, though, a comment on the newsworthiness of sexual violence.

## How newsworthy is sexual violence?

In many respects, sexual violence is highly newsworthy – after all, it brings together the two key news values of sex and violence (see Chapter 1 for more on this). Perhaps this is why sexual violence is more likely than most other crimes to make the news. In an early study, Sherizen (1978) looked at the percentage of police-recorded crimes in the US that get covered in newspapers (or 'shrinkage', as he described it). Murder was by far the crime most likely to make it into print – 70 per cent of police-recorded murders became news-reported crime. After this, rape was the next most likely crime to be reported (5%). For all other crimes, less than 1 per cent of incidents recorded by the police made it into press. What's interesting is that this observation has been replicated in more recent studies and for different countries. Sacco and Fair (1988: 117), in their analysis of all crime news during 1980 in *Vancouver Sun*, a Canadian daily, make a similar discovery – murder and then rape had by far the highest ratio of police-recorded to news-reported crime. Carter (1998), in a more recent study of British newspapers, confirms the pattern. She found that murder had the lowest 'shrinkage' rate, but noted that most news reports are about female murder victims, despite the fact that, in official statistics, victims are overwhelmingly male. She found that after murder, the second most frequently reported crime was rape, accounting for 18 per cent of all newspaper articles in the sample. This is despite the fact that, in the year the study was carried out (1995), rape accounted for only 2 per cent of violent crime recorded by police in England and Wales. In other words, the volume of news about rape is disproportionately high compared to its contribution to overall recorded crime.

It seems, then, that the news depiction of sexual violence is further evidence of what Surette (2010) refers to as the 'law of opposites' that affects media representations of crime. We considered Surette's thesis in the Introduction to this part of the book, but let's quickly refresh our memories, because his argument is particularly relevant to this chapter. Media depictions of crime, Surette argues, seem to run directly counter to the 'reality' of crime (that is, what official statistics tell us about crime). Newspapers and television shows give us the impression that crime is spiralling dangerously out of control. Yet official figures show the crime rate decreasing in most economically advanced countries. Similarly, the vast majority of recorded crime is property crime and a smaller proportion is violent crime; of the latter, the vast majority results in minor injuries. Nonetheless, it is very serious violent offences – particularly those involving murder or rape – that are likely to make the news.

Surette's thesis is certainly compelling, and, as we find below, there are all sorts of ways in which news reporting on sexual violence runs directly counter to reality. We should be careful, though, not to see the 'law of opposites' as something akin to an unstoppable and unchanging law of nature, one that (like gravity) simply 'is'. Media depictions of crime don't run counter to reality in any automatic or default way. Patterns in crime reporting are more complex than that and therefore need careful analysis and interpretation. When we look more closely at sexual violence in the news, for example, we find that some types of sex crime are far more likely to be reported than others. Also, as with news coverage of violence in general, reporting on sexual violence has *increased* significantly since the Second World War in both the UK and the USA (Soothill and Walby 1991; Lees 1995; Cuklanz 1996; Kitzinger 2004). Both of these observations need explanation, and this is another central aim of this chapter.

### Rape in the news

Let's start with the observation that sexual violence hasn't always been high on the news agenda; or, rather – to avoid the suggestion that this category of offence is becoming ever more newsworthy – its newsworthiness is rather changeful. Kitzinger (2004: 15) notes that, whilst British and US newspapers were decidedly quiet on the matter of sexual violence during the middle decades of the twentieth century, from the 1970s onwards we've seen a very significant increase in reporting in this area. She also notes, though, the zeal for reporting on gruesome and titillating cases of sexual exploitation and assault during the mid-nineteenth century, particularly in the coverage of the British Jack the Ripper case (pp. 13–14). Nonetheless, such stories often used euphemisms to refer to the sexual violence involved, and were rarely centrally concerned with rape as a crime, framing the cases instead as matters of indecency, immorality, or taking murder to be the central wrong-doing. In the 1970s, rape came to be discussed in the news as a problem in and of itself – this is how Kitzinger (2004: 15) puts it:

> Prior to developments in the 1970s, the mainstream media paid very little attention to rape: journalists even avoided the word, preferring phrases such as 'carnal knowledge'. By the end of the 1970s, in the UK and the USA, news items on rape had doubled, and increased by a much larger proportion in certain publications.

In trying to account for this increase, Kitzinger draws attention to the rise of second-wave feminism and its attempts to expose violence within the family and home – to make 'the personal political', as the US feminist slogan had it.

Whilst the awareness-raising activities of feminists might have produced a cultural environment in which sexual violence became a more acceptable subject for news reporting, it does not follow that news articles have come to frame rape in feminist terms. The fact that the news tends to focus on specific cases, rather than critical discussion of the social causes of sexual violence, for example, means that rape is rarely framed as anything other than a matter of individual pathology. What aids in this typification of rape is the focus in newspaper reports on attacks carried out by psychotic strangers. Carter (1998: 228), in her study of British newspaper reporting on rape, found double the number of articles on stranger-perpetrated rape than acquaintance-perpetrated rape. Soothill and Walby (1991: 1) also note that the typical sex offender in news reports is the 'stranger pouncing out of a bush', a crazed, 'sick' individual. Yet official statistics demonstrate that sexual violence is far more likely to be carried out by a partner, intimate, or acquaintance than a stranger. If we look at national crime statistics for the UK, USA, and Australia, 10–17 per cent of rapes with adult female victims are carried out by strangers, roughly 30 per cent by an intimate or acquaintance, and anywhere from 20 per cent (in the

USA) to 45 per cent (in the UK) by a current or former partner (see Australian Bureau of Statistics 2004; Home Office 2000; US Department of Justice 2006).

How can we explain this disjuncture between news reporting and the reality of rape? In our discussion of newsworthiness in Chapter 1, we found that a pre-eminent news value is atypicality. News outlets, the argument goes, are more likely to run stories about unusual crimes that have some sort of 'novelty value'. This is the explanation often given for why violent crime is more likely than property crime to make the news, or why stranger-perpetrated violence is, in general, deemed more newsworthy than violence perpetrated by intimates. Random attacks, the argument runs, are unexpected, unusual, and therefore more shocking. The problem with this argument is that the public perceive crime to be mainly violent, and violent crime to be mainly committed by strangers. Even many of my criminology students are visibly surprised to read the sort of statistics quoted in the previous paragraph about stranger-perpetrated rape. Put differently, if news editors and journalists prioritised unexpected stories about rape, they'd be more likely to run items on sexual assaults perpetrated by intimates rather than strangers.

Feminists offer us an alternative explanation, namely that the media perpetuate myths about rape that help prop up the patriarchal social order. The emphasis on stranger-perpetrated rape means that sexual violence is more likely to be seen as a matter of individual psychosis, rather than anything to do with social arrangements and inequality between the sexes. This means that we are free to see rape as a problem of a few sick men, rather than anything to do with the gender hierarchy. Jane Caputi (1987: 2), in an interesting study of the rise of serial sex killings in the USA in the 1970s and 1980s, makes a similar claim, arguing that the 'political factor is everywhere erased in mainstream discussion and analysis of serial murder. Law-enforcement officials and much of the mass media instead usually refer to this phenomenon as "motiveless crime", as an inexplicable epidemic of "recreational murder", the work of a mysterious new breed of "sexual psychopaths"'. Second-wave feminists who wrote about rape in the 1970s – figures like Susan Brownmiller, Susan Griffin, and Kate Millett – saw this dominant conception of sexual violence as a means of dampening critical debate about the social causes of sexual violence and its use as a form of social control. To admit that the home and the family might foster violence would, after all, be to rock the very foundation of patriarchal society. By the 1980s, Diane Russell (1982, 1986) had drawn attention to the hidden rate of rape within marriage and the fact that child sex abuse was most likely to occur within the family. Later in the decade the feminist journal *Ms* was writing about the high incidence of 'date rape' on US university campuses. For all involved in this aspect of the feminist movement, and as Mehrhof and Kearon put it, 'Rape ... is an effective political device. It is not an arbitrary act of violence by one individual on another; it is a political act of oppression ... exercised by members of a powerful class on members of a powerless class' (1971: 155). We usually see violence as a *breach* of the social order, carried out by the asocial and psychotic; here we are being asked to see it completely differently – as an act that *maintains* the status quo, occurring within perfectly 'normal' relationships. This redefinition of violence and its relationship to the social order is one of the most important contributions feminist writers have made to criminological thinking.

In short, by depicting rape as primarily a matter of random stranger violence, and neglecting its incidence within intimate relationships, news reports contribute to the idea that rape is 'sporadic as opposed to structurally generated' (Dowler 2006: 383). This typification of sexual violence as random rather than patterned is incredibly pervasive. In an article looking at the creation of the crime category 'stalking', Lowney and Best (1995) point out that the mass media were unwilling to report incidents when the term, in its earliest uses, referred to intimate partner harassment. This was the meaning of 'stalking' that was originally promoted by feminist groups in the US – and it received little mainstream cultural attention. The media did eventually take up the term, but only when it could be used to refer to celebrities being stalked by eccentric fans – when the perpetrator was a stranger, in other words. I found a similar trend in a study of the changing meaning of the crime category 'date rape' in the US news (Moore 2011). Originally coined by feminist groups and media, the term 'date rape' once referred to rapes carried out during dates. The meaning was quickly transformed by the mainstream press to refer to the surreptitious spiking of women's drinks with drugs like Rohypnol – again, to denote a form of stranger-perpetrated assault. In both cases, terms originally produced by feminist groups to illuminate the problem of intimate partner violence were co-opted by the mass media to offer a view of assault and harassment entirely in line with the dominant conception of violence. Such is the cultural discord produced by the idea that male-on-female violence occurs predominantly within intimate and familial relationships.

There are other reasons to be concerned about the treatment of rape in the news. Perhaps most troubling is the association, in some newspapers, of rape with sex and titillation. For example, some newspapers place particular emphasis on rape victims' physical appearance and previous sexual encounters. There is ample evidence to support this claim. In a study of the depiction of two rape cases in the popular Israeli press, Korn and Efrat (2004) found that the sexual history of the victims was a central theme in reporting, and concluded that this was meant to excite readers. Soothill and Walby (1991) go further, and describe reporting on rape in British tabloids of the 1970s to 1990s as part of a 'soft porn package'. They argue that from this period onwards we see the 'sexualisation of sex crime' in the British press (p. 1). Other scholars have noted a more general trend of 'tabloidisation' over the past few decades, wherein newspapers – even previously serious, broadsheet publications – have become increasingly sensationalist, vulgar, and trivialising (see, for example, Zelizer's recent [2009] edited collection). To return to Soothill and Walby, they note that the re-launch of the British newspaper the *Sun* in 1969 posed a challenge to existing tabloid newspapers and sparked a competition for market dominance. The *Sun's* strategy was to include much more overtly sexual material than had previously been the norm for tabloid newspapers. Printing pictures of topless young women (so-called 'page three girls') is perhaps the most well-known aspect of this strategy but a related tactic was to increase reporting on sexual violence. In analysing these pieces, Soothill and Walby observe that

> the reports are typically sensational and titillating, rather than serious accounts of these crimes. All manner of sexual detail is squeezed into these reports, anything from the previous sex life of a convicted rapist ('the savage between the sheets') to the newspapers' reading of the sexual history of the raped woman: 'Para case girl was "sex maniac".' (p. 3)

Such headlines urge us to see rape as a sexual act involving violence, as opposed to a violent act involving sex. Susan Griffin (1971: 66), in an early feminist account of rape, forcefully argued that rape needs to be seen first and foremost as 'an act of aggression'. She argues that we should resist seeing rape in terms of natural male sexual desire, and recognise it instead as primarily a violent act. The media emphasis on the sexual dimensions of a rape case again helps shift our attention away from crucial questions about the origin and nature of male violence.

Another problem with news reporting on rape concerns what Greer (2007: 22) calls the 'hierarchy of victimization'. Sometimes the label of 'victim' is easily awarded; in other cases the incident is treated more breezily, suggestions of victim culpability are made, and the perpetrators presented as unwitting or unlikely aggressors. When it comes to rape, certain social groups are particularly likely to be near the bottom of the 'hierarchy of victimization'. Rape victims who are also prostitutes, working class, or a member of an ethnic minority are more likely to have their victim status called into question in news reports. In contrast, victims of sexual violence who are white, young, and middle class more easily fit the 'ideal victim' criteria (see 'What makes an ideal victim?'). In a fascinating study, Meyers (2004a) looked at how the rape of African American women at Atlanta's annual Freaknik Festival was handled by the local media. The festival is a weekend-long Spring Break event attended mainly by middle-class students. Meyers notes that there have been concerns during recent years about an increase in the incidence of rape at the festival – and the victims are predominantly local African American women. In her analysis of local television news, Meyers found that women's testimonial accounts were often trivialised: for example, females' first-hand accounts about being groped were combined with images of women in short skirts attending the event. She argues that the trivialisation of these women's experiences is linked to their ethnicity and the fact that the alleged perpetrators are middle-class college students. In this sense social status plays a role in the cultural construction of victims and perpetrators.

---

### What makes an 'ideal' victim?

The first extract below is from a British newspaper article about the murder trial of Vincent Tabak in 2011 (*Daily Mail Online*, 14 October 2011). Tabak was eventually found guilty of murdering Joanna Yeates, his next door neighbour. The second extract is from the same newspaper, and concerns the murder trial of Steve Wright in 2008, the so-called 'Suffolk Strangler' (*Daily Mail Online*, 16 January 2008). Wright too was eventually convicted of murder. Both stories were accompanied by pictures of the victims and accused.

Discussion Point: Looking at the extracts from the two news items below, think about whether the victims are represented as 'ideal' or somehow blameworthy. How is this effect achieved?

'Jo's last night out'

- Jury told the 25-year-old was not drunk before her death
- She was planning to bake cakes and bread when she returned home
- Priest walking his dog spoke to Miss Yeates on her final journey

(full text available at www.dailymail.co.uk/news/article-2048622/ Vincent-Tabak-trial-Pictures-Joanna-Yeates-drinking-night-died.html)

'The Five Troubled Victims of the Suffolk Prostitute Slayer'

The photographs of happy, smiling people were the kind you might find in any family album ... [The] victims in the Suffolk murders were unexceptional women who fell into a life of drugs and prostitution that ultimately led to their death.

(full text available at www.dailymail.co.uk/news/article-508727/The-troubled-victims-Suffolk-prostitute-slayer.html).

---

Circumstantial factors also play a role in the cultural denotation of 'rape victim'. In a famous study of US newspaper articles on four high-profile rape cases during the 1980s, Helen Benedict (1993) argues that, depending on the features of a case, rape victims tended to be portrayed as either 'vamps' or 'virgins': that is, as blameworthy, provocative women who were somehow 'asking for it' or as bespoiled victims. Meyers (1997: 9) argues along similar lines, pointing to a 'culturally defined "virgin-whore" or "good-girl-bad-girl" dichotomy'. It's worth stressing, as Benedict does, that neither characterisation is positive: the 'vamp' is portrayed as complicit in her victimisation; the 'virgin' as utterly lacking in agency. Part of her book is devoted to identifying certain characteristics and circumstances that contribute to a stereotyping of the female rape victim as either a blameworthy vamp or virgin-victim. She finds the following things assist in the labelling of the victim as a vamp (p. 22):

• The victim knew the attacker
• No weapon was used
• The victim is the same class as the assailant
• The victim is younger than the assailant
• The victim is 'pretty'
• The victim has deviated from normal family/sex roles (for example is labelled a career woman or is homosexual).

The typology developed here is relatively similar to that put forward by Nils Christie (1986) in his famous article 'The Ideal Victim'. Here Christie argues that our culture uses the label 'victim' in certain cases and for certain people only – it is, in other words, not a naturally arising or objective category, but one that requires certain attributes and attitudes on the part of the victim. Some people, or categories of people, are 'readily ... given the complete legitimate status of being a victim' (p. 18); others are not. There's also, Christie observes, a set of conditions, specific to the criminal act, that are required for someone to be allowed full victimhood status: our culture stipulates that the 'ideal victim' doesn't know her perpetrator, was going about her day-to-day tasks when attacked, and was not engaging in any illegal or deviant activities at the time of victimisation. It's worth reminding ourselves here that *most* rape victims know their attackers – some know them intimately – and so are automatically denied the tag of 'ideal victim'. It's also worth noting that there's a double marginalisation in representation here: as discussed above, acquaintance-perpetrated rape is less likely to be covered in news reports than stranger-perpetrated rape and when cases *are* reported in the press the victim is more likely to be depicted as somehow blameworthy.

To return to our main point of discussion: Christie and Benedict draw our attention to the fact that the label 'victim' does not denote someone who has suffered intentional harm at the hands of a perpetrator – achieving the category or not is based primarily on the attributes and behaviour of the *injured* party. More than this, the actions and characteristics of the victim – her alcohol consumption and relationship to the perpetrator, for example – are sometimes deemed to *lessen* the culpability of the perpetrator. All this is particularly true of rape. Here victim status is particularly hard to win and attenuation of perpetrator responsibility particularly likely. One explanation for this lies in the social norms that surround sex and gender. Our culture frequently suggests that men are 'naturally' predatory and that women should take due responsibility for their own safety by, for example, not getting too drunk, walking home alone, or taking an unregistered taxi. In other words, our culture expects women to be active in avoiding sexual victimisation. All this makes it possible for the media to frame cases of rape where the victim knows the aggressor or has apparently flouted the norms of female responsibility as a problem of women choosing to endanger themselves, rather than men being violent.

It's worth pointing out that these ideas about sexual violence are evident in all sorts of cultural products and forums. Take, by way of example, what goes on in court cases concerning sex crime. In the 1990s Italian legal teams on occasion used what was dubbed the 'tight jeans defence' – that is, the defence that, in dressing a certain way, the female victim had knowingly invited male sexual interest (*New York Times*, 16 February 1999). Take, also, the distinctive syntax used by lawyers defending rape cases. Australian researchers have shown that defence lawyers in rape cases repeatedly invite the jury to see the female victim as causing the male aggressor to 'act upon her' (Larcombe 2002: 141). We might find these tactics shocking – they so clearly invite jurors to believe that men shouldn't be held responsible for their rapacious sexual desires and that women are centrally responsible for guarding against attack – but we find very similar rhetorical devices used in the mainstream culture, and most noticeably in news reporting. Take, for example, Henley, Miller, and Beazley's (1995) observations about newspaper coverage of rape. In their study of news items in the *Boston Globe*, they found that rape was more likely to be reported using a passive verb voice than other crimes (see 'Verb voice in news reporting'). Furthermore, they found that readers of news stories about rape that used a passive voice were more likely to think that the victim was partly responsible for her victimisation than those reading an article employing an active voice.

---

**Verb voice in news reporting**

Verbs are active or passive, and we can tell the difference by thinking about the role of the subject in the clause. In active verbs the subject of the sentence performs the action of the verb; in passive verbs the subject becomes removed from the action of the sentence. Take the following examples:

> The footballer allegedly raped Ms X.
>
> Ms X was allegedly raped by the footballer.

The first sentence makes use of an active voice (the footballer — the subject of the act, is clearly the doer). The second makes use of a passive voice: the footballer (still the originator of the action — the subject of the sentence) is less closely connected to the action of the sentence. Henley, Miller, and Beazley (1995) note that the use of the passive voice often involves a complete removal of the subject (the sentence would then become 'Ms X was allegedly raped').

Discussion Question: What might be the effect on readers of using either the active or passive voice in crime news reporting?

---

It's not simply the grammar of newspaper accounts that can urge us to see the victim as blameworthy and which sidelines the role of the perpetrator; the typical narrative focus, too, is squarely on the victim's behaviour and character in newspaper articles about rape. Meyers (1997: 62) argues that if a female victim is neither young nor elderly, gang-raped or attacked by someone with a mental illness,

> chances are she will be represented as somehow responsible for her own suffering because she was on drugs, drunk, not properly cautious, stupid, engaged in questionable activities, or involved in work or exhibiting behavior outside the traditional role of women. Her guilt is signified through statements – made by reporters, anchors, or interviewed sources – *that seek to explain why the crime occurred within the context of her activities.* (emphasis added)

Thus in news reports it is the victim's behaviour – and not that of the perpetrator – that appears to require an explanation.

Overall, media representations help promote the erroneous and damaging idea that there are two types of rape: rape perpetrated by strangers and involving a victim engaged in a mundane task and, on the other hand, rape that is somehow partly the fault of the victim, either because she knew the aggressor or wasn't actively guarding against sexual violence. Estrich (1987) makes a similar point when she argues that our culture draws a distinction between 'real rape' and incidents that are something-short-of-rape. So it is that an ex-UK Justice Minister, Ken Clarke, could talk about there being different types of rape – 'the serious, proper' cases, as he described them in an interview with Sky News, and then, presumably, the less serious, less-than-proper cases (Martinson 2011). Clarke was merely voicing a view that has been propagated by news coverage for some time – that is, that we can think of rape as a bifurcated crime. We might reasonably suggest that sustaining this impression is of ideological importance. For one thing it sustains the appalling idea that some instances of rape – most, if we believe the statistics – aren't 'serious' or 'proper' crimes. Moreover, by asking us to think about rape in terms of 'real rape' and 'less-than-real rape', the news encourages us to focus on the victim's behaviour and status and ignore the real issue of male violence.

## Child sex abuse in the news

Very few crimes are as likely to receive sustained attention in the news as child sex abuse, or paedophilia, as it's regularly referred to in tabloid parlance. In a study of the depiction of child sex abuse in local Rhode Island newspapers, Cheit (2003: 611) found that 'over 47% of the defendants charged in 1993 were mentioned in the newspaper at least once'. Bearing in mind the discussion about 'shrinkage' at the start of this chapter, that's an extraordinary ratio of police-recorded crime to news-reported crime. It's also worth noting that child sex abuse is the focus for a very large proportion of news reporting on sex crime. Chris Greer (2003: 102), in his study of child sex abuse reporting in the Northern Irish press, found that more than half of all the sex crime stories that appeared on the front page of newspapers distributed in Northern Ireland between 1985 and 1996 were about child sex abuse.

It might therefore come as some surprise that child sex abuse hasn't always topped the news agenda: in the first half of the twentieth century cases of child sex abuse were very rarely reported in the news, and it wasn't until the closing decades of the century that cases achieved the sort of coverage that they receive today. As Greer (2007: 41) notes, one of the most 'significant shifts in media reporting of sex crime in recent decades has been the emergence of child victims as a news staple'. There is ample support for such a statement. Kitzinger (1996), for example, analysed content in the British newspaper *The Times* and found a four-fold increase in reporting between

1985 and 1987. By the mid-1990s there was a further spur to news reporting about child sex abuse: concern about offenders re-entering society or being allowed to work and live around children (Kitzinger 1999: 136). Indeed, Critcher convincingly argues that it's only really in 2000 that the media framed the paedophile as the predominant 'folk devil' in cases of child sex abuse; before this news accounts were aimed variously at stirring up concern about negligent social workers, deviant care assistants, and preachy feminists (Critcher 2002: 527). Focusing on the depiction and treatment of child sexual abuse in the US, Lynch (2002: 536) finds a similar pattern: whilst concern surfaced in the 1980s, it was in the 1990s that coverage became particularly marked and salacious; since then, the media has come to express 'an ongoing sense of crisis about the particularly venal threat now dubbed "sex offender" and his more violent counterpart, the "sexual predator"'. The social historian Philip Jenkins (1996: 3–5), in his excellent study of the media furore in the US concerning predatory priests, also points to the mid-1980s as the start of the panic – but, again, it's in the 1990s that clergy abuse came to be seen as a 'ubiquitous and pernicious threat'.

All this is testament to the fact that the media treatment of child sex abuse altered dramatically during the last quarter of the twentieth century. A simple comparison helps highlight this shift. When Ian Brady and Myra Hindley kidnapped, sexually assaulted, and murdered 14 children in the North of England in the mid-1960s their crimes made headline news – but the sexual nature of the attacks was something that wasn't made particularly central in news reporting at the time. Indeed, the pair came to be widely known as the 'Moors Murderers'. This is in stark contrast to the manner in which such cases have come to be reported in the past two decades. In comparable cases today it is the sexual nature of the crime that is prioritised in newspaper headlines. Take, for example, reporting on the kidnap, rape, and murder of the British schoolgirl Sarah Payne in 2000. This incident received sustained newspaper coverage for over a month, with the British newspaper the *News of the World* launching a campaign for new legislation – 'Sarah's Law' – that would require the government to release the personal details of sex offenders to the public. Failing to garner government support for the new law, the newspaper under-took its own (illegal) campaign of 'Naming and Shaming' child sex offenders. Note that this time it was specifically the sexual dimension of the crime that was central in news reporting of this incident, to the extent that the entire crime (kidnap, assault, and murder) came to be encapsulated by the word 'paedophilia', a term that, in its original medical use, denotes simply a sexual proclivity.

Martin Innes (2003) describes the Sarah Payne case as a 'signal crime', a crime that is depicted and taken to be a troubling sign of a wider crime problem (see 'Signal crimes'). These high-profile cases serve as reference points in the reporting of subsequent cases, and they result in some sort of legislative change, and raise both public and media awareness of a threat. Certainly, the Payne case sparked a fresh wave of media interest in child sex abuse in the UK, with subsequent incidents – most notably the kidnap and murder of the schoolgirls Holly Wells and Jessica Chapman in 2002 – becoming the focus of intensive news coverage.

---

**Signal crimes**

Martin Innes (2003, 2004) coined the term 'signal crime' to refer to:

> an incident that is disproportionately influential in terms of causing a person or persons to perceive themselves to be at risk in some sense. In effect, the crime or incident is 'read' as a warning signal by its audience(s) that something is wrong or lacking, as a result of which they might be induced to take some form of protective action. In addition, the presence of this signal will shape how the person or groups concerned construct beliefs concerning other potential dangers and beliefs. (Innes and Fielding 2002: 5.2)

The media isn't necessarily the conduit for this signal, and we should note the importance attached here to audience reception. The concept is not meant to refer specifically to media exaggeration and distortion, but rather to a more general communicative process.

Discussion Question: Can you think of one or more signal crimes? How do they conform to the definition above?

---

Of course, concentrated news reporting on child sex abuse isn't specific to the UK. In fact, the news reporting on the Sarah Payne case mirrored US news reporting of the 1991 assault and murder of a girl from New Jersey, Megan Kanka (Kitzinger 1999: 137). In Australia, too, such cases have been the subject of immense mass media attention since the 1980s (Nelson 1984). All this begs the question: did incidents of child sex abuse become more numerous in economically advanced countries during the last quarter of the twentieth century? In an authoritative review of US statistics, Finkelhor (1994: 44) notes that both official statistics and survey data seem to suggest a 'rapidly rising number of reports'. However, he points out that such statistics are deeply misleading since a large proportion of child sex abuse has historically gone unreported, even to surveyors (p. 31). As Finkelhor puts it:

All of the observed increases could be explained simply by increased aware-ness and willingness to detect and disclose ... [one approach] to this issue has been to compare the rates of abuse for people of different ages within the same study, that is, among subjects who were recruited the same way and asked the same questions. At least five ... studies have such age group comparisons for North American women. Interestingly, all five show slightly lower rates for the youngest age group ... the surveys do not suggest any recent upsurge coinciding with the new interest in the prob-lem. (pp. 44–45)

In the UK, too, it seems that there is limited evidence that child sex abuse has become more prevalent in recent decades. In fact, one of the most reliable measures of child sex abuse rates in this country – the repeat cross-sectional household survey carried out by the National Society for the Prevention of Cruelty to Children (NSPCC) – has found a slight *decrease* in forced or coer-cive sexual activity since 1998 (NSPCC 2010: 14).

The increase in news coverage of child sex crime is not, then, a conse-quence of a rise in incidence rates. What else explains the increased media attention? As with the increase in reporting on sex crime more generally, the advent and cultural assimilation of second-wave feminism have no doubt made it more possible to openly discuss the problem of child sex abuse. However, this alone can't explain the predominance of news items on this crime – in particular, it doesn't help us explain the sensational tone of report-ing. In attempting to account for the media interest in child sex abuse, a number of scholars have argued that this crime has become the subject of 'recurrent or serial moral panic' (Critcher 2002: 527). Moral panic research is the subject of Chapter 5, but for now it's sufficient to say that a moral panic refers to a period of intense and sensationalising media coverage, punitive government reaction, and public concern about a particular issue or category of person. Moral panics invite disgust and outrage, make certain categories of people the repository for public concern, and encourage a sense of fear that is disproportionate to the problem.

There is significant support for Critcher's idea of a serial moral panic concerning child sex abuse. For example, Best (1990) points to the prolifer-ation of social problems in the US associated with child-victims from the mid-1980s, including child sex abuse, incest, Halloween sadism, and child pornography. This casts the net wider, and suggests that the media atten-tion given to child sex abuse is part of a broader serial moral panic concern-ing children as victims. Jenkins (1992) identifies a similar trend in the UK, with a string of moral panics concerning child-victims and predatory males. Both authors argue that certain claims-making groups – including child protection organisations, right-wing conservatives, and feminist groups – have amplified these problems in order to promote their organisational aims.

Other scholars interested in explaining the recent media fascination with child sex abuse emphasise that 'paedophilia' lends itself to cheap, easy reporting, thus making it particularly likely to make the news. In an interesting study of Australian news coverage, Nelson (1984) notes four factors that have made child sex abuse more likely to receive press attention:

- It allows for a focus on specific cases (and this, in turn, allows for stories to be personalised)
- It can be couched in broader discussions of familial abuse (so lends itself to thematic as well as episodic framing – see 'Episodic and thematic framing')
- An ample academic literature can be drawn upon for statistics and expert opinion (and the media have become more adept at mining these sources)
- Children have become, more generally, popular subjects for news coverage.

The last point is something that Jewkes (2011) has also remarked on, and it's worth devoting some space here to considering the current cultural preoccupation with childhood, and its role in increasing the newsworthiness of child sex abuse. The French historian Philippe Ariès (1965) points out that our ideas about childhood have changed dramatically over time. Once an important household resource with value as producers, children are now, in the economically advanced world at least, principally seen as consumers, childhood as a period of life that should be given over to play and emotional development, rather than work. Zelizer (1994) convincingly refers to this shift as involving a 'sacralization' of childhood. In economically advanced countries the decline in infant mortality and the increased state provision for welfare in old age has meant that, on average, women are having fewer children than in the past. Some suggest that one of the consequences of these developments is that the emotional value of each child within the family increases. Children have become, in Zelizer's view, scarce and therefore valuable commodities. We might see the increased media interest in child sex abuse as a reflection of this trend – this helps explain why child-victims have become the recurrent focus for moral panics over the past 25 years.

There are other reasons why child sex abuse has received so much news coverage in the last few decades. We might see the moral tone that is commonly used in news reports on this subject as serving an important social function. Children constitute, to return to Christie (1986), the ultimate 'ideal

**Episodic and thematic framing**

News items can frame events episodically or thematically. Using episodic framing means focusing on the event as an event, rather than part of a pattern. A newspaper article might, for example, tell us about an incident wherein a young man has been stabbed. Using thematic framing means presenting the event as part of a broader trend. A newspaper article might, for example, frame the incident mentioned above as 'knife crime', draw attention to it being the second such incident to occur this month and suggest that it's part of a crime wave. Crime news tends to use a mixture of episodic and thematic framing: the former allows for personalisation, the latter for generalisation.

Discussion Point: Access today's online edition of a national newspaper and identify two or three crime stories. Go through the stories carefully and identify where they use episodic and thematic framing. What is the effect of these different frames in terms of the meaning of the story?

victim' and they often embody purity and innocence in news reporting on child sex abuse. Unhindered by questions of victim culpability, these cases give us a means of participating in mutual moral outrage. This is particularly important given that a forthright moral language of evil and good, sin and shame, has less purchase today than in previous periods. The classical social theorist Émile Durkheim believed that we needed outlets for collective and emotional expressions of morality, that 'collective effervescence', as he described it, was socially functional (2008 [originally 1917]). He was thinking about the role of collective religious worship, but it's possible to argue that newspaper reporting on child sex abuse, with its campaigning tone and clear rhetoric of collective moral outrage, fulfils a similar function in today's society. Think of the broader social response to cases of child sex abuse – the jeering crowds that wait to glimpse the accused at the courthouse and the sea of flowers that are left in memoriam at a site. The news simply gives voice to this sense of mutual grief and anger.

Of course, and as Katz (1987) rightly notes, moralistic crime reporting differs markedly from the sort of religious zeal identified by Durkheim, in that the former encourages us to indulge in negative and pessimistic feelings about the social world. In its representation in tabloid newspapers at least, child sex abuse is framed as evidence of social decline and fragmentation. Newspaper articles frequently cast the problem as evidence of our society's failure to care for and protect its most vulnerable members. Take, for example, a special feature on child neglect and abuse run by the British tabloid newspaper the *Mirror*

(7 May 2001). The front page headline – 'The Lost Ones' – conveyed an idea reiterated in the main report: the problem of child sex abuse is fundamentally to do with a collapse in social morals and order (Goddard and Saunders 2001). Take, also, the recurrent suggestions, in newspaper accounts, that child sex abuse is a problem of corrupt or ineffective social authorities. In the US, early newspaper reports on child sex abuse frequently presented Catholic priests as typical perpetrators (Jenkins 1999), whilst newspaper coverage in the UK and Australia has often blamed (some would say scapegoated) child protection agencies. The overall impression given by news reports is that child sex abuse is a symptom of a broader social problem – a problem of social breakdown, both in terms of collapsing community cohesion and the failure of official social institutions and systems that are meant to protect.

The typification of the paedophile that became prominent in later news reporting on child sex abuse – that of the psychopathic attacker, unknown to his victim – might also speak of a sense of social malaise. Joel Best, in his book *Random Violence* (1999), argues that we have developed a general cultural fascination with stranger-perpetrated violence which, in turn, makes this sort of crime more newsworthy than that perpetrated by acquaintances and intimates. For Best, the main social driver of this is a decline in social cohesion and trust. As our societies have become more atomised, he argues, we have become increasingly fearful of anonymous strangers. The experience of urban dwelling is such that most of our daily contact consists of fleeting associations with strangers. This living arrangement, along with a decline in political interest and social engagement – things that might help remind us of our mutual obligations – has created a general atmosphere of distrust. Under such social conditions we can well believe, Best argues, that strangers are inherently dangerous.

Irrespective of our views on the validity of this thesis, we should recognise that news reporting on child sex abuse is a vehicle for expressions of social malaise and distrust, and that our desire for a discourse of social fragmentation (one that positions us as concerned and outraged guardians of the moral order) may go some way towards explaining the cultural preoccupation with this crime. From this perspective, news reporting on child sex abuse allows us to indulge deep-seated fears concerning social atrophy – that we're going to 'Hell in a Handbasket'. There's a more general point to be made here, and that is that crime news reflects broad socio-cultural trends, whether it's the valorisation of childhood or a sense of social breakdown. Indeed, if studying child sex abuse in the news teaches us anything, it's that media reporting does not reflect the 'reality' of crime but is a barometer of something else altogether. It shouldn't surprise us, then, that, as with news reporting on sex crime more generally, journalists and editors are selective in terms of which cases of child sex abuse get reported. Greer (2007: 23) points out that the disappearance of two British boys in 1996 failed to attract media interest, largely, he reasons, because they were male, working-class victims – in other words they lacked media currency as victims and didn't fit with the then dominant cultural script concerning child sex abuse. Cases of child sex abuse carried out by an intimate or acquaintance are also routinely ignored by journalists – after all, the media typification of the paedophile is a dangerous *stranger*, rather than an uncle or friend-of-the family. This bias is particularly pernicious because, as with rape of adults, most child sex abuse is perpetrated by acquaintances and intimates. This is confirmed in a study carried out by Wilczynski and Sinclair (1999) where they compared the depiction of child sex abuse in two Western Australian newspapers to incidents reported and responded to by the Child Protection Service. The authors found that the sexual dimensions of the cases (as opposed to the emotional harm experienced) were particularly stressed and that stranger-perpetrated incidents outside the home were over-represented. The problem with this typification of the sex offender is, as Kitzinger (1999: 145) argues, that 'it locates the threat of abuse within the individual (rather than in social, cultural, or bureaucratic institutions)'. This, in turn, 'reflects and sustains a focus on abusers as outcast from society rather than part of it' (ibid.).

## Questions for discussion

Q1)  What sort of 'rape myths' are perpetrated by the news? How are these harmful to women? Is there a particular myth that you find especially troubling/harmful?

Q2)  Why has our culture become particularly concerned with childhood/ children in the last quarter of the twentieth century? Does this cultural preoccupation explain why child sex abuse has become particularly newsworthy?

Q3)  Why is random, stranger-perpetrated violence prioritised in news accounts?

## Chapter summary

This chapter looked at the representation of victims of sexual violence in the news, focusing on rape and child sex abuse. In summary, we've considered the following points:

• Violence is newsworthy, sexual violence especially so. Studies indicate that rape has the second highest ratio of police-recorded to news-reported crime after murder.

- Whilst roughly a fifth of news reporting on crime is about sexual violence, it accounts for less than 5 per cent of police-recorded crime. In other words, news reporting on rape is disproportionately high.
- Sexual violence hasn't always topped the news agenda. From the 1970s onwards there's been a significant increase in reporting in this area, and this is partly due to the rise of second-wave feminism in the late 1960s. This political movement helped open up public debate about the problem of interpersonal violence within the home.
- The news perpetuates a number of myths concerning rape. For example, assaults carried out by strangers are more likely to make the news than those carried out by acquaintances and intimates, even though the latter type of assault is more common. The emphasis on stranger-perpetrated rape means that sexual violence is regularly framed as a matter of individual sickness, rather than anything to do with social arrangements and inequality between the sexes.
- The news also frequently urges us to see rape as a sexual act involving violence, as opposed to a violent act involving sex. On occasion the sexual dimensions of the assault become the core focus. Soothill and Walby (1991) suggest that, from the 1970s onwards, there's been a trend towards the 'sexualisation of sex crime' and document the use of titillating details in British news reports.
- Newspaper reports on rape contribute to a cultural construction of 'ideal victimhood'. A number of researchers have identified a tendency for news reports to deny full victim status to certain people by virtue of their behaviour, attributes, and social background. For example, news reports about female victims who had consumed alcohol or knew their assailant are likely to frame them as somehow blameworthy. In contrast, those who are middle class and attacked by strangers are likely to be represented as more fully victimised.
- By urging us to think of rape as a bifurcated crime – as 'real rape' versus 'not-quite-real rape' – the news helps focus public interest and debate on the issue of female culpability rather than male violence.
- Child sex abuse is an especially newsworthy form of sexual violence. In common with reporting on rape, violence perpetrated by intimates and acquaintances is less likely to make headline news than violence carried out randomly, by strangers. This is despite the fact that, again, it's the former type of sexual violence that is more common.
- News reporting on child sex abuse has increased significantly in most economically advanced countries in the last few decades, and particularly since the turn of the twenty-first century. The increase in coverage cannot be explained by an increase in incidents.

- One explanation for the increase in reporting on child sex abuse is that child-victims have become especially newsworthy over the last few decades (see Jewkes 2011). The relatively recent cultural valorisation of children and childhood may have made cases of child sex abuse the subject of particular anxieties and therefore more likely to receive coverage.
- Newspaper reporting on child sex abuse, with its campaigning tone and clear rhetoric of collective moral outrage, may also be functional in allowing for the expression of feelings of mutual outrage and moral condemnation.
- News reporting of child sex abuse might be seen as a vivid expression of shared anxieties in late modern societies concerning social breakdown and untrustworthy strangers. Newspaper articles frequently cast the problem as evidence of social atomisation and our society's failure to care and protect its most vulnerable members.

## Recommended reading

Benedict, Helen (1993) *Vamp or Virgin: How the Press Covers Sex Crime*. Oxford: Oxford University Press.

Benedict's book is based on an analysis of US newspaper coverage of four high-profile rape cases during the 1980s. She argues that rape victims tend to be portrayed as either 'vamps' or 'virgins': that is, as blameworthy, provocative women who were somehow 'asking for it' or as bespoiled victims.

Best, Joel (1999) *Random Violence: How We Talk About New Crimes and New Victims*. Berkeley, CA: University of California Press.

A great read, *Random Violence* discusses our cultural preoccupation with stranger-perpetrated, seemingly patternless violence, and suggests it speaks of deep-seated anxieties about strangers and modern living arrangements.

Carter, Cynthia (1998) 'When the "Extraordinary" Becomes "Ordinary": Everyday News of Sexual Violence', in C. Carter, G. Branston, and S. Allen (eds.) *News, Gender, and Power*. London: Routledge.

An excellent synthesis of feminist literature concerning rape in the news, Carter also presents her own analysis of newspaper coverage.

Critcher, Chas (2002) 'Media, Government, and Moral Panic: The Politics of Paedophilia in Britain 2000—1', *Journalism Studies*, 3(4): 521—535.

Critcher charts and attempts to explain the increased media coverage of paedophilia in the British press at the turn of the twenty-first century and convincingly argues that it became the subject of recurrent moral panic.

Jenkins, Philip (1992) *Intimate Enemies: Moral Panics in Contemporary Great Britain*. New York: Aldine de Gruyter.

One of several excellent studies of moral panics by Philip Jenkins, *Intimate Enemies* takes a broad view of moral panics concerning intimate partner violence in the UK.

Meyers, Marian (1997) *News Coverage of Violence Against Women: Engendering Blame*. London: Sage.

A compelling feminist analysis of news reporting on male-to-female violence.

Soothill, Keith and Walby, Sylvia (1991) *Sex Crime in the News*. London: Routledge. Soothill and Walby's analysis of sex crime in the British news illuminates, amongst other things, the sexualisation of sex crime and the tabloidisation of the British press. The book offers a great historical overview of developments and trends in the last quarter of the twentieth century.

## CHAPTER 4

# Crime news effects

Excepting situations in which we are the perpetrator or victim of crime – and those experiences are thankfully rare for most of us – we lack first-hand, direct information about crime and the criminal justice system. What, then, informs our understanding of crime? There is, of course, a wealth of data and information about crime. The government and its auxiliary agencies (the police, for example) are an important source of information releasing crime statistics and running public information campaigns. Academic criminologists and charities also provide us with useful data about crime. In truth, though, we receive most of this official information about crime by reading or watching news reports. In this sense what we hear or read about crime in the news has gone through a two-fold process of mediation: researchers and officials produce data about crime, and the media refract this picture of crime again before it comes to us. In fact, we might usefully think of there being two pictures of crime – the 'reality' of crime, as it is reflected in official statistics, and the news-spun depiction of crime. There is good reason to believe that the latter plays a more significant role in shaping the public's perception of crime. This would help explain why national crime surveys repeatedly find that the public perceive the *national* crime rate to be higher than the *local* crime rate, despite compelling evidence that the overall crime rate has dropped in most economically advanced countries. Something convinces people that there is a crime problem outside of their immediate experience and purview – and the media is surely a prime suspect!

We need only think about the content of the previous two chapters to realise how important it is to ascertain the effect of crime news on public attitudes. We saw how news reporting on terrorism tends to take a pro-state line and that articles on sexual violence whip up concern about stranger-perpetrated violence and deny certain people the label of 'victim'. These are matters that should, in and of themselves, concern us, but judging the problem of media misrepresentation also requires us to consider precisely how the depiction of, say, terrorism or sexual assault, affects public opinion and sentiment. If newspapers have a limited influence over these things, then we'd probably want to adjust how we understand the problem of media distortion. This chapter considers how the news-spun image of crime influences beliefs and attitudes about crime and criminal justice. We also ask whether news coverage plays a role in increasing people's fear of crime. This should help us qualify and extend our thinking about violence in the news.

## The effect of crime news on government policy and legislation

We'll leave aside these questions for a moment longer. For now, let's consider a more straightforward effect of crime news – its role in changing policy and legislation. Whilst the effect of news coverage on public opinion is open to question, its impact on political decisions is more obvious. Take reporting on James Bulger, a toddler kidnapped and murdered by two older children in the British city of Liverpool in 1993. In running the story, news outlets called for the government to extend the use of Closed Circuit Television (CCTV) and try the assailants in an adult criminal court. The government responded by decreasing the age of criminal responsibility in England and Wales from 14 to 10 and promoting the use of CCTV. In fact, the UK now has the largest number of CCTV cameras per square mile of anywhere in the world, and one of the lowest ages of criminal responsibility in the developed world, and at least the latter is a direct consequence of the newspaper campaigning about the James Bulger case. Surette (2010: 2–3) observes a similarly close relationship between media depictions of crime and criminal justice policy in the USA, noting that this connection is a historical one – the novel *Uncle Tom's Cabin*, Surette comments, influenced slave laws in the mid-nineteenth century. More recent examples include the impact of newspaper coverage of the kidnapping and murder of Polly Klass in California in the late 1990s. The coverage led to the creation of the 'three strikes and you're out' rule whereby a third criminal offence, no matter how serious, automatically entails a lengthy prison sentence.

All this raises the question, do legislators and policy-makers take the media to be a *barometer* or *shaper* of public opinion? If we were to go simply on the evidence provided by social scientists concerning the relationship between the media and public opinion, we'd plump for the latter. (And, as an aside, it's worth knowing that this idea – that a person or organisation acts on the presumption that media content will shape other people's views and behaviour – is referred to in the literature as 'third person effects'.) Relatively little sociological or criminological research looks at news coverage as a distillation of public attitudes; much of it instead focuses on whether and how the news sways public opinion. This body of literature is described variously as 'media effects' research (the term preferred in psychology and media studies) or 'dominant ideology' research (the term preferred in sociology). There's a related area of research in cultural studies called 'audience reception studies': this often involves looking at how an audience's interpretation of a media text is shaped by factors like gender and age. There is also a strand of writing within the criminological field of 'fear of crime studies' that focuses on the media's role in increasing our worry about crime. In all of these discrete fields of study, and as Erikson (1991: 220) notes, research tends to be focused on the media as something that leads public opinion and behaviour. Other institutions that might shape or contribute to public opinion on crime tend to be excluded in such analyses. This means that the other possibility inferred by the question above – that the media may simply crystallise public opinion, or be just one contributor to a prevailing discourse about crime and justice – isn't really given too much consideration. We return to this point at the end of the chapter, but for now I'll just say that this seems to me to be a limitation. Let's concentrate here on the literature that suggests a relationship between crime news consumption and attitudes, behaviour and fear.

---

### Third person effects

The phrase 'third person effects' was coined by Davison (1983) to describe the idea that in watching or reading an emotive media item, a person tends to believe that 'its greatest impact will not be on "me" or on "you", but on "them" — the third persons' (p. 3). In other words, we imagine that 'other people' will be deeply influenced by a media message. This is also true of institutions and political organisations: they presume that a media message will provoke unrest or anxiety amongst the public, and act on the basis of this belief. For example, a government might bring in a new law to tackle a 'new crime problem' promoted by the media, irrespective of whether there's evidence that the problem is real or that the public believe news stories about its spread. Davison (1983) uses the example of the US military's reaction to the Japanese bombardment of African American servicemen with anti-US propaganda during the Second World War. The US military attempted to counteract this threat, even to the extent of altering the composition of certain military units — and, importantly, without any evidence that the African American servicemen had been affected by the propaganda.

Discussion Questions: Can you think of an example where government officials appear to have created laws or policy purely on the basis of news coverage of crime? What are the potential problems with government officials responding in this automatic fashion to crime news?

---

## Registering crime news on our emotional radars

Let's start by thinking about the possible degrees to which we can register crime news. If we *respond emotionally* when reading or viewing a news story about crime, we might say that it's been registered on a basic level; if we can *recall* this story we can reasonably surmise that it's entered our consciousness still further; then, if we *profess or demonstrate a coinciding belief, attitude, or fear*, that story has affected us at a deeper level still; if we *change our behaviour* as a consequence of that belief, attitude, or fear (by, say, not walking home on our own or copying a crime) then we might say that our consumption of the news has affected us very significantly. At one end of the spectrum, a story produces a simple physiological reaction in us; at the other, it comes to inform our general view of crime and society to the extent that we alter our behaviour.

Most research focuses on the mass media's role in shaping behaviour and attitudes. However, there has been some work within psychology on people's emotional reception of and ability to recall crime news. Of particular note is the growing body of evidence that demonstrates that news stories that are anchored in a personal story – using episodic framing – are more likely to elicit an emotional response than news stories that are based on broad descriptions of a problem or situation (using thematic framing). Gross (2008), for example, found that a news story about mandatory minimum sentencing elicited a more pronounced emotional reaction amongst participants when it made use of episodic framing. Given that personalisation is a key aspect of crime news, we might reasonably suggest that it is particularly likely to be registered by viewers and readers on a basic emotional level. We don't simply register crime news as we read or watch it – it stays with us. Sherizen (1978: 209) found that people are more likely to remember crime news than any other type of news. When that news is negative, fear inducing, or laden with stereotypes, it is more likely to be remembered (see, for example, Lang, Newhagen, and Reeves 1996). In a fascinating study, Gilliam and Iyengar (2000) found that their participants had a greater ability to remember crime stories that conform to dominant social norms and prejudices. Most striking was their observation that a crime story is remembered more accurately if an assailant is African American (p. 567).

## A word (or two) of warning

For most social scientists, studying how crime news affects us involves making rather more grandiose claims about attitudes, opinions, beliefs, and fears. Before we take a look at some of these studies, a word (or two) of warning: there are very few studies that show a clear-cut *causal* connection between attitudes/fears on the one hand, and crime news consumption on the other. Here are some reasons why:

- It's difficult to ascertain the line of causality, that is whether consuming more crime news causes one to be more fearful of crime, or whether, conversely, being afraid of crime causes one to read more crime news. Take, for example, Driscoll, Salwen, and Garrison's (2005) study of US news users' sense of fear concerning terrorism nine weeks after 9/11. Whilst they found an association between higher levels of exposure to news coverage and heightened fear of terrorism, 'the direction of causality remains undetermined', in that 'higher levels of fear may trigger selective exposure to news for surveillance, information uncertainty reduction, reassurance, or some other gratification'. Similarly, in a study of US citizens six weeks after 9/11, Rubin *et al.* (2003) found that US people were more likely to watch news about terrorism if they were afraid of terrorism. In other words, people may *turn to* the news when they feel particularly worried about a given crime – fear and anxiety precede media consumption, rather than result directly from it.
- It's impossible to control for all extraneous variables when we're studying how attitudes, opinions, and fears are formed. When I get sunburnt (which is often) I can say, with great authority, that it was a consequence of my skin's sensitivity to sun exposure. When people come to share the view held in the news about a particular crime story – a case, let's say, that they have followed avidly – it's difficult to isolate the effect of the key variables in the same way. We might hypothesise that someone feels afraid after reading a newspaper story – after an altogether different type of *Sun* exposure! – and this is a consequence of the way in which the victim was represented in the account. It's going to be very difficult, though, to prove that it was this single aspect of representation that was instrumental in creating fear. It's much more difficult to isolate an aspect of our culture that shapes beliefs and fears than it is to identify how the interaction of our biology and environment bring about a physiological reaction.
- As a related point, we should note that there is a dizzying range of moderating factors, that is, variables that compound or lessen our susceptibility to a media message. There are certain circumstances under which I'm more prone to agree with a media message, and, equally, certain personal characteristics that make me more likely to share a particular media line. There is also a range of factors that increase my chances of getting sunburnt – my skin tone, poor application of suntan cream, and walking near reflective surfaces such as the sea. The list of factors that might lessen

or increase my chances of getting sunburn is relatively small. In contrast, the list of things that influence my reception of a media message is potentially huge, and includes use of an authoritative expert in a report, if the victim looks and sounds like me, my experience of victimisation, the frequency/extent to which I consume the media, use of sensational language, use of photographs, my sex, ethnicity, age, educational and family background, domicile – and so on. A survey might find an association between news consumption and fear of crime, but, in reality it's women aged 18–24 who have been previously victimised who are *particularly* affected (whilst, say, for men the relationship doesn't hold). This doesn't entirely undermine studies in this field, it simply means that they need to work hard to capture the nuances of the relationship between media consumption and public attitudes/fears. Graber (1980: 121) confirms this view, arguing that we should see crime news as fitting a 'modulator' model of audience effects – in other words, the influence of crime news is increased and decreased by the audience's or reader's personal characteristics and social background.

- There are problems with how surveyors measure fear. Fear is an emotional experience, one that isn't necessarily a measurable variable. Yet much of the research on media consumption and fear of crime uses survey methods – that is, asks respondents to enumerate or quantify their sense of fear (as, say '3 out of 5' or 'very high'). Moreover, there may be reasons other than a lack of fear that a respondent reports a negligible fear of crime. Social researchers have noted that men may say that they lack fear of crime because they deem an expression of fearfulness to threaten their claims to masculinity – Sutton and Farrall (2005) refer to this as 'deceptive responding'.

We'll return to some of these issues in Part III of this book when we consider how to analyse media representations. For now it's sufficient to point out that media effects research works best when confined to very narrow and isolatable relationships.

## Crime news as a shaper of public attitudes

Whilst we need to be careful about assuming a clear-cut, causal connection between news output and public attitudes, there is compelling evidence that crime news does have some influence over our ideas about crime – and we don't need to be social researchers to be able to detect this relationship! We're probably all aware that news coverage can help convince people that someone is guilty of a crime, even before they've been arrested, let alone charged or convicted. When Joanna Yeates' body was found in the British city of Bristol in late 2010, the news readily pointed the finger of suspicion at her landlord, Christopher Jefferies. Newspapers ran pictures of the man alongside jeering headlines describing him as 'Dr Strange'. He was subsequently arrested by the police, despite limited evidence that he had anything to do with the crime: he claims that this was because he had essentially been a victim of a 'trial by the media'. As it turns out Jefferies was entirely innocent: Yeates' next door neighbour, Vincent Tabak, was later arrested and convicted of her murder. Nonetheless, the damage had been done: Jefferies was perceived, in the public consciousness, to be dangerous and guilty of *something*, even after Tabak's arrest. In Autumn 2011, Jefferies successfully sued six British newspapers for libel.

Crime news doesn't simply influence our opinions about specific cases; it can shape our overall perception of crime. In fact, some researchers claim that the newspaper we read plays a more important role than personal experience of victimisation in shaping our beliefs about the prevalence of crime (see O'Connell and Whelan's [1996: 179] study of Irish citizens). That says something really interesting about how we form our ideas about crime. For other researchers, media consumption is simply the most obvious explanation for the dominant public perception that crime is a serious and entrenched problem – because it certainly can't be explained by an increase in the crime rate.

Our ideas about how best to tackle crime also appear to be shaped by our news consumption. Both Garofalo (1981) and Surette (2010) argue that watching or reading crime news encourages us to believe that the police need to be more effective in fighting crime. Others have argued that heavy consumers of crime news tend to have a more punitive attitude, and see harsh punishment and crime control as necessary in the face of an apparently spiralling crime rate (see, for example, Barille 1984; Gillespie and McLaughlin 2004; Surette 2010). This is true, too, when we look at how the representation of specific crimes affects public attitudes concerning punishment. It seems that news reporting on terrorism, for example, has played a central role in encouraging many to accept hard-line foreign policy agendas and military intervention – that the 'war on terror' is necessary and just, in other words. For example, the news's acritical adoption of the government line on the connection between 9/11, al-Qaeda, and Iraq was a significant factor in the US public's support for the strikes on Iraq (Moeller 2004; Fried 2005; Gershkoff and Kushner 2005). Other work suggests that news items on terrorism provoke different responses depending on the nature of the message conveyed, and particularly the use of graphic and troubling imagery and description. In a study that looked at US citizens' responses to emotive and non-emotive news reports on terrorism, Gadarian (2010: 469) found that 'citizens form significantly different foreign policy views when the information environment is emotionally powerful than when it is free of emotion, even when the factual information is exactly the same'. The framing of terrorism as a threat to national security and values is more likely to prompt an acceptance of whichever response – most usually the official government one – the news item describes as necessary and rightful. It's also more likely to stir up feelings of worry, and it's this idea that we turn to next.

## Does crime news increase our fear of crime?

The notion that there's an association between crime news consumption and fear of crime finds ample support. In a compelling study, Lowry, Nio, and Leitner (2003) attempted to explain the significant upward trend in US citizens' fear of crime since the mid-1990s. They point out that there wasn't an increase in the crime rate around this time – there was, though, an identifiable increase in crime news reporting from the top three US network television news channels, and this, they claim, explains the heightened levels of fear amongst the US public.

Other studies focus on more specific elements of crime news reporting and its relationship to fear of crime. For example, in a study of US citizens, Chiricos, Eschholz, and Gertz. (1997) found that frequent watching of television news was positively associated with fear concerning crime. The newspaper one reads also appears to have an effect. Williams and Dickinson (1993) analysed crime news in the ten most popular British national newspapers during a month in 1989 and compared their findings to a survey that asked people about newspaper readership and fear of crime. They found significant differences in the amount of coverage different newspapers gave to crime: the *Sun*, the country's best-selling daily tabloid, carried the most crime news (30%), whilst the *Guardian*, a left-wing daily broadsheet, had the lowest amount of crime news (5.1%). Tabloid newspapers, more generally, ran more crime stories and, what's more, these stories tended to be longer and were more likely to focus on personal violence (pp. 40–41). In the qualitative part of their study, Williams and Dickinson found that tabloid newspapers were more likely than serious broadsheet newspapers to use a fear-inducing, sensationalist tone in crime reporting. Interestingly, their survey results suggest that the differential coverage of crime in these newspapers affects people's fear of crime. They found that readers of tabloids have significantly higher levels of fear of crime than readers of broadsheets. The former estimated the rate of local crime to be far higher than the latter and expressed more serious worries about their personal safety (p. 50).

Other studies have confirmed that the style of news reporting plays an important role in shaping crime fears. In an early study, Heath (1984) analysed crime news in local newspapers from 42 US cities (a total of 1926 articles) and carried out a telephone survey to assess the connections between media consumption and fear of crime. She found that newspaper articles that portrayed local crimes as perpetrated predominantly by random strangers were more likely to arouse feelings of worry amongst participants. We already know from previous chapters that news reports generally represent violence as random. Indeed, it's reasonable to suggest that the standard news depiction of violence is particularly likely to elicit fear, and not just because articles tend to focus on stranger-perpetrated crime. Table 4.1 lists the typical violent crime as it appears in the news and considers how it might operate as a trigger for fear.

Of course, it's not just crime news that can induce fear. Various academics have noted that television crime drama can also stir up worry (Gerbner *et al.* 1980; Zillmann and Wakshlag 1987; Sparks 1992). Gerbner *et al.* (1980), for example, identified a 'mean-world attitude' amongst their participants who were heavy consumers of television, and argued that this perception – that the world is fundamentally a bad place – mirrors the impression conveyed by the mass media.

**Table 4.1**  Triggers for fear in crime news

| Standard Violent Crime Narrative in the News | Trigger for Fear | Reader/Viewer is Encouraged to Think ... |
|---|---|---|
| Story is personalised | Increased possibility of identifying with victim | 'S/he is *quite like* me/my dad/partner etc.' |
| Crime is depicted as random | Implies that anyone could be a victim | 'That *could be* me/my dad/partner, etc.' |
| Emphasis on graphic images/sensational description | Creates a sense of horror | '... and look what might happen to me/my dad/partner, etc.' |
| The victim's guilt/ innocence is up for debate | Implies that some victims are more 'worthy' than others | '... if I *am* attacked, I could be held partly responsible' |
| Social causes of crime are rarely discussed | Encourages sense of crime as unavoidable/a natural aspect of society | 'There's not much we can do to make things better ...' |
| The criminal justice system is the only real way of tackling crime | Encourages a sense that we're 'at war' with criminals | '... we need police on the streets and people in prison ...' |
| There's an urgent need for more police and prison places | Encourages a sense that we're poorly equipped to tackle violent crime | '... there aren't *enough* police on the streets and people being sent to prison' |

## Media effects as diffuse

Whilst it is useful to consider the various ways in which the standard news depiction of violent crime might induce fear amongst viewers and readers, we should beware of seeing the media as having a monolithic influence over people's attitudes and fears. We don't consume the media in a social or cultural vacuum, and when we come to agree with a news story the chances are that it has tapped into and reaffirmed long-held beliefs and attitudes. After all, we are already deeply familiar with the cultural script presented to us in news reports on violent crime – and, importantly, not simply from reading the news or consuming the media more generally. Charities run awareness campaigns about violent crime, governments incarcerate more criminals and present the police as front-line crime control personnel, mothers tell their daughters not to wear their skirts so short, friends relay urban legends about innocent folk falling prey to criminal gangs, shop keepers put up metal detectors at the entrance to their stores to check if customers are armed. In other words, the news is simply one contributor to what Garland (2001: 147) describes as our 'collective cultural experience of crime'. This should make us reflect again on the problem of ascertaining whether it is the news that causes us to believe something or feel a certain way, or whether we turn to crime news as a consequence of having certain beliefs or feelings. We don't know 'what came first' because elements of a culture simply don't operate unilaterally. In this sense we might see crime news effects as diffuse, and diffuse in all senses of the word – its influence is extensive, widely felt, but rarely monolithic, interacting as it does with other aspects of our cultural and social experience. We can say, then, that crime news is part of a cultural tapestry, *stirring up* fear and *contributing to* our overall attitudes concerning crime: the idea that it *causes us* to worry or think a certain way is in most cases overly simplistic.

This is true even when a relationship appears entirely clear-cut. A great example is the purported relationship between the popular television show *CSI* and attitudes towards evidence in criminal trials. A number of researchers have pointed to the influence of television crime drama on US jury members' attitudes towards scientific evidence – the so-called '*CSI* Effect'. The idea is that the proliferation and popularity of forensic police dramas (most notably the *CSI* franchise) have raised the public's expectations of evidence. The hypothesis is that jurors are disappointed by the level of scientific evidence proffered in criminal trials, and so have become more likely to acquit on the basis of a lack of this sort of evidence. The idea is tantalisingly plausible. Nonetheless, survey-based studies return mixed results. Shelton, Young, and Barak (2006: 333), for example, surveyed 1027 people called for jury duty in Michigan, and found that whilst there were 'significant ... demands for scientific evidence' this wasn't linked to television viewing habits. Instead, they argue, the high expectations of scientific evidence 'may have more to do with a broader "tech effect" in popular culture rather than any particular "CSI effect"' (ibid.). In other words, *CSI* is part of a broader social and cultural landscape. Looking at media representations in terms of this landscape is in many cases more fruitful than trying to examine their specific role in creating certain attitudes and fears – some of the chapters in the final section of this book attempt precisely this sort of thing.

## Questions for discussion

Q1)  Can you think of an example where crime news appears to have had a significant influence on public attitudes/beliefs/concerns? Why did this particular set of reports influence the public to such a degree?

Q2)  Why might we turn to crime news when we feel worried about a case or crime?

Q3)  How might our sex, ethnicity, and age moderate how we receive crime news?

Q4)  To what extent can we say that crime news has caused an increase in fear of crime?

Q5)  How might television drama and fiction films influence our perception and fear of crime? Do you think that crime news is more likely to shape public attitudes concerning crime than other media formats?

## Chapter summary

This chapter has considered the effect that crime news has upon us. In summary, we've considered the following points:

- Surveys suggest that the public's fear of crime is increasing, despite the fact that the overall crime rate has been dropping over the past decade in most economically advanced countries. A popular explanation for this disjuncture is that the mass media – the news in particular – have stirred up feelings of anxiety concerning crime.

- Crime news can prompt a government to change criminal justice policy and law. One explanation for this is that government officials assume that the public will automatically believe and feel alarmed by a crime news story and respond on this basis. This is known as a 'third person effect'.

- It's difficult to ascertain the precise influence the mass media have on the public. For one thing, the direction of the relationship between media consumption and public concerns isn't always clear: perhaps people turn to media coverage because they fear crime, rather than fearing crime because of their media consumption.

- Nonetheless, there is a large body of research looking at the relationship between media consumption and public attitudes, perceptions, and behaviour. A number of studies, for example, suggest that we're particularly likely to recall crime news. This is partly because we're more likely to remember stories that are negative and have a personal dimension to them, and crime news frequently has these characteristics.

- There is also compelling evidence to suggest that our perception of crime is influenced in various ways by crime news. For example, researchers have identified a connection between heavy consumption of crime news and punitive attitudes. Other studies indicate that watching or reading crime news encourages people to believe that the police need to be more effective in fighting crime.

- Researchers have also looked at the relationship between news reporting on a specific crime and public attitudes. For example, there are a number of studies that explore the impact of news reporting on 9/11, indicating, amongst other things, that the coverage shaped people's perception of foreign policy and helped legitimate the subsequent attacks on Afghanistan and Iraq.

- Factors such as the newspaper people read, level of news consumption, and the use of sensational language in reporting have all been linked to people's fear of crime.

- The average crime news item contains various triggers for fear. The emphasis on personal stories, the random nature of crime, graphic descriptions of violence, and the need for more police and harsher sentences are all likely to induce worry.

- Overall, we should recognise that crime news – and the mass media more generally – is one contributing factor to the impression we receive of crime. In most cases its effect should be seen as *diffuse* rather than unilateral and direct.

## Recommended reading

Gerbner, George, Gross, Larry, Morgan, Michael, and Signorielli, Nancy (1980) 'The Mainstreaming of America: Violence Profile No. 11', *Journal of Communications*, 30: 10–29.
An important contribution to the literature on media effects, Gerber *et al.*'s paper is based on their Cultural Indicators Research Project, a large-scale survey of US television programmes and viewers. They argue, amongst other things, that heavy television viewers, irrespective of their different backgrounds, age,

and sex, are particularly likely to acquire a 'mean-world syndrome', that is they are likely to see the world as basically dangerous and people as fundamentally untrustworthy.

Graber, Doris (1980) *Crime News and the Public*. New York: Praeger.

Graber's book looks at the relationship between US crime news and public perceptions of crime and criminal justice agencies. An early contribution to the field, but still relevant and well worth a read.

Shelton, Donald, E., Young, Kim S. and Barak, Gregg (2006) 'A Study of Juror Expectations and Demands Concerning Scientific Evidence: Does the "*CSI* Effect" Exist?', *Vanderbilt Journal of Entertainment and Technology Law*, 9(2): 331—368.

A solid, careful study of the '*CSI* Effect' which contains a good review of existing evidence as well as providing new data.

Williams, Paul and Dickinson, Julie (1993) 'Fear of Crime: Read All About It?', *British Journal of Criminology*, 33(1): 33—56.

This article is based on an analysis of crime news in ten popular British national newspapers and a survey that asked people about newspaper readership and fear of crime. Williams and Dickinson find significant differences in the amount of coverage different newspapers give to crime and demonstrate that tabloid newspapers are more likely than serious broadsheet newspapers to use a fear-inducing, sensationalist tone in crime reporting. Their survey results suggest that the differential coverage of crime in these newspapers affects people's fear of crime.

## PART II

# Conceptualising media coverage of crime

# Introduction

How can we conceptualise crime stories that receive sustained media attention? This is the central question addressed by the chapters in this part of the book. Each chapter introduces a different concept that helps us make sense of and analyse crime stories in the media. The first we cover is by far the most dominant and popular: the moral panic. Moral panics are periods of intense concern about a particular crime or category of person, such that large parts of the public come to see the incident or group as a threat to social values. The media play a key role in escalating public fears. Crucially, the threat is depicted in such a way as to encourage a disproportionate level of concern: the problem, in other words, is really of limited significance and scale. In moral panics the media play a role in sensitising the public to issues, and – beyond this – help induce undue anxiety and alarm. They also help to vilify a particular social group and participate in a process whereby members of this group are marginalised from mainstream society.

It's worth noting that research in this area quite naturally focuses on *news coverage* of crime: in using this concept researchers are interested in the media depiction of a problem as urgent, current, and real, and the news is, of course, the only format that conveys this. There are other concepts that help capture and explain crime stories that circulate in other media and formats – such as 'cautionary tale', 'crime legend', and 'cultural trauma', the foci for the other chapters in this part of the book. To be clear, this is not to suggest that news coverage of crime can't be explained by recourse to these terms. Indeed, and as I argue in the chapter on moral panics, we are far too ready to label news coverage of crime a moral panic without much consideration for conceptual clarity. The ubiquity of this concept means that almost any crime news item that receives a really significant amount of coverage is automatically described – by students, the media, and academics alike – as a moral panic. A central aim of the next chapter is to get students to apply the term more conscientiously and this might mean admitting that something that *looked*, on first inspection, like a moral panic is in fact, say, a cautionary tale.

What helps us distinguish between the four concepts in this section? I've already mentioned that moral panics are necessarily focused on news coverage of crime. Crime legends, in contrast, tend to be circulated as more informal sources of news on the Internet. Their usual form is an e-mail forward about a violent and audacious crime that befell a friend-of-a-friend – about, for example, an undergraduate who fell asleep at a party and woke to find his kidneys had been removed. They are stories that reflect our deep personal anxieties about crime, principally that we live in an amoral world of danger-ous and apathetic strangers where anything can happen. For Donovan (2004) crime legends reflect a sense of post-modern drift, a lack of trust in official sources of news and protection, and a greater willingness to believe rumours about our susceptibility to uncontrollable criminal underworlds. Crime legends receive accreditation at the margins of a culture and can stay there for years as a legendary story; moral panics, in contrast, are officially recognised reports of criminal wrong-doing that appear today and are gone tomorrow (or, at least, next month!). Moral panics rely upon a law and order discourse, crime legends on a discourse of individualism and distrust of others.

The other two concepts we look at in this part refer to crime stories that appear across media. The cautionary tale, for example, is likely to receive mainstream news coverage *and* be picked up at the cultural margins. Like the moral panic, it stirs up the public's concerns about a crime that, empirically speaking, is of limited significance and encourages us to see certain behaviour as aberrant and dangerous. However, in the cautionary tale it is not the perpe-trator's behaviour that is marginalised, but rather that of the victim and potential victim. Cautionary tales are *warnings* to possible victims – usually women – to take extra care. They frequently prescribe certain precautionary measures – 'watch your drink', take a licensed taxi, don't walk home on your own at night – and the implication, in newspaper reports and soap opera storylines, is that victims are partially responsible for their victimisation. Thus, in cautionary tales, a precautionary discourse of personal responsibility for crime is dominant.

A moral rhetoric is also apparent in mass media renditions of cultural trauma. Here, though, the focus is turned inwards. It isn't offenders of crime or individual victims that receive sustained attention, but rather a nation or group's collective identity in the face of shared grief and crisis. Terrorism, assassinations, and serious state crime can all elicit cultural trauma, and the subsequent media coverage focuses on making sense of the event for the social group involved and delineating collective values. Whilst crime legends concentrate on the personal consequences of crime, moral panics on the threatening behaviour of a deviant group, and cautionary tales on the wrong-ful behaviour of victims, cultural trauma is about a wholesale social rupture and the subsequent process of social restoration.

Table 5.1 helps sketch out further the key differences between the four concepts. It's worth noting, before we go further, that the terms actually refer

**Table 5.1** Comparing moral panics, crime legends, cautionary tales, and media representations of cultural trauma

| | Moral Panic | Crime Legend | Cautionary Tale | Cultural Trauma |
|---|---|---|---|---|
| Typically found in which medium/media format? | Newspapers and television news | The Internet (primarily e-mail forwards) | Across media (news, soap operas, e-mail forwards, glossy women's magazines) | Initially formal news (rolling news provides live, 24 hour coverage). Over time, other media incorporate references to the event |
| Intensity and time-span | Intense and short-lived, sometimes leaving a cultural residue | Slow-burning and long-lasting | Slow-burning and long-lasting | Intense and long-lasting |
| Representation of perpetrator | Folk devil — a much maligned social category of person (e.g. the young gang member) | A psychotic individual or member of a criminal underworld | Limited attention is given to the perpetrator | As a profound threat to social order, as evil |
| Representation of victim | Innocent bystanders, social values | Careless but innocent members of the public | Careless and partially culpable women | The collective, society as a whole |
| Temporal dimensions of the crime | Past incident — but an emphasis on the possibility of 'more to come' | Concurrent | Emphasis on the possible, future crime | Past incident |
| Social function of media representation | To give voice to concerns about social tensions/change | To give voice to concerns about official organisations' inability to protect individuals from random violence | To negatively frame female freedom | To allow for the working through of a social crisis and reinforce a collective identity |
| Moralising discourse | Law and order | Individualism and social distrust ('don't trust anyone') | Precautionary | Them versus Us |

to different types of phenomena: moral *panic* describes a social reaction, cautionary *tale* and crime *legend* describe a particular media story, and cultural *trauma* describes a representational process (one that is not confined to mass media contributions). However, all four concepts can be used to explain why certain events and issues elicit sustained media attention, and all provide tools for understanding why a given story 'hits the headlines' and proliferates. This is the central reason for including them together in this part of the book.

## CHAPTER 5

# Moral panic

Very few criminological concepts have become quite as widely used as 'moral panic'. We pretty much all know what an article participating in moral panic looks like – but here's an example from a British national newspaper:

*Knife Crime Soaring*
KNIFE crime has soared to a record high on Britain's streets and school classrooms, shock new figures have revealed ... One senior ministerial source admitted last night: 'We are facing a problem of epidemic proportions. ...' (*Sunday Mirror*, 18 June 2006, p. 2)

The centrality of statistics (invariably, as this article has it, '*new* figures'), the rolling out of state officials to comment on the problem, the familiar anxiety-inducing language (crime is 'soaring' to a 'record high' ...) – these are all features we readily associate with moral panic. Even news outlets frequently use the term – apparently unself-consciously – to refer to media-produced panics, and the concept has become, as Garland (2008: 9) notes, 'part of the standard repertoire of public debate'. There is a cost to ubiquity, though: imprecise usage and deflated explanatory power. If *everything* is a moral panic, it follows that *nothing* is. That's why, before we proceed, I'd like to add an important caveat: 'moral panic' is a term to be used carefully and conservatively. We – and by that I mean students, journalists, *and* social researchers – are often too quick to label a particularly sensational media story that stays in the headlines for a couple of days a 'moral panic'. That's not just a personal assessment: various academics working in the field have called for greater attention to conceptual clarity (most notably Critcher 2009). The key thing to stress is that moral panics are *more than* crime news stories that excite the public's imagination: there are certain criteria that a news story has to fulfil before we can refer to it as such. The other thing to emphasise here – and hopefully this will become evident in the other chapters in this section – is that moral panic is by no means the only paradigm available to us when describing crime news stories that receive a significant amount of media coverage. In other words we should see moral panic as simply one concept available to us for explaining a salient crime news story and be conscious that others – like crime legend, cautionary tale, or cultural trauma – might do a better job of describing media attention given to a particular crime.

## The pioneers of moral panic theory

The concept 'moral panic' was first used in print by the cultural theorist Marshall McLuhan in his 1964 book *Understanding Media* (Rohloff *et al.* 2013: 1). The term was then taken up by Jock Young (1971), one of the radical British criminologists who founded the National Deviancy Conference in the 1960s, to describe the police and media's role in criminalising young drug users. However, the phrase is more closely associated with the work of another member of that intellectual circle – Stanley Cohen. In 1972 Cohen published his PhD thesis as a book entitled *Folk Devils and Moral Panics: The Making of the Mods and Rockers*. The text quickly became a staple read within criminology and popularised the concept of moral panic. The study focused on the treatment of the Mods and the Rockers, two British youth subcultural groups that had become increasingly visible during the mid-1960s. The two groups were apparently diametrically opposed to one another in everything from style of dress to musical taste: the Mods were scooter-driving, suit-wearing teens; the Rockers preferred motorbikes, Brylcreemed hair, leathers, and jeans. On Easter Monday, 1964, the two groups came to blows in the sleepy English seaside town of Clacton. This is how Cohen (1987: 29) describes the incident:

> Easter 1964 was worse than usual. It was cold and wet, and in fact Easter Sunday was the coldest for eighty years. The shopkeepers and stall owners were irritated by the lack of business and the young people had their own boredom and irritation fanned by rumours of cafe owners and barmen refusing to serve some of them. A few groups started scuffling on the pavements and throwing stones at each other. The Mods and Rockers factions – a division initially based on clothing and life styles, later rigidified, but at the time not fully established – started separating out. Those on bikes and scooters roared up and down, windows were broken, some beach huts were wrecked and one boy fired a starting pistol in the air ...

A few scuffles, some broken windows and beach huts: what Cohen describes is a scene of low-lying, youthful deviance – nothing more serious than that. Nonetheless, 97 arrests were made and all but one national newspaper ran alarmist front page stories on the incident the following day. This societal response, Cohen suggests, was entirely disproportionate and helped vilify and then alienate the two groups. The Mods and Rockers became the repository for public anxiety – 'folk devils', as Cohen puts it – and the subject of a moral panic. Cohen famously defines the latter concept as follows:

> A condition, episode, person or group of persons emerges to become defined as a threat to societal values and interests; its nature is presented in a stylized and stereotypical fashion by the mass media; the moral barricades are manned by editors, bishops, politicians and other right-thinking persons; socially-accredited experts pronounce their diagnoses and solutions. (p. 9)

It's worth pausing to consider more deeply Cohen's definition. According to Cohen, moral panic occurs when a group or incident is held to constitute *a threat to the moral fabric of society*. As Garland (2008) has argued, the moral aspect has come to be strangely neglected in writings about moral panics; instead, and as we'll see below, the emphasis in more recent writings is on identifying the social actors involved in a moral panic. Note also that, according to Cohen, moral panic involves a *wholesale* social reaction. The 'moral barricades', as Cohen has it, are 'manned' by a range of social authorities, including (in his study) judges, police officers, politicians, and the media. Cohen argues that a key component of the Mods and Rockers moral panic was the 'operation of the control culture', that is, the implementation of heavy-handed policing and judicial penalties that served to marginalise the young people. Cohen's suggestion here is that moral panics aren't simply about mass media coverage but also incorporate a range of social institutions and authorities.

Bearing that in mind, let's turn now to take a closer look at Cohen's analysis of the media's role in the creation of the moral panic. In Chapter 3 he identifies several central aspects of media reporting that aid in this construction, including:

- Exaggeration and distortion: 'Sensational headlines [and] ... melodramatic vocabulary', such as words/phrases like 'riot', 'orgy of destruction', 'battle', 'attack', 'siege', 'screaming mob' (p. 31).
- Misleading headlines: 'Violence' (*Evening Argus*, 30 May 1966) was the headline for a report that read 'in Brighton there was no violence in spite of the crowds of teenagers on the beach' (p. 39).
- Double reporting: Newspapers reported the same incident twice, thus creating the impression that two separate violent incidents had occurred.
- Misreporting of incidents: The most important of these was the '£75 cheque story' (p. 28). Many newspapers ran a story concerning a young

man who had been arrested for obstructing the peace and fined £75 by the Magistrate. According to the media's framing of the story he had loftily said that he would write the court a cheque, something that the newspapers took to be an indication of the thoughtless arrogance of the Mods and Rockers' generation, their easy affluence and lack of respect for authority. On further investigation, Cohen finds that the young man in question actually couldn't afford the fine. As he didn't have the cash, he reasoned that offering a cheque would mean that he'd temporarily avoid imprisonment. What's important about this story is that it reflects the overall tone of newspaper reporting on the Mods and Rockers: they were feckless, middle-class youths with too much money and time, and not enough responsibility. Cohen argues that this depiction was far from the truth – for one thing, most of the young people involved in the strife were working class. Nonetheless, it served an important function in buoying up public prejudice concerning young people from these subcultural groups.

- Demonology: Cohen argues that the media demonised the Mods and Rockers (p. 41). Reports emphasised their gang-like behaviour when, in fact, the two groups were rather amorphous, at the start of the panic at least. One of the effects of framing the Mods and Rockers as organised gangs was to cast them as focused solely on causing chaos.

The Clacton incident was the first of several: in the next few years there were various clashes between the Mods and the Rockers. Cohen suggests that it was the social reaction to the early incidents at Clacton that laid the basis for an ongoing antagonism between the two youth groups. This is part of what he describes as a 'deviance amplification spiral' and it's worth devoting some space here to detailing the five-step model Cohen puts forward in chapter 6 of his book. Moral panics, Cohen argues, proceed along the following lines (p. 226):

1) First there is 'the initial problem stemming from the structural and cultural position of the working class adolescent':

   In the case of the Mods and the Rockers this 'initial problem' was boredom and disaffection.

2) The second stage constitutes the folk devil's 'initial solution' to their condition/situation:

   The Mods and Rockers engaged in low-level deviance as a way of easing their boredom and disaffection.

3) This is followed by a 'societal reaction':

The incident at Clacton was condemned in the media and by social authorities.

4) In turn we see the swinging into action of the control culture and the creation of stereotypes:

Police were more heavy-handed with Mods and Rockers after Clacton, Magistrates gave harsh sentences, and the public became convinced that the two groups were intent on disruption.

5) Lastly, the 'folk devil' becomes susceptible to higher-level deviance:

In the case of the Mods and Rockers, we see the creation of a bitter rivalry after Clacton that eventuated in further clashes.

According to Cohen there were three central reasons why the 'societal reaction' lead to increased deviance on the part of the Mods and Rockers. First, by hypothesising about future violent incidents the media inadvertently promoted further clashes between the two groups. Secondly, by emphasising the differences between the two groups, the media concretised a sense of antipathy between the Mods and the Rockers. Lastly, by employing punitive measures, such as harsh fines and heavy-handed policing tactics, the Mods and the Rockers were effectively alienated from mainstream society, thus reducing their sense of social responsibility and increasing their willingness to engage in violence.

Cohen's analysis is convincing and innovative. In suggesting that the actions of a 'control culture' – of police, magistrates, and politicians – could actually *increase* the possibility for deviance he was challenging orthodox views about the relationship between punishment and deviance. We tend to see the former as following directly and naturally from the latter: in fact, Cohen argued, punishment is sometimes pre-emptory and disproportionate and, most importantly, can actually increase the level of deviance. This idea should sound familiar to us – it certainly did to sociologically minded readers of Cohen's book. Cohen's analysis was highly influenced by the US sociologist Howard Becker's theory of symbolic interaction, part of which suggested that those pronounced and marked deviant are likely to 'live up to' that label. Much of the terminology in Cohen's book reveals his indebtedness to Becker and US sociology more generally. His suggestion, for example, that the media establish an inventory of deviant markers for the public to look out for (such as, in the case of the Mods and the Rockers, styles of dress, attitudes, and even turns of phrase) is reminiscent of Becker's work on the use of symbols in interaction. His notion that deviance is socially constructed, rather than an intrinsic feature of certain acts, also belies his affinity to Becker.

It's possible, though, to see Cohen's contribution quite differently, that is, as a consideration of the social and cultural context out of which moral panics emerge. Some of the most engaging parts of his book are directed towards interpreting the moral panic concerning the Mods and Rockers as evidence of a broader social anxiety concerning a new, more permissive society. The 1960s was the era the post-war 'baby boomers' came of age. A large group of affluent teenagers emerged who, for the first time, had significant spending power, limited responsibilities, were increasingly interested in political radicalism and subcultural movements, and seemed unwilling to practise abstinence and self-control. The counter-culture of the 1960s was synonymous with this generation's newfound freedom and sense of experimentation. Fears concerning the new permissive society were therefore directed towards teenagers, and youth subcultural groups in particular. In this sense, and as Cohen puts it, 'the Mods and the Rockers symbolized something far more important than what they did' (1987: 192). Or, as Barker (1992: 82) puts it, 'for reasons other than their crime, society was "in a mood" to find [the Mods and Rockers] a threat'.

This idea – that moral panics are products of specific socio-historical conditions – is one of the most important of Cohen's insights and, I would add, often what distinguishes subsequent successful analyses. Take, for example, Stuart Hall *et al.*'s classic study, *Policing the Crisis: Mugging, the State, and Law and Order*, first published in 1978 (and recently updated – see the 35th anniversary edition published in 2013). The book marked an important shift in moral panic studies. Whilst Cohen had been concerned with the symbolic work that goes into the construction of deviance, Hall *et al.* were interested in the function and origin of the moral panics in terms of relations of power and social control. The group of researchers who wrote the book were based at Birmingham University's Centre for Contemporary Cultural Studies (CCCS), renowned for its interest in neo-Marxist analyses of cultural phenomena. The group's case study was the early 1970s 'black mugger' moral panic in the UK. A single incident – the mugging of a Birmingham pensioner by three black youths in 1972 – sparked a media furore concerning the apparently worrying increase in muggers (and, more specifically, those of an Afro-Caribbean ethnicity). The dominant message conveyed by the media was that there was a spiralling crime problem that needed an immediate and punitive government response and this, Hall *et al.* argue, is a common and important ideological function of moral panics. In the case of the 'black mugger' moral panic tougher sanctions were brought in for theft from the person, and the police became increasingly hostile towards young Afro-Caribbean men.

Not that Hall *et al.* wish to deny that there was a growing problem of criminality amongst this ethnic minority group in the UK. They identify a 'drifting population' of Afro-Caribbean working-class young people who had been systematically marginalised and, as a consequence, criminalised (Hall *et al.* 2013: 352). Nonetheless, they argued that the idea of a mugging crime *epidemic* that needed serious attention was complete nonsense, and had more to do with political manipulation, ingrained racist attitudes, and increasing support for punitive measures of crime control than anything else. During the early 1970s – the time of the mugging moral panic – the UK, like much of the developed world, was in the grip of economic recession and, more than this, a 'state of unstoppable capitalist decline' (p. 303). This is the 'crisis' referred to in the book's title. Weathering the storm of an economic catastrophe that raised serious questions about the future of capitalism, the government became focused on tough law and order sanctions that shored up the political elite's control and legitimacy. In this sense, moral panics are of ideological import: they distract us from socio-structural tensions and justify state intervention of a punitive nature, which, in turn, helps legitimate the state's role as rightful law-maker and -enforcer. (And, as an aside here, it's interesting to note that this is the same period during which the British government was seeking to promote a pro-state line in news reporting on Northern Irish terrorism, and for similar reasons – we considered this in some detail in Chapter 2.)

Certainly, the mugging moral panic focused the British public's attention on an already much maligned social group: young Afro-Caribbean working-class men. Hall *et al.* convincingly argue that this group was made the scapegoat for public anxiety. They provide a detailed analysis of media reporting on mugging, noting, amongst other things, the widespread use of crime statistics to construct the idea of a crime wave. It is here that the media's lack of objectivity becomes most apparent: Hall *et al.* argue that there was in fact very limited statistical evidence to support the British press's pronouncement of a spiralling crime problem. There's a more general point to be made here: the crime categories that we read about in newspapers – including things like 'knife crime', 'stalking', and 'date rape' – are often media creations, produced for the purposes of a succinct headline, and with no official equivalence. This means, in turn, that there is very limited statistical data to go on. 'Mugging' is one such term: in point of fact it was originally a US crime category (like 'gun crime' and 'date rape'), and was only adopted by the British Home Office as an official crime category in 1972 – that is, the year the moral panic erupted. As a consequence, the persistent suggestion in newspapers that official crime statistics proved the existence of a growing crime problem was bogus. All this begs the question: How exactly did the term 'mugging' come to be taken up by the media? Who – or, more properly, which social institution – was pushing the idea that there was a mugging crime wave? Hall *et al.* trace the use of the term back to a set of press releases from the police: this institution acted as the 'primary definer' of the situation. The original criminal act, Hall *et al*. comment, was '*mediated* by the police investigating it; *they* provide the mugging label, and hence the legitimation for its use by the press' (p. 74). The media simply repeated, acritically, the official take on the problem.

Hall *et al*. also make a broader argument about moral panics as a phenomenon. They draw attention to the process whereby the scale and nature of a threat are amplified in public discourse – the 'signification spiral'. The panic starts with an issue being identified as a problem and quickly escalates so that, eventually, the public are urged to believe that 'firm steps' are required (p. 220). Two key factors help in the escalation of the signification spiral: convergence and thresholds. The former refers to the process whereby otherwise separate problems or issues come to be associated in media coverage and public debate: 'thus the image of "student hooliganism" links "student" protest to the separate problem of "hooliganism"' (ibid.). As Hall *et al*. (ibid.) point out, 'this indicates the manner in which *new* problems can apparently be meaningfully described and explained by setting them in the context of an old problem with which the public is already familiar'. Think, for one moment, about the concepts used to describe the range of 'new crimes' associated with the growth of the Internet – Cyber-porn, Cyber-piracy, Internet Fraud, and so on – and note the melding of established, familiar crime categories and much newer words.

The second key dimension to the signification spiral – thresholds – involves the symbolic marking out of 'limits of societal tolerance' (p. 221). Imagine a spectrum of acts, at one end of which is entirely acceptable, conventional behaviour, and at the other end deeply subversive and violent behaviour. Now imagine there to be thresholds on this spectrum. In fact we often conceive of behaviour in this way – we say that someone has crossed a line or boundary when they've done something wrong. Of course, we see a huge range of behaviours and situations as permissible and harmless, but on occasion something happens that we are invited to see as *im*permissible, as contravening shared norms. In other words an act passes the first, most basic threshold of public tolerance. An incident passes another threshold, further along the spectrum, once we are asked to see it not simply as inappropriate but as illegal. Right at the far end of the spectrum we have the last threshold: acts that are presented to us as not just illegal, but as extremely violent and troubling too. How does all of this relate to a signification spiral? Hall *et al*. point out that 'the threat to society can be escalated if a challenge occurring at the "permissive" boundary can be resignified, or presented as leading inevitably to a challenge at a "higher" threshold' (p. 222). Thus a certain style of dress – fairly innocuous in itself, but perhaps inappropriate by usual standards – might be associated with a far more serious infraction. Take, for example, a young man wearing the hood of his sweat top pulled up tight, so that it covers his face. The act in itself is harmless but it has come to be associated with acts that pass the highest threshold of public tolerance. Indeed, in the UK the term 'hoodie' is popularly used to describe someone who poses a serious threat to the social order.

Besides providing us with further concepts to analyse public discourse concerning crime, Hall *et al.* make an argument concerning the historical occurrence of moral panics. They argue that since the time of the panic concerning the Mods and Rockers in the mid-1960s moral panics have become more frequent and anxiety inducing. Looking at the social context for the black mugger moral panic, Hall *et al.* observe that 'panics follow faster on from one another than earlier and an increasingly amplified threat to society is imputed to them' (p. 218). They identify a number of reasons for this. First, by the late 1960s the mass media had become attuned to the symbols associated with a moral panic style of reporting and had come to respond more quickly in naming and promoting a problem. Moreover, Hall *et al.* argue that the escalation in moral panics, evident in both the UK and the USA, was partly a consequence of a 'law and order' campaign promoted by the political elite. A key plank of government policy and rhetoric during the early 1970s was the idea that strict punitive measures were needed to control crime. Thus a situation emerged whereby 'minor forms of dissent seem to provide the basis of "scapegoat" events for a jumpy and alerted control culture' (p. 219). The moral panic concerning mugging, they argue, took place in this distinctive social context. *Prior to* this panic the public had been sensitised to the idea that there was a general problem of social order that required punitive measures. The mugging moral panic – and others thereafter – led to an ever greater intensification of crime control measures and heightened public consciousness of the 'problem of crime'. Frequent moral panics were part of this climate of fear. More than this, Hall *et al.* argue that various state agencies stirred up and augmented panics for the purpose of shifting attention away from political and economic problems for which they were partly responsible and legitimating their crime control agenda.

## Moral panic studies in the USA

Moral panic studies started out as a distinctively British area of social research, and not just in terms of geographical location. Cohen and Young belonged to the pioneering group of British thinkers who, in the 1960s, broke away from mainstream academia to forge a new direction for British criminology. Hall *et al.* were employing a form of Marxist analysis that would come to be closely associated with British sociology for several decades. In the mid-1990s a new voice joined the debate. Erich Goode and Nachman Ben-Yehuda, two US sociologists, made their first forays into moral panic research, and their perspective has subsequently become really influential. It's worth pausing here to reflect upon the differences between British and US approaches to moral panic research. Critcher (2009: 22) makes a useful distinction between British and US scholarly work on moral panic. He suggests that the former provides a processual model because it focuses on the stages and processes through which a moral panic passes, whilst the latter provides an attributional model because it focuses on the qualities an episode should possess to qualify as a moral panic.

Certainly, unlike the work of Cohen and Hall *et al.*, Goode and Ben-Yehuda are centrally interested in operationalising the concept of moral panic – that is, in producing a measurable set of criteria by which we can categorise events as moral panics. They have, they argue, 'at least five crucial elements of criteria': media coverage must be volatile (moral panics 'erupt suddenly ... and, nearly as suddenly, subside') and disproportionate to the threat, there must be concern and widespread consensus amongst the public that the threat is significant and real, and there must be hostility toward an established folk devil (pp. 37–43). In practice, it is often difficult to establish whether a given event or episode fulfils these criteria (something admitted by Goode and Ben-Yehuda). Take the fact that many events that otherwise appear to be moral panics don't have an identifiable folk devil – swine flu and industrial accidents are just two examples mentioned by Goode and Ben-Yehuda. Do these still count as moral panics? The authors think not, and argue that 'certain conditions may cause anxiety, concern or fear but in the absence of folk devils or evildoers do not touch off *moral* panics' (p. 42).

Moral panic researchers may well find other difficulties in applying Goode and Ben-Yehuda's criteria. In this schema, a moral panic is a rapid escalation in media and public concern that reaches fever pitch: but exactly how can we distinguish a highly charged moral panic from what are simply salacious, anxiety-inducing media stories? Would we require *all* national newspapers to run a front page story on the event for, say, a *week*? Gauging consensus is equally difficult. We can't assume that a large volume of provocative news items on a subject reflects or has eventuated in public consensus that there's a genuine problem. As for disproportionality, consider the difficulties involved in working out what constitutes *too much* media coverage and public concern! Intrinsic to this task is working out the real nature of the threat – whether it is very serious, not so serious, and so on. This should strike us as a terrifically complex task, but it is, after all, what is required to make a judgement about disproportionality. Goode and Ben-Yehuda (p. 86) do offer some suggestions as to how to identify disproportionality: 'exaggerated harm, invented [statistics], the proliferation of "tall tales", comparisons across conditions, and [emphasis on] changes over time' are all, they argue, tell-tale signs that a threat has been exaggerated.

Problems of classification aside, we might note that Goode and Ben-Yehuda's schema neglects various matters that are given priority in Cohen's and Hall *et al.*'s accounts of moral panic. Notice how, in this model, there is no mention of moral panics being an expression of socio-structural tensions, the role of the control culture, or political manipulation. Indeed, for Goode and Ben-Yehuda, the primary point of studying moral panics is not to reveal their political uses or social function but rather to determine their relationship to collective behaviour, the social actors involved in their production, and whether they 'fit the mould'. In this sense, and as Critcher (2006: 27) suggests, their work on moral panics is a 'scientific and not a political enterprise'. Take, for example, Goode and Ben-Yehuda's comments on the origin of moral panics. Arguing that Hall *et al.*'s study of the mugging moral panic is 'empirically overdrawn', Goode and Ben-Yehuda (2009: 66) suggest that the notion that the ruling elite could today select and promote a particular crime problem for media coverage is 'fanciful … strictly comic book fare'. Moral panics, they argue, are more likely to be a consequence of interest groups running focused campaigns that coincide with grassroots public concern. Or, as they put it, whilst outrage at the grassroots level 'loads the gun', interest group activism 'acts as a kind of triggering device' (p. 70).

As Thompson (1998) notes, US moral panic scholars tend to focus on claims-making and interest groups much more than their British counterparts. In contrast, the latter are more interested in the role of state agencies in manufacturing moral panics. These preferences are surely partly linked to the fact that the British state's power is much more consolidated and centralised extending, even, into ownership of the country's most influential television news outlet. Nonetheless, it is interesting to note that in their analyses of British moral panics US academics still give emphasis to the role of interest groups – I'm thinking in particular of Philip Jenkins' (1992) notable study. Here Jenkins notes the increased incidence, since the 1980s, of moral panics in the UK concerning sexual violence, arguing that interest groups have played a key role in this trend. Conservative and feminist interest groups have, he argues, helped promote a distinctive set of moral panics concerning paedophilia, rape, pornography, and child abuse. These problems are often interconnected in news reporting and the public imagination, not least of all because they are couched in a similar rhetoric. Jenkins attributes this to the fact that core activist groups often run campaigns across these issues – he calls this 'problem convergence'. Jenkins also points out the increased tendency during this period for interest groups to take *indirect aim* at certain groups and behaviours rather than explicitly denouncing them as immoral – he refers to this as 'symbolic politics'. A campaign or panic becomes a *symbol for* a particular moral position. For example, in decrying the decriminalisation of homosexuality during the 1980s, British conservative campaigners focused on the possibility that children would be adversely affected; this line of argument became a screen for more explicit and prejudicial sentiments of disgust.

Jenkins' work is distinctive in its identification of certain patterns and trends in British moral panics, including the rise of a discrete portfolio of panics, the role of interest groups in promoting and shaping these episodes, and the cloaked moral indignation that characterises the campaigns. He gives us a broad view of moral panics, one that provides really useful insights, not least of all that certain interest groups are heavily involved in promoting a small range of moral panics that are similar in tone and aim. His other books, too, usefully chart the history of moral panics. Of these, I particularly recommend *Synthetic Panics*. Here Jenkins turns his attention to the USA and looks at the rise, from the early 1960s onwards, of moral panics focusing on synthetic drugs such as ecstasy, ketamine, and GHB. Despite the limited harm and abuse connected to these drugs they have been the focus of moral panics stirred up by increasingly powerful anti-drug interest groups in the USA. A key part of the rhetoric used in such campaigns is the idea that the USA is involved in a 'war on drugs'; this framing has helped make any problems related to synthetic drugs particularly newsworthy. Interestingly, Jenkins suggests that the drugs themselves serve as folk devils in these panics: they are consistently framed as evil and dangerous. This offers up the tantalising possibility that a folk devil can be not just a group or category of person but an object. In the case of synthetic panics, Jenkins argues, it is the fact that these drugs are human-made that seems particularly disturbing: this somehow pricks public fears concerning unfettered scientific and technological innovation.

## Are moral panics a thing of the past?

'Moral panic' might be one of the most widely used concepts in the social sciences but there are some who question its relevance today. It's certainly important to note that most studies of moral panics focus entirely on newspaper coverage. This is logical, of course: a moral panic is a sudden eruption of public concern about an officially accredited problem, and the news is the most suitable conduit for stirring up this sort of reaction. The reason why the focus on news coverage is a problem for moral panic studies is that official sources of news are fast becoming a thing of the past. Newspapers, as we found in Chapter 1, are experiencing dwindling circulation figures and there is some evidence that television news broadcasts, too, are becoming less

**Table 5.2** Comparing newspapers/television news and the Internet as sources of news

|  | Newspapers/Television News | Internet |
| --- | --- | --- |
| News selection | Carried out by an editor, sometimes in collaboration with journalists | Carried out by the media user (individuals click on links to read a full story) |
| Placement | Decided by an editor, sometimes in collaboration with journalists | Decided in the first instance by an editor, but shaped by users (Internet news sites commonly have a prominent list of links to the 'most read' stories) |
| Parameters of debate | Set by editors, journalists, and experts | Sketched out by editors, journalists, experts, and 'increasingly' sponsored bloggers, but with contributions from media users (in the comments section at the bottom of the piece) |

popular – as *television* broadcasts, at least. It's important to note that many of the most widely watched video clips on YouTube are clips from television news programmes. People are, then, still interested in news: *they're simply consuming it differently*. The Internet, for example, has become a key platform for receiving the news, whether that's through YouTube, a news app downloaded onto our mobile phones, or a homepage on our computers. The news updates we get on the Internet are consumed differently to those in newspapers and television, as Table 5.2 demonstrates, and these differences pose something of a problem to moral panic studies scholars.

In short, the Internet allows for media users to *choose* which news stories to read or watch and allows a far greater range of voices to contribute to a debate. It's therefore less easy for Internet news sites to set the news agenda, exert a monolithic influence over public opinion, and exclude minority views or dissenting voices – all things that have, in the past, aided more traditional news sources' participation in moral panics. McRobbie and Thornton (1995) make a similar argument concerning the role of the Internet in changing the nature of moral panics. They point to the expansion and decentralisation of the media over the past few decades. A range of new media and media outlets have sprung up: niche media for subcultures, news websites, blogs, and television channels have all proliferated over the last decade. As a consequence, there are more participants in media debates now, including bloggers, pressure groups, and charities. This, along with the fact that 'folk devils' are often supported in their own niche media (itself a consequence of media expansion), means that a particular social group is less likely to be demonised. Given all this, the authors argue, 'it is now time that every stage in the process of constructing a moral panic be revised' (p. 559).

There are other reasons to question the relevance of the moral panic concept. Ungar (2001) has convincingly argued that the sources of public anxiety have altered significantly in the last few decades. It is not primarily deviant-seeming social groups that we feel most threatened by today, he argues, but rather environmental degradation, climate change, nuclear fall-outs, and technological and scientific developments (such as genetically modified food crops). It is, in short, the risks associated with modernisation that are perceived to pose a threat to our safety. This is also a key idea behind the so-called risk society thesis, associated principally with the sociologist Ulrich Beck: indeed, Ungar is an advocate of this theory. It is the risks of late modernity, Ungar wants to argue, that are more likely to make news headlines than the traditional stuff of moral panics. Take a moment to think about the big global news stories of the last few years and you may well conclude that Ungar has a point. Sustained and intense news coverage has been directed towards the nuclear fallout in Japan, trapped Venezuelan miners, and the global economic recession. Human-made threats of *this* order are, we might reasonably argue, the big concerns of citizens and news outlets in late modern societies.

The other point that's worth considering here is whether moral panics still draw upon and advance a clear moral rhetoric. Stuart Waiton (2008) has put forward this argument, suggesting that late modern societies are in a constant state of panic, but that it is *'amoral* panics' that abound. These campaigns tend to emphasise the need for would-be victims to take extra care rather than marginalise a folk devil. Part of Waiton's argument concerns the decline of a declamatory, moralising conservative ideology and the wider acceptance of a more liberal attitude towards minority groups. Racism, sexism, overt disapproval of the working classes – all, Waiton suggests, have become less acceptable, and in turn the moral panics of yesteryear have waned.

Both Ungar and Waiton raise important points. These authors usefully draw our attention to the ways in which news coverage has changed over the past few decades and rightly argue that studies of moral panics have been slow to account for these changes. Ungar is clearly right to point out that today's news-reading public is concerned with issues beyond those traditionally dealt with in moral panics. Equally, we should carefully consider whether a discourse of morality is evident in news reporting on crimes and criminals. Nonetheless, we need only think of the newspaper handling of child sex crime, 'knife crime', and drug abuse to realise that there are still social groups and problems that provoke overt moral opprobrium amongst the public and media alike. New social conditions and media technologies might be less conducive to moral panics, but, to borrow from Mark Twain, reports of moral panic's death are greatly exaggerated.

## Moral panics as moral regulation

That isn't to say that moral panic studies doesn't need development. In fact, some of the most exciting recent work in this field is interested in how to take moral panic studies forwards, and particularly how to couch it in existing conceptual and theoretical frameworks. One of the most convincing arguments comes from the Canadian social theorist, Sean Hier (2002, 2008), who suggests that we see moral panics in terms of moral regulation. In essence, he's suggesting that we bring together two hitherto discrete areas of academic work – moral regulation theory and moral panic studies. Moral regulation theorists have drawn attention to the role of social movements and campaigns in urging a population to adopt certain attitudes and behaviours. In many instances, these movements reiterate and shore up prevailing ideas about social order and authority – they are, in other words, ideological. Corrigan and Sayer's book (1985) *The Great Arch: English State Formation as a Cultural Revolution* is widely seen as the first significant contribution to moral regulation studies. Here the authors look at the historical process whereby the British state successfully challenged religious leaders and the monarchy to become the central power broker. They argue that the state's authority was principally secured through the gradual consolidation of moral power. The presumption that it is natural and logical for the state to rule stems from our sense that the state is the rightful law-maker and -enforcer, a disinterested and legitimate arbiter in disputes, and that this particular form of social order is not just desirable but also natural. The expansion of the legislature was crucial in producing this notion of the state: the law, Corrigan and Sayer argue, came to be seen as 'an absolute authority', thus serving to underpin the moral power of the state (p. 80).

The term 'moral regulation' is used by Corrigan and Sayer to describe this process of 'normalizing, rendering natural, taken for granted, in a word "obvious" … a particular and historical form of social order' (p. 4). What sorts of campaigns and movements participate in this? Those involved in moral regulation studies have written about a range of examples, including the sexual purity and alcohol abstinence movements in the USA at the turn of the twentieth century. Both campaigns prescribed rightful behaviour, employed a clear moral rhetoric, and called for law changes (in the case of alcohol abstinence, ushering in a decade of prohibition). More abstractly, both proceeded from the principle that there are – and should be – common, shared standards of behaviour to which everyone in society should be beholden. In inviting people to imagine themselves members of a shared moral community and framing the law as the most effective instrument of this moral consensus, such campaigns performed the work of moral regulation – in other words they helped normalise ideas about the state's moral power to rule and a particular form of social order.

Alan Hunt (2003) has pointed to a historical shift in the 'moralising discourse' employed in such campaigns. Originally relying, in the nineteenth century, on an explicit and religious language of moral rectitude, such campaigns are today more likely to employ the language of risk. Instead of being told that early sexual encounters are corrupting and will lead to our moral dissolution we have our 'awareness' raised about the associated health risks. For Hunt, the latter type of campaign is still participating in *moral* regulation, despite the lack of an overtly moral language. He points out that various contemporary health awareness movements frame the individual as personally responsible for guarding against risks and, in this sense, we can detect the continued salience of ideas about blame, retribution, and waywardness.

What does any of this have to do with moral panics? As Hier (2002) points out, moral regulation theorists have generally considered moral panics to be outside of their remit. Moral regulation projects are, after all, long-term, socially entrenched movements and are directed towards self-improvement. Moral panics, in contrast, are 'here today, gone tomorrow' and are centrally concerned with marginalising the deviant behaviour of the folk devil. Moral panics signal a *rupture* in the social order; moral regulation projects involve an *affirmation* of that order. This is why the former require rapid and punitive state intervention. Moreover, in moral regulation projects 'the regulated are purported to internalize codes of moral conduct shared by the regulator' (Hier 2002: 329). In contrast, moral panics involve certain groups *not* heeding the moral precepts of mainstream society.

Why, then, does Hier believe we should see moral panics as akin to moral regulation projects? Fundamentally, both involve 'one set of persons seeking to act on the conduct of others, and they both contain an inherent linkage between the identity of the regulator and the identity of the regulated' (p. 328). They instruct us, albeit it in very different ways, in what it means to be a respectable member of a society. Both play an ideological role in drawing out for us the parameters of rightful and wrongful behaviour, whether this is a matter of prescribing what one ought to do or drawing attention to what constitutes deviance. After all, 'thou shalt *not*' is just as much a moral precept as 'thou shalt'. Thus, as Hier (2002: 332) argues, 'the convulsive power of the "panic", combined with the long-term reserve of regulatory projects, is where the real thrust of moral governance ... is to be located'.

I find Hier's argument highly persuasive. Seeing moral panics as a distinctive form of moral regulation focuses our attention on their broader social function in shoring up a particular idea of social order and the state's moral power in dealing with crime. It's not simply that a moral panic demonises a particular group – in framing the folk devil's behaviour as deviant and (often) illegal it draws upon and helps sustain familiar ideas about punishment, justice, and the right of law. In fact we might see media depictions of crime more generally in terms of moral regulation. The next chapter considers the possibility that there is another common form of media reporting on crime – the 'cautionary tale' – that also performs the work of moral regulation, this time in a way that is much closer to the campaigns and movements identified by moral regulation theorists.

---

### Exercise

In small groups, develop a working definition of the concept moral panic. In other words, consider the dimensions/attributes you believe an episode has to have to qualify as a moral panic. Using this working definition, identify two recent crime stories in the media that constitute moral panics. Write a short paragraph on each, justifying the categorisation. Now, as an entire class, discuss each group's definition and selection of moral panics.

---

## Chapter summary

This chapter has considered different approaches to moral panic. In summary, we've covered the following points:

- 'Moral panic' is an important but over-used concept in the social sciences. It refers to a sudden outburst of public fear and hostility concerning a group or event. A particular group is demonised and seen as a threat to social order. These 'folk devils' are often young, working-class men belonging to a subcultural group or gang. Public concern is disproportionate to the threat in question: distortion and exaggeration are important elements of moral panic. News reports play a key role in stirring up concern, as do criminal justice agencies and politicians.
- The concept was popularised by Stan Cohen, in his 1972 book *Folk Devils and Moral Panics: The Making of the Mods and Rockers*. This book looks at the depiction and treatment of two British youth subcultural groups.

Following a clash in the seaside town of Clacton in 1964, the Mods and the Rockers came to be perceived as deeply hostile to one another, disruptive, and a threat to social order. Cohen shows that the panic was constructed by social institutions, including the mass media.

- Cohen shows that mass media distortion is just one feature of moral panics. The 'control culture' – the police and judges, for example – also played an important role in creating a panic about the Mods and the Rockers.
- Moral panics are products of time and place. The notion that the Mods and Rockers were listless, spoiled youths with a dangerous passion for subversion and nihilism reflected broader concerns of the period about the 1960s counter-culture and the rise of youth subcultural groups.
- Cohen draws attention to a 'deviance amplification spiral' whereby low-lying deviance (in, for example, dress or attitude) can prompt harsh, punitive measures, which in turn create the conditions for higher-order acts of deviance, such as violence. This runs counter to our expectations concerning the relationship between punishment and deviance – here punishment promotes deviance, rather than offering a solution to it.
- Hall *et al.* (2013) provide another approach to moral panics. Their focus is the 'black mugger' moral panic that emerged during the early 1970s in the UK. Hall *et al.* point to a dearth of statistical evidence to support media claims of a mugging epidemic. They identify the police as the 'primary definers' of the panic, having promoted the idea of a mugging crime wave to mass media outlets. In this case at least, moral panics are manufactured by political elites and government agencies.
- Hall *et al.* point to an escalation in moral panics in the last quarter of the twentieth century. In attempting to explain this pattern, they point to the usefulness of moral panics for governments pursuing a tough, law and order agenda and seeking to deflect attention away from socio-structural problems such as poverty and unemployment.
- Goode and Ben-Yehuda (2009) provide what Critcher (2009: 22) calls an attributional model of moral panic. They suggest that we see moral panics as possessing the following core characteristics: media coverage must be volatile (moral panics 'erupt suddenly ... and, nearly as suddenly, subside') and disproportionate to the threat, there must be concern and widespread consensus amongst the public that the threat is significant and real, and there must be hostility towards an established folk devil (pp. 37–43). They also emphasise the role of interest groups and grassroots public concern in producing moral panics.
- A number of researchers have suggested that moral panics may be a thing of the past – or, at least, that we need to consider the relevance of the concept. McRobbie and Thornton (1995), for example, point out that the

expansion and decentralisation of the media over the past few decades mean that there are more participants in media debates now, including bloggers, pressure groups, and charities. This, along with the fact that 'folk devils' are often supported in their own niche media (itself a consequence of media expansion), means that a particular social group is less likely to be subject to wholesale demonisation.

- Recent changes to the way in which news is consumed may be altering the nature and impact of moral panics. The Internet offers up the possibility for people to select and contribute to news stories. This limits news organisations' ability to set the news agenda and might mean that official accounts of an event are less likely to become definitive.
- Moral panics might be seen as a form of moral regulation. Moral regulation projects and moral panics share an emphasis on instructing us in what it means to be a responsible member of society. Both play an ideological role in drawing out for us the parameters of rightful and wrongful behaviour, whether this is a matter of prescribing what one ought to do (in the case of moral regulation projects) or drawing attention to what constitutes deviance (in the case of moral panics).

## Recommended reading

Cohen, Stanley (1987) *Folk Devils and Moral Panics: The Creation of the Mods and Rockers*. Oxford: Wiley-Blackwell.

Cohen's book popularised the concept of 'moral panic'. Based on an analysis of the social reaction to the apparently warring Mods and Rockers, two British youth subcultural groups in the mid-1960s, Cohen offers a nuanced discussion of deviance amplification. It's worth reading the second, enlarged edition for Cohen's insightful Preface.

Critcher, Chas (2006) *Critical Readings: Moral Panics and the Media*. Maidenhead: Open University Press.

This collection brings together some really useful readings on moral panic. Critcher's Introduction is illuminating and the readings encompass a range of case studies and theoretical approaches.

Critcher, Chas (2009) 'Widening the Focus: Moral Panics as Moral Regulation', *British Journal of Criminology*, 49(1): 17–34.

This article argues that greater conceptual clarity is needed when using the term 'moral panic'. Critcher also makes the case for moral panics being understood as a matter of moral regulation.

Critcher, Chas, Hughes, Jason, Petley, Julian, and Rohloff, Amanda (eds.) (2013) *Moral Panics in the Contemporary World*. New York: Bloomsbury.

This collection brings together essays that consider the ongoing relevance of the moral panic paradigm. The Introduction is particularly good.

Garland, David (2008) 'On the Concept of Moral Panic', *Crime, Media, Culture*, 4(9): 9—30.

An excellent summary of work in this area, particularly Cohen's original contribution, from an important contemporary criminologist. Garland argues that the moral dimension of moral panics has been neglected in recent scholarly work.

Goode, Erich And Ben-Yehuda, Nachman (2009) *Moral Panics: The Social Construction of Deviance*. 2nd edition. Oxford: Blackwell.

Goode and Ben-Yehuda's central contribution to moral panic studies, this book considers where moral panics come from and how we should define them. Good, interesting examples are used to illustrate the authors' argument.

Hall, Stuart, Critcher, Chas, Jefferson, Tony, Clarke, John N., and Roberts, Brian (2013 [originally 1978]) *Policing the Crisis: Mugging, the State, and Law and Order*. 35th anniversary edition. Basingstoke: Palgrave Macmillan.

A classic, early study, *Policing the Crisis* looks at the role of social authorities and elites in constructing the 'black mugger' moral panic in the UK during the early 1970s. The anniversary edition contains a new and insightful Afterword, written by several of the original authors.

Hier, Sean (2002) 'Conceptualizing Moral Panic through a Moral Economy of Harm', *Critical Sociology*, 28: 311—334.

A tough read, but Hier provides a convincing case for treating moral panics as a distinctive form of moral regulation.

Jenkins, Philip (1992) *Intimate Enemies: Moral Panics in Contemporary Great Britain*. New York: Aldine de Gruyter.

Jenkins' book is notable for looking at a set of moral panics and seeking out commonalities. Here he examines the increased incidence, since the 1980s, of moral panics in the UK concerning sexual violence, arguing that interest groups have played a key role in this trend.

McRobbie, Angela and Thornton, Sue (1995) 'Rethinking "Moral Panic": The Construction of Deviance', *British Journal of Sociology*, 46 (4): 559—574.

This much cited paper considers the relevance of the moral panic paradigm given the significant changes to the mass media since the 1970s, not least of all the rise of the Internet.

Thompson, Kenneth (1998) *Moral Panics*. London: Routledge.

A good introductory guide, with particularly good chapters on moral panics concerning violence in the family and girl gangs.

## CHAPTER 6

# *Cautionary tales*

This chapter details the key features of the cautionary tale, considers some examples, and looks at their social origins. Before we proceed, it's worth reminding ourselves that not all sustained and alarming news coverage of crime constitutes a moral panic. You can test this hypothesis yourself by carefully reading the headline news for three online new sites every day for a week or so. You'll notice, amongst other things, that there are stories that recur, that are taken up by all the news sites, and are given prominence over several days. You might detect the use of a moral rhetoric in these stories – suggestions are made about blame, responsibility, the need for greater security or more punitive measures, and the deeper reasons for someone's victimisation or treatment within the criminal justice system. Some of these stories will focus on a case of individual or group deviance and, on closer inspection, turn out to be part of a moral panic. That connection is worth reiterating. Moral panics are substantially about *those who offend* (in both the legal and broad sense of the word). What's more, the deviant, in these stories, is generally male. Where do women feature in crime reporting? How can we characterise sensational, voluminous stories about *victims* of crime? The cautionary tale is a concept that allows us to answer these questions. It involves sustained media attention but it is the victim and potential victim whose behaviour is cast as deviant – and these characters are generally female.

## The cautionary tale: key features

In Chapter 3 we looked at sexual violence in the news and I made the point there that women are very frequently associated with victimhood in news reporting. On occasion, and in the cautionary tale, women's susceptibility to victimhood becomes *the focus* for media coverage. These media stories share certain characteristics with the moral panic: media coverage is voluminous and disproportionate to the threat in question and there is a clear moral rhetoric employed in reporting. The cautionary tale, like the moral panic, exaggerates the threat. Nonetheless, there are clear differences between these two forms of media coverage of crime. In the cautionary tale future and hypothetical crimes are given emphasis; sometimes news reports are nothing more than warnings about what *might* happen. As I discuss below, this is particularly the case in reporting on sexual assault where entire stories are given over to warning people to be on their guard. Take the following news item, from a local US newspaper – importantly, we learn later in the article that there have been no recorded incidents of the crime being identified as a risk here:

> *Police: Be Wary of 'Date Rape Drugs'*
> The Dubuque Police Department is reminding people ... [to] be wary of 'date-rape drugs' ...
>     Tips for prevention
>
> • Never leave beverages unattended.
> • If you suspect beverage tampering or contamination, do not consume.
> • Do not accept drinks from someone you don't know and trust.
>
> (*Telegraph Herald*, 2 October 2011, p. 12)

Lists of precautionary behaviour, like the one we find here, are a typical feature of the cautionary tale. News reports warn people to 'watch your drink', 'shred your mail', 'cover your pin', 'check taxi drivers' licences', and undertake all manner of risk rituals. The implication – or sometimes explicit message – is that *not doing so* will make one partially responsible for an attack. Crime, in the cautionary tale, is at least partly the consequence of the victim's negligence. The (usually male) perpetrator of crime, as we'll find below when we discuss some examples, is sidelined and sometimes barely mentioned in news reports.

Often, the particular precautionary message of a cautionary tale is found in media besides official sources of news, something that makes it distinct again from moral panics. One reason for this is that cautionary tales don't depend so wholly upon the official tone of news reporting for rhetorical force. They are recognised as genuine problems requiring an official response (something that marks them out from crime legends, discussed in the next chapter), but the cautionary tale is also a suitable subject matter for extended opinion pieces in glossy women's magazines, soap opera storylines, and warning e-mail forwards. Unlike the moral panic, which absolutely relies upon a formal voice of censure, a cautionary tale can be told as an informal piece of news – as a rumour, in other words. This means that it can be relayed in media formats that allow for a more 'chatty' mode of address and are less closely bound to the norms of news giving. As something of an aside here, it's worth noting that the cautionary tale is particularly likely to appear in media forms that are predominantly consumed by women – e-mail forwards, glossy women's magazines, soap operas. This is at least partly because, in many cases, the 'message' of the tale is aimed principally at women.

What also distinguishes the cautionary tale is that it is relatively slow-burning. Unlike a moral panic, which erupts and disappears suddenly, a cautionary tale tends to circulate for a number of months, sometimes years. Its existence in media and formats outside of formal news reports aids in this, of course. That it refers, in part at least, to possible future incidents is also an important reason for the cautionary tale's longevity: certainly, it means that the story's continuance does not require fresh incidents. Beyond this, the staying power of a cautionary tale probably has much to do with its reiteration of entrenched social ideas about, for example, female freedom and foolhardy victims. Indeed, the cautionary tale offers moral instruction and enjoins the reader or viewer to heed advice or suffer the consequences. In this respect it might fruitfully be seen as a form of moral regulation.

In the closing section of the previous chapter I suggested, following Hier (2002), that we see moral panics as a distinctive form of moral regulation. In marginalising the behaviour of a folk devil, moral panics urge us to express in common our shared sentiments of outrage and shore up our belief in the rightfulness of a social order in which the state and related social authorities are responsible for law and order. There is, I suggested at the end of the chapter, another distinctive form of media coverage of crime that fulfils the function of moral regulation, but in an altogether different way – I was thinking of the cautionary tale. I think we can usefully view the moral panic and cautionary tale as constituting two poles of moral regulation in media reporting on crime (see Table 6.1, below – and Chapter 5 for more on moral regulation). Both forms of media coverage are fundamentally aimed at regulating behaviour and outlining inappropriate and appropriate conduct, whether

**Table 6.1**  Two poles of moral regulation in media reporting on crime

| Cautionary Tales | Moral Panics |
| --- | --- |
| Prescribe rightful behaviour | Condemn wrongful behaviour |
| Attribute responsibility to a (usually female) victim | Attribute responsibility to a (usually male) perpetrator |
| Marginalise behaviour of the victim/potential victim | Marginalise behaviour of the perpetrator |
| Emphasise the need for **self-regulation** | Emphasise the need for **state intervention** |
| The moralising discourse is **risk and precaution** | The moralising discourse is **law and order** |

that's by marginalising deviant behaviour or prescribing precautionary behaviour. Both, in other words, can be thought of in terms of moral regulation, but where moral panics deploy a moralising discourse of law and order, the cautionary tale relies instead upon a discourse of precaution and personal risk. The next section provides some examples of this distinctive form of media coverage.

## Identifying cautionary tales

'Cautionary tale' is a term I coined in a 2009 article about the British media's handling of drug-facilitated sexual assault (see Moore 2009). Whilst helping to carry out a study of university students' attitudes towards binge drinking, drink spiking, and sexual assault, I'd decided to carry out a media analysis to better understand the popular representation of drug-facilitated sexual assault (DFSA). The phrase refers to the surreptitious spiking of someone's – generally a young woman's – alcoholic drink with a drug, popularly Rohypnol and GHB. Media interest in this offence first emerged in the USA in the mid-1990s and was quickly taken up by the British press thereafter. A decade later the story was still going strong to the extent that, of the students we surveyed, most referred to the media as their main source of information about DFSA (Burgess, Donovan, and Moore 2009). I expected the media analysis to be a reasonably straightforward adjunct to the main study. A number of scholars had referred to the media coverage of this crime, albeit in passing, as a 'moral panic', and this is what I fully expected to find. The early stage of the analysis seemed to confirm this view. The Roofie Foundation, an interest group set up in the UK to 'raise awareness' of DFSA, had prompted media interest with a highly emotive press release in 1997. Newspaper coverage of DFSA soared in 1998 with front page articles warning of a drink spiking 'epidemic'. Scotland Yard launched an official enquiry in 1999 to investigate the extent of the problem and, as our own survey established, there was significant student concern about the apparent crime problem. This level of worry was, as in classic moral panics, disproportionate to the actual threat: notwithstanding the difficulties in detecting drink spiking, various surveys and official statistics suggested that DFSA wasn't widespread.

Despite all this I hesitated to label the media coverage a 'moral panic', and for one central reason: there was no discernible 'folk devil'. In news reports the drink spiker was a vague, unseen, anonymous character – often someone never found, and whose identity was shrouded in mystery. News reports weren't asking us to take up arms against a certain group of offenders; in fact, the perpetrator of DFSA was rarely mentioned. Instead, I realised, it was the victim and would-be victim that took centre stage – *her* behaviour was the focus in reports. Most articles contained some sort of warning or directive concerning how best to avoid drink spiking; some, as the example right at the start of the chapter demonstrates, were nothing more than this. The longevity of media interest in DFSA was also a problem. Moral panics are usually 'here today, gone tomorrow'. In the case of DFSA, the coverage had persisted for over a decade, albeit with discernible peaks and troughs. Our respondents' comments about what they'd seen in the media about DFSA alerted me to another distinctive feature of media coverage that made it difficult to apply the 'moral panic' tag. Students were just as likely to refer to the drink spiking storyline in the popular British soap opera *Hollyoaks* and e-mail forwards as official news reports on DFSA. Yet in moral panics it is specifically formal, official news sources that convey the idea that the problem is widespread, serious, and real.

All of this led me to believe that the term 'moral panic' didn't adequately capture what was going on here and, more than this, that the media reports about DFSA fitted an altogether different category of coverage, one that was relevant beyond this limited case study – and that category was, of course, the cautionary tale. In subsequent work (Moore 2013) I have used the concept to describe and explain British film and newspaper coverage of such things as the 'dope girls' in the 1920s, young women who strayed, unchaperoned, into the dangerous areas of London, only to be punished for this exercise of freedom by being lured by gangs and tricked into drug addiction. More recent cautionary tales include media coverage of 'festival rape', that is, sexual assault carried out at music festivals, and 'taxi cab rape'. In the latter there is an extraordinary emphasis in news reports on precipitating behaviour on the part of the victim and warnings to potential victims (such as to always check a taxi driver's licence). The cautionary tale isn't simply applicable to the British media handling of crime. In both the USA and Australia there has been a media furore over 'sexting' – the sending of sexually explicit messages and images using mobile phones – that is, again, consistent with the style and tone of media coverage found in the cautionary tale. Moreover, the flurry of annual reports in the local US media about 'Spring Break' attacks is directed, principally, towards warning would-be victims and marginalising apparently risky female behaviour.

Whilst the cautionary tale is most often associated with stories about women's sexual victimisation, the concept can be fruitfully used to explain media coverage of non-sexual offences. In particular, media coverage of various forms of cyber-crime – Internet fraud and identity theft, for example – are possibly best thought of in this way. Certainly, it is the negligent behaviour of victims that forms the focus for news reports on these crimes, and the need to be vigilant against an unseen, unknowable menace is emphasised.

## The social origins of cautionary tales

In their classic writing about moral panics, both Cohen (1972) and Hall *et al.* (2013) see the socio-historical context as instrumental in the creation of a particular panic. Moral panics erupt during periods of social tension, when there is a need for a scapegoat or when a government needs to distract from deeper socio-economic problems and justify the existence of punitive law and order measures. In short, they happen because they chime with entrenched social attitudes and cultural currents, and find significant institutional support if they contribute to a particular agenda: they are products, in other words, of a particular socio-historical moment. This is an important insight because it forces us to recognise that moral panics are not naturally emerging: we don't panic about a particular social group because they or their behaviour are *self-evidently* abhorrent but rather because the right social and cultural conditions exist to precipitate public concern and hostility.

We can make a similar argument about cautionary tales. They emerge because the time is right for this sort of moral instruction and because we are receptive to the idea that a given crime is principally a consequence of victim negligence. In fact, cautionary tales appear to have become more numerous and frequent over the past few decades. How can we explain the salience of this form of media coverage? One explanation concerns the role of interest groups in promoting cautionary tales. Like moral panics, cautionary tales receive significant support from campaigning groups. In the case of drug-facilitated sexual assault, the British Roofie Foundation has been highly active in courting media interest. That such organisations can now draw upon a popular rhetoric of 'awareness raising' has helped strengthen their status as expert commentators in media debates. There are financial reasons for news outlets' increased reliance on press releases from campaigning organisations, as discussed in Chapter 1 (see 'Are newspapers dying out?', p. 20). Newspapers are experiencing dwindling circulation figures and, as a consequence, increased financial pressures. They have come to make extensive use of articles written by press agencies – these are cheap and reduce staff costs. Press agencies' articles, in turn, tend to be simple and acritical regurgitations of press releases from official organisations – the police, a charity, a campaign group. All this means that interest groups' precautionary messages are increasingly likely to find their way into print.

None of this explains why such messages might be deemed newsworthy – why, in other words, there is particular public support for, and interest in cautionary tales. A number of sociologists have argued that risk has become an especially salient discourse in late modern societies; since cautionary tales draw upon this rhetoric, their proliferation might have something to do with the rise of a so-called 'risk society'. The phrase is most closely associated with the work of Ulrich Beck (1992). A crucial aspect of the shift from pre-modern to modern society, Beck argues, has been the rise and assimilation of the concept of risk. Once beholden to indeterminate dangers, modern citizens developed a means of making hazards statistically calculable – the mathematics of probability and, after it, the assessment of risk. The rise of modernity signalled the extension of our control over hazards in more ways than this: floods, famine, earthquakes – many such natural disasters – became manageable and predictable. Today, Beck argues, the most pertinent dangers are human-made, such things as nuclear fallout, environmental degradation, and poisoning by toxins. Such risks are indiscriminate, Beck argues: irrespective of class, nationality, gender, wealth, and ethnicity, we all face the consequences of such problems. As discussed in the previous chapter, Ungar (2001) has convincingly argued that it is these risks that now stir up public anxiety, rather than the more traditional bases of moral panics. Certainly, the language of risk – the idea that there are shared, indiscriminate risks that require precaution and mitigation, the reference to low-risk and high-risk behaviour and risky situations – has become a central element of our culture. The dominant view, propounded by governments, interest groups, and subscribed to by large swathes of the public, is that we're each responsible for guarding against crime by being risk-aware. As Heywood (2007: 235) puts it,

> The emphasis is squarely on micro-preventative crime strategies, and as such local authorities, businesses and the public at large are encouraged to employ practical deterrents to ensure that buildings, public spaces and people do not provide 'soft targets' for the criminal. Great store is therefore placed on increased physical security and, importantly, high-profile surveillance, both public and private. The preventative value of closed-circuit television is also crucial in the 'fight against crime'. Similarly pragmatic deterrents such as secure perimeters, barred windows, 'vandal-proof' public facilities, the encryption of digital financial data, the spatio-environmental design of business premises and domestic residences, airport and school metal detectors, alarms and even better locks and bolts, all feature prominently ...

This, we might reasonably argue, is precisely the socio-cultural context in which cautionary tales proliferate.

Whilst a risk-based explanation for the current salience of cautionary tales is convincing, it fails to account for the fact that these media stories are generally directed at and involve *female* victims. The gendered nature of cautionary tales is striking, and requires explanation. Elsewhere I have suggested that cautionary tales speak of public concern about the extent of female freedom (Moore 2013). They are cautionary tales in more ways than one: they warn of a specific risk and serve as salutary lessons about what happens when women are allowed the freedom to be pleasure seeking and autonomous. Most of the cautionary tales we've discussed in this chapter – concerning drink spiking, assaults in taxis, at music festivals, and parties, women straying into the dangerous quarters of London, and the use of mobile phones for sexting – are focused on these themes. Think, for a moment, about the precautionary messages involved in these cautionary tales: don't accept drinks from strangers, don't give out your phone number to people you don't trust, don't travel on your own late at night, be careful when away from home. All of them are prescriptions that limit women's freedom, not simply by requiring them to be chaperoned, avoid certain public places, and be cautious in their relationships, but by asking them to constantly reflect upon their behaviour – to think twice before acting. It is perhaps unsurprising, given this, that cautionary tales become particularly widespread during periods of increased female freedom and involvement in public life. Since the 1970s, in most developed countries, we have seen a very significant increase in female employment and involvement in higher education, in no small degree a consequence of the second-wave feminist movement of the 1960s. By the 1990s and 2000s there was growing public concern about the effects of all this freedom, and it is in this period that we see also the proliferation of cautionary tales. In this sense we might see media condemnation of 'ladette' behaviour, female binge drinking, and increased rates of female violence as part of the same cultural landscape as cautionary tales. At the heart of such media coverage is the idea that women need *reining in*, that there should be limits to their freedom. This, I think, is the real precautionary message of the cautionary tale.

## Questions for discussion

Q1) Can you think of examples of cautionary tales in the media? In each case identify how the tale seeks to regulate behaviour.

Q2) Why do female victims tend to be the focus in cautionary tales?

Q3) In what sense is the cautionary tale a traditional story form? What, on the other hand, makes it distinct to late modern societies?

## Chapter summary

This chapter has looked at cautionary tales in the media, detailing their core features and illuminating their social origins. In summary we've considered the following points:

- Cautionary tales appear in a range of media formats, including news reports, soap opera storylines, and e-mail forwards. They give significant emphasis to the possibility of future crimes. In this type of crime story the perpetrator is sidelined and sometimes even ignored entirely. Instead it is the victim and potential victim – usually female – whose behaviour is cast as deviant.

- The moral message of the cautionary tale concerns the need for victims and would-be victims to regulate their behaviour by, for example, checking taxi drivers' credentials, watching their drinks at social gatherings so they aren't spiked, and never walking home alone at night.

- The cautionary tale is distinct from the moral panic in the following ways: it tends to be slow-burning and have longevity, it focuses on crime of the future and hypothetical acts, it appears in both informal and formal sources of news, and it marginalises female victims' behaviour rather than that of a male perpetrator.

- Cautionary tales appear to have become particularly common in the last few decades. One explanation concerns newspapers' increased reliance on press agency material and press releases. This means that advice released by awareness-raising organisations – warnings, for example, about the risks of certain behaviours and situations – is more likely to make the news. These warnings are easily transformed into cautionary tales.

- Cautionary tales make use of a language of risk. The idea that there are shared, indiscriminate risks that require precaution and mitigation is particularly salient today, The recent proliferation of cautionary tales might be part of the growth of the 'risk society'.

- The fact that cautionary tales are usually addressed to women and implicitly place blame on female victims is also important if we are to fully understand the social origins of the cautionary tale. Most cautionary tales are designed as salutary lessons about what happens when women are allowed the freedom to be pleasure seeking and autonomous. Cautionary tales have become particularly widespread during periods of increased female freedom and involvement in public life – in other words, they reflect anxieties about shifts in the gender order.

## Recommended reading

Moore, Sarah E.H. (2009) 'The Cautionary Tale: The British Media's Handling of Drug-Facilitated Sexual Assault', *Crime, Media, Culture*, 5(3).
    This article introduced the concept of 'cautionary tale'. It focuses on UK media coverage of drug-facilitated sexual assault and reveals a striking emphasis on

victim responsibility. The core features of the cautionary tale are sketched out and contrasted to those of the moral panic.

Moore, Sarah E.H. (2013) 'The Cautionary Tale: A New Paradigm for Studying Media Coverage of Crime', in Chas Critcher, Jason Hughes, and Julian Petty (eds.), *Moral Panics*. London: Routledge, pp. 33—49.
Using media coverage of 'dope girls' and 'taxi cab rape' as examples, this essay theorises the social function of cautionary tales by arguing that they operate as distinctive forms of moral regulation.

CHAPTER 7

# Crime legends

Snopes.com and Hoax-Slayer are websites dedicated to the assimilation and verification of urban legends and rumours. You might like to have a look at some of their articles on crime legends before reading this chapter.

This chapter considers the core features and themes of the crime legend and ends with a consideration of how we can explain the proliferation of crime legends over the past decade. Even if you've never heard of the term before, the chances are that you've come across a crime legend. They usually take the form of an e-mail forward sent on by well-meaning folk. The forwarded message tells an awful story about a friend-of-a-friend who has fallen victim to (or cleverly escaped) an outrageous and violent crime. Perhaps the victim has been drugged and had his kidneys removed for sale on the blackmarket, or maybe a woman has been kidnapped by a gang using the sound of a crying baby as a lure. The Internet has become the preferred platform for these sorts of crime legends – outrageous, empirically unverified stories of criminal wrong-doing, told as a rumour. The crime legend is unlike a moral panic in a number of ways: it is relayed as informal news, remains at the cultural margins (rarely influencing policy or policing), and is much more slow-burning, evolving over many years (see Table 5.1 in the Introduction to this part of the book for a fuller comparison). Though it has more in common with the cautionary tale in the sense that it relays a warning to would-be victims, in existing at the margins of mainstream culture and focusing on a dark underworld of organised crime the crime legend is distinct from this type of crime story too. However, it's worth noting that crime legends might *accompany* a moral panic or cautionary tale. Whilst crime legends might pick up on and overlap with either of these forms of media coverage there is, I think, great merit in studying them as a separate phenomenon. As the discussion below aims to show, they are a distinct form of crime story, their characteristics, in turn, revealing our deepest fears about crime.

Crime legends might initially strike us as less criminologically interesting or important phenomena than either moral panics or cautionary tales – after all, they don't prompt legislative changes or a flurry of cross-media activity. Such a view misses what's distinctive about them: their ability to tap into and stoke contemporary anxieties about modern living arrangements and the threat of random violence. Despite the unreal scenario of a crime legend, there's something deeply familiar to us about these stories. Like myths and fairytales, they grossly exaggerate our fears and echo well-rehearsed moral lessons: don't go out alone, never accept gifts from a stranger, don't trust people you don't know – *anything* could happen.

### Conveying crime legends: from word-of-mouth to e-mail forwards

The crime legend is a sub-category of the urban legend, and we need to devote some space here to considering the latter concept. We might describe urban legends as modern folklore, fantastical stories that stay with us for some time, urge us to take extra care and warn others. They are 'urban' simply by virtue of referring to modern living arrangements, the condition of living alongside strangers in anonymous cities. They are 'legends' in that they survive over time and have an unreal, folkloric quality. Brunvand (1983: 10) describes urban legends as having a 'strong basic story-appeal, a foundation in actual belief, and a meaningful [moral] message'. They are, in other words, fictional but, importantly, reflect contemporary concerns and beliefs. Urban legends might be incredible in terms of the content of the story relayed, but they must nonetheless reflect a social world that is recognisable to us. To become widespread, they must chime with deeply held beliefs about culpability, wrong-doing, and justice.

There are certain conditions under which urban legends proliferate. As Rosnow (1991) notes, we are more likely to hear and pass on urban legends and rumours during periods of uncertainty and when lines of formal news are restricted. During wars, for example, we see a growth of urban legends, particularly about leaders and battles; this is a situation where we have an especially pronounced desire for information but our access to such knowledge is restricted. In this respect, the creation and passing on of urban legends is a coping mechanism; it allows us to distil and share our fears, and feel like we have received some sort of news about what's going on. When they are delivered face to face urban legends can also function to promote a sense of community, that we're all in it together. As Brunvand (1981: xxvii) notes, this method of delivery has become increasingly rare. Today, most urban legends are transmitted via the Internet.

So too with crime legends. Whilst there has been less scholarly interest in this specific category of urban legend, there are a number of really interesting studies that help us understand the crime legend's common features. In an early article, Bonaparte (1941) describes and analyses the 'corpse in the car' crime legend, a story that became widespread in Western Europe during the Second World War. The historical context is key to understanding the story. In this legend a mysterious stranger tells a young man (referred to, in the re-telling of the story, as a 'friend-of-a-friend') that by the end of the day Hitler will be dead and he will find the corpse of an unknown person in the boot of his car. By the end of the day only the second prophecy has come true – and, in most versions of the story, the murder victim is recognised by the young man as a hitchhiker to whom he has given a lift in the past. Bonaparte points out that there's an unnerving inversion of the moral universe here: Hitler doesn't get killed, but an anonymous, unassuming stranger does. This is something we see elsewhere in crime legends, particularly in stories concern-ing good Samaritans who become victims. The rather disturbing lesson, in both instances, is that bad things happen, and to the wrong people. The other interesting thing to note about the 'corpse in the car' legend is that it clearly reflects contemporary uncertainty concerning the outcome of the war. The sociologist Gary Fine (2010) argues that rumours are functional in allowing us to rake over fears, prejudices, and uncertainties. A similar observation might be made of crime legends: they allow us to speak directly and fervently about niggling concerns – the tantalising prospect, for those involved in the Second World War, that Hitler might suddenly die, and the horrifying reality that countless anonymous strangers are dying in his stead.

Other crime legends play upon fears about the anonymity of modern social life. Take, for example, the 'razor blade in the apple' story that circu-lated in the US during the early 1980s. Best and Horiuchi (1985) describe and trace the legend. It concerns a deeply deviant fruit-packer who targets chil-dren during the Halloween period by hiding razor blades in apples. When we look more closely at the story it reflects ingrained concerns about innocent children being victimised, random, stranger-perpetrated violence, and the distance between consumer and worker/producer in economically advanced societies. The legend was so salient that it was reported by local newspapers and, when surveyed by Best and Horiuchi (1985), most people had heard of the story. This was a story that spread widely, was remembered and believed by many, and treated as serious. This goes to show that whilst a crime legend doesn't dominate the national media in the same way as a moral panic, it can certainly have a similarly far-reaching impact on public behaviour and atti-tudes. Unlike moral panics, though, crime legends tend to have absolutely no basis in reality. Best and Horiuchi convincingly demonstrate that the 'razor blade in the apple' story was completely fictional: they found no evidence of any incidents, and point out that only two people had ever been arrested for poisoning children during Halloween in the early 1980s – and both of these were guardians of the children in question.

Both the 'corpse in the car' and the 'razor blade in the apple' legends were spread predominantly by word-of-mouth. During the 1990s the Internet became a key conduit for crime legends through online forums and, increasingly, e-mail forwards. Today, the range of legends circulating in cyberspace is extraordinary: from stories about snuff films to organ theft, child abduction to car jacking, credit card fraud to drink spiking. There have even been websites set up to document and verify e-mail forwards that spread such stories, the most useful of which are Hoax-Slayer and Snopes.com. I very much recommend having a look at the crime legends detailed on these websites. One thing that is immediately striking is that there are often multiple versions of a single story. This is an important observation because it draws our attention to the fact that crime legends are products of social interaction. They're co-created, rather than issuing from a social authority or official source (as might be the case with newspaper articles). Individual recipients collaborate in creating and disseminating the story. One important consequence of this is that crime legends are incredibly malleable. They're like 'Chinese Whispers', changing slightly over time and with each re-telling. Time, place, and characters can all be edited and changed to make the story more relevant to the next recipient. This might help explain the longevity of many crime legends.

The crime legend about kidney theft is a case in point. I remember hearing this story when I was at school – and, two decades later, my university students report having read e-mail forwards relaying what is basically the same story. Brunvand notes that word-of-mouth stories about kidney theft started in the early 1990s. By the middle of the decade the story was being circulated through e-mail forwards. The story describes the experiences of a friend-of-a-friend (the narrator's girlfriend's brother or sister's friend, for example). The story runs something like this: a young man (sometimes he's a first-year undergraduate student, other times he's away on business) goes out on his own for a drink at a bar. He is approached by a pretty woman who casually invites him to a party. He goes along, drinks some more alcohol, maybe even takes some recreational drugs – the rest is a blur: he wakes up alone, naked in a bathtub filled with ice. Looking around, he notices that there is writing on his chest (in some variants it's the bathroom mirror) telling him to phone for an ambulance immediately. It turns out that he's had his kidneys removed by a gang who steals and sells organs on the blackmarket.

The kidney theft story draws upon a stock of standard narrative devices and details that we'd commonly associate with the crime legend: it's from a friend-of-a-friend, invariably starts with an emphasis that this is a 'true story', involves an underworld group of criminals, the victim is drugged and represented as overly trusting, and the reader is implored to take the story seriously and pass it on so others may be warned. We could add here that, like most crime legends, the story is without foundation. One thing that should alert us to this is the fact that there are a number of different versions of the story. When I ask my students about the kidney theft crime legend most of them have heard it – but they usually recount a story that's different in terms of things like setting, the main character's occupation, and the narrator's relationship to the victim.

## Core themes

For all their variation, crime legends draw upon a stock group of settings, villains, and victims (for a summary see 'The typical casting and staging for a crime legend'). The perennially mobile characters in our modern social world – college and university students, business travellers, hitchhikers – are frequently victims. These are categories of people who are particularly likely to be isolated (both socially and geographically) and dependent on the generosity of strangers, and both of these factors are often integral to their victimisation. Women and children are also frequently the victims in crime legends, and this time it's their physical vulnerability, willingness to trust

---

**The typical casting and staging for a crime legend**

| *Typical victims* | *Typical villains* |
|---|---|
| Hitchhikers | Hitchhikers |
| College and university students | Gangs |
| Business travellers | Car jackers |
| Women | Psychotic individuals |
| Children | |

| *Typical settings* | *Typical narrative details* |
|---|---|
| Parties | Violence |
| Motels | Elaborate cons |
| Cities | Cars and highways |
| Car parks/lots | New technology (ATMs, two-way |
| Gas stations | mirrors, etc.) |
| Shopping mall bathrooms | Babies/children used as a lure |
| Bars | The victim is surreptitiously drugged |
| | Gang initiation rites |

Discussion Question: How might we explain these recurring features/characters in crime legends?

strangers, and kindness that lead them into danger. Take, for example, the various crime legends about women being kidnapped or attacked by gangs using the lure of a crying baby.

Victims – whoever they are – are often drugged in crime legends, thus making them completely vulnerable. The drugging of the victim is often reported in a particularly salacious fashion; the reader is invited to imagine what degradations and tortures could be visited on the victim once unconscious. The lesson is that no one can be trusted and that no one is safe from the sophisticated and morally bankrupt underworld of criminal gangs. The latter are often the villains in crime legends, their awful deeds carried out for the sake of commercial interests (as in the case of organ theft) or as a means of initiating new gang members. On other occasions the villains' motives are inscrutable. Mysterious, psychotic individuals kidnap, attack, rape, and kill because of a seemingly insatiable appetite for destruction and violence.

There are also a stock of standard settings for a crime legend, frequently the deserted, impersonal, functional spaces of city life – gas stations, car parks, shopping mall bathrooms, and motels. Cars, driving, and deserted highways are frequently mentioned. Where social situations provide a setting – for example, parties and bars – the victim is generally there on his or her own. In all these cases, the victim's isolation makes him or her appear vulnerable to manipulation and attack.

## Why have we seen the proliferation of crime legends?

It's possible to see the popularity of crime legends simply in terms of their salacious and graphic representation of violence. Violence is certainly a central ingredient in many popular stories, including folktales about outlaws, action films, news articles on violence, and fairytales. Looked at in this way, the crime legend is simply part of a broader trend in story-telling. The problem with this sort of explanation is that crime legends have become particularly plentiful in the past few decades; this is something that requires explanation.

One convincing explanation lies in the growth of the Internet. If crime legends are now in abundance, this is surely because we have a new platform that specifically allows for the circulation of informal, editable, unverified stories to huge numbers of people. The Internet, in this sense, is a global rumour mill perfectly suited to the 'Chinese Whispers' quality of the crime legend. Whilst the Internet makes the spread of crime legends easier, we mustn't neglect to consider why large swathes of people would choose to participate in the creation of specifically *this sort* of story. Earlier in this chapter I suggested that we see crime legends as socially functional: they embody public anxieties and allow for the expression of uncertainty. It is unsurprising, then, that they proliferate during periods of instability and conflict. These are moments when people's access to official sources of news is restricted and there emerges, simultaneously, a strong desire to discuss and explain an unsettling situation. Whimsical, informal stories about contemporary problems fill this information gap. Urban legends and rumours allow us to displace our uncertainty and anxiety onto other, related issues. They enable us to talk, often in dramatic and cathartic terms, about the very thing that's keeping us awake at night. The 'corpse in the car' crime legend discussed above is a case in point.

Looked at from this perspective, crime legends express ingrained, shared fears, and their proliferation speaks of a very particular socio-cultural context, one characterised by uncertainty and unease. That crime legends are often about inherently dangerous strangers and the risks of modern life is suggestive of our deep-rooted and nagging concerns about social fragmentation, that is, the experience of living in situations of diminished social trust and solidarity. After all, crime legends are fundamentally about acts of random violence, and they make an awful lot out of people's trust in strangers being betrayed, from the good-natured motorist being assaulted by a hitchhiker, to the innocent businessman deceived by a woman at a bar. The overall moral message is don't trust people you don't know, because ours is a moral universe where anything is possible and no one is to be trusted.

What's particularly troubling about a crime legend is that, often, there is no escape from pernicious strangers. Take, for example, the meaning and role of the car in such stories. Cars allow us to navigate dangerous inner-city areas in safety. They promise privacy and protection: we can, after all, lock ourselves in and darken our windows. However, they also break down and can be invaded by dangerous others (hitchhikers and car jackers, for example). Crime legends – and, of course, horror films – play upon this duality. Even our attempts at producing a safe space in the urban jungle can back-fire: try as we might, strangers will intrude into our lives, and with disastrous consequences.

In sum, crime legends instruct us that strangers are dangerous, deeply deviant, and dissimulating; more worryingly, our best attempts at safeguarding our privacy can actually place us in greater peril. Not only this, but crime legends instruct us that we can't rely upon the more innocuous strangers that populate our social world – bystanders, police officers, and ambulance staff – to come to our rescue. In her account of crime legends about organ theft, Donovan (2002: 206) observes that this story requires us to see such people as completely apathetic:

> The potential witnesses [to organ theft] include 911 dispatchers, hotel personnel, hospital personnel, vendors of medical equipment, law

enforcement personnel, the victim and his loved ones, as well as the organ recipient. Only in a world without intervention, where everyone minds their own business, does this scenario make sense ...

Crime legends, Donovan argues, often depend upon us believing that *all* strangers – even those that are employed in public service – are uncaring, apathetic characters. In fact, for Donovan, the widespread perception that official social authorities are careless and negligent is a core reason why crime legends have become so prevalent in contemporary society. We have developed, she argues, a generalised lack of trust in authority figures. Certainly, over the last few decades there has been growing resentment towards politicians, law-enforcement officials, and journalists: all have come to be popularly seen as self-interested liars and cheats. Trust in criminal justice agencies such as the police and courts has dramatically fallen across the developed world in the last 50 years. Donovan suggests that crime legends distil these distinctively contemporary fears: they depict official guardians of truth and safety as ineffective and negligent and represent the dark criminal underworld of a crime legend as beyond official censure and control. In turn, crime legends enjoin the reader to accept his or her responsibility in guarding against a given threat – after all, more official sources of safety can't be relied upon. Donovan wishes to make a broader point about our credulity concerning this sort of crime story. Lack of trust in social authorities, a sense of personal responsibility in the fight against crime, and belief in a powerful criminal underworld – this social context is particularly likely to result in diminished trust in official sources of information and, at the same time, increased credulity in informal, first-hand sources of news, including personal testimony, blog accounts, and, of course, crime legends. Donovan sees this as a distinctively post-modern condition: our disdain for so-called expert opinion and formal accounts reflects a more fractured social world where old hierarchies are of limited purchase. In this sense the proliferation of crime legends is a consequence of a generalised state of uncertainty and distrust.

## Questions for discussion

Q1) What crime legends have you come across? Why do you think these particular crime stories have circulated?

Q2) How might the change in communication from word-of-mouth to e-mail forwards have changed the nature of crime legends?

Q3) To what extent do you agree with Donovan that the recent proliferation of crime legends is a consequence of the 'disintegrative nature' of late modern society?

## Chapter summary

This chapter has focused on crime legends, detailed their core features, and considered explanations for their recent proliferation. In summary, we've covered the following points:

- Crime legends are outrageous, empirically unverified crime stories spread by word-of-mouth and, increasingly, the Internet. They are a sub-category of the urban legend and take the form of rumours from a 'friend-of-a-friend'. Crime legends distil contemporary anxieties about modern social living arrangements and the risk of violence therein. Examples include the 'kidney theft scam', child abductions from malls, and car jackings at lonely gas stations.
- The crime legend is highly malleable. Like 'Chinese Whispers', the story can change with each re-telling. The setting and main characters can be easily edited, making them relevant to each new set of readers. One consequence of this process of updating is that crime legends often circulate for a significant length of time.
- The crime legend is different to the moral panic in these respects: it tends to have longevity, has an informal tone and mode of address, and is communally created (rather than produced and/or defined by social authorities). It is different to the cautionary tale in the sense that it never gains credence in official, serious news outlets.
- Despite existing in great variety, crime legends share certain core features. Victims are often good Samaritans, women, children, and the mobile characters of modern social life (for example, hitchhikers, travelling businessmen, new college and university students). The perpetrators often belong to gangs, a complex criminal underworld, or have an unexplained lust for violence and disorder. Cars and highways feature recurrently as settings, as do the deserted, impersonal, functional spaces of city life – gas stations, car parks, shopping mall bathrooms, and motels. The crime described is generally violent, and the victim is often entirely incapacitated (by, for example, being drugged).
- Another core theme is that strangers are untrustworthy, dangerous, and deceitful. The world of the crime legend is decidedly bleak, lonely, and amoral, and a core reason for this is the persistent suggestion that strangers of all types – even those we ordinarily rely upon to help and protect us – will do us wrong or ignore a cry for help.
- Crime legends seem to have proliferated over the last few decades. The increased use of the Internet is an important factor in this. The Internet allows for the circulation of these informal, editable, unverified stories to huge numbers of people.

- Crime legends tap into our sense of antipathy and distrust concerning social authorities. As trust in criminal justice agencies, politicians, the mass media, and other authorities has declined, belief in rumours and more informal sources of news is likely to increase. A more general decline in social trust is also evident in crime legends, and this helps explain the emphasis on malevolent and unhelpful strangers.

## Recommended reading

Best, Joel and Horiuchi, Gerald, T. (1985) 'The Razor Blade in the Apple: The Social Construction of Urban Legends', *Social Problems*, 32(5): 488—497.
Best and Horiuchi focus on a crime legend that circulated in the US during the early 1980s concerning a deeply deviant fruit-packer who targets children during the Halloween period by hiding razor blades in apples. The legend was so salient that it was reported by local newspapers and, when surveyed by Best and Horiuchi, most people had heard of the story.

Donovan, Pamela (2002) 'Crime Legends in a New Medium: Fact, Fiction, and Loss of Authority', *Theoretical Criminology*, 6(2): 189—214.
This article looks at online newsgroup postings and discussions about several crime legends concerning snuff films, child abductions from theme park rest-rooms, and organ theft. Donovan also reports on interview findings to ascertain the level and nature of belief in these crime legends.

Donovan, Pamela (2004) *No Way of Knowing: Crime, Urban Legends, and the Internet.* London: Routledge.
Donovan looks at crime legends conveyed by 'old' and new media, including newspapers and e-mail forwards. The focus is on how contemporary legends reflect distinctively post-modern social anxieties and a lack of trust in social authorities and official sources of news.

Hoax-Slayer (www.hoax-slayer.com)
Snopes.com (www.snopes.com)
These websites collect and chart online versions of urban legends.

## CHAPTER 8

# Cultural trauma

This chapter outlines the central features of cultural trauma and considers the role of the mass media. Before this, though, it's worth briefly considering how cultural trauma differs from other concepts we've looked at in this part of the book. In the previous chapter we looked at crime legends and found that they focus our attention on the personal consequences of violence. The social costs of crime – to a shared morality, social stability, collective way of life – are rarely a concern in these stories, and this is mainly because crime legends are about a distinctly asocial world. In contrast, moral panics explicitly invite mutual outrage and ask us to see an incident as a threat to shared values. This happens also when the media participates in cultural trauma, but the event in question is represented as so significant that it irrevocably changes a group's identity and causes a profound rupture to the social order. A sense of crisis and embattlement pervades media accounts, there is a clear concern for reaffirming shared values and a collective identity, and an acknowledgement that things will never be the same again. Take, for example, this extract from a *Washington Post* article the day after the 9/11 attacks:

*America at War*
Once more, this country has been the target of a despicable attack by elements unconcerned with the niceties of civilized human conduct. But the coordinated assaults that began yesterday morning are, perhaps, even more cowardly than the attack 60 years ago at Pearl Harbor ... (*Washington Post*, 12 September 2001, A22)

In Chapter 2 we discussed the use of a military frame in news reports on terrorism, and we see that here: the article starts with the assertion that the USA is 'at war'. It is a very particular type of war, though: one on the shared values of Western society by a brutalised, under-developed, uncivilised 'element'. It is social crisis, rather than individual tragedy, that forms the focal point here. So it is that the article goes on to speak explicitly and passionately of vengeance: the attack is on *every* US citizen, the desire for justice felt by all.

Notice also the parallel drawn between the 9/11 attacks and a previous histor-ical moment of besiegement – the attacks on Pearl Harbor. In this time of crisis, remember who we are and our shared history, the article enjoins its readers. As with personal trauma, cultural trauma requires the shoring up of self-identity, the working through of past events, and a process of sense-making – and the media often play a central role in this representational process.

## Defining cultural trauma

The theory of cultural trauma has been developed principally by a group of sociologists associated with the Center for Cultural Sociology at Yale University (see, for example, Sztompka 2000; Alexander *et al.* 2004; Eyerman 2008). In outlining the theory Jeffrey Alexander (2004: 1) notes that, 'cultural trauma occurs when members of a collectivity feel they have been subject to a horrendous event that leaves indelible marks upon their group conscious-ness, marking their memories forever and changing their future identity in fundamental and irrevocable ways.' The horrendous event in question must be 'culturally disorientating' – that is, threatening to time-honoured cultural practices and a collective identity (Sztompka 2000: 455). Acts of terrorism, wars, assassinations, and state crime potentially have this effect. It's impor-tant to note that not all social episodes or situations that appear threatening and painful are experienced as traumatic. A socially disruptive event becomes a cultural trauma through representation. In other words, it's only when an event is framed as horrific, difficult to reconcile, and an assault on the foun-dational values of a society that it becomes a cultural trauma. Thus, as Alexander puts it, cultural trauma is, 'a claim to some fundamental injury, an exclamation of the terrifying profanation of some sacred value, a narrative about a horribly destructive social process' (2004: 10).

Cultural trauma has much in common with what the anthropologist Victor Turner (1980) called social drama. Social dramas have four phases: a social rule is publicly breached, 'a sense of crisis sets in, redress is then sought, and eventually there is either recognition or reintegration of the schism' (p. 149). The key protagonists in the drama are represented as 'symbolic types' – heroes, villains, judges, and truth-sayers. Victor Turner uses the example of the Watergate scandal that engulfed the Nixon administration in the early 1970s. The original infraction – the burglary of an opposing political party's headquarters – was followed by crisis (conspiracies about entrenched political corruption), redress (the President's resignation), and cultural reintegration of the event (by becoming the subject of entertaining plays, films, and television drama).

The third phase of social drama receives particular attention from Turner. It's here, he argues, that we see a complex mix of ritual, sacrifice, judicial procedure, and scapegoating. Most importantly, during this phase we see the emergence of social reflexivity, that is, a group 'tries to scrutinize, portray, understand, and then act on itself' (p. 156). It is in thinking about redress that a social group is forced to consider its root values, what exactly is being threatened, and how best to defend and present itself. In this sense, a social drama, whilst universal in form, is also 'our native way of manifesting ourselves to ourselves' (p. 158). Put differently, a central feature of social drama is a representational process of invoking and evoking a sense of collective identity. We find this too in cultural trauma, although this concept requires a closer consideration of the cultural-historical context and the deep structures of meaning that precipitate the transformation of an incident into a traumatic event. Thus, Sztompka (2000) discusses the various triggers to cultural trauma – a prevalent 'climate of anxiety', for example – as well as certain groups' greater susceptibility to cultural trauma due to historical experiences of oppression. Such arguments draw our attention to the socially contingent nature of cultural trauma: they do not arise out of a social or cultural vacuum, but are products of time and place.

## Representing cultural trauma: the role of the mass media

It's important to emphasise here that media representation is simply part of a broader socio-cultural process of cultural trauma. In other words, this conceptual framework requires us to see the mass media as a social institution that contributes to, rather than defines cultural experience. With this in mind, let's consider the role of the mass media in cultural trauma. As we learned above, cultural trauma involves a representational process of defining the event and the role of the protagonists, attributing blame, and reiterating a collective identity. A central feature of this process is the identification of a victim and a perpetrator. As Smelser (2004: 282) puts it, 'no traumatic story can be told without tracing ... themes of suffering and blame'. There are a number of what Alexander (2004: 15) calls 'institutional arenas' for the representational process, including art, courtrooms, theological debate, and the mass media. These arenas allow for distinctive forms of representation. For example, and as Alexander points out, news reporting tends to offer us an unnuanced and, in certain circumstances, one-sided representation of events. This is because journalists are subject to various constraints: they are heavily reliant on the state for information and must report incidents succinctly. There is little room for ambiguity in news reporting on an incident: it's usually the case that one particular interpretive framework becomes dominant. Indeed, we can often detect what Eyerman (2004: 62) describes as a 'meaning struggle' in early mass media coverage of an event during which opinion leaders and organisations attempt to furnish the dominant interpretation of a trauma.

There are other ways in which the mass media are distinctive as an institutional arena for the representational process. They are particularly effective at incorporating an audience that is geographically dispersed and producing a sense of trauma beyond the social group directly affected. Benedict Anderson (1991) has argued that the growth of a national press in many European countries during the nineteenth century helped produce just such a sense of 'imagined community'. The rise of the national newspaper, with its emphasis on current affairs and pressing matters of the day, allowed large sections of the public to imagine the nation-state as a social group with distinctive values and norms – and, more than that, to imagine themselves part of this otherwise amorphous social group. Today, news is disseminated globally, principally through rolling television news channels and Internet news sites. Conscious of their diverse audience, such news outlets often frame events as having global consequences or as universally significant. This has important implications for the framing of a traumatic event and the representation of collective identity. For example, that major terrorist attacks on 'the West' can be framed as a threat to liberal democracies *around the world* is partly a consequence of the creation of an 'imagined community' on a global scale.

The mass media are, then, a particularly important site for national and international trauma, the sorts of events that ostensibly 'affect us all'. It is in such cases, as Eyerman (2008: 165) notes, that we are particularly likely to see experts, politicians, and journalists 'claiming to speak for a collective, the nation, while calling it into being'. We can see this dual process clearly in the newspaper article cited at the start of this chapter: the mode of address is directed towards the nation, and the references to past attacks and national character invoke a sense of collective identity. In such instances, Eyerman suggests, the mass media are 'performing the collective' (ibid.), thereby fulfilling an important function of cultural trauma.

Of course, the mass media representation of cultural trauma doesn't always invite the entire audience or readership to share in a sense of loss or crisis. In many instances we are positioned as spectators to a specific group's cultural trauma. An event might be framed as locally, as opposed to nationally or globally, traumatic. Take, for example, the 2002 British news story about the sexual assault and murder of two girls who lived in the small English town of Soham. The event was interpreted in the national press as a local tragedy, hence the description of the event in the mass media as the 'Soham Murders'. Newspaper reports referred to the girls as 'Soham's Roses', the local vicar became a spokesperson for the town, the church a key site for the expression of collective grief and soul-searching. In cases such as these, and as Giesen (2004) notes, the mass media become a 'third party' to cultural trauma – that is, neither victim nor perpetrator, but spectator.

A further distinguishing characteristic of the mass media as an arena for cultural trauma is that they allow for the event in question to be narrated as a story. As Giesen (2004: 141) points out, other sites for the representational process, such as academic debate or the courtroom, favour argument and abstraction. The mass media, on the other hand, 'must narrate a story about good and bad people' (ibid.). Giesen is particularly interested in film depictions of the German Holocaust, commenting that: 'the media staging of the Holocaust succeeds ... in the representation of the victims as subjects with a face, a name, and a voice. Those who have been reduced to mere objects are remembered as 'co-humans', as suffering subjects, as members of the national community' (p. 142). He also finds fault with the representation of the Holocaust in film, arguing that the atrocity has too frequently been offered up and consumed as entertainment. Certainly, it's important to note that when the story becomes the central representational form for a cultural trauma the consequences are mixed: the audience might be urged to recognise sufferers' humanness and to see the personal costs of an event, but they may also be invited to indulge feelings of titillation and pleasure.

## Crime as the precipitating event in cultural trauma

Serious crime is precisely the sort of event that precipitates a cultural trauma. Assassinations, state crimes, political fraud, terrorism – all can be readily framed as social crises. For theorists of cultural trauma, it is immaterial that these incidents are formally recognised as crimes: what matters is that they lend themselves to crisis because they contain the potential for cultural dissonance and social rupture. The assassination of the Dutch film-maker and journalist Theo van Gogh is a case in point. Eyerman (2008) provides a persuasive analysis of the incident, arguing that it precipitated a cultural trauma in the Netherlands. A vociferous critic of Islam, and particularly the treatment and place of women in Islamic culture, Van Gogh was murdered in 2004 whilst cycling to work in Amsterdam. Here's Eyerman's description of the incident:

> Both assassin and victim were cycling when Mohammed B. began shooting. The latter fired several times, severely wounding his victim. The final shots were fired as van Gogh was being chased (twice) around a parked car, while shouting 'We can still talk about this, don't do it' ... After van Gogh was dead, the assailant cut his throat with a small machete ... The killer then stuck a filet knife into his victim's body so deeply that it touched his

spine. Attached through the knife (which perhaps was meant as a dagger) was a note that contained threatening references not to van Gogh but to Ayaan Hirsi Ali [a well-known Dutch politician and advocate of Muslim women's rights]. In his pocket Mohammed B. had another, more personal note written to friends and colleagues, in which he declared his martyrdom ... (p. 5)

Mohammed B. never did become a martyr: he was apprehended soon after the attack during a shoot-out with the police.

The event elicited huge media interest. Eyerman notes that the police made early attempts to 'define and control the situation by declaring the murder a spontaneous act carried out by a single individual without a criminal record' (p. 47). This initial framing of the event didn't hold, not least of all because Mohammed B. was known to the police and the attack was clearly premeditated. A few days after the event media reporting became focused on the idea that Van Gogh had been attacked specifically for his anti-Islamic views. At the same time, Mohammed B.'s background – his conversion to radical Islam and his upbringing in a Moroccan immigrant household – received scrutiny in the press. Thus, the 'dominant interpretation' of the event quickly became: 'Theo van Gogh was murdered by an Islamic radical who was part of a terrorist group with probable links to an international network' (p. 51).

In fact, there was inconclusive evidence that Mohammed B. had murdered Van Gogh in the service of a specific terrorist group. Why, then, did this framework become dominant? One explanation lies in the possibility afforded for framing the incident as a matter of 'them versus us'. Sketching out an oppositional relationship between the assailant and collectivity is a central feature of the representational process in cultural traumas. This relationship is crystallised through denouncements that both condemn the perceived aggressor and assert shared values – both are functional in maintaining social order during periods of crisis. Eyerman (2008: 34–35) argues that the framing of Mohammed B. as an outsider – as a radical, non-Dutch, terrorist, second-generation immigrant – helped avoid a *full* social breach. By placing the blame for the event on someone who is distinctly unlike 'us', the media stemmed self-reproach and focused attention on a single rogue element in Dutch society. The dominant interpretation also allowed for the possibility of shoring up a collective identity – a sense of who 'we' are, what it means to be Dutch, and the consequences, for both, of assimilating immigrants and their diverse cultures. Despite the fact that during Van Gogh's lifetime he had been widely seen as a troublemaker, he now became 'one of us'. That he was a distant relative of Vincent van Gogh, one of the most highly regarded European painters of the nineteenth century, aided in this construction: Van Gogh became a standard-bearer for liberal, open, civilised Western society, a champion for freedom of expression. In this sense, the story of Van Gogh's murder wasn't simply, or in the end principally, about the death of a man: it was about an attack on Dutch values. In other words, the attack was framed as something that affected *everyone*. The nature, not just content, of media coverage emphasised this idea. Van Gogh's funeral was televised live, thus helping to make visible the sense of collective loss and embattlement. 'Those viewing it or who choose not to', Eyerman adds, 'could imagine themselves as either inside or outside [the collective's] bounds' (p. 48).

Cultural trauma theory requires us to consider the social and cultural context that precipitates an incident becoming a trauma. As Eyerman notes, the media's treatment of the murder of Van Gogh was shaped by, amongst other things, relatively high levels of immigration in the Netherlands, the apparent failure of immigration policy to encourage assimilation, as well as the loss of the country's colonial status (p. 4). All, he argues, have contributed to a widespread belief that Dutch values are being eroded and compromised. Eyerman notes a particularly pronounced anxiety about Muslim immigrants, especially those from Turkey and Morocco: it is these groups that are frequently represented in the Dutch media as 'clannish' and illiberal, particularly in their views concerning women and homosexuality (pp. 114–115). This social context provided fertile ground for Van Gogh's murder to become a cultural trauma.

In other cases an incident is so deeply awful and transformative that it appears destined to become a cultural trauma, irrespective of the broader social and cultural context. The events of 9/11 are a case in point. As Smelser (2004: 270) points out in his discussion of 9/11 as a cultural trauma, in their 'scope, intensity, timing, and symbolism, it would be difficult to conceive that [the attacks] would *not* be traumatic in nature'. Consider the fact that the incident is widely taken to be a seminal point in US history: we often refer to other historical events as 'pre-9/11' or 'post-9/11'. Nonetheless, and as Smelser puts it: 'The events occurred in the context of American society and American culture at the beginning of the twenty-first century, and the shape of the national reaction was intimately conditioned by that context. The reactions to similar events in other national contexts would have unfolded differently' (ibid.). The last point is crucial and helps us grasp the idea that cultural traumas are socially contingent rather than 'natural' responses to awful events. The US reaction to 9/11, Smelser suggests, was distinctive. Flag-waving became popular, as did unabashed displays of patriotism, and a certain wartime mentality prevailed. Smelser identifies further elements that marked the national response. Take, for example, the emphasis, in media reports and politicians' speeches, on the need for quick, decisive retaliation to the attacks. Smelser points out that the USA has, historically, been 'uncomfortable if it regards itself as the political aggressor, but comfortable – and very aggressive – in striking out against aggressors against itself' (p. 176). The USA's world power status, he continues, is primarily based on economic dominance, rather than imperial or colonial rule. There is, Smelser argues, limited public interest in military engagement for the sake of territorial gain. At the same time, there is a strong belief that, when confronted with hostility, it is right and just to respond aggressively. The USA sees itself, Smelser suggests, as a 'great innocent giant', one that lashes out only when provoked (p. 272). It also, he adds, has a sense of urgency and efficiency in such matters: the retaliatory attacks on Afghanistan after 9/11 were framed as a 'job that needed to be done', and this too reflected a distinctively US attitude to international justice.

The use of a forthright moral language of evil and right in media reports about 9/11 was also, Smelser argues, characteristic of the US. There is, he points out, a widespread sense of pride and regard amongst Americans for US political institutions and the country's distinctive brand of democracy. The US political system is widely held to be central to what it means to be American. Thus, any attack on US political institutions is likely to elicit strong feelings. As Smelser puts it, under such circumstances there is an 'uncritical sense of sacredness, sometimes bordering on martyrdom' in public debate (p. 277). In the case of 9/11, there was an important spur to this moral rhetoric, namely the existence of an opposing position, voiced by the Arab world, that the attacks were a consequence of the historical oppression of Muslims, perpetrated principally by the USA. As Smelser (ibid.) notes, 'when two antagonists confront one another, each armed with the sure conviction that it has been traumatized by the other, we have an unfailing recipe for a polarization of the pious, rigidity of ideological positions, and violence perpetrated in the name of the holy'. In such instances, when an incident seems to portend ongoing hostilities and potentially catastrophic social rupture, the cultural trauma is likely to be framed as sacred in character.

## Questions for discussion

Q1) Can you think of your own examples of cultural trauma? What makes these incidents cultural traumas rather than moral panics?

Q2) What is the role of the mass media in representing cultural trauma?

Q3) What sort of social conditions increase the chances that a crisis will become a cultural trauma?

Q4) Can the mass media conjure up an 'imagined community' on a global scale? What impact does this have on the creation and experience of cultural trauma?

## Chapter summary

This chapter has introduced academic work on cultural trauma, described the role of the mass media in the representational process, and considered examples of crimes that have sparked cultural traumas. In summary, we've considered the following points:

- Cultural trauma refers to the process whereby a group or society come to represent an event as causing a profound rupture to the social order. A sense of crisis and embattlement pervades media accounts, there is a clear concern for reaffirming shared values and a collective identity, and an acknowledgement that things will never be the same again.
- Serious crime is precisely the sort of event that precipitates a cultural trauma. Assassinations, state crimes, political fraud, terrorism – all can be readily framed as social crises.
- Cultural trauma isn't a 'natural' response to awful events. Not all negative, harmful events become crises, and the scale of the event is not decisive in this process. Instead, we should see a response to an event as socially contingent. Smelser (2004), for example, highlights the distinctiveness of the domestic response to the 9/11 attacks.
- There are a number of different 'institutional arenas' for cultural trauma (Alexander 2004: 15). The mass media are one of them and play a distinctive role in the representational process. In this arena the event is likely to be depicted in terms of a story, with a clear demarcation between 'good' and 'evil', a dominant interpretation of the situation is likely to be produced quickly and then hold, and stories lack nuance and ambiguity.
- News outlets today often have a global reach. This has important implications for the framing of a traumatic event and the representation of collective identity. For example, that major terrorist attacks on 'the West' can be framed as a threat to liberal democracies *around the world* is partly a consequence of the creation of an 'imagined community' on a global scale.
- Eyerman's (2008) analysis of the societal response to the assassination of the Dutch film-maker Theo van Gogh demonstrates the importance of a core oppositional relationship – of 'them' versus 'us' – in cultural traumas. Eyerman (2008: 34–35) argues that the framing of the assailant as an outsider – as a radical, non-Dutch, terrorist, second-generation immigrant – was an important dimension of the ensuing cultural trauma. By placing the blame for the event on someone who is distinctly unlike 'us', the media stemmed self-reproach and focused attention on a single rogue element in Dutch society.

## Recommended reading

Alexander, Jeffrey *et al.* (eds.) (2004) *Cultural Trauma and Collective Identity*. Berkeley: University of California Press.

This edited collection of essays ranges across case studies and lays out the theory of cultural trauma. Alexander's and Smelser's essays are particularly illuminating.

Eyerman, Ron (2008) *The Assassination of Theo Van Gogh: From Social Drama to Cultural Trauma*. Durham, NC: Duke University Press.

Eyerman provides a detailed analysis of the assassination of the outspoken, anti-Islam Dutch film-maker Theo van Gogh. The study sketches out the representation of the main characters in the event and provides an in-depth discussion of the socio-historical context that gave rise to the ensuing cultural trauma.

## PART III

# Analysing the media

# Introduction

Many students let out a groan at the very mention of methods of collecting and analysing data. They often find this aspect of their academic training obtuse, dull, and self-serving. Why bother *describing* a method when you could be actually *doing* research? Those who feel this way are in good company. The eminent sociologist Max Weber once suggested that his discipline was beset by a 'methodological pestilence' adding 'It is almost impossible to find [an] essay in which the author – in the interests of his reputation – has not found it necessary to add some "methodological" remarks ... In order to walk, it is not necessary to know the anatomy of one's legs' (Max Weber in Oakes 1975: 13). Certainly, good researchers are responsive, flexible, and see their methodology in terms of an active process of doing research, rather than a staid description of how they went about things. The good researcher is always ready to adapt and extend her techniques, and that willingness to yield to curiosity is something that no one can teach – although I perhaps wouldn't go so far as to suggest that it's as instinctive as walking. What *can* be taught are tried-and-tested, well-honed approaches to studying social phenomena. In fact, whilst I share Weber's concern, I think research methods training is more like giving someone directions than teaching someone to walk. Our metaphorical lost person will hopefully have the good sense to choose a reachable destination – that's something his friendly instructor can't have much of a hand in. He also might have an intuition about how to get from A to B (he's not been *here* before, but he's got a vague idea of how to reach his destination). Nonetheless, it's sensible to get directions, if only to save time. Once our traveller has learned the most commonly taken path he can, of course, choose to take a scenic route, or maybe over time he'll find a shortcut that he can pass on to others.

This part of the book outlines several approaches – shortcuts included! – to analysing crime stories in the media. We start with the most popular and oldest technique, content analysis, before turning our attention to narrative and then discourse analysis. There are other techniques for media analysis, of course, including semiotic and textual analysis. I've chosen to focus on these three simply because they're widely used and, in my experience, student friendly. The chapters are structured so that the first half gives practical information on the use of the given technique and the second half discusses examples of studies that use the method. Even if you're not particularly interested in learning how to carry out a content analysis, it's worth reading ahead because you'll hopefully find the discussion of particular studies worthwhile. The studies discussed cover a wide range of media and formats: newspaper articles, rap music, primetime television shows, and crime films. Some techniques of analysis are particularly suited to particular media, as we'll find out in the following chapters (sometimes by looking at studies that have chosen methods that are distinctly unsuitable). Each chapter ends with suggestions for a workshop session so that you can put the skills you've learned to practical use.

## A preliminary observation

All of the methods outlined in this part of the book assume the media to be a key influence on public sentiment. In fact, we usually find that there is a connection between a researcher's method of analysis and her study's overall conception of the media. Sociology students will be well versed in this argument. The early weeks of a sociology methods course are often devoted to exploring the relationship between choice of method and a researcher's conception of society. Researchers who see society as something that exerts an external influence over us – as something beyond the individual and small social group's direct control – will choose methods that allow them to spot the relationship between our membership to social groups and behaviour or attitudes. Researchers who see society as something that is created collaboratively and through social interaction will choose methods that allow them to take a close look at group life. In other words, sociologists routinely ask the question 'What is society, and where does it reside?' and their answer shapes their choice of research topic, method of data collection, and analysis.

Those carrying out media-based research would gain much from thinking along similar lines. Ask yourself this deceptively simple question: How does your study conceive of the media? As a shaper of attitudes? As contributing to existing cultural scripts? If so, then the methods and techniques discussed in this part of the book are for you. You should be aware, though, that there is another way of approaching media representations of crime. In some instances our answer to that question 'How do you conceive of the media in your study?' is 'As *instructive*, as *vivid* depictions of human behaviour, as something that *deepens* our understanding'. Another way of putting it is to say that 'media output' can of course constitute art. In these circumstances we should approach a media text differently, with a sense of its artistic value in mind, and recognise that it might be able to *contribute* to, rather than *demonstrate* a criminological argument. This is why many law students are required to watch Hollywood trial movies: they teach them more about the subtleties of legal defence or jury decision-making than any criminological theory!

Researchers might choose to analyse a film, painting, or novel for a similar reason – because, *in itself*, it illuminates or advances an argument.

The last part of this book approaches the media in this way. We look at, amongst other things, what a television Western can tell us about the evolution from lawlessness to lawfulness, what crime novels can demonstrate about the distinctive pleasures of detection, and what a close analysis of *A Clockwork Orange* can add to our understanding of rehabilitation. For now, though, we concentrate on studying the media as the carrier or influencer of cultural trends.

## Developing a research question

The first stage in any research project involves devising a research question. The first golden rule here is that the question has to be answerable. This will seem like a really obvious comment, but a very significant number of students opt for questions that they'll never be able to answer. You need to be particularly careful when opting for a research question that suggests a causal relationship between the media and public attitudes or behaviour. As we discovered in Chapter 4, it's very difficult to ascertain a clear-cut relationship between these two things, and studying anything but the narrowest of media effects is going to pose considerable problems. The following research questions make precisely this type of error:

- Has the media made people afraid of terrorism?
- Has the introduction of web-based news made people less susceptible to moral panic?
- Has *CSI* made juries more trusting of scientific experts in criminal trials?

Think carefully about what we would need to demonstrate in order to answer these questions in the affirmative. We'd need to show that the media are the public's only or main cultural resource and that before news reporting on terrorism, web-based news, and *CSI* the public were free from fear, panic, and trust respectively. We'd also need to demonstrate that it is the media that have shaped public attitudes, and not the other way round. It's perfectly plausible, for example, that those who trust scientific experts in criminal trials are more likely to watch *CSI*. In short, any attribution of causality to the media needs to be considered very carefully indeed.

The second golden rule for devising a research question is to think carefully about what sort of information you'd need to gather in order to answer the question. Anything that focuses on how the media has shaped beliefs, attitudes, and behaviour will require you to carry out an audience reception study as well as a media analysis. This involves using surveys or interviews to examine people's perception of media output. If you're not able or prepared to do this sort of research, you should think again about the parameters of your study. Students often end up with a far more modest research question than what they originally had in mind. That's a good thing! It means that you've been through a process of revision and thought more deeply about what you need to do to produce a sufficient answer to your question.

The last rule is a simple one: be as focused as possible. Take the following questions:

- How has the media perpetuated stereotypes about rape?
- How are offenders of crime depicted on television?

These might be great essay questions, but they're too vague to work as good research questions. Which medium are you interested in studying? Within that, is there a specific genre or format that you're focusing on? Is there a specific case you're going to home in on in your analysis? Which timeframe and geographical region are you going to be looking at? These are all parameters that you need to decide early on, and mentioning them in your research question will keep you focused on the task in hand. Bearing all this in mind, the above questions might be developed to become:

- What 'rape myths' were evident in US newspaper reporting of the 1992 Mike Tyson trial?
- How are male offenders of violent crime depicted in the second season of *CSI: Miami*?

### Accessing data

If you're studying a film, television series, or Internet site accessing data is relatively straightforward. Newspapers are clearly a different matter. You could, of course, buy newspapers – say, three national titles each day for a week. There are good reasons for wanting to get print copies of newspapers. For one thing, it allows you to see how stories are arranged and look at the use of photographs. In many instances, though, we want to study large numbers of newspaper articles and over a long period of time. In such cases you have a couple of options. Many newspapers have an online edition or archive you could use. Or you could use Nexis®, an electronic database of newspapers from around the world, amongst other things. Most university libraries have access to this database: ask your librarian to show you how to access it if you need help. In terms of its newspaper holdings, the database contains items from many European and US newspapers, both national and local. In some cases the holdings go back some 50 years. The guidance notes below will help you use the database.

*How to search through the database*

You may well find that using Nexis® is rather intuitive. You'll notice that you can change the search parameters according to the following.

- Search terms: Remember that if you search for a phrase (like 'gun crime') you need to contain that phrase within speech marks. Alternatively you can use AND to indicate that the articles returned need to include two or more search terms. For example, you could enter gun AND crime or terrorist AND Islam AND suicide into the search box. You can search for all words incorporating a word stem by using an exclamation mark. Say, for example, you wish to search for articles about burglary. Not all articles will use this term, and this means that your search will omit a good number of relevant items. By searching for the term 'burgl!' the database will return articles that feature words such as burglary, burglar, burglars, burglarise, and burgled, thus increasing the pool of relevant articles. You can also specify where the phrase/word appears in the newspaper article, and that's of great use. For example, you may want to limit your search so that the word/phrase is 'In the Headline' or has '3 or more mentions'. A drop-down box in 'Search Terms' allows you to do this. Try leaving 'anywhere' as the parameter in an early search and you'll see the consequence in the Results Page: lots of articles that make very minor mention of the crime in question.
- Sources: If you click on the drop-down box that says 'All English Language News' you can see a range of parameters for searching through publications. You can, for example, choose 'UK National Newspapers', or 'UK Broadsheets', or 'Asia Pacific News', or 'US News'. Have a look at the different options.
- Excluding certain items: You might have noticed that you can tick a box to 'Exclude Newswires'. This means that you'll be removing articles written by press agencies (see Chapter 1). Sometimes it's a good idea to leave this unticked: that way you can see the original wire copy on which other newspaper stories are based.
- Duplicate versions: Always put the setting to 'On – High Similarity'. It's often the case that several versions of the same newspaper are published on one day (colloquially referred to as the 'early' and 'late' editions of a newspaper). Nexis® often stores all versions for a given day, and this means that you run the risk of double counting an article that appears in both the early

and late editions. Nexis® will detect this if you put the 'Duplicate Versions' setting to 'On' and exclude duplicate copies of an article from the search results. Once you get your results some of the articles will have a 'Read Similar Articles' link – if you click on this it'll take you to a list of other articles in the database that have the same or very similar content.

- Dates: Finally, you can specify the dates for which to run your search.

### Reading the results

Nexis® will return a list of newspaper headlines which link to the full article. Have a look also at the left-hand column of the Results Page. Here the database has streamlined the results into 'Newspapers', 'Newswires', etc. This allows you to have a look at the articles in a single publication that include your search term. Narrowing the results by clicking on, say, *'Daily Telegraph'*, might allow you to find an interesting trajectory in reporting – it's worth, in the early stages of using Nexis®, having a look at this sort of thing.

It's tempting to simply jot down the results returned by Nexis® and push on with another search. Resist this temptation. Instead spend time carefully checking your results, especially if this is the first time you've searched for a given term/word. Click on several headlines returned by Nexis® to read the full articles and ask yourself: is the term I searched for being used to refer to the crime I had in mind? On occasion our search phrase/word has more than one meaning. Bear in mind that many of the words we use for crimes (like rape, assault, fraud, theft) are used metaphorically in newspapers and when discussing things that are nothing to do with crime. Take the phrase 'siege'. A newspaper article that uses this term might be referring to a hostage situation, but it might be using the term metaphorically, to refer to, for example, a politician being 'under siege' by business leaders.

You need to have a careful look at the results to check that they reflect the intended meaning of the search terms. If you find some odd results think about:

- 'Cleaning' the data – that is, going through and deleting any irrelevant results. If the results are small enough in number you can simply check by hand.
- Changing your search terms (by searching for siege AND hostage, for example).

Once you are confident that the search terms used are appropriate and capture what you intended, you can push on and extend your search to other years/months/newspapers.

*Limitations*

Nexis® is a brilliant resource, but it does have its limitations. For one thing we can't actually look at the article as it originally appeared in the newspaper: we don't know whether it was accompanied by a picture or where it was positioned on the page. Most importantly, perhaps, we don't know what sort of weight a story was given relative to other news stories. You might decide that the problems with Nexis® are insurmountable, in which case you need to go and analyse print copies of a newspaper. One last brief word of warning. It's easy to get carried away with Nexis®. Remember that results need interpreting: a chart showing us the 'ups' and 'downs' of newspaper coverage is pretty useless without explanation and theorisation.

## Sampling

So you've got a workable research question and figured out how to access the media texts. The next hurdle is deciding how to select a sample of texts to study. If you're studying a relatively recent crime category in the news or a particular film-maker's work then perhaps you can incorporate all relevant items in your analysis. In many instances that's impractical and you have to select a number of cases to study. Students often find this a really daunting prospect: they know they don't have time to study *all* the relevant television episodes, films, or newspaper articles, but they're loath to omit anything from the study. The important thing is to select a sample carefully and logically, and describe how you did this in your write-up.

Let's work through an example of how we might go about selecting a sample. Let's say I want to study the depiction of rape in the British news. I'm planning to do a focused study of 20 articles using discourse analysis (see Chapter 11). How do I select my 20 articles from all relevant cases? I need to find a sensible and logical method of selection. I could, for example, choose a particular incident that received lots of news coverage and look at all articles on that subject. I could choose a single publication and search for all articles from a randomly selected month. In other words I could narrow my search according to topic, publication, and timeframe. There's another way of going about things. Let's say I don't want to narrow my search in this way – I want to be able to include any article about rape written in a UK national newspaper from the 1970s to the present day. I use Nexis® to bring up all relevant results. This list is my sampling frame – that is, the list of all cases that fit my inclusion criteria. Unfortunately, Nexis® has returned several thousand results! How do I pull out 20 articles to study from this huge list? One way is to employ a method of simple random selection, perhaps by choosing every

125th newspaper article. You might want to make sure that you include articles from broadsheets and tabloids, or from across the timeframe. Using this sort of selection criteria – making sure that broadsheets and tabloids each make up 50 per cent of your sample, for example – is referred to as stratified sampling.

A similar set of principles holds for studying visual media. You might, for example, choose films by a particular director of action or horror films to look at the depiction of homicide in Hollywood movies, or you could randomly select episodes of a television detective drama to carry out an analysis. Of course, you could select television episodes or films on the basis that you feel them to be particularly revealing and interesting representations of something. That's perfectly legitimate. The important thing is that, in writing up your analysis and discussion you acknowledge how you came to choose a particular group of texts to study.

## CHAPTER 9

# Content analysis

This chapter describes the technique of content analysis and then discusses two studies that make use of the method of analysis – to varying degrees of success, as we'll see below. Content analysis is the oldest and most popular technique for analysing mass media content. The reason for the method's popularity is simple: it allows for systematic, replicable analysis of media texts. Historically, content analysis has been used as a purely quantitative method. The technique I favour has both a quantitative and qualitative dimension – that is, it can be used to assess the volume of media coverage for a particular subject and carefully examine the use of language. In other words, the form of content analysis detailed below allows us to answer the questions 'How much media coverage of $x$ has there been?' and 'How was $x$ depicted?' I prefer this approach for the simple reason that our answer to the second question qualifies our answer to the first. Put differently, there's little point in knowing that 20 per cent of a newspaper is devoted to reporting on crime if we don't know the tone, slant, or focus of this reporting.

Content analysis is a method that is particularly suited to print media, and is favoured by researchers studying newspaper content. In fact, if we were to look back over chapters in the first section of this book we'd find that most of the studies cited – on, for example, 'shrinkage', reporting styles of newspapers, and the pro-state bias in news reporting on terrorism – made use of content analysis. The popularity of content analysis amongst those studying the news is due to the centrality of measurement in this method of analysis, and the relative ease of this sort of endeavour when examining news output. Think of it like this: we need only measure the amount of space devoted to a particular report or count the number of references to a particular word to get a sense of how much newspaper coverage has been given to an issue, event, or person. Measuring coverage of an issue or event is far more difficult when it comes to television programmes and films.

Content analysis has its limitations, then. Besides the fact that it's not really suited to studying visual media, it's not particularly useful for in-depth critical sociological enquiry. For those interested in analysing media messages in depth and understanding their relationship to the broader culture, other techniques of analysis are more suitable – but more on this in Chapters 10 and 11.

## Quantifying media content and examining use of language

Let's work through the two stages of content analysis. The quantitative dimension of the analysis involves examining how much of the media content is devoted to a particular subject. The key thing here is to devise counting rules and stick to them. This is harder than it might sound. For example, in counting how many newspaper articles there are about rape in a national newspaper, do you include stories that make minor mention of rape or only those that are predominantly about rape? How do you account for placement and length? Do you give differential weighting to stories that appear on the front page? Or consider the task of counting news item references to the perpetrator's ethnicity. If an image of a perpetrator is used, how do you count this?

The best option is to spend some time carefully reading a selection of items with an open mind about counting procedures and set about answering the above questions. Apply your rules systematically and include a note in the report briefly outlining how you counted items. Say I'm carrying out a study of 'gun crime' in the news. I might end up with an analysis schedule that looks something like the one shown in Table 9.1.

Table 9.1 is primarily for the purposes of carrying out the analysis; we'd neaten it up in order to use it in our report or essay. We could, of course, also count certain themes or details in the news reports. We might decide to count how many articles in our sample contained reference to the assailant's ethnicity or a statement from the police. All such things can be incorporated into a counting schedule such as the one below.

**Table 9.1** Example of a preliminary analysis schedule

| |
|---|
| Number of headline mentions of 'gun crime/attack' |
| Number of articles* about 'gun crime/attack' |
| Average word count for articles* |
| Number of front page articles |
| Average** page placement |

*Only those articles that mentioned 'gun crime/attack' three or more times were included in the count.
**The average here refers to the mode.

Another way of extending the analysis is to add in variables that we think might have influenced the volume of coverage. We could, for example, fill in the table above for each year of a given decade, thus allowing us to see how the volume of reporting has changed over time. We could choose a particular period and fill in the table for three different newspapers, thus gaining a sense of variations in reporting across publications. There are lots of different ways of presenting this information – Figures 9.1 and 9.2 give you a sense of how you might go about doing it.

Charts need interpretation and discussion. Note that both Figures 9.1 and 9.2 have footnote sections that detail how the data was collected. It's really important to abide by this convention in your write-up. There should always be a written discussion of a chart, too. We might say, for example, that looking at Figures 9.1 and 9.2 we can observe that the *Washington Post* contained the most coverage of 'gun crime': the average article length is longer than for the other two titles, and we can clearly see from Figure 9.1 that it has the highest peak in reporting. In contrast the *Washington Times* has the lowest average article length and, unlike the other two publications, reporting clearly trails off post-2007. How can we explain this pattern? We might think about the political slant and usual concerns of each of these publications – perhaps the *Washington Post* has a historic interest in reporting violent crime, or gun crime in particular. We'd probably want to know what it is that sustained interest in 'gun crime' post-2007 for the *Washington Post* and the *New York Times*. We'd certainly be interested in finding out what happened in 2003 to spark interest across the three publications. Was there a short-lived moral panic concerning 'gun crime' at this point? Was there a celebrity or

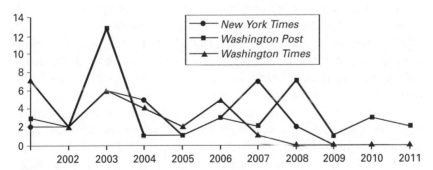

**Figure 9.1** Comparing the number of articles about 'gun crime' in three US national newspapers, 2001–2011

*Source*: Data gathered using Nexis®. Reproduced by permission of Reed Elsevier (UK). Limited trading as LexisNexis.

*Note*: Articles included in the sample made 'major mention' of 'gun crime' (that is, the phrase was contained in the headline, first paragraph, or index notes for an item).

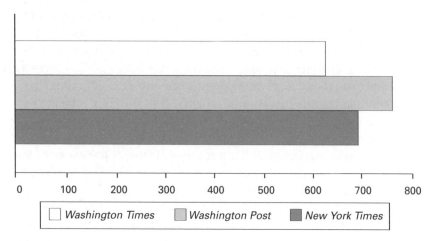

**Figure 9.2**   Bar chart comparing the average word count of newspaper articles about 'gun crime' in three US national newspapers

*Source*: Data gathered using Nexis®. Reproduced by permission of Reed Elsevier (UK). Limited trading as LexisNexis.

*Note*: Articles included in the sample made 'major mention' of 'gun crime' (that is, the phrase was contained in the headline, first paragraph, or index notes for an item). Thirty-eight articles from *the Washington Post* were included in the sample, 28 from *The New York Times*, and 27 from *the Washington Times*.

child involved in a case – anything that would make 'gun crime' particularly newsworthy? Most importantly, was there a 'real' increase in 'gun crime' at this point? To answer the last question we'd need to look at trends in official crime statistics as a comparator – always an interesting task if you're studying crime in the news (as we found in the Introduction, in our comparison of news reporting and official statistics on 'knife crime', see pp. 4–7).

Most of the questions we'd want to ask about the above picture of 'gun crime' in the news require us to take a closer look at news coverage, and this is where we turn to the qualitative dimension of content analysis. Qualitative content analysis involves a careful examination of the use and intended effect of language in a text. If a sample is small enough you might choose to include all items in this part of your analysis. If your sample is very large you can legitimately opt to select a sub-sample for this stage (see the discussion about sampling in the Introduction to this part of the book). The first stage of the qualitative analysis is to discover the general slant and tone of coverage – positive or negative, anti-police or pro-police, hysteria inducing or relatively neutral. You should identify commonly used words or phrases (or groups of words and phrases) that help produce this tone. Essentially you're trying to find out how a subject is characterised and the role of language in producing this effect. This might mean looking at such things as:

- Use of metaphors in reporting (the metaphors of the epidemic and war are frequently used in crime reporting)
- Use of emotive language
- Juxtaposition of certain images or words
- Motifs (for example, images or ideas that are commonly associated with a story).

Let's take a look at the start of an article in the *New York Times* about a play teenagers performed concerning the problem of 'gun crime' and have a go at carrying out a qualitative content analysis. We'll take an article from the 2003 peak in news reporting entitled 'Spreading the Message About Gun Crime'.

> The three teenagers ... brashly performed a history of their own, telling of gun violence that kills their friends and plagues their schools and neighborhoods ... [to illustrate] how gun violence demands attention beyond the places where children tote guns ... The skit was one of a series of public service messages developed by local, state and federal law enforcement agencies. (*New York Times*, 20 July 2003, p. 3)

The article is relatively characteristic in tone. When we look at the other pieces for 2003, almost all of them frame 'gun crime' as a pressing policy issue and a current political concern. A number of newspaper articles discuss changes to legislation that were contemporaneously being discussed by Congress. All this helps explain the increase in news reporting during 2003. When we look closely at the use of language in the extract above we might notice several interesting things:

- 'Gun crime' is associated with young people (notice the emotive reference to 'children tot[ing] guns')
- It is certain inner-city communities that are affected
- 'Gun crime' is represented as a very serious and entrenched problem (notice the use of the metaphor 'plague')
- Awareness raising is vaunted as a solution to the problem
- It is a problem that requires official action.

Our qualitative analysis would proceed with a careful examination of other items in our sample or sub-sample. Our aim, again, is to spot patterns in reporting and representation. Is the metaphor of a 'plague' used elsewhere? Are young people associated with 'gun crime' throughout? How are inner-city neighbourhoods generally characterised? If we find that a specific phrase or word is used frequently we might decide to extend the quantitative part of our analysis and count how many times it appears in all the articles in our sample. As I said in the Introduction to Part III, it is important to be responsive and flexible when carrying out research. The studies discussed in the next section do just that.

## Thinking through content analysis: studying homicide in the British news and references to violence in rap lyrics

We're going to be focusing on the following two studies in this section of the chapter — I recommend that you have a read of them before continuing:

* Peelo, Moira, Francis, Brian, Soothill, Keith, Pearson, Jayn, and Ackerley, Elizabeth (2004) 'Newspaper Reporting and the Public Construction of Homicide', *British Journal of Criminology*, 44(2): 256—275.
* Kubrin, Charis, E. (2005) 'Gangstas, Thugs, and Hustlas: Identity and the Code of the Street in Rap Music', *Social Problems*, 52(3): 360—378.

One of the best ways of understanding the shortcomings and benefits of content analysis is to have a look at studies that use this technique. We're going to start with a discussion of a straightforward content analysis and then turn to a study that is more innovative in its use of the techniques discussed above. Our first example is Peelo *et al.*'s (2004) study of British newspapers' coverage of homicides (that is, recorded cases of murder, manslaughter, and infanticide). The analysis involves a pretty straightforward counting exercise, and in that sense it gives a good idea of the remit of content analysis. Homicide in the news is potentially a huge subject, so the researchers chose a specific timeframe and particular publications for the analysis. They compared news reporting on homicide in three national newspapers – *The Times*, the *Mail*, and the *Mirror* – during 1993–1996. They found that 'newspapers ... are not producing just one clear message about homicide. Certainly there are "family resemblances" between newspapers in selecting homicide stories ... [but] each newspaper produces its own distortion' (p. 273). This is something to be alert to in your own research. Certainly, you should avoid treating the mass media as homogenous, and presuming that there is a single dominant interpretation of events in the news. A careful content analysis is precisely the sort of technique that can help enumerate the differences in reporting across news publications.

A core point of interest for Peelo *et al.* is the disjuncture between the news depiction of homicide and the 'reality' of homicide as it's reflected in official crime statistics. Their study therefore involves comparing the media-spun image of homicide to the official picture of homicide we get in statistics. They used the Home Office's Homicide Index as their source of official statistical information. This database provides basic information on, amongst other things, the final suspect for a case, the victim, motive, and method of killing. They then worked out how many of the homicide cases during the period of study (n=2685) were covered by the three newspapers. They found that 'just under 40 per cent of homicide cases appeared in at least one of the newspapers' (p. 261). You might recall from Chapter 3 that Sherizen (1978) described the ratio of police-recorded crime to news-reported crime as shrinkage. Content analysis is particularly useful in working out this ratio, as Peelo *et al.*'s (2004) study demonstrates.

Interestingly, the three newspapers studied often reported on different homicide cases:

> Only 14 per cent of homicide cases were reported in all three newspapers, while 17 per cent were reported in just one of the three newspapers. In terms of the 1,066 cases reported in at least one newspaper, 35 per cent were reported in all three newspapers and as many as 42 per cent were reported in just one of the three newspapers. (p. 261)

As Peelo *et al.* (ibid.) point out, this suggests that 'newspapers are making different decisions according to the case characteristics'. The researchers proceeded to work out whether there were patterns in the sorts of homicides reported by each newspaper. Their observations are really interesting – here's a selection:

- 'Faction and racial killings showed the greatest discrepancy in reporting – *The Times* reported half of the 38 killings of this type, whereas the *Mirror* reported only just over a quarter (26 per cent)' (p. 272). Peelo *et al.* note that, as a proportion of all homicides they reported, *The Times* is significantly over-representing this type of homicide.
- *The Times* was much more concerned with homicides caused by shootings than the *Mail* and the *Mirror* (ibid.).
- The *Mail* was less likely to report homicide involving an Afro-Caribbean victim or incidents where a homosexual was murdered by a partner (p. 274).

Peelo *et al.*'s study is an exemplary content analysis. It is careful, convincing, and focused. Moreover, the researchers were flexible enough to respond to findings, following up their early observation that there are significant differences between newspapers' reporting of homicide with a closer look at the differential weighting the three titles give to certain types of homicide.

A less successful, but nonetheless interesting study based on content analysis is Kubrin's (2005) work on references to violence in US rap music. Based on an analysis of 403 song's lyrics, Kubrin sets out to 'examine how rappers' lyrics actively construct violent identities for themselves and for others. It explores the ways in which violence is justified and accounted for in terms that clearly resonate with the code of the street' (p. 361). Her point of departure, then, is the idea of a 'street code': the code of conduct for gang members' relationships in black, disadvantaged urban US communities. She uses Anderson's (1999) conceptualisation of this code to develop a list of its core features (see Kubrin 2005: 368):

- Respect
- Willingness to fight or use violence
- Material wealth
- Violent retaliation
- Objectification of women
- Nihilism.

Notice that the core themes that inform the media analysis come from an existing academic theory. This is one of several strategies for choosing which key features and themes to investigate in your analysis (see 'Identifying core features and themes in the analysis', below).

Kubrin then carefully analysed her sample of rap lyrics and counted the number of times these aspects of the street code are affirmed. Her sample consisted of songs on rap albums that had gone platinum (that is sold over one million copies) during the period of 1992–2000. This gave her a sampling frame – that is, a list of all possible cases that fit the inclusion criteria – of 1922 songs. From this list, she randomly selected 632 tracks to study. After analysing 350 songs she found that she was no longer making any fresh observations. At this point she decided to code another 53 songs, just to make sure that she had indeed reached saturation point. This means her eventual sample was 403 tracks. The main findings from her quantitative analysis (p. 369) were as follows:

- Sixty-eight per cent of the songs referred to respect: this was the most frequently mentioned aspect of the street code
- Violence was referred to in 65 per cent of the songs
- Material wealth was mentioned in 58 per cent of the songs
- Violent retaliation was mentioned in 35 per cent of the songs
- Nihilism was a theme in 25 per cent of the songs
- Twenty-two per cent of the songs contained lyrics that objectified women.

---

**Identifying core features and themes in the analysis**

Content analysis is often used to detect common themes and features of media coverage. How, though, do we develop a list of themes to look out for? This is often a difficult task that requires careful attention. Here are the strategies mentioned and used in this chapter:

- Derive a list of themes/features by carefully reading through a sub-set of items. Keep reading items until you can no longer identify new themes (this is the strategy suggested in the short analysis of 'gun crime' above).
- Use an existing academic theory or concept to develop a list of core themes (Kubrin's strategy for studying rap music's reference to a 'street code').
- Draw upon official data to derive categories for analysis. In Peelo *et al.*'s (2004) study the researchers compared official statistics on homicide to news reporting on homicide. The themes for their media analysis were based upon the information contained within the official Homicide Index. The latter contained information on, amongst other things, the method of murder, victims, and final suspect. These became the core themes for the media analysis.

Discussion question: What are the possible drawbacks and advantages to using each of these techniques?

---

Kubrin supplemented her findings with a qualitative analysis that focused on the depiction of violence in the songs in her sample. Here Kubrin discovered that references to violence were frequently used to bolster a rapper's reputation and demonstrate a community's or gang's level of social control:

> Rappers are virtually fixated on 'respect'; they tell listeners that no one should tolerate disrespect and are clear about the consequences of such behavior, which can include death for the 'perpetrator'. Whether referenced only in passing or explained in more detail, the message is clear. There may be severe penalties for disrespect. (p. 372)

There is much to praise in Kubrin's study. She does a good job of integrating the quantitative and qualitative strands of her analysis. Notice, also, that she altered the parameters of the study as she went along; this is precisely the sort of responsiveness that is required in research. She also checked for inter-rater reliability by getting another researcher to code a sub-set of her sample (see 'Inter-rater reliability', below). The coder's results matched closely with

### Inter-rater reliability

Counting is central to content analysis. What makes this task difficult is the fact that the meaning of the items we're counting can sometimes be debatable. It's easy to count how many times the phrase 'gun crime' is used in a set of newspaper articles, but it's more difficult to count how many times an article makes reference to violence. How can we trust that the researcher's counting procedures are sound and reliable? This is where inter-rater reliability comes in. It refers to the level of similarity that exists between two different counters' score sheets. Say I count 20 references to police ineptitude in a set of newspaper articles about a homicide and my fellow counter finds only ten. That's a really significant disparity. The results lack reliability, in other words. It's always a good idea to test for inter-rater reliability when carrying out a content analysis. If the gap between the two counts is large, then go back to the drawing board and have another think about what should get included and excluded from a count. This will tighten up and strengthen the analysis.

Exercise: In pairs, choose a recent online newspaper article concerning crime. Read it carefully and separately, then decide on some themes for a content analysis — don't, at this stage, identify examples from the text. Now re-read the article — separately, again — and highlight/underline each piece of text relevant to your themes. You're coding the text. Finally, check your coding against your partner's to find out the extent to which your analyses overlapped. How would you refine/narrow your themes in light of this exercise?

Kubrin's, thus strengthening her claims. This is a strategy that is often used in content analysis; the method lends itself to replication, and demonstrating that the findings stand up to a test of objectivity lends greater weight to the analysis.

Nonetheless, there are a few problems with the research. Take the fact that music is primarily an aural medium, yet the analysis here is textual. Lyrics are only one element of a song; we'd surely want to know how words and musical arrangement combine to produce meaning here. It would matter greatly if, for example, the lyrics to a rap song were delivered slowly, loudly, without accompaniment, at the end or start of the song, and so on. There's a broader point to make here: we must choose research methods that suit the medium being studied. We need to ask ourselves what are the core features of a medium and whether a particular method will allow us to take full account of these features. Content analysis works very well for media texts that rely heavily on written or verbally delivered texts – newspapers and talk-based radio shows, for example – but we run into difficulties when we use it to study media output that has a strong visual or complex sound component. Of course, you can attempt to adapt the techniques to quantify these sorts of media content, but great care would need to be taken in doing this. You'd need to be alert to the possibility that in producing a counting schedule for, say, a filmic depiction of gang life, the analysis would be unable to accommodate the relevant representational features. The two other research methods covered in this part of the book – narrative and discourse analysis – would probably serve you better.

Kubrin's study also sheds light on the difficulties faced in interpreting media content. The most obvious problem she encountered was that rap lyrics sometimes need decoding: 'kiss' can mean 'kill', 'gristle' refers to a 'face', and so on. Kubrin makes use of an online rapper's dictionary to help make sense of the song lyrics, but it's not always that easy to locate an interpretive tool for content analysis. Songs or literature produced by a niche media or subcultural group – anything non-mainstream, in fact – may well make use of terms and images that a researcher will struggle to decode.

You might also have wondered about Kubrin's counting schedule. What constitutes a song lyric that 'objectifies women', for example, and what about the possibility that some lyrics were delivered with irony or undercut by the musical accompaniment? As we discussed at the start of this chapter, counting is not a straightforward task in content analysis. Some things are easier to quantify than others. A newspaper article that mentions 'gun crime' or 'gun violence' in the first two sentences and headline can probably be counted as an article 'about' gun crime. We might be less satisfied with the suggestion that a song that contains a reference to a woman's body is objectifying women.

Kubrin concludes that rap music is an 'interpretive resource', a means of explaining and making sense of the street code: 'the code supplies an interpretive schema for seeing and describing violent identity and behavior, and the lyrics are treated as reality-producing activities' (p. 375). Moreover, she suggests that rap music renders violence normative and acceptable – simply a way of life. All this begs the question: interpretive and normative for whom? Kubrin suggests that rap music is being *put to use* by someone. Does rap music make manifest the street code for rappers themselves, their fans, or those living in economically disadvantaged black neighbourhoods? The problem is that Kubrin doesn't collect data that allows us to answer these questions. It is a media-based analysis, and this means we can only speak about the *intended* effects of media output. In this respect her study offers us another important lesson: make sure that the analysis supports a conclusion, or else make clear that your extrapolations are speculative.

## Chapter summary

This chapter has outlined the uses of and problems with content analysis. We learned that this technique allows for systematic, replicable analysis of media texts. Historically, content analysis has been used as a purely quantitative method to assess the volume of reporting on certain topics, but it can incorporate a qualitative dimension that involves carefully examining the use of language. By way of summary we might note that content analysis is particularly useful for:

✓ Looking at the volume of media coverage
✓ Comparing the volume of police-recorded crime to news-reported crime
✓ Producing a study that can be replicated – your findings can be checked and verified
✓ Assessing differences in media coverage or representation over time, across countries, or publications
✓ Discovering and quantifying the key themes in media coverage
✓ Detecting common phrases/words in reporting.

By contrast, it isn't particularly suited to:

× An analysis of narrative structure
× Identifying the use of certain discourses
× Non-print media
× Analysis of images.

A careful content analysis involves:

• Thinking about the parameters of the study, both in terms of the timeframe to be studied and the publications to be used
• Clearly labelling charts/tables
• Checking for inter-rater reliability
• Having clear and logically developed categories of analysis
• Considering whether the technique of analysis is suitable for the chosen topic and medium.

## Recommended reading

Krippendorff, Klaus H. and Bock, Mary Angela (eds.) (2009) *The Content Analysis Reader*. London: Sage.

An edited collection that brings together a large number of essays about content analysis and studies using this technique of analysis. The book gives an excellent insight into the history and uses of content analysis.

Krippendorff, Klaus H. (2012) *Content Analysis: An Introduction to Its Methodology*. London: Sage.

Now in its 3rd edition, Krippendorff's book offers an excellent and practical introduction to content analysis. There are really useful chapters on sampling, reliability, statistical tests, and the uses of computer programmes. Highly recommended.

Neuendorf, Kimberly, A. (2002) *The Content Analysis Guidebook*. London: Sage.

Clear and engaging, Neuendorf's book is student friendly and accessible. A range of interesting examples and media are used to demonstrate the uses of content analysis.

Riffe, Daniel, Lacy, Stephen, and Fico, Frederick (2005) *Analyzing Media Messages: Using Quantitative Content Analysis in Research*. London: Routledge.

Clearly written, this textbook offers a step-by-step guide to carrying out quantitative content analyses of various media.

## Workshop session

The following tasks usually take about two hours to complete. Both tasks should be done in small groups of two to four people.

### Task one

You've been asked to produce a content analysis of news reporting on the disappearance of Madeleine McCann. Carry out the following tasks:

- Devise a research question
- Devise a basic counting schedule. Consider how you might extend the analysis by looking at the influence of certain variables (for example, newspaper title, country, timeframe) and the volume of reporting on certain themes
- Use a newspaper's online edition or Nexis® (see the Introduction to this part). Focusing on specific newspapers find out how many articles about the McCann case appeared in the year after she went missing
- Selecting a couple of newspapers for a closer analysis, identify common themes/words used in reporting
- Integrate these themes/words into your quantitative analysis. Do certain terms appear more frequently In certain publications?
- How might we account for the use of language in reporting?

### Task two

In his book *Folk Devils and Moral Panics*, Stanley Cohen identifies the key features of the news reporting on the clashes between the Mods and the Rockers in the mid-1960s (see Chapter 5 for more on this book). These include:

- The two groups were described/pictured as belonging to two distinct gangs: the Mods and the Rockers
- The young people were described/pictured as 'invading' Clacton from London
- Motorbikes and scooters were frequently mentioned/pictured
- The young people's affluence was a common theme
- The young people were described as coming to Clacton with deliberate intent
- Acts of violence and vandalism were given emphasis in reports
- The cost of the damage was emphasised
- The loss in trade was emphasised

In pairs consider these themes and answer the following questions:

- How might we explain these core thematic interests in media reporting?
- What do you think Cohen means when he writes that such themes gave rise to a 'composite picture' of the Mods and the Rockers?

## CHAPTER 10

# Narrative analysis

This chapter looks at forerunners to narrative analysis, gives practical tips on how to carry out an analysis, and ends with a discussion of studies that make use of the technique. First, though, a few comments on the general uses and ethos of narrative analysis. As Auden (1948) observed, crime has a ready-made narrative arc: social order is disrupted by a deviant act, the guilty are sought and generally identified, and, finally, justice is done or thwarted. If the crime itself constitutes the beginning of a story, the social reaction to it – detection, judicial enquiry, and punishment – provides its middle and end. The narrative potential of crime helps account for the extraordinary popularity of crime as a subject for films, television shows, and novels – but more about that in Part IV of this book. For now I want simply to note that crime is excellent material for a story. Narrative analysis aims to detect and then account for a text's narrative, and so offers a useful means of studying crime in the media. Those using narrative analysis believe that the individual details of an event are assembled by a story-teller in such a way as to produce a narrative. This will strike some readers as obvious – but it will strike others as highly contestable. Take, for example, a newspaper article. Some would see this as a neutral relaying of facts and information. It constitutes a story in as much as the event itself has a beginning, middle, and end, but the journalist isn't *producing* the story – the facts speak for themselves.

A central premise of narrative analysis is that there are various ways of telling a story, that the details and 'facts' can be marshalled differently and with distinctive effects. A similar principle applies to conversation in everyday life. When someone tells me a story about a friend, they are choosing to emphasise certain details, characters, and contextual elements. In passing on that story, I might stick really faithfully to the original script – but I might, of course, have a different take on the rumour, and add my own spin on things. My take on events will reflect a distinctive set of biases and assumptions, themselves reflective of broader cultural currents. Narration, as Parisi comments (1998: 239), 'inevitably involves political assumptions, ideology, social values, [and] cultural [stereotypes]'. What this inevitably means is that, whilst there are different ways to tell a story, certain versions predominate because they confirm or chime with dominant assumptions and values. A central task of narrative analysis is to uncover the implicit values that inform the stories that become particularly salient and widespread in our culture.

Before we take a closer look at narrative analysis, it's worth pointing out that this is generally a qualitative technique of analysis, and one suited to print as well as visual narrative-based media. As we'll see below, narrative analysis involves looking closely at the structure, characters, and motifs used in stories, and this sort of focused analysis tends to be based on a small sample. We could, of course, clinically outline the stages to a story – and as we'll see in the next section, some have tried to do just this – but generally speaking those using narrative analysis prefer rich description.

## Structuralism as a forerunner to narrative analysis

Structuralism was an important forerunner to narrative analysis. The work of the Russian structuralists Vladimir Propp and Tzvetan Todorov is particularly noteworthy. Working in the late nineteenth century, Propp (1968) studied the structure of 100 Russian fairytales and identified a common story arc. After an opening event, Propp argued, these stories follow a standard course of events. He identified 31 narrative stages to the Russian fairytale: not all stories contain all 31 elements, but they contain most, and, importantly, the stages appear in the same order. Somebody, usually the hero, leaves the security of the family and sets out on a voyage of discovery. He is then given an interdiction – that is, warned of doing something or going somewhere – which he ignores. The villain then enters the story, and so starts a battle between him and the hero. There are double crossings, obstacles thrown in the hero's path, and then eventually punishment of the villain and reward for the hero. Propp also identified eight character types in fairytales: the hero, the villain, the dispatcher (responsible for the hero's original departure from the family), the hero's helper, the princess (whom the hero often marries at the end of the story), the princess's father, the donor (someone who gives the hero a magical item or skill), and the false hero (someone who claims the hero's achievements and/or princess-bride as his own).

Propp was able to show that even stories as seemingly idiosyncratic as fairytales share a narrative structure and stock of characters. This is a central feature of the structuralist approach to textual analysis. As Lévi-Strauss, one of the most prominent practitioners of this approach, put it, structural analysis is 'the quest for the invariant, or for the invariant elements amongst superficial differences' (2005: 2). We can see this emphasis on the invariant also in Todorov's (1981) writing about narrative structure. All narratives, Todorov argued, share a basic story structure. A story begins by showing us what settled order looks like, a deharmonising event occurs, bringing disequilibrium, the disruption is acknowledged and countered, and equilibrium is regained (though it is different in kind to that at the start of the story).

Narrative analysis, too, requires an alertness to shared story elements. It differs from structural analysis in important ways too. First, scholars using narrative analysis often draw attention to the salience of a story structure in terms of the wider culture. The fairytale form is a classical story of good-triumphing-over-evil, one that is deeply embedded in our culture and easily identifiable in contemporary films and novels (just think of *Lord of the Rings*!). We can point to other such narrative forms: 'fallen woman' stories, for example, or 'the underdog triumphs' stories (both based on biblical stories – of Eve in the Garden of Eden, and David and Goliath). Whilst Lévi-Strauss was committed to understanding myths in terms of broader socio-cultural structures (he was, after all, an anthropologist), Propp most certainly wasn't. This is something that scholars have been very critical of – take Dundes' comments, in his introduction to the 1968 edition of Propp's book: 'Clearly structural analysis is not an end in itself! Rather, it is a beginning, not an end. It is a powerful technique ... inasmuch as it lays bare the essential form of the folkloristic text. But the form must ultimately be related to the culture or cultures in which it is found' (Dundes 1968: xiii). As we'll see in the final section of this chapter, narrative analysis takes seriously the injunction to relate a story form to the broader culture.

Secondly, unlike Propp's work, many studies using narrative analysis identify several dominant narrative structures. On occasion there are competing interpretations of an event – in, say, the stories told by different newspapers or niche magazines – and narrative analysis is alert to this. In fact, we can often detect counter-narratives in the media. Finally, narrative analysis requires greater attention to the use of language in stories than structuralist analysis. Propp and Lévi-Strauss were fundamentally interested in the form a story takes: for those using narrative analysis, the content and tone of a story are just as important.

## Analysing narratives

The starting point for any narrative analysis is to identify one or more dominant narratives within the texts in a sample. We're going to work through an example by looking at two newspaper articles about the murder of Stephen Lawrence. They provide two different versions of the same story – both represent narratives that were popular in the wider press at the time. Lawrence, a black British student, was stabbed and killed by white youths in 1993. The alleged assailants were acquitted in a criminal court due to lack of evidence. The inaction of the police was widely condemned as racially motivated, but only some time after the incident. The subsequent enquiry into the matter found evidence of 'institutional racism' in the British police force. Here are two abridged newspaper articles, from *The Times* and *Daily Mail*, reporting on a development in the case not long after the murder – read them carefully, and have a think about the differences between the two stories:

*Inquest halted on stabbed schoolboy*
A CORONER halted an inquest yesterday into the killing of a black school-boy after a lawyer told him that three new murder suspects had been identified.

The A-level student was stabbed at a bus stop in Eltham ... allegedly in a racist attack.

About 2,500 people have been interviewed in the murder investigation, which has involved 1,000 lines of enquiry.

(*The Times*, 22 December 1993)

*Three suspects named in race murder hunt*
POLICE were yesterday handed new evidence on the murder of black schoolboy Stephen Lawrence.

Mr Michael Mansfield, QC, representing the Lawrence family, said three possible murder suspects had been identified ... He claimed police had seen some of the new evidence but had decided not to take the matter further.

Stephen, an A-level student who hoped to become an architect, was killed at a bus stop in South-East London.

(*Daily Mail*, 22 December 1993)

If, on a first read, you can't see any difference between the two articles, have another read, thinking about the following:

- The differences between the headlines
- Who are the key actors and what are their relationships to one another?
- How the central protagonists/organisations are characterised
- The description of Lawrence.

The two stories should now strike you as significantly different, despite the fact that much of the information conveyed is the same. In *The Times* article the coroner and the Lawrences' lawyer are the chief protagonists. We learn that the coroner has halted a trial because the lawyer has discovered new evidence. The *Daily Mail* article starts rather differently. The police take the centre stage: the emphasis is on them being handed new evidence. There's a hint at police neglect here, and this impression is confirmed later in the article (in part of the text not reproduced here) when we are told that the police have already faced criticism in handling the case. *The Times* is totally quiet on this subject, and instead ends with a comment on the enormous scale of the police operation. You might also have noticed the different weight given to the idea that this was a racial attack. Just look at the headlines: *The Times* runs with 'Inquest halted on stabbed schoolboy' and the *Daily Mail* runs with 'Three suspects named in race murder hunt'. Both newspapers refer to Lawrence as a 'black schoolboy' in the first sentence, but while *The Times* refers to the crime as a 'killing', the *Daily Mail* uses the much more resonant word 'murder'. In the full versions of the articles *The Times* makes two fleeting references to the idea that the attack is racially motivated, even neglecting to note that the alleged perpetrators are white. The *Daily Mail*, in contrast, makes five such references, in the headline, opening few paragraphs, and in the description of the attack in the closing paragraphs. We're also given much more information about Lawrence in the full *Daily Mail* piece.

In short, the two articles draw upon the same material to create substantially different stories: one is about a lawyer halting an inquest into a stabbing of a black teenager on the basis of new evidence; the other is about police being handed new evidence on a racially motivated attack. One is a relatively antiseptic description of legal procedure; the other an implicit attack on the police. The contextual information provided is key to producing these different stories: they prompt us to make sense of the news in a particular way. The first article refers to the scope of the police enquiry, giving the impression that they're working hard to solve this case. The second article couches news of the evidence in terms of alleged police negligence. A narrative analysis would proceed by assessing the narrative structure and content of further articles. If the two narratives identified above appear to be the dominant ones the analysis would move on to consider why they came to predominate in the British press.

For those feeling a bit daunted by the prospect of carrying out a narrative analysis, the good news is that there are structured ways of doing this sort of study. Lieblich, Tuval-Mashiach, and Zilber (1998) suggest four different approaches to narrative analysis: you can carry out a holistic-form, holistic-content, categorical-form, or categorical-content reading. Advocates of either one of the holistic approaches set out to analyse the narrative as a whole in terms of structure or meaning. A holistic-form analysis aims to chart an entire narrative's structure, a holistic-content to decipher a narrative's overall meaning or message. Others favour a less ad hoc approach, and look for specific themes and categories in story-telling or focus on certain characteristics or a specific part of the narrative: these are categorical-content and categorical-form readings respectively.

What these different types of readings alert us to is the importance of deciding, early on in the analysis, whether you wish to look at the whole story, or just part of it, and whether you wish to focus on story structure and/or story content. Different research questions require different approaches. If you are interested in understanding the role of female characters in forensic detection, for example, then you might carry out an analysis of *CSI: Miami*, focusing just on those episodes or scenes that involve female detectives. If you're interested in understanding how court proceedings are represented in television news bulletins, you might choose to carry out a holistic-form analysis that looks at how a court case unfolds in the media.

In other words, different topics take you in different directions. The direction a categorical reading takes is heavily dependent on the specific categories and themes the researcher is interested in. Holistic-content and -form readings tend to be more exploratory analyses and are guided by a standard set of questions, some of which overlap.

Questions for a holistic-content reading:

- Is there a central event/incident/focus? (For example, a crime, a relationship, an accident, the release of new evidence.)
- What is the overall message of the story? (Is it a story of blame, good versus evil, etc.?)
- Are certain motifs, metaphors, and descriptions used recurrently? (For example, 'racial attack'.)
- Who are the key characters? How are they represented? Are we asked to identify with certain characters? Are certain characters responsible for the main action of the story? Is there someone/something to blame?
- Where is the story set?

Questions for a holistic-form reading:

- What and who gets mentioned/presented to us first? (In, for example, a headline, or the opening scene of a film.)
- Is there a central event/incident/focus? (For example, a crime, a relationship, an accident, the release of new evidence.)
- Is there an apotheosis and/or resolution to the story?
- What is the story's beginning, middle, and end?
- Who does/gives what to whom?

- What contextual information is provided to help us make sense of an event/incident? At what point in the story is it provided?

These are the sorts of questions that might guide your early endeavours at narrative analysis. You may well find that one or two story elements – the setting for a story and its resolution, for example – are of particular importance in achieving a particular effect. It is perfectly acceptable to focus on these elements in writing up your analysis. You might also find that what starts out as a holistic-content or -form analysis becomes a categorical analysis. Take our reading of the two articles about Stephen Lawrence above. After describing the two different stories being told, we might decide that the role and representation of the police is of central importance, and make this our focus for analysing subsequent articles and writing up our findings.

Once you are confident that you have isolated a dominant narrative or set of narratives the next stage of a narrative analysis is to ascertain how they reflect and reinforce broader cultural processes. Perhaps we'd want to argue that *The Times* article above helps obscure racial conflict and the article in the *Daily Mail* offers a counter-narrative concerning the problem of institutional racism. Be aware that this is often the part of the analysis that requires the most work: you're moving from empirical observation to theorisation, and the success of the analysis often rests on how well you perform this feat. The final section looks at a couple of studies that do a really good job of drawing out the wider implications of a narrative's structure and content.

## Visual narrative analysis: studying *Superman*

> We'll be analysing the first *Superman* comic-book below. If you want to get the most from this exercise, you can download and read the comic book yourself — it's only 15 pages long and you can buy a copy very cheaply from the iBooks store, amongst other places.

Narrative analysis can also be used to study stories based on or involving images. The same type of questions pertain, but the researcher must also be sensitive to visual effects – or audiovisual effects if the story in question is a film or television programme. Let's have a look at another example to think about how we might study images using narrative analysis. We're going to analyse the very first *Superman* comic-book story, originally published in the USA in 1938 by Action Comics. We might start with a holistic-content and -form analysis and this would reveal, amongst other things, that the story is about a radical, superhuman vigilante, driven by the desire to serve as 'champion of the oppressed'. The narrative structure is composed of seemingly discrete episodes of vigilantism – Superman gains a last-minute reprieve for an innocent woman about to go to the electric chair, halts an incident of domestic violence, hangs a tough guy out to dry on a telephone pole for harassing and kidnapping Lois Lane, and investigates a dodgy senator talking suspiciously to a lobbyist. I say seemingly discrete – these extensive endeavours into crime-fighting help sketch out a coherent picture of a world that is rotten throughout – from the city street to the private home to the halls of political power. The backdrop to Superman's exploits is a world of political corruption, inertia on the part of state officials, and interpersonal violence, a world that needs its 'destiny' to be 'reshaped', as the final caption puts it. The image in this final panel works also to reinforce the tone of radicalism – the image of Superman thrusting out his chest to break a chain circling it may remind us of Marx and Engel's famous enjoinder to the 'workers of the world' in the *Communist Manifesto*: 'you have nothing to lose but your chains' (2004 [originally 1848], p. 258).

If this sounds like a deeply unfamiliar Superman, note the historical period for this version of the story. With European peace in disarray and the troubling rise of fascist groups and governments, the Superman of the late 1930s is explicitly a superhero fit for a dissolute and anxious society. This Superman represents a possibility for rescue from social and political turmoil. In turn, crime and violence in this world have a social origin – the bad guys, in other words, are symptomatic of bigger, social problems. They are, quite literally, cut from the same cloth: one thing that might strike us, when reading this story, is that most of the wrong-doers are dressed in precisely the same emerald green. Of the six characters that are antagonists, criminals, or engaged in immoral activities, four are dressed in clothes predominantly of this colour.

Colour is used expressively in *Superman* and serves an important narrative function, in this case to suggest that what might appear like unconnected misdemeanours – a case of domestic violence, corrupt behaviour on the part of a politician, and a jeery tough guy kidnapping a woman who takes his fancy – are evidence of a general social malaise. Inertia, physical weakness, and cowardice also characterise the wrong-doers in this story: the wife-beater faints in Superman's arms, the governor's snide butler hides behind a gun, the tough guy is easily overcome when separated from his car and cronies, and the main physical feature of the corrupt senator is his corpulence. One important theme here is the idea that the new technologies of urban life – cars, skyscrapers, and intruder-proof doors – are artificial and inferior sources of protection, and hiding behind or within them is enfeebling. Superman is, by contrast, associated with natural, easy speed and strength. He may have come from another planet but, as panel 8 emphasises, his is a strength comparable to that of the grasshopper or the ant. The most obvious visual marker of Superman's natural agility is the frequent use of motion lines, but there are other features of the narrative that help emphasise this characteristic. The images of Superman often compare him to human-made machines and imposing structures and in such a way as to emphasise that he can move faster and reach higher – he leaps over skyscrapers, easily beats trains and cars, and deflects bullets. Again, there's an implicit suggestion here that this society's sources of power are second rate and that's principally because they're artificial.

A central and recurring feature of this early superhero narrative, then, is the idea that Superman constitutes a deeply natural force for good in a world that has been set off course by immorality and its over-reliance on technology. Interestingly, that Superman is from another planet does not undermine his naturalness, in this version of the story at least. He is different from normal folk, but not fundamentally so. His alienness is still important, though: it means he can promise alternative ways of doing things in a world that is bad from top to bottom. At the same time, Superman's value system – specifically, his interest in protecting the weak and disdain for the misuse of power – is deeply familiar to us. When we really scrutinise this narrative we find that Superman's quest is to *return* society to a state when basic values pertained – before power was artificially created and when the physically strong protected the physically weak.

---

**Exercise: Gender in *Superman***

There are other observations we might make about the use of colour in this *Superman* comic-book story. If you've been reading the story alongside this analysis you might have noticed that Lois Lane is dressed in the same red and blue colours as Superman for her date with Clark Kent.

How should we make sense of this in terms of the characterisation of Lois? Is she 'standing in' for Superman (who is absent for much of the action)? Or does it suggest she's his equal and natural partner?

Think more generally about the role of women in this story — are they villains, victims, heroes? How do the images contribute to this representation? Extending the analysis in this way means embarking upon a categorical narrative analysis.

---

## Thinking through narrative analysis: studying female criminals in the news

We're going to be focusing on the following two studies in this section of the chapter — you'll get more from the discussion if you read them before continuing:

- Meyers, Marian (2004b) 'Crack Mothers in the News: A Narrative of Paternalistic Racism', *Journal of Communication Inquiry*, 28(3): 194—216.
- Barnett, Barbara (2005) 'Perfect Mother or Artist of Obscenity? Narrative and Myth in a Qualitative Analysis of Press Coverage of the Andrea Yates Murders', *Journal of Communication Inquiry*, 29(1): 9—29.

The two studies we're going to be looking at in this section of the chapter are both feminist critiques of mass media coverage of female criminals. It is no coincidence that they share this characteristic. Narrative analysis, far more than content analysis, allows us to reveal the underlying prejudices and ideologies that inform media representation. Stories, after all, reflect our often unwitting biases, preferences, assumptions, and expectations.

This is certainly the argument of Marian Meyers, who suggests that the US news depiction of 'crack mothers' tells us a story 'about African American women, motherhood, and addiction' (2004b: 195). She points out that the US news has grossly exaggerated the problem of 'crack mothers', and at the same time ignored other, less culturally salient ones. Whilst crack cocaine use amongst African Americans and Latinos has been widely promulgated by the news media as a serious social problem, heavy drug use amongst affluent white populations has been all but ignored (p. 200).

Meyers uses narrative analysis to examine a seven-part newspaper series, 'Growing Up With Crack'. The series ran for seven days during 1998 in the *Atlanta Journal-Constitution*. It's a small-scale, focused study. Moreover, the articles were all written by the same person, in the same newspaper, and with a specific aim in mind. All of these are important observations: as mentioned in the introduction to this chapter, narrative analysis is generally a qualitative technique, and this means that generalisability is of limited concern.

Producing a holistic-content reading, Meyers identifies a dominant narrative of redemption in the articles she studies, and within that four central themes:

(1) redemption from addiction is possible for the few who are dedicated and hard working, (2) the state's child protection services and politicians

are largely to blame for the plight of crack babies, (3) crack addicts are the victims of a 'demon drug' over which they have no control, and (4) the dedication and compassion of exceptional individuals is necessary to redeem mothers and save the children. (pp. 195–196)

She also identifies five dominant character types in the stories: the victim (the crack mother's child), the addict, the hero (committed to 'saving' victims), the villain (the state welfare system and politicians who ignore the problem), and foot soldiers (front-line workers such as social workers and volunteers). Fundamentally, Meyers argues, the dominant narrative found in stories about 'crack mothers' constitutes a form of paternalistic racism, 'of a white, professional middle-class working to save women and children of the black underclass' (p. 196).

Meyers is also critical of the way in which the children of African American 'crack mothers' are represented as victims of uncaring politicians and welfare systems. Here's how she puts it in her concluding remarks:

By defining the problem facing the children of female addicts as one of an uncaring and unresponsive bureaucracy, the series further denies that the subordinate position of women within the drug culture and society at large, as well as the abusive relationships, poverty, and violence they endure, are connected to the material conditions of their and their children's lives. (p. 214)

Meyers is referring here to the idea that social class, ethnicity, and gender intersect to produce profound inequalities that are difficult to escape. All three structural positions interact also in creating the distinctive media image of the 'crack mother': what's important about this typification is not just that the people in question are female, but also that they belong to a particular ethnic minority and inhabit a place low down on the socio-economic scale. Narrative analysis is particularly suited to capturing the multidimensional nature of media depictions. Content analysis, in contrast, pulls out specific categories for analysis, and can prohibit us from understanding the complexity of media representation.

Meyers is also able to think about the stories in terms of what's omitted, and, again, that's a task for which narrative analysis is particularly suited. 'Missing from these stories', she comments, 'are the men responsible for addicting these women and/or impregnating them – the crack dealers and the men who exchanged crack for sex'. 'The omission of these men', she points out, 'leaves the female crack addict solely responsible for her situation' (p. 213). She is able to make this observation because she has looked at the narratives holistically: this means that she can comment on the overall story told, not just key words or phrases used.

Barnett (2005), in her study of the US news depiction of the Andrea Yates case, achieves a similarly rounded view of the newspaper stories she analyses. She also uses narrative analysis, but whilst Meyers is concerned with the overall message of the story told, Barnett is concerned also with studying story form. The Yates case received widespread media attention, and Barnett compares coverage in a national news magazine and a local newspaper from the month the incident occurred (June 2001) to the month of Yates' sentencing (March 2002). The details of the Yates case are relatively simple: Yates, a Texan housewife to a good Christian family, killed her five children seemingly without motivation. Directly afterwards she calmly phoned the police and her husband to report the incident. With a history of post-partum depression, Yates had been receiving medical and psychiatric help for a number of years. She was eventually sentenced to life imprisonment for the murders.

The subsequent news stories, Barnett comments, 'attempted to explain what seemed inexplicable: how Yates, a woman described as devoted to her children, became violent' (p. 10). Barnett's analysis is guided by three central research questions (p. 11):

1) What collective narratives did news stories tell about Andrea Yates and the murders of her children?
2) How did these narratives challenge or reinforce cultural myths about women and femininity?
3) How did these narratives challenge or reinforce stereotypes and myths about motherhood?

Notice how she's concerned with the relationship between news stories and myth. 'Journalists', she argues, 'frequently use the old to illustrate the new, and, in so doing, their narratives rely on and reinforce cultural myths' (p. 14). In revealing dominant stories, narrative analysis points out for us the indebtedness of our culture – even those elements which style themselves as 'news' – to traditional stories of redemption, temptation, female sin, bravery, self-sacrifice, the underdog, and (in this case) betrayal and just deserts.

Barnett's sample consisted of 45 articles from a local newspaper and seven items from a national news magazine. In employing narrative analysis she uses Foss' (1989) framework to examine the central elements of the narrative, that is, the events, characters, setting, narrator, temporal relationships, and causal relationships (Barnett 2005: 14–15). In doing so, Barnett combines a holistic-content and -form analysis. She identifies two dominant narratives in news reports: 'the narrative of the traitor, constructed to apportion blame, and the narrative of the quest, constructed to right a wrong' (p. 15). In terms of the latter, Barnett finds that the narrative form closely resembles the classic narrative structure identified by Todorov:

> A state of equilibrium exists (a family appears happy); an action occurs (the children are murdered); the disruption is recognized (police and the judicial system intervene); an attempt is made to repair the disruption (the trial is held); and equilibrium is restored (Yates is found guilty and sent to prison). (Barnett 2005: 19)

The other dominant narrative – that of the traitor – characterises Yates as a Judas Iscariot figure who tricked her husband, friends, and doctors into falsely believing that she was a regular and loving mother. This traitorousness was often given a distinctively gendered meaning in news reports. As Lloyd (1995) once observed, women who commit acts of violence are often judged by the culture and criminal justice system to be doubly deviant: once for their crime and again for being female. As a consequence female perpetrators of violence are often marginalised and subject to particularly harsh punitive measures. We can see this clearly in the news handling of the Andrea Yates case:

> News stories ... presented a narrative of a woman who betrayed her sex. The collective narrative in news accounts of the Andrea Yates murders was one of a woman who defied nature, who destroyed instead of nurtured. By murdering her children, Yates betrayed, not only her family and faith, but her femininity. (Barnett 2005: 16)

Barnett identifies three counter-narratives to this dominant narrative of the traitor: 'Yates' husband as a traitor to his family, the medical community as a traitor to Yates, and Yates' mind as a site of betrayal to reason and logic' (ibid.). The last of these is particularly interesting. Barnett suggests that the idea that Yates was insane – becoming a traitor to her 'real' self – served as a counter-narrative to the dominant idea that she was evil. She points out that the notion that women who kill are either insane or evil is a common 'dual categorization' in Western cultures. What was practically ignored in news reporting, she argues, was the possibility that the 'young mother might have been exhausted, helpless, overwhelmed, frustrated' – feeling trapped and oppressed, in other words, by the experience of motherhood (p. 19).

Barnett also notes important differences between local and national news reporting, specifically in terms of setting:

The primary setting in the *Newsweek* articles was the other world of Andrea Yates's mind, which writers described as a sort of haunted kingdom, dark and mysterious and full of agony and pain … In contrast, the *Chronicle's* settings were external – the house where the children were killed, the jail, the courtroom, the city of Houston, and the state of Texas. (p. 21)

The differences in setting reflected differences in attribution of blame. *Newsweek* tended to see Yates as insane and therefore blameless. The local newspaper tended to see Yates as an evil trickster and therefore blameworthy. In attempting to explain these differences, Barnett alludes to local newspapers' role in restoring social order and *Newsweek's* interest in mental health issues. It's important to note that Barnett didn't set out to examine the different settings in news reports: taking a holistic view of the narratives allowed her to observe that this was a particularly salient feature. This is another important difference between content and narrative analysis: with the former the researcher is looking for evidence of predetermined themes and content; with the latter the researcher derives the core features of a narrative from a close reading of the stories told.

## Chapter summary

This chapter has outlined the uses of and problems with narrative analysis. A central premise of narrative analysis is that there are various ways of telling a story. Nonetheless, certain versions predominate because they confirm or chime with dominant assumptions and values. A central task of narrative analysis is to uncover dominant narratives and counter-narratives and then work out their relationship to wider cultural currents, prejudices, assumptions, and social norms. Narrative analysis involves looking closely at the structure, characters, and motifs used in stories, and this sort of focused, qualitative analysis tends to be based on a small sample. By way of summary we might note that narrative analysis is particularly useful for:

✓ Detecting dominant stories, in terms of both form and content
✓ Examining stories in their entirety and understanding them on their own terms, rather than looking only at material that fits predetermined categories and themes
✓ Analysing print and visual, narrative-based media
✓ Uncovering the prejudices and ideologies that underpin media representation
✓ Considering the relationship between media representation and broader cultural motifs/currents.

By contrast, it's not particularly suited for:

× Quantifying media output
× Analysing a large volume of media content
× Analysing media items that don't make use of obvious and/or linear narrative structures, for example, paintings
× Making generalisations about media content.

A careful narrative analysis involves:

• Selecting a small enough sample to carry out a detailed analysis
• Reading/viewing/listening to items in the sample to discern dominant narratives and counter-narratives
• Potentially narrowing the study to concentrate on certain narrative features, such as location or the characterisation of the victim
• Considering how the narratives identified reflect and reinforce broader cultural processes, prejudices, and social norms
• Considering whether the technique of analysis is suitable for the chosen topic and medium.

## Recommended reading

Fulton, Helen (ed.) (2006) *Narrative and Media*. Cambridge: Cambridge University Press.
  This brilliant book explains how a wide range of media formats construct narratives.

Lieblich, Amia, Tuval-Mashiach, Rivka, and Zilber, Tamar (1998) *Narrative Research: Reading, Analysis, and Interpretation*. Thousand Oaks: Sage.
  Lieblich *et al.* explain how to carry out holistic and categorical readings of narratives and take the reader through their own analyses.

## Workshop session

You might like to consider integrating the exercise above, 'Gender in Superman' (pp. 183—185) into this workshop session.

The following task usually takes one hour to complete. It should be done on your own or in pairs.

### Task

You can use Nexis® or an online website for this exercise (see the Introduction to this part of the book for tips on using the former).

Identify a recent high-profile court case. Choose a small selection of ten newspaper articles on the case — these can be from a range of national newspapers, the same publication, or (like Barnett) from one local and one national title. Produce a holistic-content and -form reading, and identify dominant narratives in the coverage. Look out for counter-narratives. Once you have done this, answer the following questions:

- How do the narratives reflect and reinforce cultural norms and ideologies?
- How might you develop the study into a categorical-content analysis?
- How would someone using content analysis have analysed the news coverage?

CHAPTER 11

# *Discourse analysis*

This chapter introduces Foucauldian and critical discourse analysis, gives practical tips on how to carry out an analysis, and ends with a consideration of three studies using these techniques of analysis. First, though, we need to get a firm sense of what constitutes a discourse. It's best to start with an example – consider the following two statements:

'Weddings are really important to me — that bit where the Vicar asks you to think about the couple's relationship to God reminds me of what it's all about ...'

'I *love* weddings: the dress, the horse-and-carriage, the first dance ... It just makes me think of those old films; you know, where everything is just far *simpler* ...'

Both speakers want to tell us what a wedding is, and they do that by explicitly referring to objects we'd associate with religion and romance respectively and by using rhetorical flourishes to emphasise the value of either interpretation. For the first speaker the couple's relationship to God is 'what it's all about'. For the second, the romance of a wedding harks back to the 'good old days'. In noticing such things we're recognising different discourses. A discourse refers to a form of communication – verbal, written, pictorial, or gestural – that promotes a certain view of ourselves, others, or the world in which we live. We might say that in the first statement above weddings are framed in terms of a religious discourse, in the second in terms of a romantic discourse.

It's worth noting that neither of our imaginary speakers actually mentions the words religion or romance. A discourse finds indirect expression, in this case through ideas about what we should value. The other thing to point out here is that discourses are culturally embedded: that is why we need only the most fleeting of cues – a reference to 'the dress', to God with a capital 'G' – to ascertain the writer's or speaker's view on things. To put it differently, a discourse is something we're really familiar with both in terms of the mode of expression someone uses and the content of that expression. When someone talks about ethnic minorities 'stealing our jobs', starts a sentence by saying 'I'm not racist, but ...', or refers to migrants as foreigners we probably have a sense that these are coded forms of racism. There is, we might say, a certain vocabulary of racism – and of sexism, nationalism, ageism, etc. Recognising this vocabulary is an important first step in discourse analysis.

As mentioned above, images, gestures, and spatial arrangement can also reflect a particular discourse. When I walk into one of my colleague's book-lined offices I immediately soak up the cues that this is the space of a middle-class professional: the framed Manet prints, the satirical cartoons cut out from serious newspapers, and the half-empty cafetière on the table all impress upon me the serious work of critical contemplation that goes on within. (As something of an aside here it's worth pointing out that counting the number of books in that office – the sort of work done by those favouring content analysis – would tell us nothing about the discourse of middle-class professional life.) Discourse analysis, then, can involve studying the *non*-linguistic cues that gesture towards a particular construction of reality and identity.

Another important observation to make here is that discourses are all-encompassing. Discourses *seep into* what we say, how we behave, our gestures, affecting who we associate with, what we buy, wear, and watch on television – to name just a few things. Academics often refer to such things as discursive practices to stress the fact that a discourse isn't 'just' words on a page or spoken – it enters into our lives. Take, for example, the dominant discourse in our culture that women are the natural child-rearers: health personnel direct questions about a child's health to the female partner, baby food is marketed as following 'Mother's Own Recipe', child-rearing handbooks contain mainly pictures of the baby with a mother, advertising uses the knowing slogan 'Mums Know Best', children's clothes are positioned next to women's clothes in department stores, and schools address messages in a child's homework diary to Mrs so-and-so. Our culture is saturated with images and texts that reinforce the idea that women are the default parent. In other words, representations help *naturalise* this idea, thus making it very difficult to challenge the convention that women do child-rearing better than men. In fact, we can go further than this: when we openly refuse or fail to accede to a dominant discourse – we might think of a woman who goes back to work after a week, 'leaving' her newborn child with a male partner – we risk losing our claim to a social identity, in this case traditional femininity. In this sense discourses *constrain* us: they set the parameters of rightful and wrongful behaviour. It follows, then, that opting into or out of a discourse can have serious consequences in terms of our social position and identity. These are precisely the sort of things that those using discourse analysis are interested in. Their aim is to deconstruct, account for, and critique discourses. As with narrative analysis, this requires that we have a sense of a discourse's relationship to wider social structures and cultural currents.

## Approaches to discourse analysis: Foucault and Fairclough

There are a number of different approaches to discourse analysis. Here I'm going to discuss Foucauldian discourse analysis and Fairclough's version of critical discourse analysis. The first derives from the work of the French philosopher and social theorist, Michel Foucault. He never really offered a thoroughgoing account of discourse analysis, but his books *Discipline and Punish* (1995) and the first volume of *History of Sexuality* (1990) might be thought to follow this approach. They are historical analyses in which Foucault traces the emergence and shifts in discourses concerning punishment and sexuality respectively. Foucault employs two central techniques: he digs down, looking for the historical root of a particular discourse; and, on discovering particularly important historical moments in the evolution of a discourse, he takes a focused look at a range of documents from that period. 'Digs down' is an apt expression here: Foucault saw his technique as archaeological.

A closer look at Foucault's arguments in *Discipline and Punish* and the *History of Sexuality* helps us understand precisely what it means to carry out a Foucauldian discourse analysis. The former is particularly interesting and relevant to our purpose. *Discipline and Punish* looks at the changes in punishment in Western European societies from the eighteenth to the twentieth centuries, in particular the decline of corporal punishment – the 'spectacle of the scaffolding', as Foucault puts it – and the birth of the prison. Foucault's thesis might be summed up as follows: where once these societies favoured public and physical punishment of the body they now favour a covert disciplining of the mind. Foucault elsewhere describes this as a historical shift from 'sovereignty' to 'governmentality', from a situation where people obey rules out of fear for a figure-head, to a situation where power is hidden and we are asked to see ourselves as responsible citizens, absorbing a code of behaviour because it's the 'right way' to act. This, Foucault believes, is partly the remit of the prison: to inculcate and acculturate, to transform wrong-doers into model citizens. The point is that, during the historical period under study the widely accepted meaning of punishment changed – there was, in other words, a shift in discourse.

What is central to the Foucauldian approach is the idea that a discourse participates in a process of social construction. In fact, this basic tenet underpins many approaches to discourse. Social constructionists believe that our ideas about the world, ourselves, and others are socially produced, rather than naturally arising. Take the widely held view that women are more emotionally astute than men. For social constructionists, this sort of belief reflects complex social processes of learning and acculturation rather than any biological or 'real' difference between the sexes. Not only this, they argue, but a scientific discourse of sexual difference helps confirm the legitimacy of the gender order, for example by suggesting that men are emotionally incapable of doing 'women's jobs' like nursing or elderly care. In this sense, discourse structures our way of looking at the world and ourselves. If you can grasp this, you're well on your way to understanding the point of discourse analysis. Again, an example from Foucault's work will help. In his series of books on the history of sexuality, Foucault argues that sexuality came to be seen as a really central element of self-identity during the late nineteenth century. The rise of this discourse was inextricably linked to the rise of a particular body of knowledge, namely psychoanalysis. This is an important facet of discourse: it lays claim to being authoritative, often by virtue of being accredited and supported by a group of experts who claim for it a superior take on reality. To return to my main point here: it's not just that the ways in which we spoke about sex and sexuality changed during this period: we came to see ourselves and others as possessing a sexual orientation. Today this idea is so normal as to appear uncontentious, but Foucault's point is that sexuality is just a socially produced set of categories. In this sense, a discourse constructs ways of thinking, acting, and looking at the world. Take, again, Foucault's argument in *Discipline and Punish*: the idea that punishment is better directed at minds rather than bodies has come to define how we think and talk about things like capital punishment and what we do about things like prison overcrowding. Our views on such things appear absolutely natural, indisputable, and objectively correct – such is the power of discourse.

Wooffitt (2005: 148), in his assessment of Foucauldian discourse analysis, points out that this approach is not only about identifying how discourses construct ideas about ourselves and the world in which we live, but also how they instruct us to 'participate in social life' and 'furnish us with subject positions'. In other words, from a Foucauldian perspective, discourses inform things like social roles and interaction by sketching out a social order and our place within it. Put differently, and as alluded to in the introduction to this chapter, discourses help keep us in our place. For those who follow the Foucauldian approach to discourse analysis, this method is a critical tool for revealing both the constraining and socially constructed nature of discourse. This is an important point for those considering following the Foucauldian approach: this approach is customarily a tool in a broader project aimed at social critique.

A similar point can be made about the second approach to discourse analysis considered here: critical discourse analysis (CDA). I'm going to focus on Norman Fairclough's version of CDA, partly because I think it's the most useful but also because Fairclough has written extensively on the subject. Students wishing to pursue CDA further would do well to consult some of these texts, particularly the revised 2010 edition of *Critical Discourse Analysis: The Critical Study of Language* and his 2003 book *Analysing Discourse: Textual Analysis for Social Research*. Fairclough's approach to critical discourse analysis, like Foucauldian discourse analysis, is focused on social critique. The former 'aims to contribute to addressing the social "wrongs" of the day (in a broad sense – injustice, inequality, lack of freedom, etc.) by analysing their sources and causes, resistance to them and possibilities for overcoming them' (2010: 231). We can say, then, that critical discourse analysis is an explicitly political endeavour, aimed at revealing the power structures that underpin discourses. Teo (2000: 12) points out that 'the word ['critical', in 'critical discourse analysis'] signals the need for analysts to unpack the ideological underpinnings of discourse that have become so naturalized over time that we begin to treat them as common, acceptable, and natural forms of discourse'.

Fairclough draws upon the work of Foucault, but is especially influenced by Marxist theorists of ideology and hegemony and the field of semiotics. As we'll see below, his is a more structured approach to discourse analysis, and he has written extensively on how to approach this type of study. As he points out, we might differentiate between approaches to discourse analysis on the basis that some offer focused analyses of the linguistic features of individual texts and others look at a collection of texts in more general terms. Foucault's work, for example, sketches out a set of historical shifts in discourse, but rarely enters into a detailed analysis of the use of grammar, pronouns, and verbs in a particular text. Fairclough aims to unite the two approaches by looking at the relationship between abstract social forces such as hierarchies based on social class, gender, and ethnicity, and texts.

## Analysing texts using discourse analysis

This section draws together the observations made above and offers some practical tips on how to carry out an analysis. We focus here on the analysis of text-based material – the section that follows offers some insights into using discourse analysis to study audiovisual material. Discourse analysis is a qualitative technique and, as with narrative analysis, this means that the quality of the study relies heavily on the skill and sensitivities of the researcher. Bear this in mind when choosing to use discourse analysis. Remember also that both Foucauldian discourse analysis and critical discourse analysis are customarily used for a political or critical purpose – to reveal the way in which texts manifest socially constructed discourses that constrain our behaviour or help institute injustices and inequalities.

If you have decided that discourse analysis is a suitable method, the next step is to decide what particular form of discourse analysis you want to use. If you're interested in tracing the historical roots of a discourse and taking a macro-approach you might consider using Foucauldian discourse analysis. There are two main ways of embarking upon this sort of analysis: by devising a list of themes and/or discourses to look out for and then coding the articles accordingly or by starting with the texts themselves and noting discourses that emerge during your careful reading of them. The first is what is called a deductive technique: we start with a list of relevant themes and/or discourses and then turn to the object of study. Let's say you want to look at the portrayal of terrorists in crime films. You might start with a list of themes, derived from existing literature on this subject – perhaps you'd want to look for an association of terrorism with Islam, anti-Western sentiments, and pre-modern ideas. You would proceed by focusing on these particular themes in the crime films in your sample, with the aim of establishing whether there is a dominant discourse of, say, Islamophobia. In this example existing studies have indicated a popular discourse and pointed to themes in reporting through which this discourse manifests itself. In other cases scholarly work will suggest the dominance of a particular discourse and you'll need to work out yourself which themes might contribute to this representation. Michelle and Weaver's (2003) study, discussed in the following section, makes good use of this sort of technique.

The alternative approach noted above involves eschewing predetermined categories of analysis and starting with the texts themselves. This is often referred to as an inductive technique. This isn't to say that you shouldn't consult any existing literature and go into the study entirely blind to what previous studies have found. Herbert Blumer (1954: 7) argued that existing concepts and theories should give us an indication of 'the direction along which to look'. They should serve, he argued, as 'sensitising concepts', rather than definitive categories of analysis. Let's work through an imaginary example. Say you want to look at changes to discourses surrounding domestic violence in women's magazines. Perhaps you'd start by choosing a single publication and read all relevant articles over a 20-year period, looking for substantive shifts in how the issue is dealt with. One conclusion you might draw – and this is simply by way of example – is that where this form of violence was once discussed using a medical discourse (with male perpetrators seen as psychopathic, the crime itself as rare) a feminist-oriented discourse has become more predominant (with this form of violence seen as relatively widespread and symptomatic of wider social inequalities between the sexes). Such an analysis would go on to consider the changing social context in which this shift has occurred, referring perhaps to the rise of feminism and the growing recognition that intimate relationships can be the site of abuse. The key thing with this sort of analysis is to closely and carefully read or watch the items in your sample.

One common question students ask about using Foucauldian discourse analysis in an inductive fashion is 'How exactly do I spot a discourse?' Always my initial answer to this is: 'By reading the items in your sample very closely!' If you're feeling daunted by this task, you might use the following questions to guide your reading:

- How is an issue, group, or event framed? (For example, is an event framed as an accident, an act of God, fate, the consequence of evil wrong-doing?)
- Can you discern a particular perspective or line of argument being developed? (For example, is the media item urging us to accept a particular argument about an event, issue, or group? Does it prioritise or affirm one perspective over another?)
- Are certain words/phrases repeated?
- Can you discern any connection between the phrases/images used? (For example, does a newspaper article consistently refer to an incident using military imagery/terms – perhaps there's a reference to a 'war on drugs', the state mounting a 'mission' to tackle the problem, 'front-line' personnel mounting a 'fight'?)
- What is the setting for the story? (A hospital, courtroom, church meeting? Thinking about this can help you work out if there's a particular vantage point that is being prioritised.)
- Are there particular experts or sources of wisdom/knowledge? (Do newspaper articles in the sample use predominantly quotes from police spokespeople? Do television shows under analysis base discussions of criminality on the results of forensic tests?)

You might, of course, choose to follow Fairclough's version of critical discourse analysis instead. This is a form of analysis that involves a more focused analysis of texts, looking at things like syntax structure and verb use. Fairclough suggests analysing texts in terms of genre, style, and discourse – these three elements overlap, of course. Genre refers to the type of interaction or communication under study and the social relations reflected therein. The job interview is a genre, as is the newspaper editorial, television sports commentary, and university lecture. We can detect a genre by looking at the use of language in a text. Look at the following example:

> Rome was once a great city — the centre of the civilised world. We owe the Romans a great deal. Many significant aspects of our day-to-day existence and social system are directly descended from the Romans: our sewage system, our legal system, much of our language, and medicine. So when people ask 'What did the Romans do for us?' the answer is 'They provided the pillars of civilisation — and in that they were unique' ...

We immediately recognise this as a lecture – we are being taught something here (pretty badly, but still ...). How do we know this? For one thing claims are categorical and factual: 'Rome *was* once a great city'. The speaker is apparently an authority on the subject. Our position is that of the uninitiated learner. Sentences and clauses are paratactic: that is, they lack connecting phrases or words such as 'likewise', 'as a consequence', 'therefore', 'because'. Sentences and clauses that do use such terms are described as hypotactic. Each style of expression achieves different effects. In the case of our speaker above the use of a paratactical style means that no comment is qualified and no complexity enters into the account. It's a relaying of information.

We could imagine the text presented differently. If, say, we were having a chat with a friend and he was relaying the same sort of information, we'd expect a different language and genre – he'd say something like this:

> I've heard people say that Rome was a great city once. How do they put it? 'The Centre of the Civilised World', something like that. Some people say that we owe the Romans an awful lot — I guess you've heard that too, right? It's because so much of what we see and do every day is due to the Romans. It's amazing — I always think so, anyway — that the sewage system we have now was created by them ...

Here the speaker makes it clear that the facts he relays are second-hand ('I've heard people say that ...') and implies that the listener shares the same sort of knowledge base ('I guess you've heard that too, right?'). The speech reflects a more equal relationship with the listener: the speaker is careful not to suggest that he possesses knowledge superior to whoever's listening. Notice, for example, the use of the first-person here to impress upon us that this is mediated knowledge that might be seen differently by different people ('It is amazing – I always think so, anyway ...'). This text's genre – the type of interaction and relations reflected therein – might be described as an informal conversation.

The second element of a text Fairclough recommends analysing is its style. In Fairclough's terms, this chiefly means looking at 'the sort of identity which is projected in the text for its author'. 'We can see this', Fairclough adds, 'in terms of what the author is implicitly committed to by the way the text is written – being a particular sort of person, claims about what is the case, value claims about what is good and desirable' (2010: 271). In the case of the first speech about Rome above, we might say that the speaker is presenting himself as an expert; in the case of the second the style of prose is that of a knowledgeable peer. The third textual feature Fairclough suggests focusing on is discourse. Discourse refers to 'semiotic ways of constructing aspects of the world (physical, social or mental) which can generally be identified with different positions or perspectives of different groups of social actors' (p. 232). This is similar to the definition of discourse we started the chapter with: we're looking for clues concerning how the speaker or writer constructs the issue in question and his relationship to it. In the first speech above the speaker valorises a specific social form – ancient Rome – as the pinnacle of civilisation. We might characterise this discourse and the speaker as politically conservative and Eurocentric. In summary, Fairclough's approach involves looking closely at texts in terms of the use of language, the speaker's or writer's self-presentation and style, and which perspective is favoured.

## Thinking through discourse analysis: studying mass media depictions of incarceration, domestic violence, and gang violence

We're going to be focusing on the following three studies in this section of the chapter — you'll get more from the discussion if you read them before continuing:

- Mason, Paul (2006) 'Prison Decayed: Cinematic Penal Discourse and Popularism 1995—2005', *Social Semiotics*, 16(4): 607—626.
- Michelle, Carolyn and Weaver, Kay C. (2003) 'Discursive Manoeuvres and Hegemonic Recuperations in New Zealand Documentary Representations of Domestic Violence', *Feminist Media Studies*, 3(3): 283—299.
- Teo, Peter (2000) 'Racism in the News: A Critical Discourse Analysis of Reporting in Two Australian Newspapers', *Discourse and Society*, 11(1): 7—49.

Discourse analysis is suited to a wide range of media, and in the discussion below we range across studies of television documentaries, Hollywood films, and newspapers. The three articles make use of different types of discourse analysis: Mason's study uses an unstructured, inductive form of discourse analysis, Michelle and Weaver's study uses a deductive form of discourse analysis that seeks to ascertain the prevalence of predetermined discourses, and Teo's study uses critical discourse analysis. The studies also have wildly different foci: the first looks at how prison films reinforce a discourse of penal populism, the second looks at the attribution of blame in a New Zealand documentary television series on domestic violence, and the third argues that Australian newspaper reporting on Vietnamese gang violence contributes to a racist discourse. Despite their differences, though, they share a critical outlook and an interest in understanding how ideas about criminality are socially constructed.

We'll start with Mason's study of prison films. Paul Mason uses Foucauldian discourse analysis to study 28 films released between 1995 and 2005. He starts by observing the popularity of prison as a solution to crime for both governments and the public – often referred to as penal populism. His aim is to consider how the dominant discourse of incarceration in prison films reinforces the popular idea that prison is necessary and legitimate as a form of punishment.

Mason's analysis is unstructured, guided simply by the aim of understanding the meaning of incarceration in the films under study. He opts to develop close readings of the films that are sensitive to the medium he is studying. He considers, amongst other things, opening shots, use of musical soundtrack (often referred to as non-diegetic sound), use of sound effects (often referred to as diegetic sound), editing, choice of shot (long-shot, panning shot, etc.), as well as things like dialogue, costume, and mise-en-scène (see 'Film and television analysis: some key terms'). He identifies two central elements to the discourse of incarceration in prison films: 'the graphic exploitation of violence and sexual assault' and 'the representation of prisoners as dehumanised other and deserving of harsh treatment' (p. 611). Both, Mason argues, efface critical consideration of the role and legitimacy of prison as a form of punishment.

In arguing that graphic displays of violence are central to the popular depiction of the prison, Mason points to the use of opening shot sequences. He identifies three typical openings to prison films: the long-shot of the prison accompanied with loud and aggressive rap or rock music, a set of shots that follow someone through the process of being incarcerated (usually ending with a point of view shot as the prisoner sees other prisoners – in the dining hall or yard – for the first time), and a set of shots that follow a visitor through the process of being admitted to a prison (usually involving various 'aural cues of incarceration' – jangling keys, buzzers, gates closing, locking doors, etc.). All three openings reinforce the idea that prison is violent and dangerous. This construction is evident also in the 'pre-emptive talk' about rape and assault between prisoners and other prisoners, loved-ones, and guards, as well as scenes of what Mason calls set-piece brutality (such as fights erupting suddenly in the dining hall and rapes in shower blocks). Mason

---

**Film and television analysis: some key terms**

Here are a few terms that might prove useful in studying and analysing film and television.

- Shot: Typically refers to the distance between the objects being shot and the camera. In a close-up the camera is very close to objects. A long-shot gives us a full view of a character or object, thus allowing us to see someone or something in its physical context. A long-shot is often used at the start of a film or programme to help set the scene (when used in this way it's referred to as an establishing shot).
- Panning shot: The camera sweeps round from left to right or right to left.
- Point of view shot: A shot that appears to let the audience share the visual point of view of a character (as if we're looking through his/her eyes).
- Shot sequence: A selection of shots (perhaps a close-up of one character is followed by a long-shot, and then a close-up of a given object).
- Montage: A collection of short shots are strung together to represent the passing of time. In contemporary Hollywood film such sequences are often accompanied by a musical soundtrack.
- Diegetic sound: Sound that is part of the world being filmed (for example, from a radio a character turns on, the sound of a door opening).
- Non-diegetic sound: Sound that is not part of the world being filmed (for example, a voiceover).
- Mise-en-scène: The arrangement and creation of a particular scene (by, for example, arranging characters and props in a shot and using a particular camera).

---

points out that the association of prison with violence could give rise to an anti-prison discourse in the films he looks at. Instead violence in prison films is decontextualised, graphic, and titillating – or, as Mason puts it, 'the discourse remains entrenched in the violence itself rather than in denunciation of it' (p. 614).

The second dominant element of the incarceration discourse in prison films – the dehumanisation of prisoners – works to render prison a legitimate form of punishment. Mason points out that in most prison films the protagonist is treated sympathetically – as someone who has been wrongly convicted, given an overly harsh sentence, or is in prison for the first time. Part of this representation involves dehumanising the rest of the prison population: the world of the prison that the new inmate enters is deeply threatening, often conveyed in an iconic panning shot of the prison yard, filled with tattooed, muscular men with shaven heads, lifting weights and ominously grouped into cliques (p. 617). The inmate population is frequently referred to in the aggregate as a bunch of 'murderers', 'rapists', or 'animals'. The consequence of this construction, Mason argues, is that 'prison [appears] necessary to keep these psychotic deviants caged and incapacitated' (p. 616).

We might characterise Mason's study as inductive: his analysis is guided by a close reading of the films in his sample. In contrast, Michelle and Weaver (2003) set out to ascertain the predominance of a set of discourses in three television documentaries about domestic violence in New Zealand. Sponsored by the police in the mid-1990s, and part of a media campaign, the documentaries are now mainly used as educational aids in schools. All three documentaries – *Not Just A Domestic* (1994), *Not Just A Domestic: The Update* (1994), and *Picking Up The Pieces* (1996) – devote a very significant amount of coverage to testimonial accounts from couples dealing with domestic violence or individuals who witnessed violent incidents within the family as children. The first documentary consists mainly of intimate interviews with five couples – together and individually – as they tackle the violence within their relationship. These sequences are intercut with interviews with expert commentators. In the second documentary we return to see how some of the couples from the first documentary have fared. This programme focuses on the capacity of violent men to change. The overriding message of both documentaries is that 'seeking intervention [is] a catalyst for change' (p. 288). Both are explicitly aimed at educating men, and make use of male actors with a macho, laddish persona as presenters to help achieve this aim. The third documentary is different in focus and content, although it retains the emotional testimonial as a central form of presentation. This documentary is focused entirely on three women's personal experiences of domestic violence (one of them is also the presenter) and two men's childhood experiences of witnessing their mothers being abused. The programme emphasises the effect of violence on children.

In analysing the documentaries Michelle and Weaver draw upon Damian O'Neill's work on social science discourses concerning domestic violence, which suggests that five core discourses prevail in this area (pp. 286–287):

- A medical pathology discourse (the idea that domestic violence is a pathology of the individual)
- A discourse of romantic expressive tension (the idea that domestic violence is a reaction to social and family pressures, such as unemployment)
- A liberal humanist instrumentalist discourse (the idea that domestic violence is a rational, end-oriented behaviour used as a mechanism of control)
- A socio-systemic discourse (the idea that domestic violence is a consequence of dominant social values and norms concerning gender)

- A discourse of *tabula rasa* learning (the idea that the perpetrators of domestic violence have learned their behaviour through childhood experiences and becoming desensitised to violence).

The three documentaries studied made use of the five discourses, but to varying degrees and give primacy to certain discourses. Michelle and Weaver argue that the discourses of romantic tension, *tabula rasa* learning, and medical pathology are predominant, whilst the more critical discourses of socio-systemic failure and humanist instrumentalism are rarely in evidence. In fact, they argue that the documentaries continually gloss over the fact that it's predominantly men who commit this form of violence by referring to the problem as 'family violence'. All three documentaries, they suggest, attribute diminished responsibility to male perpetrators. For example, in *Not Just A Domestic* a male perpetrator's suggestion that he used domestic violence as an instrument of control (the humanist instrumentalist discourse) is undercut by the voiceover and presenter suggesting that his acts are in fact evidence of a pathology (p. 290). In turn, the programmes suggest that the female victims are partially responsible for the violence. Take the fact that women's testimonial accounts of abuse are often followed by the presenter asking 'Why does a woman keep on going back to such a man?' The implication, Michelle and Weaver point out, is that it's the victim's behaviour, rather than that of the perpetrator, that needs explaining.

Michelle and Weaver argue that 'violent men are further exonerated through the overwhelming textual focus on personal narratives and the location of specific (and externalised) causal factors in the personal histories of individual perpetrators' (ibid.). The emphasis on personal biographies – a popular technique in contemporary documentaries, referred to by the authors as 'intimization' – means that the problem of domestic violence is framed as an individual rather than social problem. Take also the fact that institutional failure is rarely discussed across the three documentaries. For one of the couples that we return to in the second documentary the violence has continued: we learn that the male partner has recently been released without conviction after attacking his partner. The voiceover relays this information whilst showing us images of the couple relaxed and happy. The incident is framed – by the couple, as well as the documentary – as a 'slip': the fact that the courts have failed to prosecute an act of violence isn't acknowledged, let alone seen as problematic. Once again, the authors argue, male violence is rendered acceptable.

Like Michelle and Weaver, Teo (2000) is interested in how a discourse constructs ideas about blame and responsibility. He uses critical discourse analysis to study Australian newspaper coverage of a Vietnamese gang of drug dealers, the 5T. Teo analyses a total of nine articles published during the mid-1990s in two Sydney-based daily newspapers, the *Daily Telegraph* and the *Sydney Morning Herald*. One of the gang's leaders was murdered during the period of study, and some of the articles focus on this event. Teo carries out his analysis in two stages. First he looks at his sample as a whole to uncover the discursive strategies used across the texts – by 'discursive strategies' he means lexical techniques that contribute to the production of a discourse. For example, Teo points out that headlines and stand-firsts frequently emphasise police control over the situation and the gang's depravity. He finds that the articles often use a technique of generalisation to conflate the 5T with the Asian and Vietnamese population in Australia, thus contributing to negative stereotypes about these ethnic groups. He identifies a pattern of quotations, whereby experts from the ethnic majority are much more likely to be quoted than members of the Vietnamese population. Moreover, where they are used, quotations from the Vietnamese population are often anonymous and appear towards the end of the article. Finally, Teo points to a problem of over-lexicalisation in the newspaper articles he studies: 'over-lexicalisation results when a surfeit of repetitious, quasi-synonymous terms is woven into the fabric of news discourse, giving rise to a sense of over-completeness' (p. 20). For example, a female lawyer's sex and gender might be repeatedly referred to in an article, whilst a male lawyer is simply and only a 'lawyer' (ibid.). In the case of news reporting on the 5Ts, Teo finds that the gang's youthfulness and their extreme violence are repeatedly asserted. Thus, 'while the powerless are silenced, they are over-lexicalised with a ... largely unsavoury characterization' (p. 23).

The second stage of Teo's analysis involves taking a focused look at two articles taken from either end of the study period and closely studying syntax structure, or what he calls the articles' 'micro-structure'. He goes through both texts and carefully looks at each sentence and clause to determine the ordering of information (thematisation) and which people or groups are presented as active and passive (transitivity). By unpacking syntax structure, verb use, and subject positions he is able to decipher the intended effect of each text. The first article, for example, shows the drug dealers to be in control of the situation and the police to be ineffectual. This is evident simply by looking at the thematisation of sentences, that is, what is given priority. After being told about the police's patrolling of a certain area, we are informed that 'About 100m down the road' drug dealers continue to sell their wares:

> our attention is drawn to the physical proximity between the police and drug-dealers. This creates an incongruous situation in which the effect of the police only extends to the immediate locality and not beyond, where just '100m down the road', 'more people are selling drugs', seemingly

oblivious to the police. Moreover, again by thematizing 'After 20 minutes' in the following clause, our attention is drawn to the transient effect of the police, as 'immediately', after the police leave, 'The pushers are back in business'. (pp. 29–31)

Teo is looking here at the order of information in sentences, and particularly at what is foregrounded. He also considers the agency attributed to certain people and groups, as well as the relationship between groups' actions. Again, the first text makes the police appear inactive; they rarely do or say things. In contrast, the drug dealers 'sell', 'say', 'look', 'loiter' – they are associated, in other words, with a whole range of verbs that attribute action to them. Moreover, the drug dealers' actions seem only vaguely affected by the police's behaviour:

> The causal relationship between the arrival of the police and the leaving of the drug-dealers is, at most, only hinted at and not structurally realized as in a potential construction like: *At 6.30pm, the police arrive, causing the youths to scarper*. Instead, what we get is a sequence of independent clauses – the police arrive, the youths scarper, more people are selling drugs down the road, the police leave, the pushers are back in business – strung together in a paratactic relationship, suppressing the potential dependency relationship among them. (p. 27)

Here Teo suggests that the relationship between clauses – how they are 'strung together' – produces a particular effect. In this case, the use of a paratactical style makes it seem that the drug dealers are unaffected by the police's behaviour.

The combined effect of such grammatical patterns is to render the 5T intrinsically dangerous and criminal. In his analysis of the second article, from later in the study period, Teo notes an altogether different patterning: here it is the police who suddenly appear to be in charge of the situation. He observes the dominance of a militaristic language in the second article to describe the police's response to the gang. This, too, Teo suggests, reduces the possibility for the audience understanding the actions of the 5T: here the gang is akin to an external enemy, an assailant requiring deadly force. Overall, Teo argues, the discursive strategies used in the newspaper articles about the 5T are decidedly racist: the voices of gang members and those living in affected communities are sidelined and obscured, the gang's behaviour is depicted as beyond comprehension, in terms of utter criminality and mindless violence, and the gang's ethnicity is emphasised. As with the other two studies considered above, Teo's study is an exercise in revealing how texts reinforce pernicious stereotypes and social inequalities.

## Chapter summary

This chapter has outlined the technique, uses, and problems with discourse analysis. By way of summary we might note that discourse analysis is particularly useful for:

- ✓ Uncovering the ways in which texts reinforce inequalities, stereotypes, and social norms
- ✓ Studying how texts construct ideas about ourselves, others, and the world in which we live
- ✓ Focused analysis of a small number of texts, both in terms of their micro-structure (clause by clause) and their macro-structure (as entire stories)
- ✓ Studying visual media.

By contrast, it isn't particularly suited to:

- × Assessing the volume of media coverage
- × Analysing a large number of media texts
- × Making generalisations about media coverage.

A careful discourse analysis involves:

- Selecting a small enough sample to carry out a detailed analysis
- Deciding on a particular approach for the analysis – deductive or inductive, Foucauldian or critical discourse analysis – and devising a strategy to carry out the analysis accordingly
- Reading/viewing/listening to items in the sample to discern dominant discourses
- Considering how the discourse(s) identified feed into broader ideas and prejudices
- Considering whether the technique of analysis is suitable for the chosen topic and medium.

## Recommended reading

Fairclough, Norman (2003) *Analysing Discourse: Textual Analysis for Social Research*. London: Routledge.
  Fairclough's brilliant introductory textbook makes use of a wide range of examples across media formats. Highly recommended for those wishing to carry out detailed linguistic analyses.

Fairclough, Norman (2010) *Critical Discourse Analysis: The Critical Study of Language*. London: Longman.

A huge and comprehensive collection of Fairclough's most important writings on critical discourse analysis.

Gee, James Paul (2010a) *An Introduction to Discourse Analysis: Theory and Method*. London: Routledge.

A best-selling introductory guide to discourse analysis as a theory and technique of analysis. Makes use of a good range of examples.

Gee, James Paul (2010b) *How to do Discourse Analysis: A Toolkit*. London: Routledge.

The companion text to Gee's *An Introduction to Discourse Analysis*, this book is a practical guide aimed at researchers using discourse analysis. There are useful practice exercises for students to develop their skills of analysis.

Machin, David and Mayr, Andrea (2012) *How To Do Critical Discourse Analysis: A Multimodal Introduction*. London: Sage.

Offers a good, clear guide to critical discourse analysis. Highly recommended for those wishing to carry out detailed linguistic analyses.

Paltridge, Brian (2012) *Discourse Analysis: An Introduction*. London: Continuum.

A student-friendly textbook that explains the theory and technique of discourse analysis. Makes use of a range of engaging examples.

## Workshop session

The following tasks usually take two hours. Both tasks should be done in small groups of two to four.

### Task One

In Chapter 14 we look at the *CSI* franchise. There we discuss the programme's representation of detection as primarily a scientific pursuit and its lack of interest in the social determinants of crime. Analyse the first 15 minutes of an episode of *CSI* — it can be of your choice, from any of the series. Your aim is to answer the following two questions:

- How is a scientific discourse used to construct the process of detection?
- Is any explanation offered for criminal behaviour? Can it be described in terms of a particular discourse (for example, psychological, medical, sociological)?

Pay particular attention to the following:

- Use of opening shot
- Use of diegetic and non-diegetic sound
- Use of montage (in opening credits, etc.)

- Dialogue between the characters
- Costume
- Setting.

*Task Two*

Choose one of the following topics:

- Honour killings
- School shootings
- Internet hacking.

Identify a particular case, either from memory or by searching the Internet. Using Nexis® or a newspaper's online resources (see Introduction to Part III for notes on using the former) select five newspaper articles about the case. Read each carefully, paying particular attention to how the problem is constructed and the allocation of blame.

- Can you detect a dominant discourse?

Now carry out a micro-structure analysis on one article. You might like to refer back to the summary of Teo's study, above. Have a look at:

- Which pieces of information are given priority in a clause
- The verbs associated with each individual/group in the article
- The use and ordering of quotations
- The description of the assailant (young, male, black, etc.), and whether particular features are emphasised.

What does this analysis tell us about the representation of the perpetrator(s) and victim(s)?

## PART IV

# Fictional worlds of crime, justice, and order

# Introduction

This part of the book focuses on fictional and semi-fictional crime stories. We discuss, amongst other things, HBO's television Western *Deadwood*, the film *A Clockwork Orange*, Agatha Christie and Raymond Chandler's detective novels, the television programme *CSI*, Hollywood legal dramas of the 1950s and 1990s, and reality crime television series *Cops*. The chapters explore what fictional renderings of revenge and retribution can teach criminologists, changing ideas about detection and courtroom justice, and representations of police-work, prison, and rehabilitation. They weave together focused readings of specific media texts, general observations about mass media representations, and discussion of social theory. In doing so they resemble the course-work essays traditionally required of students taking 'Crime and the Media' courses. You might, then, find a pedagogical value in these chapters as exemplar essays – but, quite beyond that, they help us extend our understanding of the 'cultural landscape of crime'.

We'll come back to this matter in the Conclusion. For now, and by way of introduction to this part of the book, our interest lies in explaining the growth of crime fiction as part of the rise of modernity. Popular crime stories such as the ones discussed are so plentiful today that it's difficult to imagine our culture without them. Nonetheless, crime hasn't always been a media staple and unlike, say love, tragedy, and comedy, crime isn't a traditional basis for story-telling in most cultures (with the notable exception of the Icelandic Sagas). There's a simple explanation for the relatively recent growth of interest in crime stories (and then, as we'll see below, a number of not so obvious ones). It was the development of fully-fledged, formal criminal justice systems in the early nineteenth century that furnished the subject matter for modern crime stories. It was during this historical period that we start to see the creation of big, state-run prisons, designated law courts, and state-sponsored police forces, and many of our favourite crime stories today take this modern, bureaucratic system of law and order as a backdrop.

For Michel Foucault, there's another important aspect to the relationship between the growth of crime fiction and the emergence of official systems of criminal justice. In *Discipline and Punish* he famously argues that the modern European criminal justice system instituted a new way of dealing with lawlessness. The rise of incarceration as the standard form of punishment in the early nineteenth century marks an important shift in the exercise of power. Where social authorities once used corporal punishment to keep the population in check, they began instead to go to work on reforming the criminal's mind and behaviour. Incarceration and investigation became the main tools of criminal justice, rather than torture and execution. One of the consequences of this was that justice, once a public spectacle, came to be hidden behind locked prison and police office doors. Modern crime stories allowed people to continue to see and in some sense experience justice and punishment being done – and it's worth noting here that detective fiction became a recognisable genre at the roughly the same point that the prison became the standard form of punishment (but more on this in Chapter 14).

All this suggests that popular crime stories are at least partly functional. The courtroom denunciation, the police case and capture, the official inauguration to prison – all such episodes in novels, films, and television programmes dramatise the otherwise hidden and bureaucratic world of criminal justice. More than this, they transform what was once a 'physical confrontation' into an 'intellectual struggle between criminal and investigator', thus mirroring the shift from corporal punishment to discipline (Foucault 1995: 69). For Foucault, the disciplinary techniques of the modern criminal justice system still depend upon violence, albeit a sanitised, sublimated form of violence. That crime fiction enables us to watch various forms of violence being enacted may also help explain its distinctive appeal – that's something you can judge for yourselves when reading the chapters below.

## CHAPTER 12

# *Revenge and retribution in* Deadwood

---

**Recommended viewing**

This chapter provides a close reading of the opening episode of the television Western *Deadwood*. You'll get more out of this chapter if you watch the episode too. You might like to buy the first series of *Deadwood* or see if your local lending library has a copy for hire.

---

The cultural commentator Robert Warshow suggested that 'the two most successful creations of American movies are the gangster and the Westerner: men with guns' (1956 in Warshow 2002: 105). This chapter is concerned with the latter creation, though it's worth acknowledging, as Warshow does, that 'men with guns' are a staple of American cinema. Guns, he goes on to argue, 'constitute the visible moral center of the Western movie, suggesting continually the possibility of violence' (p. 109), though, as he astutely comments, this is done in such a way as to invite us to consider the social function of violence.

We make similar observations here about the social meaning of violence, though our focus is rather different to Warshow's: I want us to consider what the pilot of the television Western *Deadwood* (2004, dir. Walter Hill) can tell us about the transition from revenge to retribution as a form of justice – or, as I put it, from unruly to rule-based justice. This is a matter of great significance: the creation of a nascent criminal justice system is a seminal moment in a community's evolution from nebulous social group to fully-fledged society. Given this, it might strike us as rather odd that scholars in criminology and legal studies are rather quiet on the issue of how and why a community institutes criminal justice. One reason for the apparent lack of academic interest is the profound difficulty in studying communities that go through the transition from lawlessness to lawfulness. Such communities are difficult to identify and access, and if we wanted to study them post-transition using official documents we'd be hindered by a lack of resources – the sophisticated bureaucracy that collates such information tends to appear *after* a society has developed a full criminal justice system. Besides this, reading about policies and legislation wouldn't really allow us to understand the nature of community support for formal laws, the difficulties in establishing legal authority, or the interests that are served by such developments.

It is, then, extraordinarily difficult to locate the necessary empirical evidence to ascertain how a community institutes criminal law. We do, though, have access to artistic renderings of this process. Many film and television Westerns offer us a vivid depiction of the slow and often difficult shift from lawlessness to lawfulness. Many have noted that the Western is fundamentally about the institution of a legal framework – Pippin (2009: 225) puts it particularly well when he suggests that many Westerns are about 'the early, struggling stages of modern bourgeois, law-abiding, property-owning, market-economy, technologically advanced societies in transition from, mostly, lawlessness (or corrupt and ineffective law) ...'. It's worth noting that Westerns are distinct in having this thematic concern. Nowhere else in our culture do we get this sort of insight – indeed, in the legal dramas, detective stories, and prison shows that dominate today's media the criminal justice system is more generally a given, a feature of modern bureaucratic society that just 'is'. Westerns give us a rare insight into a pre-bureaucratic period of law creation, a historical moment when the need, purpose, and control of a nascent criminal justice system were contentious matters. Studying *Deadwood* can deepen our understanding of such matters.

## Morality, law, and order in the Western

I also hope that approaching *Deadwood* from a criminological perspective can add something to scholarly work on film and television. There is a huge literature within film studies on the Western. This is partly because there is a wealth of fine examples from this genre. Jim Kitses' (2004) *Horizons West* provides a brilliant and detailed discussion of key films in the genre: his book demonstrates, amongst other things, the sheer breadth of film Westerns. The Hollywood Western enjoyed an extended 'golden age'. John Ford's *Stagecoach* (1939) is widely seen as the first great Western and launched John Wayne's career. Ford went on to direct a string of acclaimed Westerns, notably *The Searchers* (1956) and *The Man Who Shot Liberty Valence* (1962). The 1950s and 1960s also ushered in a set of Westerns that were darker in tone. Take, for example, the string of Westerns directed by Anthony Mann during the 1950s, and starring James Stewart. The actor's ability to play inscrutable, morally confused characters was key to the success of *Winchester '73* (1950) and *The Man From Laramie* (1953). Sergio Leone's films – *A Fistful of Dollars* (1964), *For a Few Dollars More* (1965), and *The Good, The Bad, and The Ugly* (1966) – were further notable additions to the genre. The films confirmed the star status of Clint Eastwood, and, unlike traditional Westerns of an earlier age, depicted a messy moral universe. Also of note is Sam Peckinpah's *The Wild Bunch* (1969). Here the traditional Western is the backdrop to the sickeningly violent exploits of a gang – thus showing, in graphic detail, the costs of honour and justice.

Film scholars have had plenty of inspiration, then, when it comes to the Western. The noted film critic and theorist, André Bazin, dedicated two essays to the genre, 'The Western: American Film *par excellence*' (1971a) and 'The Evolution of the Western' (1971b). In the former Bazin famously argued that the Western is 'unalloyed myth' (p. 143), telling stories of deep cultural resonance – of freedom and social constraint, of good versus evil, of male honour and female virtue. Bazin argues that film as a medium is perfectly suited to this sort of story-telling. He points out that no other medium could create epic stories of this type. Take the possibility offered by long and panning shots to capture the wide open space of the 'Wild West'. These shots help convey a sense of geographical vastness, as well as an undeveloped social world – they're integral, in other words, to achieving the overall effect of the Western.

Like many other film scholars, Bazin is particularly concerned with the Western's contribution to a myth about society building, and the role of law and morality in this endeavour. In the Western, he comments, '[The white Christian] imposes simultaneously his moral and his technical order, the one linked to the other and the former guaranteeing the latter' (1971a: 145). Morality is the basis for law creation in Westerns, Bazin argues at various points, and law creation in turn 'guarantees' social order. The relationship is summed up in his suggestion that 'it is only law that can impose the order of the good and the good of order' (ibid.).

The notion that the Western dramatises the relationship between morality, law, and order – and in that direction – is found throughout film studies accounts (we find it, for example, in Kitses 2004). Amongst criminologists this rendering of the relationship is often referred to as a natural law perspective. It's a view that's been criticised for implying that legal systems emerge from a social vacuum and for ignoring the ideological struggle that is involved in instituting formal law. More sociological approaches see legal systems as emerging once a community becomes self-conscious of itself *as a* community. Rule-based law doesn't carve out right and wrong for what Bazin (1971a: 145) calls a 'primitive amoeba of a civilization'; it is an institution that emerges at a rather late stage of social development, and generally to shore up an existing social structure. In this sense rule-based justice is reflective more of social conditions and power relations than a natural moral conscience: those involved in its institution must persuade and if necessary force a community to accept its legitimacy. Criminology students are rather fond of this argument concerning the origin of criminal law, but in the absence of fleshed-out examples of this process in action it's more an article of faith than anything else. *Deadwood* gives us a rare insight into the difficult shift from unruly to rule-based justice, depicting it as a violent and ideological struggle with ambivalent outcomes. In doing so it not only deepens our criminological understanding, but also broadens our sense of what the Western can achieve – or, at least, what this particular television Western has achieved.

Of course, none of this is to suggest that Bazin is *wrong* in his reading of traditional film Westerns. Many Westerns of the 'golden age' sketch out precisely the sort of relationship between morality, law, and social order that he identifies – *The Man Who Shot Liberty Valence* immediately comes to mind. The relationship between law and order is imagined rather differently in *Deadwood*, and more along classical sociological lines. In the few academic commentaries on *Deadwood*, the show's emphasis on the relationship between commercial interests, law and governance, and social order is a central concern (see, for example, Hark 2012; Jacobs 2012). 'What is different about *Deadwood*', Jacobs notes, 'is its fundamental shift of emphasis ... to the mercantile dimension of settlement, exploring the nature of capital not as a disrupting, civilising force – say in the depiction of the corrupt railroad or cattle barons – but as a necessary condition of settlement with all its alienating and violent consequences' (2012: 60).

That *Deadwood* differs from traditional film Westerns in its depiction of law and order demonstrates the changefulness of the Western as a genre. For Westerfelhaus and Lacroix (2009) *Deadwood* is most certainly a product of time and place. They argue that the show embodies 'post-9/11 angst'. Of particular note is what they see as the unsatisfying nature of retributive justice in the programme and the characters' lack of a moral compass; both, they argue, reflect concerns in the US that the state's response to 9/11 was inadequate and illegitimate.

*Deadwood* reflects other, broader cultural currents. In a post-counter-cultural period, a sociological discourse that emphasises the role of capitalist interests in shaping social values and systems has become more resonant. In turn, the idea of an inherent moral conscience has lost purchase: we prefer to see such things as culturally relative now. A similar point has been made about recent film Westerns, most notably the Oscar-winning *No Country For Old Men* (dir. Ethan and Joel Coen, 2007). Devlin (2010) suggests that most of the characters in this and other recent Westerns are nihilistic: they operate in a muddy moral universe without straightforward distinctions between good and evil. This, Devlin argues, is a reflection of a broader cultural condition, in particular a sense of ambivalence concerning traditional moral codes.

Whilst there is much value in pursuing the relationship between an individual Western and its cultural and historical milieu, this chapter takes a rather different focus. Before we turn to consider more deeply what *Deadwood* can tell us about the emergence of rule-based justice, we briefly consider the historical backdrop to the Western.

## The West and the Western

In a 1921 book about the meaning of western expansion for American history, the influential historian Frederick Jackson Turner described 'The West', as a 'form of society, rather than an area':

> It is the term applied to the region whose social conditions result from the application of older institutions and ideas to the transforming influences of free land. By this application, a new environment is suddenly entered, freedom of opportunity is opened, the cake of custom is broken, and new activities, new lines of growth, new institutions and new ideals, are brought into existence. The wilderness disappears, the 'West' proper passes on to a new frontier, and in the former area, a new society has emerged from its contact with the backwoods. (Turner 1921: 205)

Notice the repetition of the word 'new' here: it is this ever evolving, ever new social life of 'the West' that forms the backdrop to most film and television Westerns. Notice also Turner's suggestion that 'free land' has a 'transforming influence' on established traditions and institutions. The clamour for land, property, and wealth produces a new social order and with it new sets of rules. Not that all land was 'free' for the taking. During the early nineteenth century, the USA had achieved expansion by buying land in the West from Spain and France. What they couldn't acquire quite so readily was the large areas of land belonging to Native Americans. In 1832 Congress declared that all land west of the Mississippi River belonged to Native American tribes (Brown 1997: 412). The declaration wasn't to stand for very long: the events of the next half-century – the Californian gold rush of 1849, the end of the Civil War in 1865, economic recession in the eastern states – all drove mass migration westwards (Brown 1997: 78). So it was that Turner could claim in 1921 that 'up to our own day American history has been in a large degree the history of the colonization of the Great West' (1921: 1).

Up until the 1890s territorial expansion remained patchy: significant areas of land had an indeterminate relationship to the USA, and states' borders changed as land was successively re-claimed and re-lost by Native Americans. Frontier camps emerged in contested territory or right at the margins of accepted boundaries. People moved en masse to these camps because of the promise of business and wealth – perhaps the camp had become a stop-off point on the cattle trail (this was how Dodge City came into being), or a railroad was being built nearby and there was work available, or there were rumours that the surrounding hills were full of gold (this is why so many US settlers moved to the Black Hills in the 1870s). Cattle, trains, and gold: these were key drivers of the nascent US economy during the mid- to late nineteenth century.

This is the social backdrop to most Westerns. It is, of course, what makes the Western so quintessentially American – the 'American film *par excellence*', as Bazin puts it. Films in this genre are intimately tied up with the story of how the USA came into existence; they reconstruct US history. They affirm a sense of national identity in other ways too. Take, for example, the central figure of the cowboy. Semi-nomadic, with an intuitive sense of justice, seeking fortune and adventure, he unites two characteristics that are often seen to define the American character: he's a pioneer and an individualist. Take also the interest many Westerns have in the balance between social control and liberty. Maintaining the balance in this relationship is also a core feature of the US constitution: man is born free, but must also acknowledge the rightfulness of a higher set of rules, both man- and God-made. Many Westerns focus on the fact that individual freedom – to trade, roam, avenge – is circumscribed by a community's need for rules and peace. Looked at from this perspective, the Western offers us a fascinating insight into the relationship between the individual and society. Mitchell (1996: 3) argues along similar lines, and suggests that we see the genre as bringing together a 'set of problems recurring in endless combination', most fundamentally the need for order and justice on the one hand, and the need to protect personal freedom and honour on the other. Many Westerns, he points out, focus on the difficulty in instituting law in circumstances where traditional and personal forms of justice might be more appealing. When we look closely at particular Westerns, we can see that what's really interesting is the tension that exists between these two systems of justice, and the process whereby a formal system of retribution becomes de facto. The opening episode of *Deadwood* alerts us to the subtle problems of this shift in justice – but before we get on to that, a brief introduction to the television series.

## Introducing *Deadwood*

Deadwood is a real place, and many of the characters in the television series are based on people who lived in or visited the camp (such as 'Wild' Bill

Hickok, 'Calamity' Jane, and Wyatt Earp). Produced by David Milch for HBO, *Deadwood* ran for three seasons from 2004 to 2006. The series traces the evolution of a camp of gold prospectors into a fully-fledged town during a one-year period, from mid-1876 to mid-1877. In the commentary to the DVD of *Deadwood*, David Milch says that the main thing that inspired him to create the series was the 'fact that Deadwood had no laws'. *Deadwood* explores the consequences of lawlessness and what's involved in the shift towards a more formal social system. At the start of season one the camp's legal status is unclear: the fledging town has 'order more or less, but no law whatsoever', as Milch puts it. In fact, this is what draws many people to the place, whether it's Wild Bill Hickok, who believes that warrants for his arrest don't apply in Deadwood, or gold prospectors thinking that the lack of legal red-tape will somehow advantage them. The camp is technically within Sioux-controlled territory, but many members of the camp expect the area to become an annex of the Dakota territory in the USA – and this is precisely what happens at the end of season two.

## Unruly and rule-based justice in *Deadwood*

*Deadwood*'s opening scenes vividly depict a society in transition from informal justice based on revenge to justice based on impersonal retribution. The programme opens not in the camp, but in a Montana prison-house. The town's Marshal, Seth Bullock (Timothy Olyphant), is holding Clell Watson (James Parks) prisoner for stealing a horse owned by Byron Sampson (Christopher Garga). Watson attempts to bribe Bullock to release him, but is interrupted by the arrival of a liquored-up Byron Sampson and mob. Sampson was the one who called in the law to deal with Watson, but he's changed his mind: the mob's come to fetch Watson from the prison-house and exact some rough justice. 'Why don't you *climb out* from behind your badge and your *big brick* building?' Sampson jeers at Bullock. His implication is clear: the law is a cowardly mechanism for exacting punishment, its status and power artificially derived. Sampson's challenge to Bullock prompts a change in perspective. Barring the opening establishing shot, we've remained entirely within the safe confines of the prison-house up until this point. Sampson's contestation of official legal power prompts the camera to move outside, and we're offered a side-view of the mob facing the prison-house (see Figure 12.1). A wall of human men with shotguns and flaming torches confronts the darkened prison-house, bars lining its windows. Unruly justice meets rule-based justice face on.

Bullock's response to Sampson's goading is to drag Watson out onto the terrace of the prison-house and hang him there and then; better for the

**Figure 12.1**  The mob confronts the law

prisoner to hang 'under colour of law' than at the hands of an angry mob. Seeing that Bullock means to hold an impromptu execution, Sampson shoots into the sky: violent retaliation should be *his*. He jeers at Watson not to make the jump. '... Or what?' the prisoner responds incredulously, 'you'll *kill* me?' The scene captures something that criminological accounts couldn't hope to convey with the same sort of clarity and conciseness: the end-goals of both formal and informal justice are *precisely the same*. Formal justice gains its authority from exactly the same source as revenge: *the threat and ready use of violence.*

In this respect the opening of *Deadwood* offers up a powerful critique of formal justice by inviting us to think more deeply about what distinguishes formal and informal justice. If the opening scenes encourage us to think 'not very much at all', it's worth considering what *does* separate unruly and rule-based justice here. In fact, one of the great values of these opening scenes is that they don't entirely dismiss formal law. Bullock's dogged and seemingly disinterested adherence to the rules of retributive justice is of particular note here. The Marshal appears to be absolutely unimpeachable. In the prison-house Watson desperately tries to engage Bullock in conversation, but Bullock remains aloof, and every answer he gives is an attempt to stop dead the conversation. He makes the gesture of pouring Watson a cup of coffee, but doesn't hand it to him directly through the prison bars, instead setting it down within arm's reach. Watson responds to the gesture by apologising for grazing Bullock's arm whilst trying to avoid capture. There is no suggestion that Bullock harbours a desire to revenge *this* wrong. Watson suggests that, when his time comes, God will look unfavourably on his having shot a 'legally ordained' man. 'He may have heard worse stories' the Marshal retorts, his nonchalance suggesting that *this* judge certainly has.

In short, the opening scenes establish that Bullock operates in complete conformity with the deeply impersonal logic of formal law and justice. For him, this case is one of many, some less grievous, some more, the prisoner deserves basic civility and comfort, but nothing in the line of genuine contact, and his personal injury is no cause for retaliation or vindictiveness. In contrast, the principles and purpose of those bent on revenge are rather more questionable. Sampson's desire for violent retaliation is sharpened by liquor, and the mob has been bribed with money and booze.

Looked at in this way, formal law can offer something that revenge can't: cool abstraction and methodical application of rules. What it doesn't constitute, in the opening scenes of *Deadwood*, at least, is a position of moral superiority. Watson's death is horribly violent, the law affords him no protection from unnecessary pain and humiliation, no last indulgences, no final appeals. Watson's wide-eyed objections to Bullock's plan to hang him there and then – he hasn't yet seen his sister, hasn't had the chance to say his goodbyes, and can't see how the drop from the porch step is going to be enough to hang him cleanly – are entirely ignored. 'I'll help you with the drop' Bullock answers simply (Figure 12.2). The horror of what is about to happen – or, more specifically, what Bullock is about to go through with – registers on the faces of the waiting mob. In disquiet and confusion their faces turn slightly and their limbs gain a lightness, as if they're suddenly not at all sure why they're here, and certainly not sure that they want to see *this*. Watson makes the jump. Bullock calmly steps down from the porch and, eyes fixed on the mob, firmly tugs at Watson's waist, a loud snap confirming that he's broken the man's neck. The camera lingers on the dying man's feet scrapping wildly against the floor and then finally becoming lifeless. It's a graphic scene that's likely to leave us feeling deeply ambivalent about the role of formal law in exacting punishment. Bullock has made the death easier, but by killing Watson with his own hands he's shown that formal justice, like revenge, amounts to one man brutalising another.

It's difficult to see how formal justice has the moral high ground in administering this punishment. The execution is a straightforward assertion of the primacy of formal retribution as a response to wrong-doing – it's an expression of power and authority more than anything else. There's no consideration of whether Watson *deserves* this punishment – or punishment at all – or whether the sentence is proportionate to the crime. Here formal justice has an inexorable and terrible logic. The point is made again later in the episode when we see Deadwood's bar and brothel-owner, Al Swearengen (Ian

**Figure 12.2**    'I'll help you with the fall': formal justice by any means

McShane), administering punishment to Trixie (Paula Malcolmson), a prostitute who has taken the law into her own hands and shot a client who was attacking her. Taking Trixie into his office, Swearengen angrily asks why she didn't call out for help when the attack started – in other words, why she didn't make recourse to the usual rules and mechanisms for dealing with misdemeanours in the brothel. 'You don't shoot nobody, 'cause that's bad for my business', Al continues. Trixie is resigned to her fate and plaintively asks Al to get on with dishing out her punishment. Al erupts, throws Trixie across the room, and pins her to the floor with his foot. As with Bullock's hanging of Watson, Swearengen's violent attack reasserts the authority of formal rules and procedures. It's nothing personal – in fact, at the end of the episode we find out that Trixie is his lover. In both cases rule-based law is inelastic, uncompromising, and especially punitive when dealing with threats to its legitimacy – that is, when others try to wrest control of justice by means of revenge.

What makes Swearengen's brutal attack on Trixie particularly difficult to watch is our sense that she is absolutely beholden to this man and his rules. Her social position – particularly her gender and occupation – leave her vulnerable to violence. The law of the brothel, it seems, offers limited protection from these wrongs; in fact, it places clients' safety above that of the prostitutes. Looked at in this way, retributive justice operates as a means of keeping people in their place. (And if we for one moment doubt that this set of observations is applicable to modern legislation, we might remember that many jurisdictions have only recently come to see the serious and long-term abuse of a female by a male partner as a mitigating factor for killing a husband or boyfriend.)

Thinking along these lines might prompt us to consider more deeply the relationship between rule-based justice and power. This puts me in mind of Miller's (1998) brilliantly argued essay about the difference between revenge and retribution. Miller suggests that John Wayne Westerns showcase what he calls 'wild justice', a form of justice that has come to be seen as morally repugnant in most other areas of our culture. Miller sketches out a standard argument concerning the development of criminal justice around the world. This argument runs thus: traditional societies relied upon revenge as an informal way of dealing with lawlessness – in more modern societies retribution has taken the place of revenge. The shift depended upon a change in public attitudes towards revenge. Revenge came to be cast as an emotional response to an injury. Retribution, in contrast, was framed as an impersonal and officially sanctioned response to a wrong. Modern, economically advanced societies are apt to see retribution as morally preferable: it appears measured, applies abstract, universal principles, and gives due regard to circumstance. For Miller, this is more ideological gloss than reality: the state frequently fails to weigh cases objectively, doesn't satisfy an emotional desire for retaliation, and often uses extreme violence to achieve its ends. Thus he asks that we 'rid ourselves once and for all of the notion that revenge and honour are part of some pre-social, pre-cultural, wolfish human nature' (pp. 165–166). More than anything, Miller argues, we should recognise that the state has a vested interest in promoting the idea that it has the sole right to punish, that retributive violence is justified and humane, and that revenge is irrational.

The opening scenes of *Deadwood* dramatise the historical shift from revenge to retribution and in doing so reveal the process to be deeply messy and contradictory. The opening episode helps illuminate the difficulties that arise when formal, rule-based justice is on the ascendancy and informal justice is still in the process of being phased out. One thing that is amply clear from watching *Deadwood* is that, during this phase of social development, unruly justice poses a more significant ideological threat to rule-based justice than common-or-garden rule-breakers. So it is that formal law must at some point label older bases for justice as criminal. In other words, its reach and application must extend to those seeking justice under a different banner to the criminal law: this is central if rule-based law is to establish its jurisdiction and overall authority. Thus we are urged to accept as a basic tenet of civilised society that if you call the law in, you can't then call it off to exact some justice of your own, as Bullock tells Sampson in the opening scene.

The opening episode of *Deadwood* reveals something else about the shift from unruly to rule-based justice, and that is the interests that are served in establishing formal, retributive justice. 'No law *at all* in Deadwood? – Is that true?' the jailed Watson enquires of the Marshal. Answering in the affirmative, Bullock explains that Deadwood is built on Indian land. Watson is astonished: 'No laws at *all*. *Gold* you could scoop up from the streams with your bare hands ...'. So it is that the central relationship between easy, democratically distributed wealth and the absence of a formal legal code is drawn out for us even before we enter the camp – and when I say democratically distributed wealth I mean, of course, *amongst men*. Deadwood has gold for the taking – no rule-book or law-man is going to stop you simply scooping up whatever you find. When one has accumulated a significant amount of gold, though, a lack of laws becomes a problem – but more on that below.

For now let's consider further the depiction of Deadwood as a nirvana for the free-wheeling, self-made man, a place immune to the muddy disputes about public revenge and retribution that we've seen played out in Montana. At the end of the opening scenes described above Seth Bullock hands over his Marshal's badge and rides out of town to begin a new life. Next time we see him he's entering Deadwood to set up as a market trader, hoping to make his fortune like all the rest. We follow him into the camp and get our first close-up view of Deadwood. Shifting to a point-of-view shot, we share Bullock's first impression of the camp. It's overwhelmingly busy and noisy, packed with newcomers and traders hawking their wares, hastily written signs indicating the going prices. New buildings are being erected, but the camp is predominantly a series of makeshift dwellings. There's no brick prison-house here, no sign of established civilisation. Instead what we get is a surfeit of filth and mud. The place looks *primordial*, given over wholly to that most basic of human relationships: exchange. As Erin Hill (2006) points out, this is not the 'wild west' of rodeo shows and gun-slinging cowboys; it's the west of dog-eat-dog commerce and capitalist expansion. The lack of formal rules and officials in Deadwood appears to allow for unhindered enterprise and wealth creation. In fact, we soon learn that the camp residents' experience of freedom and unconstrained prosperity is conditional upon their place in Deadwood's social hierarchy and their relationship to key power brokers. There is a social order in *Deadwood*, and in time this order will give rise to a more formal system of governance – by the end of the first season the camp has a local council and Seth Bullock has been made sheriff.

## Concluding discussion

Something resembling law comes to Deadwood principally because those with power – more specifically, those with capital – have a vested interest in the camp becoming self-governing. As the camp expands and the possibility of incorporation into the USA becomes more real, those with the most to lose commercially become increasingly interested in the function of law and local government in protecting their interests. An absence of laws might open up novel opportunities for wealth creation, but once capital is accumulated it begets power, then law and governance: nowhere is this relationship made more piercingly clear than in *Deadwood*. Nor, we might add, could we easily find such a succinct and vivid depiction of the transition from unruly to rule-based justice. In these respects its achievements are distinctive as a Western and as a contribution to criminological thinking.

## Questions for discussion

Q1)  Can you think of other media representations of lawlessness? What do they suggest about the relationship between morality, law, and social order?

Q2)  Can you think of other media representations of revenge? What do they suggest about the value and meaning of unruly justice?

Q3)  What other media texts have you come across that might enrich our understanding of the causes of crime and/or the function of justice?

## Recommended viewing

The following film Westerns are highly recommended:

John Ford (dir.) (1939) *Stagecoach*. USA: United Artists.
John Ford (dir.) (1956) *The Searchers*. USA: United Artists.
John Ford (dir.) (1962) *The Man Who Shot Liberty Valence*. USA: United Artists.
Anthony Mann (dir.) (1950) *Winchester '73*. USA: Universal Pictures.
Anthony Mann (dir.) (1953) *The Man From Laramie*. USA: Columbia Pictures.
Sam Peckinpah (dir.) (1969) *The Wild Bunch*. USA: Warner Bros.

## Recommended reading

Bazin, André (1971) 'The Western, or the American Film *par excellence*', in H. Gray (ed.), 2 vols, *What is Cinema?* Berkeley: University of California Press, pp. 140–148.
Bazin's famous essay sees Westerns as epics, revolving around certain core myths and particularly suited to film as a medium. Highly recommended.

Hark, Ina Rae (2012) *Deadwood*. Michigan: Wayne State University Press.
Hark's book looks at the production of *Deadwood* and explores central themes, such as use of language, violence, and the lawlessness.

Jacobs, Jason (2012) *Deadwood*. London: BFI.

A brilliant little book based around close readings of scenes from the series. Highly recommended.

Kitses, Jim (2004) *Horizons West: Directing the Western from John Ford to Clint Eastwood*. London: BFI.

Kitses' book provides an excellent overview and evaluation of key film Westerns. A great resource for those interested in the genre.

Lavery, David (2006) (ed.) *Reading Deadwood: A Western to Swear By*. London: I.B. Tauris.

Lavery's edited collection is accessible and covers a wide range of topics, including law and order in *Deadwood*.

Miller, William Ian (1998) 'Clint Eastwood and Equity: Popular Culture's Theory of Revenge', in A. Sarat and T.R. Kearns (eds.) *Law in the Domains of Culture*. Ann Arbor: University of Michigan Press, pp. 161—202.

A really stimulating essay that looks at the depiction and meaning of revenge in Westerns starring Clint Eastwood. Highly recommended.

# *Prison and rehabilitation in* A Clockwork Orange*: thinking afresh about 'what works'*

---

**Recommended viewing**

This chapter looks at the representation of prison and rehabilitation in the film version of *A Clockwork Orange* (1971 USA, 1972 UK, dir. Stanley Kubrick). You'll get more out of the discussion if you watch the film — it's readily available for purchase and hire.

---

One of the most pressing problems for criminal justice systems in economically advanced countries today is high and rising prison numbers. The problem is steadily becoming a crisis – just consider the situation in the UK: according to the Ministry of Justice (2009) between 1995 and 2009 the prison population increased by a massive 66 per cent. In this same period we've seen a significant decrease in recorded crime. In other words, the increase in prison numbers isn't due to an increase in the number of people being convicted of crime. The story is the same for much of Europe. The gravest problem of spiralling prison numbers, though, is faced by the USA. The Norwegian criminologist Nils Christie captures the situation very well in his brilliant book *Crime Control as Industry*. The book is peppered with worrying statistics – for example, that at the turn of the new millennium 'close to 5% of the [US] population from 18 to 44 [were] under the control of the penal law system' (2000: 34). *Five percent* – and the situation has only worsened since then. For most criminologists, Christie included, there's a simple conclusion to draw from all this: we're locking up too many people – in some countries, it's more than at any other point in recorded history. Prisons are becoming seriously overcrowded and dangerous, and too many people who find themselves there have committed minor infractions (or haven't even been convicted – a significant proportion of those in prisons in the USA and UK are awaiting trial, a wait that is becoming ever longer as the criminal justice system becomes increasingly stretched).

This is the 'real-life' backdrop to mass media representations of the prison. Given the scale and urgency of the problems identified by Christie and others we might reasonably expect some sort of cultural response – a glimmer of recognition in mass media depictions of prison life that we can't go on like this, that prison might not be working. This isn't pure idealism. In the mid-nineteenth century the great British novelist Charles Dickens was eager to show up the problems with failing prison systems in the UK and USA. Later in the chapter we'll consider a more recent media text that urges us to think critically about punishment – we're going to look at how the film version of *A Clockwork Orange* (1971 USA, 1972 UK, dir. Stanley Kubrick) illuminates the problems with prison and rehabilitation. In truth, such critical representations of prison are rare today. Instead, mass media representations of the prison tend to promote the idea that the large prison facility is a central and necessary solution to crime. It's to this set of media depictions that we now turn.

## Prison drama and penal populism

Of all the different elements of the criminal justice process, imprisonment is the one about which our knowledge and experience are most restricted. We can, after all, see police on our streets, walk into a police station (if not an interview room), attend a court session, and even watch the legislature at work – but, for most of us, the internal parts of a prison will remain firmly behind closed doors. How do we know about what goes on in prisons, then? The question should arouse more than an idle curiosity in us: after all, this is the principal way in which our societies have chosen to punish serious crime. The great likelihood, as Wilson and O'Sullivan (2004: 8) point out, is that prison dramas are the central source of our ideas about prison and prisoners – after all, these are far more stimulating and accessible than 'any number of unread, dry and dusty government reports, or campaigning documents of penal reform organizations'.

There are certainly enough prison dramas to whet our appetite. A number of academics have noted the increased popularity of television prison dramas in the last two decades, with shows like the British, ITV-produced *Bad Girls*, the popular, HBO-produced programme *Oz*, and, more recently, the US-produced *Prison Break* given primetime slots. In film, prison drama is an enduringly popular genre – just think of the popularity of films like *Escape from Alcatraz* (1979, dir. Don Siegel), *The Green Mile* (1999, dir. Frank Darabont), and *The Shawshank Redemption* (1994, dir. Frank Darabont). Some of these television and film prison dramas raise critical questions about prison as a form of punishment – for example they often represent prisons as unsavoury places that breed criminality. What they tend not to do, though, is ask us to think about the purpose of prison or question its very existence.

Mason (2006) makes a similar observation in his discourse analysis of 28 prison films released between 1995 and 2005 (a study discussed at some length in Chapter 11). Mason argues that these films work to obscure critical discussion about the value of prison by representing prison violence in a titillating manner and depicting prisoners as animalistic and 'deserving of harsh treatment' (p. 611). The second point is particularly interesting. Mason notes that the protagonist in most prison films is someone who has been wrongly convicted, given an overly harsh sentence, or is in prison for the first time – someone, in short, with whom we're meant to feel a good deal of sympathy. Dehumanising the prison population reinforces our affiliation to the central character. Thus, the world of the prison that greets the new inmate is typically deeply intimidating and zoo-like – Mason points to the iconic panning shot of the prison yard, showing scores of loosely grouped, tattooed men lifting weights (p. 617). The likely impression the viewer gains from all this is that prison is a necessary evil 'to keep these psychotic deviants caged and incapacitated' (p. 616). It's an impression that finds ample support across our culture – as Mathiesen (2000: 144) notes: 'In the newspapers, on television, in the whole range of media, the prison is simply not recognised as a fiasco, but as a necessary if not always fully successful method of reaching its purported goals. The prison solution is taken as paradigmatic ...'. It is for these reasons that academics commonly see the popular representation of prison as feeding 'penal populism'. The phrase refers to the broad public support that now exists in many economically advanced countries for harsh forms of punishment, particularly incarceration. We should recognise the broader cultural backdrop to the rise of penal populism – after all, prison dramas alone haven't given rise to these sorts of sentiments. Amidst moral panics about youth violence, television series on gangs, and politicians' pronouncements on the 'problem of crime', there's been an evident shift in public attitudes so that crime control – rather than, say, due process – is popularly seen as the most important aim of criminal justice agencies today. The naturalisation of prison in mass media depictions – the persistent suggestion, in other words, that prison is necessary and a solution to crime – is just one factor promoting penal populism, and, we might reasonably surmise, the trend towards ever bigger prison populations.

## How and why do we punish?

The other thing to observe here is that prison is the form of punishment that receives by far the most mass media attention. Yet there are, of course, numerous forms of punishment. Punishment, in its broadest sense, means 'to pay a penalty' – that could mean being fined, having to give over some of your time to do community service, having to give up your freedom for a period of time, or having to undergo some sort of rehabilitation. All of these are penalties enforced by official criminal justice agencies for committing a crime. The emphasis on prison in mass media representations means that 'the prison solution is taken as paradigmatic', as Mathiesen puts it (2000: 144). In other words, we're provided with a very narrow conception of punishment and offered limited possibilities for thinking about how else our societies might deal with offenders of crime.

Central to any consideration of *how* we punish is the question of *why* we punish. Let's spend some time here thinking about the various purposes of punishment – it'll prove useful in the discussion that follows of how the film *A Clockwork Orange* understands the uses of punishment. Standard criminological thinking sees punishment as having several important social functions: to incapacitate offenders and thus protect communities, deter criminals, enable social restoration, achieve retribution by offering 'an eye for an eye', reintegrate the offender into society, and discourage reoffending. Debates about how we should punish – particularly political debates – tend to see a couple of these functions as primary, the others as secondary. Interestingly, these ideas about what should constitute the main functions of punishment change over time. In the UK today politicians show some interest in the use of punishment to enable social restoration, but, really, political debate is focused on retribution and discouraging reoffending as the core functions of punishment. When we look back to the middle of the twentieth century, though, reintegration was popularly seen as the central purpose of punishment by British politicians and the public.

Looking at these shifts in political debate helps us to understand what politicians mean when they talk about 'what works' in relation to punishment. We should be aware that politicians often have specific aims in mind when pronouncing on what's working and what's not. When the British politician Michael Howard famously announced in a 1993 speech that 'prison works' he was referring to the idea that it appeared to have deterred and incapacitated criminals – it was based on his interpretation of the crime rate rather than, say, a consideration of whether prison had promoted offenders' reintegration into society.

The film *A Clockwork Orange* asks us to approach the question of 'what works' rather differently, in terms of the individual offender's experience of punishment. We're asked to think about 'what works' in ethical, and not just utilitarian, terms – in particular, about what's involved in attempting to change people. Let's turn now to consider how the film understands these matters.

## Punishment in *A Clockwork Orange*

The film *A Clockwork Orange* is an adaptation of a 1962 Anthony Burgess novel of the same title. According to Burgess 'A Clockwork Orange' refers to an old cockney phrase 'queer as a clockwork orange' (meaning extraordinarily odd, or 'queer to the limit of queerness', as Burgess puts it – in Dexter 2008: 200). He also suggested that the book's title was a play upon the Malaysian word *orang*, meaning man (Burgess lived in Malaysia for several years and was fluent in Malay) (p. 201). The two explanations for the book's title are equally convincing – *A Clockwork Orange* is about a deeply odd world of inhuman, unfeeling people.

The novel – and in turn film – is set in the near future in the UK and offers a bleak vision of social life. Like the book, the film focuses on the exploits of Alex (Malcolm McDowell), a teenage delinquent who appears to have an unquenchable thirst for violence and disorder, as well as a disconcerting love of Beethoven's 9th symphony. Alex is the leader of a truly nasty gang, marked out by their bizarre dress (all-white outfits, bowler hats, and heavy black boots), invented language ('nadsat'), and regular participation in what they refer to as 'ultra-violence'. We watch the gang viciously attack a homeless man and a rival group of teenagers. Then, with his fellow gang members ('droogs') Alex breaks into a couple's house. He beats the husband, leaving him paralysed for life, and then rapes the wife. It's a deeply sickening assault, all the more so because the attack on the woman is accompanied by Alex gleefully giving a rendition of 'Singin' in the Rain'. Alex's violent crime spree continues the following day: he breaks into the mansion of an eccentric woman ('cat lady') and viciously beats her – and this time the attack is fatal. Alex is duly arrested and convicted for the crime, and is sent to prison.

Prison is very obviously a site of social control in *A Clockwork Orange*. The formal admission process Alex goes through provides a stark example. Barking orders, the officious admitting officer demands that Alex carries out each aspect of the procedure absolutely correctly (see Figure 13.1). First he needs to take a small footstep backwards to remain behind a white line. Then Alex hands over his possessions rather too hastily for the officer's liking: he must do it again, this time more slowly and carefully. There is, we soon realise, no practical necessity for these rules. Their enforcement is primarily

**Figure 13.1**  Being made to toe the line: Alex is admitted to prison

about engendering compliance rather than ensuring the procedure runs smoothly. It's therefore unsurprising that Alex is vaguely bemused at the situation – he toes the line (literally and metaphorically) but there's no suggestion that the experience is affecting or meaningful for him.

One conclusion we might draw from this is that an important feature of prison life – in *A Clockwork Orange*, at least – is that offenders are required to obey rules without asking why. The aim is to get offenders to become more yielding in general and more likely to follow social rules in the round. The implicit idea here is that making someone act a certain way is a powerful form of discipline, something that may well put us in mind of Foucault's (1995) argument in *Discipline and Punish*. Here Foucault points to an important historical shift in punishment during the early nineteenth century. This was the point at which many European countries started to favour prison as a form of punishment over public torture (although the shift was in fact a very slow one). The modern prison, Foucault points out, forced prisoners to internalise rules and routines. The aim was to transform them into obedient citizens by making them into 'docile bodies' (1995: 136). Discipline of this order is attempted in institutions beyond the prison, of course, and we should be aware that Foucault was trying to establish the importance of this form of social control in a range of modern organisations and settings. For example, school pupils and army recruits are also commonly taught a basic rule of discipline by being made to wait on a specific spot or in a strict line – in borrowing this technique, Alex's treatment in being admitted to the prison may seem very familiar to us.

One inherent problem with discipline as a technique is that making some-one act a certain way – whether it's a pupil, soldier, or prisoner – may have no effect on how he feels or thinks or what he values. *A Clockwork Orange* offers us an insight into this problem. Take, for example, the scene in which prisoners attend a religious service – we join them during a rendition of the hymn 'A Wandering Sheep'. The lyrics are displayed on an overhead projec-tor at the front of the room: '… I was a wandering sheep, I did not love the fold / I did not love my shepherd's voice, I would not be controlled …'. The men's lack of commitment is palpable – and ironic, given the lyrics of the hymn. Many are evidently distracted, messing around rather than singing: one prisoner belches loudly, another makes lip-pouting gestures at Alex. The guard shouts at the men to behave themselves and sing – it's another heavy-handed attempt to exert control, and its failure is evident. Given the lyrics of the hymn we're likely to imagine that the men's lack of commitment extends beyond the simple matter of not singing nicely and sitting up straight: they are refusing too the identity of the reformed character described in the song. The scene provides a vivid depiction of the difficulties in trying to change offenders. You might be able to make people say the words 'I was a wandering sheep … [who] would not be controlled' but this doesn't mean they believe the message or are admitting to the self-image portrayed therein.

The other thing that is striking about this scene is the mutually reinforc-ing relationship between the disciplinary techniques of the prison and reli-gion. Here the prison system produces rules for conduct and religion provides a discourse that valorises subservience. The relationship is evident elsewhere in the film. The chaplain shows particular interest in Alex and is eager to convert him. Alex, in turn, is happy to receive Bible lessons – because, he adds in a voiceover, he finds great pleasure in reading about the various bloody episodes in the Bible. Without internalising the values and principles that underpin the Christian faith Alex is unable to see the Bible as anything other than a thrilling story of violence and vengeance – its moral lessons, in other words, are lost on him. A similar problem makes Alex and his fellow prison-ers unable to accommodate themselves fully to the rules of the prison: that the deeper purpose of these rules is unclear and left unexplained means that a genuine change in subjectivity and attitude is highly unlikely. We might add here that the film is also suggesting that we see prison rules and Bible stories as potentially *reinforcing* Alex's value system: after all, the Bible *is* in parts deeply violent and the enforcement of the prison rules reflects a certain pleasure in domination.

The overall lesson in these scenes is that forcing compliance is a poor means of bringing about genuine change in people, and may be particularly counter-productive when directed at people with domineering, violent personalities. Certainly, it doesn't work for Alex. Desperate to escape prison, he signs up for a pioneering rehabilitative therapy, the Ludovico Technique. Created by an enterprising politician and set of scientists the therapy appears to entirely cure prisoners of their criminality. The party in government is of course delighted by the prospect: it means they can claim to have solved the problem of crime once and for all.

The treatment is fundamentally a form of aversion therapy and involves Alex being made to watch images of violence whilst being drugged and played music by his beloved Beethoven. There's a twist, though: whilst the therapy does stop Alex from being able to act violently, it does not remove his desire for violence. Every time he is in a situation that is in any way violent – and any time he hears a Beethoven symphony – he is paralysed by agonising nausea.

The treatment is judged a success and Alex is released from prison, free to start his life as a reformed character – or, at least, incapable of acting violently. He quickly runs into difficulties. For one thing, his inability to witness and carry out violence means that he's unable to defend himself. He meets and is attacked by people from his old life, including his own gang who – even more astonishingly – are now police officers. Eventually he runs into the couple he attacked before entering prison. Locking Alex in the attic room of their house, they torture him by playing Beethoven's symphonies, knowing that he'll have an adverse reaction to the experience. Unable to bear the agony Alex jumps out of the window and wakes to find himself in hospital. The Minister of the Interior visits him – it transpires that Alex has become a media celebrity and the press have been holding him up as a victim of the government's over-zealous interventions in prisoner rehabilitation. The film ends with Alex's aversion therapy being somehow reversed and him being returned to his 'normal' violent self – he is 'cured', as he puts it. Alex's rehabilitative therapy might seem extreme and bizarre, but it's worth reminding ourselves that our societies use similar forms of punishment – for example, some sex offenders are required to take incapacitating drugs. In the 1970s, the idea of curing offenders by making them undertake therapy was particularly popular. Stanley Cohen took umbrage with this approach in his first book, *Images of Deviance*, written during this period. Cohen believed that a therapeutic approach to punishment was deeply problematic, not least of all because it implied that crime was an individual, as opposed to a social problem. To suggest that what criminals principally need is medical treatment, he argued, means seeing their problem as organic and nothing to do with such things as socialisation, social norms, or subcultural codes of violence: 'Thus the sexual offender is not degenerate but sick: he has a 'kink', a 'warped mentality', or a 'twisted mind'. These labels are comfortable ways of looking at things, because they leave us with the satisfaction of knowing that the problem is *somewhere out there ...*' (p. 11, emphasis added). And, we might add, somewhere *in him* – nothing to do with *us*, at any rate. In other words, the idea that crime is illness and punishment should consist principally of therapy precludes more radical interpretations of crime as, say, an expression of social alienation or marginalisation – as an issue requiring a political, social response. So it is, Cohen argues, that '[psychiatrists] have ... legitimized the creeping tendency to write off or explain away every political conflict or racial disturbances as being the work of "mere hooligans" or "the lunatic fringe"' (p. 20).

Treating Alex as a lunatic whose first need is for therapy means ignoring the social context in which his violent tendencies have developed. The film is certainly critical of this – after all, Alex isn't portrayed as an aberration: instead we're asked to see his world as *wholly* bad and violence as endemic. The rehabilitation programme undertaken by Alex not only leaves these broader social problems unresolved; it serves as a flat denial that violence can be anything other than evidence of an individual pathology. It's also, we might add, a deeply unpleasant form of punishment. Rehabilitation and therapy are traditionally seen as part of an educative-curative model of punishment, an approach that is often heralded as being more humane and liberal than earlier, corporal forms of punishment. In the context of the film, though, the curative-educational model of dealing with offenders is deeply intrusive. In fact, Alex's treatment closely resembles torture: strapped down, with his eyes forced open with metal pins, he clearly finds the therapy appallingly painful and begs for it to be stopped (see Figure 13.2). In this way Alex's treatment might make us think about the ways in which modern forms of punishment – even those which can be labelled humane, curative, or rehabilitative – still involve work upon the body.

Of course, Alex's rehabilitative treatment is unusual in involving this level of physical pain. Rehabilitation today is much more likely to involve things like educational programmes for prisoners and post-release mentoring. If we look at the principles that underpin current ideas about the purpose of rehabilitation, though, they're strikingly close to those informing Alex's treatment. In the UK today, and in other countries besides, rehabilitation is understood by politicians in rather narrow terms, to mean the discouraging of reoffending (just look, for example, at how the government understands its so-called 'rehabilitation revolution' – see Nick Clegg's May 2013 speech for an insight). In this conception of rehabilitation it's specifically behaviour, rather than values, attitudes, or feelings, that's the intended site for change.

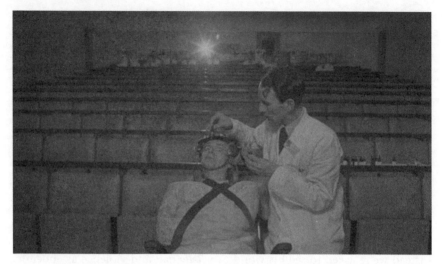

**Figure 13.2**   Rehabilitative treatment as corporal punishment

It is precisely this instrumental view of rehabilitation that informs Alex's therapy in *A Clockwork Orange*, and the film vividly depicts the problems with this approach. For the politicians and scientists who have pioneered Alex's treatment all that matters is that he is physically unable to commit crime again. Their understanding of rehabilitation and its purpose is informed by narrow political interests in driving down the crime rate and influencing public opinion. Alex's needs – his overall well-being and reintegration – are a secondary concern. In turn, this means that the ethical problems with his treatment – and with behaviour-focused rehabilitation more generally – are ignored. The prison chaplain notes precisely these sorts of problems with Alex's treatment. He is outraged to find that the prisoner's rehabilitation has involved nothing more than the simple removal of his ability to be violent. That Alex is now unable to be bad means, by extension, that he's also unable to choose to be good. Thus, the chaplain complains, he is denied the opportunity to lead a genuinely moral life. The Minister of the Interior is unperturbed by the chaplain's complaints: 'we are not concerned with motives, with the higher ethics', he retorts. The aim, he adds, is simply to cut crime and lessen the burden on prisons. Besides, he adds, 'the point is that it works' – if, we might add, 'what works' is conceived of in narrow terms, as referring just to the portion of an offender's future behaviour that is classed in official terms as criminal. That the treatment can work in this narrow sense and still be, by anyone's standards, an absolute failure is really illuminating – it might, for example, prompt us to think further about the purpose of punishment.

## Concluding discussion

In showing us that a bad society invariably does bad things to bad people *A Clockwork Orange* prompts a critical consideration of our own society's approach to punishment. It might make us recognise, for example, that rehabilitation can succeed in the narrow sense of stopping reoffending but fail to attend to the social sources of misery and harm that promoted a life of crime in the first place. The film suggests something further: rehabilitation of the individual (however that's conceived) is less likely to succeed if the society in which violent crime occurs isn't also the subject of reform. Another way of thinking about this is to say that, for rehabilitation to work, the society for which the offender is being 'made fit' must offer a meaningful alternative to a life of violence. What happens if, in the society in question, brutality has become a mundane aspect of social life? This is the case in *A Clockwork Orange*. Violence is endemic in this world – even Alex's old gang, who are now *police officers*, give him an appalling beating after his release.

The film suggests that this sort of society struggles to make rehabilitation work, and for two central reasons. First, the offender will probably be unable to sustain a life without violence – because if violence doesn't come *from* him, it will almost certainly come *to* him. Secondly, the offender's overall well-being and reintegration are unlikely to be primary concerns in any rehabilitation programme produced by such a society. Instead, quick fixes aimed at stopping reoffending are likely to be favoured, irrespective of their ethical problems. The film demonstrates that these quick fixes are unlikely to be effective in their own terms: long-term socio-psychological processes like the cultivation of a value system or moral code – the sorts of processes that enable people to freely choose to be law abiding – aren't served particularly well by bursts of therapy, temporary initiatives, or being made to follow rules unthinkingly.

## Questions for discussion

Q1)  Can you think of other films and television series that might reinforce penal populism?

Q2)  Why have we seen the recent growth of prison dramas on television?

Q3)  Identify another film or television series that illuminates problems with punishment. What is the basis for its critique?

Q4)  Why might it be a problem that prison is over-represented in the mass media as a form of punishment?

## Recommended reading

Mason, Paul (2006) 'Prison Decayed: Cinematic Penal Discourse and Popularism 1995—2005', *Social Semiotics*, 16(4): 607—626.
Mason carries out a fascinating discourse analysis on 28 prison films and argues that these films reinforce penal populism. Highly recommended.

O'Sullivan, Sean (2001) 'Representations of Prison in Nineties Hollywood Cinema: From *Con Air* to *The Shawshank Redemption*', *The Howard Journal of Criminal Justice*, 40(4): 317—334.
O'Sullivan analyses four Hollywood prison films of the 1990s and considers their effect on public attitudes to incarceration.

Saunders, David and Vanstone, Maurice (2010) 'Rehabilitation as Presented in British Film: Shining a Light on Desistance from Crime?' *The Howard Journal of Criminal Justice*, 49(4): 375—393.
Saunders and Vanstone provide close, sensitive readings of four British films that feature the rehabilitation process. They suggest that these films illuminate the long-term, complex process of desistance. Highly recommended.

Wilson, David and O'Sullivan, Sean (2004) *Images of Incarceration: Representations of Prison in Film and Television Drama*. London: Waterside.
Ranging across examples from the USA and UK, Wilson and O'Sullivan discuss the impact of popular representations of prison on public attitudes and its relationship to the reality of prison life.

## CHAPTER 14

# Stories of criminal detection from Christie to CSI

Raymond Chandler, in his wonderfully acerbic 1944 essay 'The Simple Art of Murder', suggested that good detective fiction gives us a sense of 'what goes on in the world' (1988: 11). This euphemism nicely captures the distinctive charm and achievement of the genre: stories of criminal detection sketch out for us what our social world can be like at its worst, they ask us to abandon any childlike notions of security and basic goodness, and acknowledge that *this* type of bad stuff is possible in *this* type of social world. Put differently, detective fiction asks us to think about where evil resides and the shape it takes under particular social conditions.

This chapter focuses on three sets of detective fiction: Agatha Christie's fiction of the (mainly) 1920s and 1930s, Raymond Chandler and Dashiell Hammett's novels of the 1930s and 1940s, and the contemporary television series *CSI*. The aim of this chapter is a rather broad one: to compare how each set of detective stories sketches out the social world of crime and the nature of detection, and to discuss both in relation to socio-historical context. Before we turn to these case studies, though, a brief discussion of early detective fiction and the relationship between styles of detection and characterisation.

## Early detective fiction

Try this experiment: seek out an online best-seller list for one of the big high-street booksellers and count how many of the top 50 books for that week are detective novels. It's probably at least a fifth, and perhaps as much as half. At the time of writing, best-seller lists in the UK are (still) dominated by books by Stieg Larsson, Jo Nesbo, and Henning Mankell. I'm sure that none of this is news to you. What might surprise you, though, is that detective fiction has been amongst the most popular of genres since the novel's emergence as a mass literary form in the early nineteenth century. Other genres and sub-genres come and go, but detective fiction has retained its popularity through the decades. In fact, forget Charles Dickens: the best-selling British novelist of the Victorian period was the master of suspense and intrigue, Wilkie Collins. His novels *The Woman in White* (1859) and *The Moonstone* (1868) are now widely regarded as literary classics, and they happened also to be extraordinarily popular amongst the reading public at the time. The second of these books is often taken to be the first notable detective novel, though this is contestable (see, for example, Evans 2009: 25–26). What we do know is that Collins' book was widely seen as an important early contribution to the genre: T.S. Eliot described the book as 'the first, the longest and the best of modern English detective novels' (cited by Kemp in Collins 1998: vii).

The other notable early contributor to detective fiction lay across the Atlantic to Collins. Edgar Allan Poe, the great nineteenth-century American author of the macabre, is often heralded as the first to create a detective-protagonist in short story form. His literary detective, C. Auguste Dupin, was introduced in *The Murders in the Rue Morgue* (1841) and appeared as the central character again in *The Mystery of Marie Roget* (1842) and *The Purloined Letter* (1844). Dupin is a privately hired detective, part-dilettante, part-genius whose detection is characterised by intellectual leaps quite beyond us mere mortals – only he could entertain the possibility that an escaped *orangutan* could be the perpetrator of the terrible murders on the Rue Morgue. He may well put us in mind of that other famous nineteenth-century fictional detective, Sherlock Holmes. Indeed, Conan Doyle was influenced by Poe's work, and Dupin is clearly a forerunner to Holmes. For this reason, amongst others, Poe is often described as the most important originator of the modern detective fiction genre. Certainly, Dupin is, in many ways, the quintessential literary detective. Take the fact that, despite being a recluse, he becomes a celebrity amateur detective, showing up the police's shameful lack of imagination in solving serious crime. How familiar this sounds to any enthusiast of Sherlock Holmes or Hercule Poirot! Moreover, and as Stern (1941) notes, Poe introduced the convention of using the detective's (rather more human, rather less brilliant) sidekick as the narrator (think of Dr Watson and Hastings).

## Styles of detection and characterisation

We can make another observation about Dupin: he is a master of induction. That is to say, he engages in the task of detection with a completely open mind, assimilates the facts, and assiduously scrutinises everything related to the case to build an explanation evidence-up, as it were. This distinctive method of logical inference has become a hallmark of detective fiction. Induction isn't the only detective style in town, though. The other notable technique used by fictional detectives is deduction. The deductive detective starts with a theory or hunch, and then collects evidence to substantiate it – the television detective Lieutenant Columbo (Peter Falk) and Christie's literary creation Miss Marple are good examples of detectives who use this sort of approach. In thinking about specific examples like this it's easy to see that style of detection, inductive or deductive, is a facet of characterisation in crime stories. Marple's powers of detection are intimately connected to her nosiness, intuition, and inconspicuousness as an observer. This, really, is the only type of detection available to her: Marple, you may recall, is an elderly lady belonging to polite society. We'd be mistaken, then, to imagine that she *chooses* a style of detection: deduction is what's available to her and what's convincing to us, in terms of her social status and position. Similarly, Peter Falk's Columbo is a shabby, bumbling, working-class homicide detective – he is also deeply intuitive and has a profound understanding of human behaviour. This is the basis for his detection, and, again, it's closely related to his social status. The sorts of balletic intellectual leaps practised by the likes of Dupin depend largely on academic knowledge and the ability to acquire that knowledge at speed. The characterisation of Marple and Columbo effectively precludes them from detecting in this way.

What can we say about the relationship between induction and characterisation? Induction, as practised by Holmes and Dupin – and, after them, Hercule Poirot – is an expression of extreme rationality and complete open-mindedness. In both cases this sets them apart from the often irrational, incompetent, and work-a-day police detectives. Thus Holmes tells his sidekick Dr Watson in 'The Sign of Four', the second of Doyle's numerous stories featuring Holmes, that he is not merely the 'only unofficial detective' in London, but the most decent one of all:

> I am the last and highest court of appeal in detection. When Gregson, or Lestrade, or Athelney Jones [police detectives] are out of their depths – which, by the way, is their normal state – the matter is laid before me. I examine the data, as an expert, and pronounce a specialist's opinion … (Doyle 1999 [originally 1890]: 64)

If Marple and Columbo are possessed of the singular gift of intuition, Holmes and Dupin are endowed with a similarly rare quality: mental dexterity and objectivity. This, after all, is what makes Holmes an expert, what characterises his 'peculiar powers', as he puts it – it is the ability to systematically discount facts and hypotheses until he is left with only one possible explanation, however extraordinary. Most importantly, perhaps, detection is framed here as *scientific work* (the references to data, specialists, and experts are deeply suggestive of this). Just as Marple and Columbo couldn't conceivably develop and manifest the necessary traits to undertake this sort of work, Holmes and Dupin could not hope to develop a keen and emotional understanding of the human psyche. In the world of the detective story, this is often explained in terms of the inductive detective's energies being fully absorbed in purer intellectual pursuits (or, as in the case of a modern-day inductive detective like Lisbeth Salander, having an organic mental disability that precludes social awareness). What's also important, though, is that both Holmes and Dupin are free from financial concerns – Dupin finds a wealthy sponsor and Holmes is of good stock. This means that both detectives are at liberty to pursue esoteric intellectual endeavours (Holmes, we learn, has written several books, one on footsteps, another on cigar ash). It's a sort of freedom that the down-at-heel Columbo and the elderly spinster Marple could never hope to have. In this sense, social class and access to wealth help decide what sort of detective a character can become.

There's a more general point to be made here: fictional detectives, even those that appear to possess super-human talents, are products of their social world. We can go further than this and say that detective stories reflect social conditions, prevailing values, and contemporary ideas about crime and order. This, at least, is the premise of this chapter. This observation might seem counter-intuitive: detective stories often seem to have the same sort of hold over us as the eternally absorbing puzzle. This, I think, is to ignore detective fiction's rootedness in time and place. Just think, for one moment, of the British and US public's ongoing love of Poirot television mysteries: part of the appeal of these programmes is that they represent a social world that seems so quaint to us now. So it is that modern adaptations of Christie's novels are still set in a bygone age (and, as something of a contrast, it's worth reflecting on the fact that so many adaptations of Shakespeare plays *are* ripped from their original setting). However much the mysteries themselves might seem to appeal to ingrained and unchanging human interests, Christie's stories, unlike, say, Shakespeare's, are redolent of a certain period and society.

### Detective-work in Christie's novels: rooting out the bad apples

If Collins, Poe, and Doyle were important originators of the detective fiction genre, the British author Agatha Christie was the first to really popularise it worldwide and across social groups. Often referred to as the 'Queen of Crime', Christie is the best-selling crime writer of all time. Her first novel, *The Mysterious Affair at Styles*, was published just after the First World War, in 1920, and introduced her most famous literary creation: Hercule Poirot. Christie was a prolific author, and her work spans several decades. What interests us here, though, is her writing during the 1920s and 1930s. This was a period known as the 'golden age' of detective fiction. Christie might have been the most popular progenitor of this literary tradition, but she was not the only one. The interwar years in the UK saw an extraordinary growth in crime writing, giving rise, in 1930, to the creation of The Detection Club, a group of mainly British crime writers eager to forge a collective identity and literary movement. Christie belonged to the group, as did the formidable Dorothy L. Sayers (creator of the aristocratic detective Lord Peter Wimsey), G.K. Chesterton (creator of the cleric-cum-detective Father Browning), and Gladys Mitchell (creator of Mrs Bradley, consulting psychoanalyst to the Home Office).

However distinctive the golden age protagonist-detectives appear on first sight, they share certain important traits. First, with the notable exception of Miss Marple, most of them are inductive detectives – that is, they are led by the evidence and develop a theory 'bottom-up'. This was one of the core principles of The Detection Club: fictional detectives should develop solutions by studying the facts and without recourse to instinct, emotion, or prejudice.

Another shared trait amongst the golden age detectives is that they are amateur or private detectives: put differently, very few are working on behalf of the police (even if they have previously done work for Scotland Yard or an individual police force). Thirdly, almost without exception, they come from outside the social group that falls under suspicion; they might belong to a different age group or class (as is the case with Jane Marple, Inspector French, and Lord Wimsey) and often arrive on the scene as visitors. Hercule Poirot is perhaps the clearest example of the detective-as-outsider: Christie makes frequent references to his foreign accent and mannerisms. That the golden age detectives are outsiders is really important because it gives them a certain objectivity in examining the situation, marks them out as one of a handful of characters who are above suspicion, and therefore makes them reliable sources of information. (There are notable exceptions to this: in Christie's 1926 novel *The Murder of Roger Ackroyd*, for example, Dr Sheppard serves as the amateur detective and narrator – he is also, it turns out, the murderer.)

In most cases, then, the detective of the golden age is in a position to judge objectively – and this is just as important as his or her ability to rationally consider the facts (to deploy, as Poirot so often tells us, 'the little grey cells'). Judging, in other words, is a matter of one's social position as well as cognitive abilities in golden age detective fiction. Bearing this in mind it's worth noting that many of the detectives in these books share another characteristic: they often represent a social authority, such as the church (in the case of Father Browning), the medical establishment (Mrs Bradley), or the aristocracy (Lord Wimsey). In such cases the vantage point of the detective is not simply that of the outsider but also the respected authority figure.

Books in this sub-genre of detective fiction share other characteristics. For one thing, the crime is always murder; for another, the social group under suspicion is always relatively small in number and clearly defined. To read a book from this era is, generally speaking, to read about a contracted social world of an extended family, the goings-on of a single street or household, a small community, or group of hotel guests. Sometimes the mystery is set in a space where access is strictly limited to the small group of suspects, such as an island or remote holiday destination. The smallness of the social world of the novel is a crucial feature of golden age fiction, often becoming intrinsic to the inductive process of discounting explanations and eliminating suspects. Take, for example, Christie's 1939 novel *And Then There Were None* (originally published as *Ten Little Niggers*, the title of an old English nursery rhyme). The novel is set in a mansion on a sparsely inhabited island and focuses on ten suspects (eight houseguests and two servants). One by one the suspects are killed off, leaving the real murderer – or so we are lead to imagine. A similar technique is employed by Dorothy L. Sayers in her 1931 book *Five Red Herrings*, often thought to be one of her best. Set in a remote Scottish community popular with artists, the murderer has to be one of six local painters. The book proceeds by giving due consideration to and then discounting the five 'red herrings'.

There are several important insights we can make about this feature of golden age fiction. Focusing our attention on a small group means that the detective's and reader's powers of logical inference and induction can be narrowly directed. Fundamentally, these novels are about spotting an aberration in a specific social group – not in the social world as a whole. As we'll see later, this is in contrast to the messy worlds of uncontainable violence and crime depicted in contemporary US detective fiction. In golden age fiction crime has a very specific location and is isolatable: the detective's job is to root out the wrong-doer (or wrong-doers) and return this once peaceful social world to tranquillity. This is precisely what the poet and cultural commentator W.H. Auden found so appealing about these novels. In a 1948 article in *Harper's* magazine, Auden tried to account for his love of British golden age detective fiction. For him, 'the interest in the detective story is the dialectic of good and evil' (p. 406). Suggesting similarities to the story structure sketched out by Aristotle for tragedy, Auden usefully identifies the standard movement of the classical detective story (p. 407). We start, he notes, in a state of 'false innocence', the period before the murder where everything seems (but clearly is not) harmonious. The murder takes place, precipitating a 'revelation at the presence of guilt' within the social group. Guilt is then falsely located, as evidence mounts against certain suspects, who are later revealed to be innocent. Then we have the 'location of real guilt' and catharsis caused by the arrest of the real guilty party. Finally 'true innocence' is achieved.

In this schema, golden age detective fiction is centrally about restoring order. Indeed, Auden suggests that the most successful novels of this genre are set in Eden-like places. Here, there is a vested and shared interest in locating and isolating guilt and re-finding peace. The cathartic process of detecting and detaining a wrong'un depends, Auden wants to argue, on our having a sense that the social world of the novel is worth saving, worth putting back together. Murder appears all the more disruptive in such social situations, the corpse 'shockingly out of place', not simply because it's a corpse, but because it absolutely does not belong *here* – 'as when a dog makes a mess on a drawing room carpet' (1948: 408). The dog that relieves himself in the street is just doing what dogs do; when he does it on the smart carpet in a smart lady's house, his difference to us higher animals is more apparent. So it is that, in golden age fiction, the corpse on the drawing room carpet signifies extreme, inexplicable evil – it is the symbol of an animalistic violence not belonging to *this* society. For Auden this is part of the appeal of golden age detective fiction: it invites us to think about murder as a disruption of social values and order. Take the fact, Auden writes, that so many golden age detective novels are about the well-to-do. Many, he comments, are set on esteemed college campuses and invite us to consider the possibility that men of learning – academics and their star pupils – could be brutal murderers. The device is successful partly because extreme acts of cruelty run so obviously counter to universities' atmosphere and ethos of civilised conduct. To entertain the possibility that a college professor is a murderer is to consider not just the possibility for human violence but that someone *like this* could have strayed.

That golden age fiction makes us think like this could make this body of literature rather subversive. It might mean, for example, that we're urged to consider the possibility that the upper social classes – college professors and all! – have no special claim to moral authority after all and that murder is symbolic of there being something rotten about this social group as a whole. Interestingly, this is precisely *not* what we're asked to imagine in golden age fiction. This is not to deny the virtues of this fiction, particularly the work of Christie. I fully agree with Mary Evans' (2009: 59) comment that there is great critical value in Christie's fiction because 'nothing in the social world [of these novels] is quite as it seems'. Nonetheless, it's clear that Christie's books aren't meant as institutional critique – and this makes them somewhat unlike much recent detective fiction where a corrupt politician, police officer, or corporate boss is most certainly symptomatic of a broader institutional problem. (Anyone who's read Stieg Larsson's Millennium trilogy – or watched the David Fincher films based on these books – will have a sense of this.)

In contrast, in golden age fiction, the detective's problem is a specific, rather than general one. Poirot's famous revelation speeches at the end of Christie's novels point the finger at an individual; they don't denounce the upper-middle class as bad to the core. In fact, in Christie's novels it's frequently the case that the perpetrator turns out to have been masquerading as a member of the upper-middle-class group and is in fact a down-at-heel commoner or, worse, a member of the criminal class. In Christie's 1938 book *Appointment With Death*, for example, the murderer, Lady Westholme, turns out to have had a shadowy past as a criminal. Enjoying an educational tour of Jerusalem with her husband, she realises that someone in the holiday party recognises her from her past life – and she kills so that her former identity won't be revealed. The implication here is that, in acting in this way, the perpetrator has been unable to shake off her past life – once a criminal, always a criminal. Here the problem for the upper-middle class is that it is permeable, that imposters can enter its ranks without being vetted and infect it with the seedy values that make murder possible.

In other cases, the villain turns out to be a genuine member of the social group, 'respectable people gone bad', as Scraggs (2005: 43) puts it. Interestingly, in these stories, the motivation for murder is often connected to a desire to maintain status (classically, to avoid bankruptcy, loss of fortune, and scandal). What's important about such stories, as Scraggs notes, is that full scandal is inevitably averted, rather than realised. The job of the detective is, fundamentally, to contain the problem and thus maintain the 'upper-middle class status quo' (p. 47). It's worth remembering here that golden age detectives are privately recruited or amateur sleuths, and in many cases their loyalties lie with the group under investigation, and sometimes even the murderer. This helps explain why, on occasion, Poirot allows the murderer to escape arrest (as is the case in Christie's *Death on the Nile*) or decides not to pursue the guilty party (as is the case – famously – in Christie's *Murder on the Orient Express*). Thus, Scraggs argues, the golden age detective shares with the group of suspects 'a broad concern to avoid unnecessary scandal about the upper-middle class' (p. 43). Certainly, in Christie's fiction, the story ends not just with social order restored (as Auden has it), but with the social class system reinforced by a cathartic weeding out of imposters and ne'er-do-wells. It's worth remembering here that Christie was particularly prolific and popular during the inter-war years. Her novels are, in one sense, a comforting reminder of the resilience of the British social system: after all, they tell us stories about the elite being rocked, but not crumbling, of order temporarily breached, but not destroyed altogether.

## Detective-work in hard-boiled fiction: stepping inside the underworld

If the world of a Christie novel is basically a good one, the world of a hard-boiled detective novel is basically bad. In a 1944 essay entitled 'The Simple Art of Murder' Raymond Chandler, one of the most influential authors of this strand of US detective fiction, offered a stinging attack on his British counter-parts. One of his central complaints was that the golden age detectives were very thin characters, mere instruments to mystery solving, rather than actu-ally inhabiting the social world they studied. This is true, but principally because golden age detectives' authority to judge is due in part to their distance from the social world. Different fictional worlds require different types of fictional detectives. That the golden age masters of 'rare knowledge [live] ... psychologically in the age of the hoop skirt' most certainly would preclude them from possessing the sort of knowledge, smarts, and susceptibil-ities required by the modern hard-boiled detective (Chandler 1988: 4).

For Chandler golden age British fiction followed an 'arid formula' (p. 12), was too contrived and joyless. He contrasts this strand of literature to the work of Dashiell Hammett, the US crime writer. 'Hammett', Chandler wrote, 'took murder out of the Venetian vase and dropped it into the alley', thus giving 'murder back to the kind of people that commit it for reasons, not just to provide a corpse; and with the means at hand, not with hand-wrought duelling pistols, curare, and tropical fish' (p. 14). This sort of detective fiction – so distinctively North American, so seedy, and direct – quickly came to be referred to as hard-boiled. If the British authors of the golden age had domi-nated worldwide sales in the 1920s and early 1930s, it was the American writ-ers, most notably Chandler and Hammett, who became the up-and-coming stars of detective fiction in the mid-1930s and 1940s. This is partly because several of their novels were adapted to become Hollywood movies, thus shoring up interest in the hard-boiled sub-genre. Chandler's *The Big Sleep* (dir. Howard Hawks, 1946) and Hammett's *The Maltese Falcon* (dir. John Huston, 1941) are perhaps the most famous of the hard-boiled novels to be transferred to the silver screen. Humphrey Bogart played the lead detective role in both, showing up the fundamental similarities between the characters of Philip Marlowe (Chandler's creation) and Sam Spade (Hammett's protagonist). Both are fast-talking private eyes with a susceptibility to female charms.

Both are also men of basic integrity operating in a criminal underworld of corruption, money laundering, gambling, drug running, and bribery. The world of the hard-boiled detective, Chandler points out, 'is one in which gangsters can rule nations and almost rule cities, in which hotels and apart-ment houses and celebrated restaurants are owned by men who made their money out of brothels, in which a screen star can be the fingerman for a mob ...' (p. 17). What Chandler is describing here is the shadowy criminal rackets that underpin legitimate enterprises, a just-out-of-sight criminal world. Like golden age fiction, this is a sharply defined social world, albeit one that needs to be uncovered. The hard-boiled novel is fundamentally about an *under-world*. There are borders to this world; for example, the novels frequently make mention of the nice, safe parts of town.

It is, of course, a world in which Poirot and Marple would have absolutely no place. An entirely different order of detective is needed for the world of the hard-boiled novel, one whose ability to detect comes principally from an acute social awareness rather than any skillful inductive technique or social distance – Chandler, again:

> He talks as the man of his age talks, that is, with rude wit, a lively sense of the grotesque, a disgust for sham, and a contempt for pettiness ... He has a range of awareness that startles you, but it belongs to him by right, because it belongs to the world he lives in. (p. 18)

Hard-boiled detectives, unlike their golden age predecessors, are fully part of the social world they investigate: and the world they inhabit is filthy with corruption, enervating, and above all else dynamic. At the start of Chandler's 1939 novel *The Big Sleep*, Philip Marlowe is called to the mansion of the vener-able old General Sternwood. Chandler juxtaposes a world of old wealth with the down-and-dirty world to which Marlowe belongs. Approaching the mansion, Marlowe observes:

> a broad stained-glass panel showing a knight in dark armour rescuing a lady who was tied to a tree and didn't have any clothes on but some very long and convenient hair. The knight had pushed the vizor of his helmet back to be sociable, and he was fiddling with the knots of the ropes that tied the lady to the tree and not getting anywhere. I stood there and thought that if I lived in the house, I would sooner or later have to climb up there and help him. He didn't seem to be really trying. (p. 3)

Marlowe is a knight for a new social world, where old customs no longer apply, nothing is certain and fixed, politeness is no longer needed (in sex, and all things besides), and standing still means losing out.

Most importantly, it's a world in which everyone under investigation is to some degree implicated in crime and wrong-doing, despite appearances to the contrary. Of course, in a Christie novel, too, not everything is as it seems: little old ladies can be first-rate detectives and the guilty party can turn out to be the well-to-do man of repute. Eventually, though, the wrong-doer will be rooted out and order restored. In a Chandler or Hammett novel, there is no such happy resolution. At the end of *The Big Sleep*, we find out that Sternwood's youngest daughter is a murderer and his eldest daughter an accessory to the crime – and that's it. This refusal to end peacefully – to put things back together again – is a common feature of hard-boiled novels. Perhaps the best example of this is Hammett's 1930 novel *The Maltese Falcon*. We open with Sam Spade being approached by a forlorn and beautiful Miss Wonderly, apparently looking for her missing sister. The meeting is part of an elaborate con: she turns out to belong to a criminal underworld and murders Spade's partner in order to implicate a fellow criminal. Spade turns Miss Wonderly – or, as we soon learn, Bridgit O'Shaughnessy – over to the police, but there's no sense of relief or resolution here: Spade has fallen in love with her, and is effectively condemning her to death. (And, as something of an aside here, it's worth pointing out that names matter greatly in hard-boiled fiction: General Sternwood is as leaden and old-fashioned as his name suggests, whilst Miss Wonderly turns out to be falsely named in all ways imaginable.)

As in other hard-boiled novels, the characters of *The Maltese Falcon* completely lack redeeming features: there's no honour amongst thieves here, no loyalty to anything or anyone, and, importantly, no innocents to be protected. No one in the criminal underworld of the hard-boiled novel is to be trusted – not even a detective. Not only does Sam Spade hand O'Shaughnessy over to the police, he seems relatively unaffected by his partner's death, and pockets bribes. The other main character of the book, O'Shaughnessy, is almost wholly dissimulating; we suspect that even her advances to Sam Spade have been for the sake of self-preservation. In fact, almost every female character in hard-boiled novels turns out to be criminally inclined and double-crossing – and the more beautiful or vulnerable they appear, the more deeply deviant they end up being. O'Shaughnessy is perhaps the quintessential female dissimulator of hard-boiled fiction – but Vivian, in *The Big Sleep*, is a similarly slippery character, as is Orfamay Quest in Chandler's *The Little Sister*. What is particularly striking about these female characters is that they initially appear helpless, innocent, and virtuous – they appear distinctly and traditionally feminine, in other words. That they are often the most vicious and double-crossing characters is an important part of these novels' overall effect in showing us a world turned upside-down. It's worth noting here that this sub-genre of detective fiction was mainly produced during the 1930s and 1940s. During the early years of this period, the USA was experiencing a profound economic depression, started by the catastrophic and sudden Wall Street Crash of 1929. This was an era when rich men became poor men overnight and social institutions that once appeared utterly trustworthy suddenly failed. Hard-boiled literature shows a social world ruled by invisible and malevolent forces where no one can be trusted and no one's status is set in stone: this is also, in some sense at least, the world of the Depression Era USA.

## Detective-work in *CSI*: routine investigations

We move on now to consider the portrayal of detective-work in the popular contemporary television series *CSI: Crime Scene Investigation*. We're making a large jump, then, both in terms of medium and historical setting. We'll do some catching up in a moment to work out how we got from hard-boiled novels to *CSI* – but first, a few words to introduce the series. First aired on the US network CBS in 2000, *CSI* focuses on the criminal investigation work of a forensics team based in Las Vegas. The programme is centrally about detection as a scientific process involving the careful examination of a crime scene for physical evidence and then the use of electronic databases and scientific equipment to identify the perpetrator. The opening credit shots for the programme clearly indicate that this is the show's focus. Over the (now familiar) strains of The Who's 'Who Are You?' shots of each character are interspersed with quick flashing images of, amongst other things, X-rays of various parts of the body, blood splatter, a science equation and table, controlled explosions, police tape being drawn across a crime scene, a graph, an evidence inventory, teeth being studied (presumably for the purpose of identification), and a microscope view of the contents of a petri dish. The montage is punctuated with bright, flashes of light – sometimes from diegetic sources (torches and explosions), but otherwise simply as an effect unrelated to the images we see. This use of light, combined with the speed of the images, is supposed to evoke something about scientific testing and computer technology – the fact that they appear to provide instantaneous results and 'illuminate a situation'.

The show generally opens at the crime scene: we begin, in other words, not with the social milieu or personal life of perpetrator, victim, or detective, but with the aftermath of a crime. As the story develops, the key revelatory moments come with the results from, variously, analysis of fingerprints, CCTV images, phone conversations, clothing fibres, and bodily excretions. A breakthrough in scientific analysis – with, say, the identification of the weapon from blood splatter – tends to prompt a flashback to the scene of the crime. The implication is clear: scientific analysis allows us to *precisely* picture what happened and how. In other ways, too, scientific testing is shown to give a privileged view of crime. For example, an electronic database search or the act of looking down a microscope is customarily marked in *CSI* by a computer-generated shot incorporating a flash zoom: the idea is to represent processes of testing and searching that are otherwise mechanical and invisible to us.

These are the sorts of features that characterise *CSI* – and they're deeply familiar to anyone who's watched the programme. Such was the show's immediate popularity, that CBS quickly developed a franchise: *CSI Miami* was launched in 2002 and *CSI NY* in 2004. The original programme remains the most popular. In fact, reliable indicators suggest that it is the most watched television series in the world. In 2012, and for the fifth time, the show won the prestigious International Television Audience Award for a Drama TV Series at the Monte Carlo Television Festival – the award is given to the television drama series with the largest worldwide audience for that year. Its extraordinary popularity has led some academics to talk of a 'CSI Effect' wherein the show has come to influence people's expectations of criminal investigation to such a degree that jury members in the US feel a case to be substantially weakened by a lack of physical and forensic evidence (see Chapter 4 for more on this).

In truth *CSI* is part of a broader trend in detective fiction: it doesn't stand alone, exerting a monolithic influence, in other words, but is part of a now dominant sub-genre. Even if you haven't watched *CSI*, you may well have caught one of the many other television shows that follow a similar formula, such as *Law and Order*, the British-produced *Waking the Dead*, and, more recently, *Dexter*. How did we get from hard-boiled fiction to detective dramas about forensic investigation? How and when did the private dick give way to the CSI team? Two related shifts in detective fiction are really important here: the rise of fiction that focused on detection as the purview of state-hired and -trained investigators, and the emergence of a strand of fiction that takes detection to rely centrally on scientific testing. Interestingly, both developments were first evident in the original medium for detective fiction – the novel.

A handful of novels in the first half of the twentieth century focused on the detective-work of the police – so-called police procedurals – but this period really belonged to the Poirots and then Sam Spades of the detecting world. As Scraggs (2005: 92) notes, it was in the second half of the twentieth century that we see police procedurals become really popular. The US author Ed McBain's 87th Precinct novels were important early contributions to this sub-genre, as were the novels by the British writers P.D. James and Ruth Rendell about Inspector Adam Dalgliesh and Inspector Wexford respectively. As Scraggs (2005) points out, the rise of the police procedural novel coincided with the creation of a welfare state in the UK and the growth of the public sector across most economically advanced societies. The rise of the police procedural, in other words, reflects the growth of modern bureaucracies, and, as part of that development, modern criminal justice systems.

It is this distinctive socio-historical context that gives rise to stories about the police's everyday pursuit of criminal detection. Given this core feature of police procedurals, it is perhaps unsurprising that this sub-genre made an easy transition into television. After all, this medium lends itself to depictions of detection as a job – as tiring, repetitive, and routine. This might help explain why police procedurals have come to dominate our television schedules: indeed, many of us are more familiar with Inspector Wexford, Morse, and Inspector Dalgliesh as characters in television programmes, rather than novels. A similar fate perhaps awaits Henning Mankell's police detective, Wallander.

Early police procedurals paved the way for programmes like *CSI* by presenting detective-work as an everyday, state-sponsored activity. A further important development in detective fiction occurred in the early 1990s when the novelist Patricia Cornwell started to write police procedural novels that focused on the work of a forensics team, and in particular the lead investigator, Kay Scarpetta. In these books detection is the job of scientific experts working for the police and it is physical evidence – gathered from autopsies and crime scene investigation – that proves to be the most important tool in identifying the perpetrator. It has become, of course, a much emulated formula, particularly, again, by television programmes.

## Concluding discussion

We end this chapter with a discussion of the similarities and differences between *CSI* and previous detective fiction. Let's think first about what *CSI* shares with golden age and hard-boiled detective fiction. Looked at from one perspective, the basic concerns of detective fiction haven't changed that much: the crime is still, almost always, murder, the detective often a rational-inducer piecing together evidence to create an overall picture of events. Moreover, *CSI* detectives share with their golden age predecessors a scientific approach to detection. For the former this scientific approach means using certain tools to solve crime and for the latter it involves a particular mental process – in other words, in *CSI* the machine serves as a detective, whereas in golden age fiction the detective tends to think like a machine. The distinction is important, and for reasons that we return to below.

The *CSI* detectives are also, like their golden age predecessors, focused on the work of restoring order. As the CSI Catherine Willows comments in the pilot episode of *CSI*, 'we restore peace of mind, and when you're a victim, that's everything'. If *CSI* shares with golden age fiction an interest in restoring order, it shares with hard-boiled fiction a certain vision of the social world as intrinsically dangerous and troubling – and irreparably so. Like the novels of Chandler and Hammett, *CSI* is set in a city mired by criminality. Here it's Las Vegas that provides the backdrop, and the various possibilities the city offers for hedonism and excitement – gambling, drug taking, and alcohol –

are frequently implicated in crime. This isn't to suggest that *CSI* urges us to consider how social problems might cause crime. In fact, there are very rarely deep reasons for committing a crime in *CSI*: murder is often the unintended consequence of someone lashing out and losing their temper with a loved-one, or recklessness and misunderstanding on the part of the perpetrator. Overall, murder rarely has a rational basis in *CSI*, and this is particularly true of the various storylines where the CSI team has to deal with a serial killer (indeed, the very first case, in the pilot episode, is a signature killing).

The world of *CSI* is, then, a bad place. Unlike the world of the hard-boiled novel, though, it is an amoral universe without any real shape. In Chandler's and Hammett's novels, generally speaking, bad things happen to bad people in the bad areas of the city. In the world of *CSI*, evil resides anywhere and everywhere: killers can be deranged psychopaths, but they can also be (and more frequently are) spouses, lovers, friends, colleagues, daughters, and reckless strangers. If golden age novels show us a contracted, genteel social world and hard-boiled novels help us imagine a powerful criminal underworld, *CSI* is about an amorphous social world of random and often inexplicable violence. Another way of looking at this is to say that the world of *CSI* lacks social structure. Again, this is in sharp contrast to previous types of detective fiction. The events of a golden age and hard-boiled detective novel take place in social worlds with distinct hierarchies and structures – they allow us to enter the echelons of the upper-middle classes, or the subterranean world of crime bosses, their lackeys, and molls. Violence, in these stories, has a social context and explanation, and has some sort of relationship to power and status. This is rarely the case in *CSI*, and where a murder does reflect these sorts of interests – as is the case, for example, in season one's 'Pledging Mr Johnson', where a college student murders one of his peers because he suspects him of coming on to his girlfriend – the desire to maintain or thwart power is a purely private concern, rather than a manifestation of complex social hierarchies. This might make us think again about the meaning of order in *CSI*. In Auden's formula, the classical detective story ends with social order fully restored. This is impossible in the world of *CSI*: properly speaking, there is no social order to be restored, just the possibility of finding 'peace of mind' for individuals.

The fictional CSI detectives provide a type of detective-work that is perfectly suited to this distinctive world of crime and victimisation. For example, it seems particularly important that *CSI* – like other police procedurals – portrays detection as a work-a-day pursuit carried out by a team of professionals. In a world in which anyone can be victimised, violence becomes a more everyday concern. Under these social circumstances, individual detectives aren't shipped in to solve specific and discrete problems. Instead teams of professional detectives are needed to perform the ongoing work of surveillance and crime control. It's notable, given this, that most episodes of *CSI* feature more than one case: crime, and so detection, never ceases in this social world. Crime is not, as is the case in golden age fiction, an aberration to be cleaned up, nor, as is the case in hard-boiled fiction, something that might be contained to certain quarters: it spills out everywhere.

In this respect *CSI* vividly reflects how we have come to perceive the problem of crime in the twenty-first century. In most economically advanced countries, there is a widespread perception that crime has become a problem of epidemic proportions. Politicians speak of the need to wage 'war' on drugs and terrorism, surveys indicate that most people imagine crime to be increasing, and mass media outlets frequently proclaim the need for more police and prison places. For criminologists, this is all rather bemusing – the overall rate of crime has been on a steady *decrease* since the mid-1990s in most economically advanced countries. Why, then, does public perception run so dramatically counter to reality (as it's presented in official statistics, at least)? There are lots of possible explanations. Perhaps the rate of unrecorded crime has increased, leading to a disjuncture between official data and personal experience. Another argument – and one I favour – is that the perception that crime is spiralling out of control is connected to our sense that we live in an increasingly atomised, amorphous social world. Post-modern social theorists commonly suggest that, since the 1970s, we've seen a loosening of social ties and expectations and a valorisation of individual desire and identity. More of us move away from our home-towns and norms related to social class, gender, and nationality appear less fixed and deterministic. In this sort of world, strangers are a more significant feature of our everyday lives, our social world appears less clearly structured, and it might be less clear what we can expect from people in given social situations – combined, these give rise to a belief that there's a real risk of random violence. Put differently, when we feel that those we live alongside are fundamentally similar and known to us, violence is likely to be a relatively marginal concern. In contrast, when we feel that our social world is inhabited mainly by people we don't really know or recognise as particular social types, random violence is likely to become a more central concern.

This isn't to say, of course, that we imagine all crime to be carried out by strangers (though this might be a particular source of worry for us). What we can reasonably suggest, though, is that modern living arrangements and social conditions have given rise to a distinctive set of fears: that crime is widespread and mainly random, can happen anywhere, that there is no likely perpetrator or victim, and that what is therefore needed is ongoing surveillance and detection. If we see *CSI* as a distillation of these fears, we might well wonder whether it also offers up a model moral arbiter in its depiction of the contemporary detective. Here, too, a comparison with earlier forms of detective fiction is useful. In golden age fiction, the detective's ability to judge comes from his or her position as a social outsider to the group being investigated and, in certain instances, his or her status as a social authority figure. In contrast, in hard-boiled fiction, the detective's authority comes from his closeness to the social world under investigation, his sense of familiarity with the pecuniary and bodily temptations that make crime possible. In *CSI*, the detectives' authority does not principally reside in personal characteristics or status – and this marks the programme, and the forensics police procedural sub-genre, out from other forms of detective fiction. In *CSI* it is science and technology that provide the privileged vantage point usually reserved for the lead detective. As Cavender and Deutsch (2007) argue, *CSI* invests science with moral authority.

There's more going on here than a simple valorisation of scientific testing and electronic databases as a means of determining 'the truth' of a situation. What's also important to note is that detection in *CSI* is an antiseptic pursuit, a process, as Gever (2005: 446) observes, that is principally mechanical rather than based on human endeavour. Thus the detectives are absolved from much of the moral responsibility involved in detection: after all, it's test results, rather than them personally, that distinguish guilt. We might add here that the fact that detection is carried out by a team in *CSI* helps also to limit individual liability for the outcomes of detection.

As audience members we might find this comforting. Ours is a culture characterised by a grave sense of doubt concerning the possibility for impartial human judgement. Take, by way of example, the fact that we now ask judges in serious criminal trials to apply a formula to calculate an offender's sentence rather than use their discretion and personal judgement. In *CSI*, the problems of human error and prejudice appear to be cancelled out by the fact that denouncements can be made in an objective manner, through scientific tests and electronic searches. This says more about our scepticism concerning human impartiality than the actual workings of the criminal justice system. Our criminal justice system relies very heavily on human skills of detection: after all, database checks are devised and interpreted by criminal justice personnel. That *CSI* obscures all this indicates its – and our – discomfort with the idea that detection is fundamentally a matter of human judgement.

## Questions for discussion

Q1)  Why is detective fiction so enduringly popular?
Q2)  How might we explain the recent emergence and appeal of forensics police procedural television programmes such as *CSI*?

Q3)   What are the core similarities and differences between *CSI* and golden age fiction? How might we account for the differences?

## Recommended fiction

*The Big Sleep* (dir. H. Hawks, 1946). USA: Warner Bros.

Chandler, R. (2000 [originally 1939]) *The Big Sleep and Other Novels*. London: Penguin.

Christie, A. (1948 [originally 1938]) *Appointment with Death*. London: Penguin.

Christie, A. (2007 [originally *Ten Little Niggers*, 1939]) *And Then There Were None*. London: Harper.

Collins, W. (1998 [originally 1868]) *The Moonstone*. London: Penguin.

Doyle, A.C. (1999) 'The Sign of Four' in A.C. Doyle *The Original and Complete Illustrated 'Strand' Sherlock Holmes: Vol. I*. London: Wordsworth, pp. 64–113.

Hammett, D. (1982 [originally 1930]) *The Maltese Falcon, Dashiell Hammett: The Four Great Novels*. London: Picador.

*The Maltese Falcon* (dir. R.D. Ruth, 1941). USA: Warner Bros.

Poe, E.A. (2009) *Edgar Allan Poe: The Complete Short Story Collection*. London: CreateSpace Publishing.

## Recommended reading

Cavender, Gray and Deutsch, Sarah K. (2007) '*CSI* and Moral Authority: The Police and Science', *Crime, Media, Culture*, 3(1): 67–81.
Based on a close analysis of episodes of *CSI*, Cavender and Deutsch's article focuses on the moral authority afforded to the police and science in *CSI*.

Chandler, Raymond (1988 [originally 1944]) 'The Simple Art of Murder' in R. Chandler *The Simple Art of Murder*. USA: Vintage, pp. 1–18.
Chandler's brilliant essay compares British golden age crime fiction and hard-boiled fiction from the USA. Highly recommended.

Evans, Mary (2009) *The Imagination of Evil: Detective Fiction and the Modern World*. London: Continuum.
A wide-ranging, sociologically oriented, and insightful discussion of detective fiction and its relationship to modern sensibilities. Highly recommended.

Gever, Martha (2005) 'The Spectacle of Crime, Digitalized: Crime Scene Investigation *and Social Anatomy*', *European Journal of Cultural Studies*, 8(4): 445–463.
A discussion of the use and meaning of scientific imagery in *CSI*.

Scraggs, John (2005) *Crime Fiction*. London: Routledge.
Scraggs' book provides a good overview of crime fiction. The discussion of Christie's novels is especially useful.

# Passing judgement: the 'double trial structure' of four Hollywood legal dramas

**Recommended viewing**

We compare two Hollywood trial movies from the 1950s to two Hollywood trial movies from the 1990s in this chapter:

Sidney Lumet (dir.) (1957) *12 Angry Men*. USA: MGM, United Artists.
Otto Preminger (dir.) (1959) *Anatomy of a Murder*. USA: Columbia Pictures.
Francis Ford Coppola (dir.) (1997) *The Rainmaker*. USA: Constellation Films.
Alan J. Pakula (dir.) (1993) *The Pelican Brief*. USA: Warner Bros.

You may well find you get more out of this chapter if you watch at least one film from each period.

From Erle Stanley Gardner's books about the fast-talking defence barrister Perry Mason to the recent rash of television programmes set in the law firm and courtroom, the criminal trial is an enduringly popular subject for drama. To be more precise, the *Anglo-American* version of the trial is an enduringly popular subject. Scholars of criminology and legal studies will be well aware that there are various different judicial systems around the world, and that we generally speak of there being two main types of trial: one following an inquisitorial model, favoured by much of continental Europe, and one following an accusatorial or adversarial model, used in the USA and UK (and most of the latter's ex-colonies). In the inquisitorial system, the trial is generally characterised as a collective search for the truth: the judge takes a more active role in proceedings, much more documentary evidence is used, and the overall aim is to uncover what happened. In the adversarial system, the trial is a battle between legal advocates. The idea is that the truth will 'out' if two opposing parties, represented by legally trained orators, put their different versions of events across. The judge is a referee in this system, and the lawyers dominate proceedings. It is this model of criminal justice, and this allied version of the serious trial, that dominates film and television representations of the judicial process – to such an extent that you'd be forgiven for thinking that this was *the only* type of trial.

Why is this version of the trial so prevalent in the mass media? One explanation lies in the dominance of the Hollywood film and television industries. It's perhaps no surprise that US film directors and script writers should choose to tell stories about their native systems of criminal justice. There's a further curious observation to be made here, though, and that is that the USA and the UK are pretty much the *only* producers of legal dramas: this simply isn't an important genre for either the established Indian and French film industries, or the growing Iranian and South Korean film industries. One possible explanation for this is that the adversarial system has more cinematic potential than the less intrinsically dramatic inquisitorial system. Another possibility is that film conventions peculiar to Hollywood lend themselves particularly well to depicting the adversarial courtroom: that *this sort* of trial suits *this sort* of cinema, and *vice versa*. Take, for example, the Hollywood convention of cross-cutting between two people. This is brilliantly suited to conveying the to-and-fro battle of wits between the two legal advocates in the adversarial courtroom. The structure of the classical Hollywood film – as in most classical European story forms – includes a final climax and resolution. The adversarial trial, with its final denouncement of 'guilty' or 'not guilty', is well suited to precisely this sort of narrative structure.

Given all this, it is perhaps unsurprising that legal drama has been a terrifically popular film genre in Hollywood for many decades and, as Silbey (2007: 131) points out, has been around since the very early years of cinema. The film legal drama flourished during the late period of the so-called 'Golden Age' of Hollywood cinema – the 1930s to the 1960s. Indeed, in the American Bar Association's 2008 list of the 'Top 25 Trial Movies' more than a quarter were released during the period 1957–1962 (Brust 2008). This is the period during which Gregory Peck played Atticus Finch in *To Kill a Mockingbird* (1962, dir. Robert Mulligan), Agatha Christie's screenplay *Witness for the Prosecution* (1957, dir. Billy Wilder) was realised, and Henry Fonda took on an entire jury in *12 Angry Men* (1957, dir. Sidney Lumet).

This chapter provides an analysis of two of the films from Hollywood's Golden Age and two Hollywood legal dramas from the mid-1990s, a period that saw a resurgence of interest in the genre. In comparing these films I've found it particularly useful to think about what Clover (1998) describes as the 'double-trial structure' usually found in legal dramas. In most films in this genre, Clover suggests, a defendant is put on trial and, by way of a sub-plot, an idea or principle is 'on trial' too. Think, for example, about the film *Philadelphia* (1993, dir. Jonathan Demme), in which Andrew Beckett (played by Tom Hanks) sues his former employer for wrongful dismissal. He claims that his boss fired him after finding out that he was homosexual and HIV-positive. The trial is about deducing Beckett's employers' motivations for firing him, but the film also asks us to think about the wider issue of discrimination, its basis, extent, and personal consequences. Social values, as much as an individual corporation, are 'on trial' here. Before examining the 'double trial structure' of the four films chosen for analysis in this chapter, we consider some core themes in legal dramas, namely the courtroom as a place of performance, spectatorship, and judgement.

## Places of performance, spectatorship, and judgement: the courtroom in legal drama

Courtroom proceedings lend themselves to dramatisation. Take, by way of example, the nature of the news coverage given to celebrity trials during the 1990s, such as those of Michael Jackson and O.J. Simpson. Fox, Van Sickel, and Steigel (2007) convincingly argue that news outlets reported on the events as if they were soap opera storylines, with television news channels even broadcasting dramatic reconstructions of courtroom sessions. Coverage of these so-called 'mega-trials', they argue, tended to blend a mode of address associated with neutral news reporting and a style that is meant to titillate and entertain – hence Fox *et al.*'s suggestion that this type of news coverage constitutes 'infotainment'. There are, of course, all sorts of explanations for the rise of the 'mega-trial' – including the rise of a 'Celebrity Culture', the trend towards tabloidisation in news reporting, and the relative cheapness of this sort of coverage. We should also recognise that today's journalists and news broadcasters are simply seizing upon the courtroom's potential as a place of performance. Courtrooms are, after all, often organised as auditoriums, and judges and lawyers dress for their parts (most evident, of course, within the British system where legal representatives wear robes and wigs). Papke (1999: 474) points out that 'trials were ideal for the early film industry' because of the relative ease of producing a film set for a courtroom: the latter is easy to light and sound travels well – partly, we might reasonably surmise, because it is already, by design, a place that promotes performance.

Many film legal dramas – the main subject of this chapter – ask us to think about the courtroom as a space for performance. Take, for example, the conventional establishing shot used in films at the start of courtroom proceedings or the summing-up session: the camera pans across an empty courtroom and the vacant rows of jurors' chairs. It's a curious convention: films and television programmes rarely incorporate shots of what are essentially *unpeopled sets*. Far from this disrupting our experience as viewers by making us suddenly conscious that we're watching a film, the sight instead chimes with what we imagine a real-life courtroom to be like: a set, akin to that of the theatre, constantly ready to receive a fresh set of characters to perform and spectate.

When we look closely at individual legal dramas we find that many are centrally concerned with the idea that the jury are spectators to a performance. Take, for example, the 1907 film, *Falsely Accused!*, described by Clover (1998: 259) as the first trial movie – it's certainly a very early example. The film opens with a shot of a young woman holding a bloody knife over her father's dead body: she's subsequently accused of his murder (falsely, as the title of the film suggests). Her case looks desperate, until her boyfriend discovers that a film camera was left running whilst the murder took place, capturing the entire attack. He gets the film processed and shows it in the courtroom, thus revealing – to both the audience and jury at once – the truth of what happened. As Silbey (2007: 141) notes, the scene collapses the distinction between the courtroom and film theatre and asks us to recognise the affinity between the jury's and film spectator's role as judges.

The scene also relies upon the idea that film can disclose the objective truth of a situation. As Silbey (ibid.) has it, 'the film glorifies the capacity of film to reveal and clarify the world'. In this sense, Silbey argues, film has 'an inherent affinity' to law: 'Both stake claims to an authoritative form of knowledge based on the indubitable quality of observable phenomena. Both are preoccupied (sometimes to the point of self-defeat) with sustaining the authority that underlies the knowledge produced by visual perception' (p. 131). The claim is a little over-stretched, but we could certainly say that judging – witnessing and determining the truth of what happened – are central pursuits for both a film audience and a jury. We can draw the connection out further. Moving and still photographs appear to simply show us something or someone – they give the illusion of unmediated perception. Films often challenge our sense of there being a straightforward connection between visual perception and reality by reminding us that, in some cases, appearances deceive, we see what we want to believe, and what we see is restricted by our vantage point. These are also central problems faced by a jury in weighing up witness testimonies. Given all this, legal dramas are potentially deeply revealing of the judicial process, not just in terms of giving us an idea of what that process might be like but, more importantly, in terms of prompting us to think about the contingent nature of truth and the problems of partiality in witnessing and judging.

## Golden Age legal drama: law on trial

We turn now to examine *12 Angry Men* and *Anatomy of a Murder*. Both are excellent examples of the Golden Age Hollywood legal drama. Famously, *12 Angry Men* focuses on a jury's deliberations, with the action taking place almost entirely within a jury room. The film begins – after an establishing shot of the courthouse and a travelling shot through the halls of justice – with a judge's closing remarks to a jury. He runs through a well-rehearsed script: this is a serious case (first degree murder), the jurors must 'separate fact from fancy', and establish whether or not the defendant is guilty beyond reasonable doubt. The verdict must be unanimous for a sentence to be passed, and, such is the gravity of the charge, a 'guilty' verdict will mean that the defendant – a young man of 18 – is automatically sent to the electric chair. The action moves to the inside of a small chamber, the space taken up mainly by a long table – this is the jury room and the setting for most of the film. As we watch the jurors file in they remove jackets, loosen ties, mop sweat from their faces, light cigarettes, and glance at their watches. This is the hottest day of the year – and the fan doesn't work. No one, it seems, particularly wants to be here, and certainly not for too long. They busy themselves with anything but court business: one guy opens a newspaper to find out about his shares portfolio, another starts doodling, and others are chatting. 'Let's vote', one juror offers, 'and then we can all get out of here'. The men are asked for a show of hands for a 'guilty' verdict: eight hands shoot up; another three slowly join them. Only one stays down. It belongs to juror number eight, played by Henry Fonda (we only learn the character's name in the final scene – in fact, we're only given two names during the whole film: even the defendant is referred to throughout as the 'kid'). 'There's always one' a juror mumbles off-screen. 'You really think he's innocent?' another asks incredulously. 'I don't know', Fonda replies simply. Why, then, the others want to know, is he so keen to stall proceedings on this appallingly hot day? There's a baseball game on soon, after all. 'It's not easy to raise my hand and send a kid off to die without talking about it' is Fonda's answer: 'he's had a pretty miserable eighteen years and I just think we owe him a few words, that's all'. This is the opening premise of *12 Angry Men*: eleven jurors are convinced a man is guilty of murder and are immediately ready to send him to his death; a twelfth (Fonda) thinks there's reasonable doubt. The film clearly validates Fonda's position: conspicuously dressed in a light-coloured suit, he slowly demolishes the other jurors' arguments and reveals glaring holes in the case. The defending lawyer wasn't up to much, he protests at the start: it certainly seems that way, as he convincingly tears his way through what originally seemed like conclusive proof of the young man's guilt.

What's more important than Fonda's dismissal of the apparently water-tight case, though, is his slow unpicking of the other jurors' prejudices. The two jurors most fiercely set on finding the young man guilty are clearly prej-udicial: one because of an ingrained racism (the defendant appears to be Hispanic); the other because of deep-seated feelings of antipathy towards his own no-good son. In one famous scene, late on in the film, the bitterly racist juror number ten (Ed Begley) vents his anger after realising that all but three of them have changed their verdict to 'not guilty'. He launches into a long, vitriolic monologue that ends with him asking the others: 'This kid on trial here, his type, well don't you know about them?' 'There's a danger here', he adds, more softly now because it's obvious he's lost the argument: 'Don't you know these people are dangerous … they're wild …'. In a minimalistic and basically unchanging mise-en-scène, camera movement helps produce a sense of story and character development – so, too, in this scene. The camera starts with a mid-shot of the speaker and slowly moves out to show other jurors standing up one by one and turning away from him: the effect is to distance the audience, like the jurors, from the appallingly racist views being expressed. Juror number ten finally runs out of steam and, realising his marginalised position, takes up a corner spot away from the others. Our hero-protagonist, juror number eight, starts speaking again and the others re-take their seats at the table: he is fully at the heart of proceedings by this point in the film. 'It's always difficult to keep personal prejudice out of a thing like this', he begins. As he delivers the speech the camera, having achieved some great distance from the vitriolic juror number ten, slowly returns to a close-up of Fonda. We even get, at the end of this scene, a direct look to camera. The implication is clear: this is the morally superior position, one that we are supposed to share.

Such devices make *12 Angry Men* feel rather hokey. Certainly, the film is declamatory about the value of certain abstract principles that underpin the US jury system: the importance of such things as reasonable doubt, unpreju-diced jury deliberation, and burden of proof. It's particularly notable that characters' names are withheld from us: it's a rather heavy-handed way of reinforcing that what matters is the role people play in the legal system rather than their personal identity and status. It's important to recognise, though, that the film is more than a straightforward assertion of the US legal system. For one thing, it's a vivid depiction of the practical difficulties in getting juries to adhere to the principles that ensure a free and fair trial. In particular, the film shows that humans tend to make quick and instinctive decisions about someone's guilt, and that this mental process is somewhat at odds with that required by the serious trial where jurors must decide whether the prosecu-tion has proved, beyond reasonable doubt, that someone is guilty. Looked at from this perspective, criminal law and judicial procedure are under scrutiny in *12 Angry Men* – and they don't come out terribly well. After all, we don't end the film feeling that all is basically right with the jury trial. The evidence against the young man is overwhelming, and it's entirely possible, as juror number eight comments, that the jury is talking themselves into letting a guilty and deeply violent man go free. Whatever the truth of the situation, we can't help but be struck by the fact that eleven jurors have been easily talked into and then out of finding someone guilty of murder. In this sense, the film prompts a deep ambivalence about the role of rhetoric in the judicial process, in both the courtroom and jury room.

Certainly, our overall impression of the deliberation process is that 'it's not an exact science', as one of the jurors puts it. Rhetoric, prejudice, and peer pressure all introduce biases, and their effects are often hidden. Take, for example, the reasoning of juror number four (E.G. Marshall). Throughout the film he insists on the importance of approaching the case objectively and concentrating on the facts. He is the most reasonable and consistent in his argument about the defendant's guilt and is the penultimate character to change his verdict to 'not guilty'. He does so for one simple reason: he suddenly realises that his observations have been led by a presumption of guilt rather than any methodological assessment of the facts. One of the key bits of testimony comes from a neighbour who claims to have witnessed, through her bedroom window, the defendant stabbing his father. Several of the jurors comment that they saw marks on the witness's nose that suggest she wears glasses – it's an important observation because, of course, she wouldn't have been wearing glasses in bed when she claimed to have seen the defendant. Juror number four's discomfort is obvious: he can remember those marks too, but he simply hadn't *seen* them before, he says. The implication is that he has somehow been partial in what he *has* seen and factored into his objective assessment of the case.

*Anatomy of a Murder* (1959, dir. Otto Preminger) is interested too in the problem of partiality in the criminal trial, but here the focus is on the construction of a defence case and its tenuous relationship to truth and reality. The film focuses on Paul Biegler (James Stewart), a lawyer who half-heartedly agrees to defend a homicide case. The case has already achieved notoriety: Lieutenant Manion freely admits to killing a man – Barney Quill – after learning that he'd raped his wife. Biegler hesitates in accepting the job of defending the lieutenant, not least of all because the Manions don't really present themselves as ideal clients: the defendant is insolent, Mrs Manion distractingly flirty. Moreover, from a legal point of view the case is difficult to defend – as Lieutenant Manion originally frames it, at least. The central problem – in terms of legal defence – is that, after learning of his wife's assault,

Manion waited a full hour before going out and killing Quill. In legal terms, he has no justification for the act, despite his insistence that he has 'unwritten law' on his side. There's no such thing, Biegler retorts, only technical legal rules: the jury will need a 'legal peg' on which to hang a 'not guilty' verdict.

Early on, then, the film draws a distinction between 'unwritten' and 'written' law. The idea is that formal, 'written' law should be seen as something distinct from our instinctive sense of what constitutes justified violence: part of a lawyer's job is to help a defendant shape his version of the facts in such a way as to fit legal definitions. This, of course, may mean shaving-off details that are unnecessary to the storyline of the case and adding story elements to conform to a legally accepted script. In short, we're being asked to see the criminal law in terms of a narrative formula into which 'real' events must be fitted. In *Anatomy of a Murder* this is seen as a standard feature of the legal process. Biegler's initial refusal to coach Manion into constructing a defence story is seen as inappropriate lawyerly conduct: maybe 'you're too pure ... for the natural impurities of the law', teases his legal associate.

This conception of the law as being 'naturally' impure helps obscure the ethical problems with the practice of witness coaching. Biegler clearly finds his friend's argument persuasive. On returning to see Manion he decides to nudge him in the direction of a more legally acceptable defence. He explains that, of the four ways he can defend a murder charge, three are straightforwardly inapplicable to this case – the murder can't even be framed as legally justified because Manion left a significant amount of time between finding out about the attack on his wife and carrying out the murder. To be 'not guilty', Biegler adds, more slowly now, Manion needs to latch upon an *excuse*, not a *justification*.

Biegler is careful to add that he's not *telling* the defendant what to say but is simply explaining the legal process. Still, his intimations are rather obvious. 'What excuses are there?' Manion wonders aloud, clearly mulling things over. 'I must have been mad', he offers, suddenly looking up at Biegler for affirmation that this fits the bill. Anger won't cut it as an excuse, the lawyer points out, looking for the necessary and legally appropriate qualification on Manion's part. 'I mean I must have been *crazy* ... am I getting warmer?' is the defendant's response.

This is just the first step in story construction for the defence. Manion quickly gets the idea, and his testimony thereafter (both to Biegler and in court) is directed principally towards underwriting a plea of 'irresistible impulse', a variant of the temporary insanity defence. He now claims to have significant gaps in his memory and experiences disassociation when remembering the events of that evening. There are other ways in which the defence's case is clearly a work of construction. Take, for example, Biegler's coaching of Manion's wife on how to dress appropriately for the courtroom (thus guarding against the risk that the jury see her as having provoked her attacker). Even Biegler's performance in the courtroom is a clever ruse: finding himself up against a slick prosecution team he presents himself as a plain-speaking underdog.

In this film, at least, legal defence is centrally the work of creating and then casting an overall impression, one that is in the service of legal rules and jury manipulation, and not necessarily the truth. The grand illusion works: Manion is acquitted. In the final scene of the film, Biegler turns up at the Manions' trailer to collect his fee, only to find that they've skipped town. Lieutenant Manion has left a note, though: he had an 'irresistible impulse' to leave. The implication of the joke is clear: dressing it up and giving it a fancy name might make a repellent act excusable in the clinical terms of the law, but in terms of real-life experience it's another matter.

As with *12 Angry Men*, we're probably left feeling deeply ambivalent about the uses and procedure of the criminal trial in *Anatomy of a Murder*. It's important, I think, that both films deny us a final sense of justice. In both cases, we're left feeling unsure that the defendant is innocent (or even 'not guilty'). Instead, we've been asked to see the truth as contingent and constructed, and the principles of criminal law as complicit in this. Setting is important in achieving this effect. The vast majority of scenes across the two films occur in the courthouse, or else in prisons and police offices. The consistency of setting is particularly marked in *12 Angry Men*, where the jury room is the setting for all but a handful of scenes. The opening scene of this film is a shot of the front of the courthouse. In *Anatomy of a Murder* we start with an outside shot of the defence lawyer's office. In both cases it's clear that these films are fundamentally about the legal system. Both, too, emphasise the pivotal role of the articulate advocate in this system – whether that's the principled juror or the canny defence lawyer. Silbey (2007) suggests that this conception of the legal process chimes with more general principles of US jurisprudence and citizenship, and specifically the rather romantic idea that one man, speaking freely and rationally, can make all the difference. When we think carefully about *12 Angry Men* and *Anatomy of a Murder* we might conclude that the films illuminate the problems with this ideal: both trials are decided on the basis of one man's interventions, but not at all satisfactorily, and most certainly not with a sense that this has been expedient to the truth.

## Legal drama of the mid-1990s: corporate greed and political self-interest on trial

We skip forward several decades now, and consider a couple of legal dramas from the mid-1990s. This was a period when legal drama was experiencing something of a resurgence in popularity: the television series *LA Law* (NBC) was launched in 1994 to wide acclaim, a few years later Fox launched its popular show *Ally McBeal*, and throughout the decade John Grisham's novels – most of them legal thrillers drawing on the author's experiences as a lawyer – were topping the best-seller book charts. Hollywood too was busy producing legal dramas again. In both the late 1950s and mid-1990s, then, the judicial process seems to have a particular cultural salience – comparing legal dramas from each period is really instructive in understanding the changing cultural meaning of the trial and legal process.

We'll be looking at two films in this section of the chapter, both of which are adaptations of John Grisham novels: *The Pelican Brief* (1993, dir. Alan J. Pakula) and *The Rainmaker* (1997, dir. Francis Ford Coppola). They are just two of a large number of highly popular Grisham film adaptations released in the mid-1990s, including *The Client* (1994, dir. Joel Schumacher), *The Firm* (1993, dir. Sydney Pollack), and *A Time to Kill* (1996, dir. Joel Schumacher). *The Pelican Brief* is about a law student's bid to bring to justice those responsible for the killing of two US supreme court judges. Motivated by the fact that her law professor (and lover) is old friends with one of the victims, Darby Shaw (Julia Roberts) decides to research the case. She has a hunch that there must be a connection between the legal judgements made by the two men that helps explain the motivation for the killings. On closer inspection it turns out that both judges had consistently ruled against cases involving environmental destruction. Shaw alights upon a theory: a powerful oil tycoon ordered the judges' killings because he believed they would obstruct his plans to set up a high-polluting business on an island inhabited by pelicans. She writes a legal brief alleging as much – the 'pelican brief' of the film's title – that subsequently gets into the hands of the FBI, who have been tasked by the President with investigating the judges' murders. They're keen to investigate further, but there's an obstacle. The businessman accused of ordering the killings provided very significant financial support to the President during his election campaign. On seeing Shaw's brief, the President promptly orders the FBI to drop their investigation and instead recruits the CIA to pursue other leads and quiet Shaw. Finding herself the object of government persecution, Shaw joins forces with an investigative journalist, Gray Grantham (Denzel Washington), and together they write a newspaper article that details the argument of the pelican brief and implicates the White House in covering up the crime.

*The Rainmaker* (1997, dir. Coppola) is also substantially about the perils of corporate greed. The film's protagonist is Rudy Baylor (Matt Damon), a new law graduate who can't find a job. Desperate to avoid going bankrupt, he joins forces with an ex-insurance assessor turned lawyer, Deck Shifflet (Danny DeVito). They take on the case of a down-at-heel couple, the Blacks, whose son Buddy is dying from leukaemia because their insurance company refused to pay out for a bone marrow transplant. The odds are stacked against them: the insurance company has hired a slick and experienced legal team and this is Baylor's very first case (his courtroom delivery is often faltering and light on patter, his movement around the courtroom clumsy). Baylor wins, of course: we wouldn't expect any other conclusion given how much is made of him being the underdog. The characterisation is one we're familiar with in legal dramas – just think again about Paul Biegler in *Anatomy of a Murder*. It's worth remembering, though, that it's Biegler himself who's responsible for constructing the idea that he's a legal underdog as a means of currying favour with the jury: the David and Goliath story that usually characterises legal drama is here used to canny effect in the creation of a legal defence. Thus, in *Anatomy of a Murder* we are asked to see the lawyer-as-underdog characterisation as a rather cynical legal ploy to manipulate the jury. In *The Rainmaker* we are the ones being worked upon; we are asked to believe that there are good guys and bad guys here, *genuine* Davids and Goliaths.

In *The Rainmaker* this battle is played out between a down-at-heel, young lawyer with a low-income client and the advocates of a wealthy, uncaring, and negligent company. Impossibly calm in the witness box, the company's CEO (Roy Scheider) addresses Baylor as 'son'. Baylor ignores the slight and directs the executive's attention to the fact that his company pays out on a very small number of claims. A report from the company's medical committee frames investment in clinics and medical resources as '*financially justified*': money, Baylor adds, is the only thing that matters to this company, not the health needs of their clients. In summing up he returns to this point and draws attention to the vast sums of money spent by the insurance company on legal representation and political lobbying. As in *The Pelican Brief*, corporate wealth is seen to beget legal and political influence.

*The Rainmaker* – and many other Grisham film adaptations besides – is interested in a rather broad set of relationships between government, big law firms, and big business. The legal process and courtroom proceedings are of interest, but to a lesser degree than in *12 Angry Men* and *Anatomy of a Murder*. It's notable, for example, that in *The Rainmaker* the first 40 minutes of the film concern Baylor's difficulties in securing a legal position and tapping into the lucrative world of the law firm. Even after embarking upon the legal case Baylor's personal life remains a focus: a number of scenes are devoted to his heroic last-minute passing of the bar exam that allows him to represent the Blacks in court and his blossoming relationship with a female victim of domestic violence.

In *The Pelican Brief* the focus is fully on the pre-trial process, something that we find in a number of other film adaptations of Grisham's books from this period. In *The Firm*, for example, a new lawyer (Tom Cruise) discovers that the legal firm he's just joined has links to the Mob. He must covertly gather evidence on their activities to help the FBI bring them to book. This emphasis on the pre-trial process of evidence gathering opens up narrative possibilities. Freed from the courtroom, the legal advocates in *The Pelican Brief* and *The Firm* get involved in car chases, shootings, and espionage. The protagonists in both films are smart and articulate, like their trial movie predecessors of the late 1950s, but they must also undertake all sorts of stunts – including escaping exploding cars and running from contract killers. In fact, both films are best described as *legal thrillers*, incorporating elements of the legal drama and the action film.

It's worth pausing for a moment to consider the relatively recent emergence and success of this new hybrid genre (of which the Grisham film adaptations of the mid-1990s serve as useful examples). The success of the legal thriller can be explained in part by the dominance of the action film genre since the 1970s and, relatedly, an increased reliance on spectacle in Hollywood cinema. Film scholars routinely draw a distinction between narrative and spectacle: the former tends to be used to refer to a storyline, the latter to more stand-alone, awe-inspiring displays. It's perhaps easiest to think about the two concepts in relation to the film Musical: the story is interspersed with big, showy musical numbers. The relatively new genre of the Hollywood action film is one in which spectacle often exists in a particularly tenuous relationship to narrative: these films tend to 'exalt the sheer spectacle of the image', as Nelmes puts it (2003: 164). You might have experienced something like this yourself when watching an action film or thriller: an extended chase, big explosion, or shoot-out seems to be included simply for the purposes of visual stimulation.

It's sometimes suggested that the rise of the action genre marks a shift towards a more spectacle-oriented Hollywood cinema – and that films today are more focused on stimulating the senses then coherent story-telling. This is to ignore the fact that cinematic spectacle was a fundamental component of early cinema, as Tom Gunning (1990) has pointed out. It's also to imagine that narrative and spectacle are mutually exclusive, the former always demanding a complex cognitive response, the latter a more base affective reaction. The dramatic courtroom scenes of the classic 1950s legal dramas are, for example, rather difficult to place in terms of their relationship to spectacle and narrative. What we can say, though, is that legal dramas from the mid-1990s rely upon set pieces borrowed from the action film genre, and that the spectacle of these scenes rarely has anything to do with the legal process.

There is much that nonetheless makes *The Pelican Brief* recognisable as a legal drama. Like *Anatomy of a Murder* and *12 Angry Men*, the film starts with an establishing shot of a law building, namely the Supreme Court of the United States (used also in the opening shot of *The Rainmaker*). The film also includes a number of scenes that showcase the skill involved in legal advocacy. Take, for example, an extended scene from a university law class – shots of attentive students listening to the fluent argument of their professor confirm that, like the courtroom, this is a place where those skilled in legal oratory perform. The law professor's speech focuses on the idea that, as he puts it, 'passion and self-interest are threats to liberty'. In most Grisham film adaptations, it is the second of these that seems particularly dangerous. 'Everyone is assuming that the motive is hatred or revenge …', Darby Shaw wistfully comments on the mass media coverage of the judges' deaths. What if, she wonders aloud, it's good old-fashioned material greed that's the motive? It's not, of course, just the actions of greedy businessmen that have deleterious consequences – what's also 'on trial' in this film is the self-interestedness of politicians. 'Never fails to amaze me what a man'll do to get an oval office', one of the judges comments before his untimely death. By the end of the movie we probably share his sense of incredulity at the lengths to which politicians in this film are willing to go to realise their ambitions.

## Concluding discussion

Most of the Grisham film adaptations of the mid-1990s confirm the view that power and money corrupt: most people will *do anything*, it seems, to raise a profit margin, enjoy the high life of corporate largesse, and maintain their political standing. Crimes of the rich and successful are callous and indirect: judges with views that risk derailing a business enterprise can be disposed of and those on a low income who become sick can be sacrificed for the sake of a company's bottom line. The world is a bad place in these films, dominated as it is by big business and cynical politicians. This helps explain why, in most Grisham film adaptations, the hero-lawyer is acting for the prosecution, and not the defence, as is more frequently the case in Golden Age legal dramas of the late 1950s. In the former the threat to all things good and right comes from without, in the latter it comes from within, that is, from the 'impurities of the law' itself. Of particular note here is the fact that many Grisham film adaptations, including *The Pelican Brief* and *The Client*, end with the central character being granted protection by the authorities and going into hiding – such is the powerful reach of politicians and corporate executives. The struggle in both *The Pelican Brief* and *The Rainmaker* is to bring these power brokers to justice, and the law is an instrument in this – even whilst lawyers as a professional class might generally not be. The latter point is an important one: these films put the law 'on trial' only in so far as they critique its practitioners' tendency to cede to corporate greed. This helps account for the tendency for the hero-lawyer to be newly qualified in these films (or, in the case of Darby Shaw, still a student). Unused to the financial benefits that come with a high-powered legal career, these characters are not yet inured to a culture of greed and self-interest (or, in the case of *The Firm*, they stand on the threshold of this sort of life and thus must grapple with the dilemma of choosing wealth or doing the right thing).

The central problem with law in these films, then, is the people who practise it, not the problems inherent in the legal process. This is particularly evident in *The Rainmaker*. In one of several voiceovers, Baylor tells us about his experience of law school: during the first year, everybody was friendly; by the last year it had become a cut-throat environment with students vying for the best-paid graduate positions. That, he adds, is just what lawyers are like. It seems that the only possibility for lawyerly salvation in Grisham film adaptations is giving up on a high-powered law career, and this is precisely the course chosen by the protagonists at the end of both *The Firm* and *The Rainmaker*.

What we get in the Grisham film adaptations of the mid-1990s, then, is an altogether different critique of law to that found in the Golden Age legal dramas of the late 1950s. Legal processes and principles are not 'on trial' here, law is not a discrete social institution, rather it is conceived of in terms of a professional group and commercial enterprise. This might help explain the limited number of scenes set in law buildings in these films, relative, at least, to the amount of time we spend in prisons, police offices, and courts in *Anatomy of a Murder* and *12 Angry Men*.

It's not coincidental, I think, that the film legal dramas of the mid-1990s tend to paint a rather simplistic picture of the law, crime, and right and wrong. There is a distinctly neat moral universe in these films: the good guys and bad guys are easy to identify, the former always win the case, the latter always lose, and simple greed and self-interest are the root of most serious crime. Above all, the judicial process is an undoubtedly sound mechanism for dealing with misdemeanours. In contrast, in both *Anatomy of a Murder* and *12 Angry Men*, we can't be sure whether the defendant is guilty or not, people's motivations (as criminals, lawyers, and jurors) are often difficult to discern, and we're left feeling deeply ambivalent about the legal process. These films suggest that there are intrinsic difficulties in ensuring that the truth will prevail in court. All this has implications for the role of punishment, too. Like juror number eight in *12 Angry Men*, we may well feel uneasy about the prospect of a young man being put to death because his lawyer was too lazy and ill-equipped to put up a proper defence. In this film and *Anatomy of a Murder* we're asked to think about what it means for a defendant to have a fair trial and, linked to this, when and how we should punish. Such considerations are of limited interest in *The Pelican Brief* and *The Rainmaker* where, instead, any tactics to derail the defence are deemed legitimate and punishment is seen as necessary.

These observations are broadly similar to the findings of Lenz (2003) in his comparison of Hollywood crime films from the 1930s to the 2000s. He categorises films according to whether they support a 'due process' or 'crime control' model of criminal justice, described by Lenz as liberal and conservative respectively. In his schema, a liberal depiction of crime and justice is one that foregrounds the defendant's right to a free and fair trial, and a conservative depiction is focused on the need for a punitive response to crime. Films of the early 1960s, he argues, tend to take a more liberal approach to crime and justice whilst conservative depictions have become more dominant since the 1970s. A reasonable objection might be made at this point about the difficulty – and, indeed, desirability – of fitting films into such categories. It's nonetheless worth noting that the cultural-historical shift identified by Lenz finds ample support in criminological accounts of changing attitudes towards crime and justice. The eminent US criminologist, David Garland (2001), for example, suggests that, before the 1970s, policy and legislation in the USA and UK were focused on offender rights and rehabilitation and, since then, we've seen the rise of more punitive measures to tackle crime. It may be that legal dramas reflect this shift. Certainly, our close reading of two films from the late 1950s and two films from the mid-1990s suggests a lessened interest in matters of due process and the problems with the judicial process as a whole.

## Questions for discussion

Q1) Identify two or three film legal dramas. How would you describe their 'double trial structure'?

Q2) What is the distinctive appeal of mass media representations of the criminal trial?

Q3) Why might film legal dramas have become less interested in critiquing the judicial process?

## Recommended reading

Clover, Carol, J. (1998) 'God Bless Juries!', in N. Browne (ed.) *Refiguring Film Genres*. Berkeley: University of California Press, pp. 255–277.
    Clover's chapter discusses the early trial movie *Falsely Accused!* and looks at the representation of juries in US films.

Lenz, Timothy, O. (2003) *Changing Images of Law in Film and Television Crime Stories*. New York: Peter Lang.

Lenz compares Hollywood crime films from the 1930s to the 2000s and argues that, from the 1970s onwards, crime films have taken a more conservative approach to crime and justice.

Silbey, Jessica, M. (2007) 'A History of Representations of Justice. Coincident Preoccupations of Law and Film', in A. Masson and K. O'Connor (eds.) *Representations of Justice*. New York: Peter Lang, pp. 131—154.

Silbey's chapter is a stimulating read and suggests that law and film share certain core concerns and characteristics.

## CHAPTER 16

# 'Real-life' crime and police-work in Cops

**Recommended viewing**

You'll find it helpful to have watched at least one episode of *Cops* before reading this chapter. I focus my discussion on episodes from season 20, but it's not necessary for you to restrict your viewing to this season.

*Cops* is a documentary-style crime television series that follows US police officers as they go about their day-to-day work on the beat – that, at least, is the premise. The programme was launched by Fox in 1989 and is now into its 25th season. This makes it one of the longest-running television shows in the USA and it is still broadcast in a primetime Saturday evening slot – all this is testament to the long-term appeal of this type of show. Indeed, even if you haven't seen an episode of *Cops*, the chances are that you've seen something like it: programmes like BBC1's *Coppers* and CBS' *Rescue 991* have been very successful in emulating the format. A central feature of these programmes – and what is central to their appeal – is that they appear to show us what crime and policing are *really* like. The camera simply follows the action, jolting round suddenly to take in a new and unexpected event, bobbing along as it is conveyed quickly by a running cameraman trying to keep up with a chase. Suspects and police officers stumble over their words, their speeches ostensibly unscripted. All this gives the impression that we're seeing as distilled a version of reality as is possible on television – as the show's executive producer put it, '[*Cops* is] as pure as you can get in documentary film making' (John Langles in Prosise and Johnson 2004: 73). This chapter sees *Cops* differently: as highly selective in its representation of police-work and crime. Before we turn to this idea, though, we consider why reality and documentary-style television shows about crime have become so popular over the last two decades.

## The rise of 'real-life' crime television

*Cops* is just one of many reality and documentary-style crime television shows. Some of these programmes focus on the work of the prison service, but most are about street-policing. In fact, Palmer suggests that the police are amongst the 'best-represented profession on television' today, and that this is a consequence of the volume of reality and documentary-style television programmes that focus on police-work (2003: 52). He's thinking in particular of the extraordinarily popular and long-running shows *Crimewatch UK* (BBC) and *America's Most Wanted* (Fox). These shows are live and sketch out a crime using reconstructions, interviews with victims, and police evidence. The public are invited to contact the police with leads via the show, and we can see phone and computer operators in the studio busily responding to phone calls and e-mails. Here it is the police and public's mutual work of detection that is 'real' and live. More recently, we've seen the emergence of reality crime clip shows that rely on police CCTV footage, programmes like *Police, Camera, Action!* and *World's Wildest Police Videos*.

The point is that whilst *Cops* uses a very specific documentary-style format it belongs to a broader class of television programme in which 'live' and 'real' crimes are the central focus. We can trace this television sub-genre back to the mid- to late 1980s – this was the period when *Crimewatch*, *America's Most Wanted*, and *Cops* were first launched. Fishman and Cavender (1998: 7) convincingly argue that the proliferation of reality and documentary-style crime television shows during this period was in part a response to growing public concern about crime. *Cops*, and shows like it, confirm the view that crime is a serious and widespread problem – after all, 'drugs, crime, and threats to the family and to safety generally are the stock-in-trade of these shows' (ibid.). The police are invariably presented as a 'front line of defense against such threats' (ibid.). In this sense, *Cops* supports a Manichean world-view: it sketches out a comfortingly simple world in which the 'good guys' work always and tirelessly in the public interest and the 'bad guys', though unspeakably bad, are at least obviously so.

Programmes like *Cops* also confirm to us that crime control (rather than, say, fostering community relations) is the central purpose of policing, and this too was an idea that had become particularly salient during the period in which reality crime shows emerged. We encountered a similar argument in the previous chapter, in our discussion of how changes in Hollywood legal dramas reflect shifts in public attitudes. David Garland (2001) suggests that, before the late 1970s, the criminal justice system in both the USA and UK was more welfare-oriented, focused on maintaining standards of due process and reintegrating offenders. The interests of society and the offender, Garland notes (2001: 180), were not seen as diametrically opposed to one another: the answer to crime was to bring about social reform *and* reform of the individual offender. Over the past few decades, he argues, there has been a cultural shift towards crime control: now we are asked to believe that the only way of tackling crime is to pre-emptively punish wrong-doing, punish harshly, and incarcerate early in the cycle of deviance. Central to this shift is a change in how we conceive of society. Dealing with crime once meant re-forming the social bonds that tie us to one another. In other words, society had a non-physical existence – it meant feelings of solidarity and shared values. In current discussions of crime, Garland notes, we tend to think of society in terms of *space*: we talk about how to keep our streets 'clean' and 'free' of criminal elements (pp. 182–183).

Garland's work is helpful in understanding the emergence of reality crime television shows. Like legal Hollywood dramas of the mid-1990s, these shows suggest that a punitive criminal justice system is the only and natural response to crime. They also participate in the idea that the central task of the police is to protect society by 'cleaning up' crime. In this way, and as Eldridge notes of television news, reality crime television shows like *Cops* aren't 'neutral products' that show us an unmediated reality (1995: 41). They, too, 'carry the dominant messages of our society', in this case messages concerning the nature of crime, the average criminal, and the role of the police. Let's turn now to consider how and why *Cops* attempts to create the impression that we're watching police-work as it really is.

### The camera as a neutral spectator in *Cops*

Let's start with a rare example from *Cops* where the illusion of an unmediated reality is temporarily broken. In the first episode of *Cops'* twentieth season ('Coast to Coast') we accompany a police officer following up a call about an incident of domestic violence. All the key players are pulled out into the street – the alleged offender (wobbly and stoned), his father who intervened in the assault, and the female who made the complaint. The alleged victim seems woozy and the police officer asks to see some ID. She performs a half-turn and instinctively shows it to the camera. The officer leans over and pulls the card away, muttering that *he* asked to see it. The scene reveals something of great importance about *Cops*. Despite the illusion that the camera has a barely there presence that has no impact on events, everyone in *Cops* is aware – sometimes acutely – that they are being filmed. In this particular scene we can say something more: the female victim is conscious that the exchange is *for the camera and audience's benefit*. In fact, her action suggests that she sees the camera, rather than the cop, as the source of authority here. It's a brief moment that explicitly undermines the idea that *Cops* is showing us real-life exchanges between police and civilians. There are other ways in which what we see in *Cops* is far from being an unmediated reality – but more on that below. For now I want us to consider further how the programme creates a sense that we're watching real-life crime, because this is fundamental to what the format sets out to achieve.

Chief amongst the techniques used to achieve this effect are camera position, shot sequence, and the emphasis on live action. Consider, for one moment, the Hollywood film conventions concerning the filming of conversations between characters: we generally cross-cut to a close-up of each speaker in turn. Now think about how reality television shows such as *Cops* capture conversations: here a mid-shot usually captures both speakers in the frame and the camera is positioned to give us a side-on, profile view. Instead of cutting, the camera moves and zooms to convey the rhythm of the exchange. Like a silent umpire in a tennis match, the camera casts its sight – *our* sight – one way and then the next, pausing and focusing to take in something of note. The camera isn't omniscient here; it doesn't give us a privileged view of proceedings (in the way that the intimate close-up of a Hollywood star in a film might). Instead its movement and placement suggest its role as an unobtrusive spectator.

Take, also, the convention in *Cops* of filming a police officer from the passenger or back seat of the squad car (see Figure 16.1). This is how the vignettes in the programme are often introduced: the camera is positioned next to a police officer as (usually) he speeds along in a car and explains either his love of the job, the various risks he faces day to day, or what he knows about the incident to which they're travelling out. What's made clear in these scenes is that the police officer is first and foremost at work, his mind primarily on the task in hand, rather than the interview or camera. The camera and by extension the audience are simply along for the ride. When we arrive at the destination, the cop usually leaps out of the car and we're left, momentarily, looking at his empty seat (see Figure 16.2). It's a fleeting shot, but distinctive to *Cops* and deeply suggestive. The point in showing a scene vacated is to give us the impression, again, that the camera is playing the part of a human observer, that observation is naturalistic, rather than contrived. The camera as a barely there spectator is slow (slower than the police, importantly), lumbering, possessed of a limited vantage point, catches as much as is humanly possible (but not more – that would be to suggest contrivance), and reacts to, rather than pre-empts, action.

This last point is particularly important given the emphasis on live action in *Cops* and other reality shows about the criminal justice system. The impression we get from *Cops* is that scenes aren't arranged and strung together

**Figure 16.1** The camera comes along for the ride ...

**Figure 16.2** ... but is too slow to keep up with the police

purposively. Instead, what we see appears to be dictated by what's *actually* happening, whether that's a sudden chase, a fraught conversation between police officer and suspect, or a search for evidence. What helps convey this is the tendency to include a police officer's description of events as an addendum to the live action. For example, a jolty chase through back streets is often followed by one of the officers, now perfectly calm and collected, delivering to camera a summary of what's just happened (see Figures 16.3 and 16.4). To the first-time viewer of *Cops* it's rather an odd convention: we're essentially talked through the scenes that we just witnessed, and the repeating of the event rarely adds anything to our understanding. To see these speeches in this way, though, is to miss the point: their main purpose is to confirm that the live action scenes we've just seen weren't produced and ordered for our sake and with the aim of achieving narrative consistency. That we found the live action perfectly easy to follow (as is usually the case in *Cops*) is beside the point: by providing a commentary the programme-makers are emphasising the integrity of the action shots as live footage.

The convention is interesting for another reason: by relaying events twice, first by offering us a view of events as they occurred and then by providing expert testimony, *Cops* asks us to approve the police's institutional framing of a situation. If the live action shots urge us to believe that we're watching a raw and unedited version of events, the subsequent police commentary asks us to see the police as efficient in assimilating that event in official terms. This ability to see and frame a criminal event in a way that the general public can't – to recognise an offender as a certain category of person, the chase as emblematic of a certain kind of crime – is something that might at once impress and comfort us. Certainly, it suggests that an official order can be brought to bear on the disordered scenes of disorderly behaviour in *Cops*.

The other point to make here is that the combination of footage that appeals to our visual senses (live action shots) and police testimony emulates the way in which evidence is presented in a courtroom. I'm thinking, in particular, of the way in which closed circuit television (CCTV) evidence is used in trials. The connection between the live footage in *Cops* and from CCTV cameras goes beyond the way in which the former is framed by expert commentary and verification. As discussed above, *Cops* works towards the idea that the camera is a barely there spectator to events, responsive to changes in action, its only purpose to pick up everything that goes on from its limited vantage point. Like a CCTV camera, the *Cops* camera is an instrument of surveillance. In fact, it's reasonable to suggest that the former has in some way provided the basis for the latter. With the proliferation of CCTV cameras over the last few decades we've got used to a certain style of surveillance – I'm

**Figure 16.3** The chase, unedited ...

**Figure 16.4** ... and the subsequent police framing

thinking not just about our expectation that public areas will be subject to video surveillance but also that this form of observation yields a particular set of images (that is different to, say, sketches from the courtroom observer or photographs from the war reporter). All this is to say that CCTV footage has a recognisable tone and structure, fundamental to which is the idea that surveillance of a given area is total and free from human design. We've been culturally sensitised to this style of observation, and the type of live footage provided in *Cops* draws upon our expectations concerning the possibility for neutral, mechanical, all-seeing surveillance of a situation. This may also help explain the rise of reality crime television programmes from the mid- to late 1980s: this, after all, was the period during which CCTV surveillance first came to be widely used in the USA and UK.

For Foucault, this style of observation is fundamental to the exercise of power in modern societies. In *Discipline and Punish*, he suggests that European societies underwent a key transformation in the operation of social control during the early nineteenth century. Where corporal punishment was once used as an expression of raw power, more subtly coercive disciplinary techniques, directed at getting the individual to internalise certain norms of behaviour, have now come to predominate. This shift, Foucault argues, is reflected in the decline of the public execution and the rise of the prison during the early nineteenth century. Corporal punishment provides support for social prohibitions by creating a climate of fear focused on the desire to avoid pain. Prisons, Foucault suggests, also help prohibit certain ways of acting and thinking by forcing the inmate to conform to a daily routine of activities laid down by the institution. These different principles of control, he suggests in his later work, can be used to describe whole social systems of power. Sovereignty is a system in which power is expressed physically and based on fear. Governmentality is a system in which power is expressed by urging citizens to internalise rules and self-regulate. The latter is achieved partly through creating a situation of total surveillance: once we've accommodated ourselves to the idea that we might be being watched at any given moment, we can internalise standards of behaviour. Foucault's famous example is the panopticon, a prison design created by the British philosopher Jeremy Bentham in the late eighteenth century. Panopticon means 'all-seeing eye', and this immediately gives us an insight into what Bentham was hoping to achieve with his prison. At its centre is a tall viewing booth from which guards can see all the corridors in the building without being seen in turn by the prisoners. The important thing is the *possibility* for total surveillance offered by such a vantage point: this spatial arrangement, as with CCTV cameras, creates a self-consciousness that one *could* be being scrutinised right now (even if there's a chance that the guards are on their break at this precise moment, or the camera has no film in it). For Foucault, one thing that's really important about this vague feeling that one could be under surveillance and subject to censure is that power is hidden and the individual must *self*-censor. This means, amongst other things, that the institutional gaze is depersonalised. It doesn't issue from a specific person, seen and present to us, but instead from a built edifice or instrument that represents the possibility for complete surveillance of our actions.

It may seem like we've travelled rather far from our original concern here, namely footage from CCTV cameras and *Cops*, and what they might have in common. Foucault's concern, after all, is with the *subject* of surveillance, whilst our core concern in this chapter is with the *products* of surveillance. What strikes me as useful, though, is Foucault's observation that one of the important functions of power in modern society is that it seems impersonal and unbiased in its application – so too, I want to argue, with the fruits of its surveillance. Records and images must be produced in a disinterested fashion if we are to accept the evidence of wrong-doing contained therein: that is a prerequisite for modern juries, judges, and television viewers of reality crime shows. We can turn this on its head: for those eager to affirm a certain view of wrong-doing, *achieving* a disinterested style and tone and *obscuring* the institutional basis for power are important rhetorical strategies. This might mean, for example, creating the illusion that a camera is simply responding to events, rather than exercising any specific social authority. In the case of the CCTV camera, this illusion is easily produced and sustained: the camera appears to respond in an utterly mechanical fashion. In the case of the camera in *Cops* things are a little different. Here the camera acts as a *human* spectator – it is a car passenger or sprints along for a chase. We are nonetheless asked to believe that the camera is compelled, *by human desire alone*, to follow the action.

In short, whether we are a jury watching CCTV evidence in the courtroom or a viewer of *Cops*, it's easy to form the impression that we're watching a neutral and simple relaying of events as they happened. In this sense the operation of the camera appears not to suggest any institutional affiliation. This isn't really true, of course. The CCTV camera has been placed and funded by an organisation interested in observing certain types of people and places, its images extracted, selected, edited, and interpreted by a criminal justice agency interested in proving something. Despite appearances to the contrary, the images in *Cops* are subject to all sorts of decisions about framing, the soundtrack, shot sequence, mise-en-scène, and editing. Fishman and Cavender (1998: 4) point out that for each half-hour episode the programme-makers must select from hundreds of hours of footage and 'editors delete uninteresting video and add clips from a program's file of stock footage'. All this undermines the idea that *Cops* is made simply by turning a camera on and following the police at work. In fact, and as we discuss below, the choices made in the production of *Cops* work towards a depiction of the police that is unrelentingly affirmatory. Before that, though, let's briefly consider *Cops* as a television programme that consolidates a particular picture of police-work and crime.

## The selective view of police-work and crime in *Cops*

We proceed here on the basis that *Cops* actually gives us a rather narrow and selective view of police-work and crime: how, then, might we characterise this portrayal? This might seem like a difficult task given that an important aspect of *Cops* is its use of vignettes that appear to bear limited relation to one another: the stories move between different police forces, states, cities, crimes, and suspects. This fragmentary structure is itself deeply evocative of a particular conception of crime and police-work, conveying, as it does, the impression that crime is a nationwide problem requiring much the same style of policing irrespective of location. There is also a discernible criminal type in *Cops*. The ensemble cast of suspects in any single episode of *Cops* generally share certain core characteristics: they are mainly male, almost always young and intoxicated (drunk and/or stoned), and often African American. Victims, in contrast, are rarely seen or heard.

Crime also takes a standard form in *Cops*. It is street-based (never white-collar or corporate), usually happens at night, drugs are frequently its root cause, and it is a constant problem. The work of the police is, in turn, unending. To reiterate this point, at the end of each vignette the soundtrack continues for a few moments longer over the customary fade and black screen. The same device is used at the start of the next vignette: we hear the soundtrack before we see the accompanying images. What we mostly hear during these lead-outs and lead-ins is a police officer talking or the distinctive fuzzy sounds of a police radio. It's a distinctive *Cops* convention, and gives a clear message that police-work is an unending pursuit that goes on after the cameras have stopped rolling (in an *unchanging* fashion is also the important implication).

Through all this, *Cops* consolidates a view of crime as serious, stemming from specific parts of the population, drug oriented, and widespread. Tough crime control measures seem like the only reasonable response to this world of crime: this, at least, is how the relationship is set up in *Cops*. Police dogs and helicopters are often deployed, handcuffs inevitably used, stop-and-searches performed with seeming impunity, and guns frequently pulled on suspects. The impression we're given is that such measures directly answer to the crime problem in US cities. What also helps legitimate this style of policing is the distinctly pro-police line established in *Cops* – and it's that to which we turn next.

## *Cops* and the pro-police line

That *Cops* is heavily biased towards the police's perspective is clear once we have accepted that we're not really watching a direct relaying of events and that the camera is not a neutral observer. We've already noted that live action is often followed by a police officer's reporting of events to camera. This is just one way in which their view of things is prioritised. Take, by way of another example, the programme's opening theme tune, 'Bad Boys', a song by reggae group Inner Circle. We hear the opening chorus – 'Bad boys, bad boys / Whatcha gonna do, whatcha gonna do / When they come for you?' – sung over lilting, upbeat music, with the word 'COPS' emboldened on our screens by a flashing light that emulates that of a police car on an emergency call. It's a gung-ho opening, one that clearly marks the start of a chase in which the 'good guys' will valiantly pursue easy-to-identify villains. The vignettes that follow show us one 'bad boy' after another being pursued, apprehended, interrogated, handcuffed, and stationed in a police car for dispatch. The suspect's guilt is very rarely ever in doubt, at least for the police officers giving chase. Take, for example, the last vignette of 'Evidence … What Evidence?' (season 20). The police are looking for the perpetrator of an armed robbery, and have been told to look for someone carrying a backpack. We join them in the pursuit of a young man who ran away when he saw the police cars pull up. We find him hiding in a garden. He doesn't have a backpack or any incriminating evidence on him, but that doesn't seem to matter. 'Why are you running from us?' a police officer asks accusingly. 'I just saw some cars pulling up and I ran' the suspect replies, adding, 'I was scared'. The conversation turns to the matter of the missing backpack, which the suspect claims to know nothing about. Another police officer claims to have seen him with it from a distance during the chase. 'Now you're calling my partner a liar', the police officer leading the interrogation says, 'man up and be a little bit honest'. 'Why I gotta be lying?' the suspect retorts. It's a reasonable question, but not in the world of *Cops*. Despite the voiceover at the start of each episode telling us that 'all suspects are innocent until proven guilty in a court of law', someone is automatically presumed guilty if he runs away from the police. 'Here's the thing', a young police officer explains to camera earlier in the same episode, 'people don't run from the police unless they have a reason to run from the police'. What he means by this is that people don't run from the police unless they've just committed a crime, but we might immediately be able to think of lots of reasons to run from the police quite beyond being a criminal, such as a lack of trust, fear, confusion, or instinct. For those belonging to certain social groups – particularly ethnic minority groups – the police might not be a benign social authority to be submitted to readily.

None of this is countenanced in *Cops*. In fact, we're asked to accept the logic that those who run are liars and criminals – after all, we see them being arrested and taken away. The police's view of things remains unchallenged: they *always* get the right man. Prosise and Johnson (2004) make a similar observation about pretextual stop-and-searches in *Cops* and *World's Wildest Police Videos* always leading to the uncovering of serious crime. In only showing successful stop-and-searches, these programmes offer a powerful legitimation of this highly debatable police practice. That a disproportionate number of the suspects undergoing pretextual stop-and-searches belong to ethnic minority groups in both programmes 'sends a clear but disturbing message': 'Stopping minority drivers or pedestrians when police notice minor traffic infractions or anomalies in behavior, such as possessing out of state plates, or because they are "acting squirrely", or because they are "acting suspicious or something", is appropriate because it invariably leads to incarceration of serious criminals' (p. 86). There's a more general point to be made here: by never raising the possibility that the wrong person is being interrogated and arrested, shows like *Cops* ask us to believe that the police's view of a suspect is decisive.

This point is often stressed in the closing scene of a vignette. At the end of the vignette described above from 'Evidence … What Evidence?' we watch the police dust for finger and shoe prints. 'It helps further show that he was the one who committed the robbery' a police officer adds in a voiceover as the screen turns black in preparation for the closing credits. 'He won't be doing that again', another officer comments at the end of a domestic violence vignette in 'Coast to Coast' (season 20). The police are almost always given the last word in *Cops*, and these final comments very often assume a suspect's guilt – and that, as they say, is the end of the story. In this sense the police are represented as law-enforcer, judge, and jury in one. This is a distinctive feature of police-work in *Cops*, one that is not at all coterminous with official ideas about the police's role but might be reassuring to an audience keen to imagine that crime can be dealt with so easily and unilaterally.

## Concluding discussion

This chapter has outlined the various ways in which *Cops* takes a distinctly pro-police line. Discussing a wide range of reality police shows, Palmer

(2003) makes a similar observation. He points out that *Cops* and programmes like it seem to offer us 'as unguarded a representation of the police as is imaginable' (p. 59). On closer inspection, though, reality police shows are so acritical of the police's actions 'that they risk being read as public relations exercises' (p. 53). Palmer suggests that television shows about the police – whether they're drama based or documentaries – have historically inclined towards a positive depiction of police-work (though there are important variations within this, with early police dramas, such as the BBC's *Dixon of Dock Green*, tending to paint a view of police officers as community-oriented, benevolent, and gentle, rather than heroic and street-smart). In this sense, the pro-police tone and message of *Cops* is nothing new. What is distinct, though, is the use of conventions from documentary and reality television to convey this attitude. Unlike earlier police dramas, we're asked to imagine that the camera in *Cops* does not prioritise certain events and views, but is simply capturing police-work and crime as it happens, as it is. That the police come off very well indeed in this show is, we are encouraged to believe, a simple consequence of them being very good at their jobs – the positive impression *Cops* gives of the police's role appears not to have been artificially produced, in other words. Creating the illusion of first-hand, unmediated reality is, I have argued above, an important part of *Cops'* rhetoric, a powerful means of affirming a decidedly selective and narrow view of crime and police-work.

## Questions for discussion

Q1)  What is the distinctive appeal of reality and documentary-style crime television series?

Q2)  How can we explain the relatively recent emergence of reality and documentary-style crime television programmes?

Q3)  In what senses are we provided with a partial representation of crime and police-work in *Cops* and programmes like it?

Q4)  Are there media representations that provide us with a different perspective of police-work to that created in series like *Cops*?

## Recommended reading

Fishman, Mark and Cavender, Gray (eds.) (1998) *Entertaining Crime: Television Reality Programs*. New York: Aldine de Gruyter.
An edited collection of essays that analyse television reality programmes. Fishman and Cavender's Introduction to the book is particularly useful and recommended.

Jermyn, Deborah (2007) *Crime Watching: Investigating Real Crime TV*. London: I.B. Tauris.

Dealing with mainly British examples, Jermyn's book looks at a wide range of reality and documentary crime television formats. There's a particularly good, focused analysis of *Crimewatch UK* and a discussion of the social context out of which the programme emerged.

Palmer, Gareth (2003) *Discipline and Liberty: Television and Governance*. Manchester: Manchester University Press.

Palmer adopts a Foucauldian approach to studying reality television. There are several chapters focusing on reality crime television here.

# Conclusion

Most books about the mass media are replete with examples of bad practice and misrepresentation. This book has them too – we've learned that reality crime television shows provide a partial depiction of police-work, news about rape reinforces certain myths about sexual violence, and contemporary prison films represent incarceration as the primary solution to crime. There's much wrong, too, with the overall picture of crime in the mass media. Across the media texts we've looked at – from *Cops* to crime news, *CSI* to e-mailed crime legends – the dominant impression of crime is that it's mainly violent, random, out of control, and requires tough sanctions. We've discussed, at various points, the fact that this is an erroneous picture of crime: for one thing, in most economically advanced societies overall crime is on the decline, and has been for several decades.

The disjuncture between the media-spun image of crime and the 'reality' of crime often prompts much finger-wagging and hand-wringing. In fact, it's become popular to decry the mass media as an institution, to suppose that journalists are bad to the bone, Hollywood directors and television producers deeply conservative. The mass media have become an easy target for remonstration and recrimination – the press especially so. Consider, for a moment, the recurrent scandals over the past few years concerning news organisations. As I started writing this book a public scandal erupted concerning British journalists' hacking of a murder victim's mobile phone. As I end this book news headlines are filled with salacious stories of press intrusion and maleficence that have come out during the British government's Leveson Inquiry into press standards. Such articles raise legitimate concerns, of course, but the usual tone and language of reporting reflect a deep sense of public hostility towards the British press as an institution – to the extent that we might reasonably say that news organisations and journalists have latterly (and partly by their own doing) become folk devils. It's an interesting cultural development, not least of all for its diffuse effects upon the culture. An anti-press mood has, for example, aided the growth of citizen journalism and crime legends, dependent, as both are, on people's sense that mainstream news outlets don't deal in the truth and, instead, informal, personal sources of news have currency.

In fact, it's more precise to say that an anti-press mood is a reciprocal part of a bigger socio-cultural trend, of which citizen journalism and crime legends are also contributing factors. The depth of ill-feeling towards news organisations is at least partly to do with a more general, zeitgeisty sense of cynicism that holds the mainstream press, Hollywood, and primetime television to be actively involved in producing a grand illusion. In popular thinking today, religion is no longer the opiate of the people – the mass media are, and, like religious ideologues, mainstream media producers are believed to be involved in an intentional project to hoodwink and dissimulate. Take the fact that, when I tell people that I've been writing a book about crime and the media, they usually respond by saying something like 'Oh, the media, yes, they distort *everything*, don't they? It's shocking what they get people to believe ...'.

Implicit to this view is the idea that the problem of media distortion is primarily one of journalistic inattention and error, proprietarial bias, and media-producers' conscious desire to peddle a conservative ideology – and, to put it simply, I don't think those are really compelling factors. Focusing on these issues often means discussions about media representation become circular: we find ourselves arguing that the mass media distort because, well, that's just what the mass media *do*. We need to ensure that the current climate of cynicism concerning the mass media doesn't stop us from looking at the deeper social and cultural explanations for the overall picture of crime that dominates the mainstream media – and that means looking beyond individual media-producers and the mass media as an institution. After all, journalists, editors, film-makers, and media funders make decisions that are informed by a deep-seated and intuitive sense of what will sell, what will chime, and what is meaningful. In other words, *we* are forever in their minds, and not as empty vessels waiting to be filled with media nonsense. Media-producers know that people *turn to* crime stories when fearful or for confirmation of their worldview. The mass media might accentuate these feelings and give shape to these views, of course, but they don't operate unilaterally, nor is their influence monolithic. In fact, and as we've found throughout the book, many crime stories echo and reinforce *existing* cultural scripts. Take, by way of example, cautionary tales in the mass media (the subject of Chapter 6). These stories warn women to be forever alert to risks to their safety, recognise their personal responsibility for avoiding victimisation, and adopt precautionary measures – by, for example, watching their drink so it isn't spiked with drugs, not taking an unlicensed taxi, and not being alone at night in public. Like moral panics, cautionary tales tend to exaggerate and misrepresent a threat. Rather than seeing this as a deliberate attempt on the part of media-producers to mislead, we should recognise that cautionary tales make it into news headlines, soap opera storylines, and women's glossy magazines because the risks described are salient to us and, in their themes and tone, find validation throughout the culture. Charities urge us to be 'aware' of risks to our safety, neighbourhood watch schemes recommend crime prevention, and insurance companies require us to recognise our responsibility in guarding against crime. More obviously, perhaps, cautionary tales reflect a set of expectations, engrained in our culture, concerning women's responsibility to avoid sexual violence.

In short, films, televisions shows, novels, and news articles are products of a culture, a particular historical moment, and set of social conditions – they might be *more* than this (as we saw in our discussions of *Deadwood* and *A Clockwork Orange*), but they are always *at least* this. In fact, crime stories are particularly resonant of social context, dealing, as they so often do, with contemporary ideas about moral boundaries, the form evil takes, the uses of violence, how we should punish, who has the authority to judge, and how to allocate blame. In dealing with these matters, crime stories tell us about ourselves and do so in a way that unites new fears and more traditional sources of hostility and faith – this is what distinguishes them as stories and marks out their incredible value for sociologists and criminologists.

What sort of things do current crime stories tell us about our shared fears, prejudices, values, and preoccupations? The question is best answered by identifying recurring narrative features in the crime stories we've considered in this book – some of them are specific to contemporary stories and others are more universally relevant.

## Recurring narrative features in contemporary crime stories

*1)    Violence is the preserve of anarchists, psychopaths, the irascible, and the weak-willed*

The societal factors that influence crime and deviance – inequalities based on social class, ethnicity, and sex – are routinely ignored in contemporary crime stories. In fact, in some stories the world depicted appears devoid of social structure. Just recall, for one moment, the amorphous social world of random violence in *CSI* where everyone's at equal risk of victimisation and anyone could be a criminal. In the world sketched out by *CSI*, violence is carried out by those who are emotionally and psychologically predisposed to act as enemies of order – anarchists, psychopaths, the irascible, and the weak-willed. Those who carry out violence are unpredictable, their motivations often incomprehensible, their characters unfixable. This is the dominant characterisation of violence not just in forensic police procedural shows, but also reality crime TV programmes, crime news, and e-mailed crime legends. Take the popular idea in British newspapers during the 1960s that the fractious Mods and Rockers were merely anarchist youths – not, as Cohen (1987) demonstrates, disenfranchised and disaffected. Or take the media rendering of Irish Republicans as 'immoral alchemists of anarchy' (Hayes 2003: 150) rather than a group whose violence had a political and historical context.

The cultural association of violence with anarchy, psychopathy, and irascibility is so definitive as to preclude certain acts of aggression being described as violence at all. Acts of violence carried out by the state, for example, are more usually described in terms of retaliation, punishment, and justice – this, at least, was the argument in Chapter 2 where we considered terrorism in the news. Here we found that the words 'violence' and 'criminal' are rarely used to refer to acts of aggression carried out to sustain a social order. Our culture also routinely denies that mainstream social values and norms might give rise to violence. In our discussion of rape in the news we found that sexual violence is rarely framed as anything other than anomalous acts carried out by a few psychopathic men rather than anything to do with the gender order. That the news gives more coverage and emphasis to stranger-perpetrated rape, rather than assaults by acquaintances and intimates, helps obscure the idea that violence might be a consequence of socially prescribed living arrangements, relationship structures, and inequalities between the sexes.

Of course, not all media texts deny the multifarious uses and meanings of violence, and those that illuminate the complex relationship between violence, power, and social order can be extraordinarily valuable to sociologists and criminologists. For example, and as we found in Chapter 12, the television Western *Deadwood* vividly depicts what happens when a society makes the shift from revenge as the dominant method of exacting justice to a more formal system of retribution. Here we found an ideological battle played out between informal and formal justice, with violence at its core. In our discussion of the film *A Clockwork Orange* (Chapter 13), too, we considered the difficulties in reforming violent individuals if a deeply violent society isn't also subject to reform.

## 2) Those responsible must be denounced

Not all crime stories involve the allocation of blame – in fact, in Chapter 15 we considered two 1950s Hollywood legal dramas (*Anatomy of a Murder* and *12 Angry Men*) that were centrally about the difficulties in determining guilt. As we discussed there, this rendering of the judicial process is a distinctive feature of Golden Age trial movies. Today, most courtroom-based dramas involve a dramatic denunciation that unambiguously allocates guilt – I'm thinking, of course, about the fact that the character assassination in the courtroom is often the climatic episode in many legal dramas. Moral panics, too – that most fundamental crime story of the late modern period – operate by marginalising deviant behaviour and rooting out the 'folk devil'. In both trial dramas and moral panics, denunciations work by emphasising the otherness of the denounced person – it must be made clear that she or he is uncivilised, immoral, incomprehensible to rightminded people, not, in short, one of us. As Garfinkel (1956: 423) once observed of 'status degradation ceremonies', 'the denounced person must be ritually separated from a place in the legitimate order, i.e., he must be defined as standing at a place opposed to it. He must be placed "outside", he must be made "strange"'.

Garfinkel's language here draws our attention to the fact that the ordeal of a denunciation is something that individuals, rather than institutions or organisations, are put through. The spatial metaphors of being separated from, different to, placed outside of the mainstream social order require as their object an individual person – someone who can be rhetorically transformed into a discrete, visible thing to be set aside. The linguistic difficulty in denunciating an institution or organisation helps explain why contemporary crime stories (and, it might be added, our criminal justice system) tend to direct blame at the individual level. In Chapter 11 we discussed Michelle and Weaver's (2003) discourse analysis of a set of New Zealand documentaries about domestic violence and their observation that blame is never directed at the criminal justice system or welfare support services. Nor, they argue, are the male perpetrators of violence generally held to be blameworthy in these media texts. Instead, various dramatic devices work towards an impression that the female victims of violence are to blame. We can draw two conclusions from this in terms of our wider discussion of blame here: first, blame can be allocated implicitly (through such things as tone and framing) and not just explicitly (through denunciation rituals) and secondly, blame can be levelled at victims as well as offenders.

Mary Douglas (1986: 59) makes a similar observation, and suggests that societies typically direct blame in two directions: towards outsiders and victims. Outsider-blaming urges us to recognise someone as 'not one of us'. Certain types of outsiders tend to predominate in contemporary crime stories – young, working-class men, those belonging to subcultural tribes, ethnic minority groups. Victim-blaming involves vilifying those who have shirked their personal responsibility for self-protection – in contemporary crime stories these are usually young women exercising their freedom or mothers failing in their parental duties. There is an obviously gendered dimension to blaming: outsider-blaming tends to focus on marginalising *male* deviance, victim-blaming on marginalising *female* deviance. Many contemporary crime stories have one of these narrative features – moral panics, for example, are focused on outsider-blaming, cautionary tales on victim-blaming (as we discussed in Chapters 5 and 6). What both forms of blaming share is a moralising tone, albeit differently directed: offender-blaming involves an outside threat to the moral order being identified, whilst victim-blaming involves a moral lesson being delivered.

### 3)   Something we all cherish is under threat

It follows, then, that an important element to crime stories that involve outsider-blaming is the sketching out of a moral order and, with it, a sense of who 'we' are – and here we return to Katz's argument (explored in Chapter 1) that crime stories are fundamentally moral tales. Katz's interest lies specifically with crime news, but his observations are pertinent to the mass media more generally, particularly his suggestion that people turn to crime stories not because of a desire for information, nor to be thrilled by unusual events, but because 'crimes may be especially telling about other things of interest to readers' (Katz 1987: 50). Crime stories, Katz argues, give us the opportunity to mull over moral dilemmas and rehearse collective values. Crime news, he suggests, is selected on the basis that it is likely to prompt feelings of mutual outrage, have a clear moral dimension, and feed into a shared sense of identity.

In this way, crime stories can play a protective role, helping to defend cherished ideas and expressing a sense of mutuality. This is particularly true of mass media representations of cultural trauma (the subject of Chapter 8). Cultural traumas involve a transformation of a negative event into a social crisis – we considered media coverage of 9/11 in the USA and the assassination of Theo van Gogh in the Netherlands as examples. The mass media's role in producing these cultural traumas centrally involved rehearsing the affective ties that bind an imagined community, sketching out a sense of 'them versus us', and reinforcing the sacred value of a national way of life. One thing that's fundamental to these crime stories is a rhetoric of consensus: a collective 'we' is confidently conjured up and mutual agreement on the nature of the threat is presupposed.

It's not just in mass media representations of cultural trauma where we find an articulation of ideas and values that 'unite us all'. Crime stories involving child-victims also frequently enjoin us to feel that something we all cherish is under threat. A number of researchers have identified a recent increase in crime stories concerning child-victims and perpetrators (see, for example, Jewkes 2011). In thinking about explanations for the increase in reporting on child sex abuse we considered how the cultural valorisation of childhood might have made crimes involving children particularly salient (see Chapter 3). We also noted a moral tone in news reporting: articles frame these crimes as a destruction of childhood innocence, an affront to common decency, and emblematic of a 'broken society'. That crime stories about child sex abuse frequently rely upon this discourse of social breakdown might also help explain the increase in news reporting on this subject – they are, in a sense, cathartic and expressive. Certainly, in asking us to think about threats to what we cherish, such crime stories allow for the expression of shared anxieties about the possibility for evil in our world.

### 4)   In process we trust

In their analysis of changes in British crime news reporting 1945–1991, Reiner *et al.* (2003: 22) observe the emergence of a less unrelentingly positive depiction of the police in the late twentieth century. They point out that 'the police and other authorities are portrayed as increasingly immoral or irrelevant' (p. 31). Our close readings of crime stories such as *CSI*, *Cops*, and legal dramas indicate something slightly different, but we can certainly agree that there has been an important shift in the representation of criminal justice agencies and personnel. In Chapters 14 and 15 we looked at historical shifts in detective fiction and legal dramas respectively and, in both cases, found that what dominates contemporary stories is the idea that crime is endemic. In turn, the police and judiciary are taken to be necessary in the fight against crime. In reality crime television programmes such as *Cops*, for example, we're urged to see police-work positively, and this is specifically because it appears to answer a really urgent and serious problem of violent crime. *Individual* police officers and lawyers might be shown to be untrustworthy, immoral, or inept in contemporary legal dramas and detective stories, but the *institutional processes* they undertake are of unquestioned value. This attitude has a real-life equivalent: lawyers are popularly seen as self-interested and, of late, the police as prejudiced, but we most certainly have not given up on the idea that the police and the judicial process are the foremost answers to the problem of crime – in fact, we often think there need to be *more* police and *more* crimes being tried in serious courts. As something of an aside here, it's worth noting that we encountered a similar argument in Chapter 13 about contemporary prison dramas (see Mason 2006): these crime stories might be lightly critical of prison life, but in depicting offenders as deeply threatening and animalistic they also help to sustain the idea that incarceration is a necessary and natural solution to crime (and, again, something we need *more* of).

Another way of looking at all this is to say that the criminal justice system is frequently represented as a technical and ongoing solution to crime today.

Previous crime stories have suggested a rather different conception of crime and its solutions. In detective fiction of the golden age, for example, detection is periodically useful, rather than an ongoing pursuit, and its purpose is to recreate social order. Consider, also, the perspective offered by Hollywood legal dramas of the 1950s: these films were often interested in the inadequacies of law and the judicial process as a response to crime. Today, crime stories are less likely to urge a critical perspective towards the criminal justice system – instead it's seen as a set of neutral mechanisms for dealing with crime. Take our discussion in Chapter 15, where we found that criminal law and the judicial process are rarely 'on trial' in contemporary Hollywood legal dramas – the threat to justice invariably comes from outside the courtroom (from politicians and corporate leaders trying to manipulate the legal process), rather than from within, as was the case in many films of the Golden Age. In Chapter 14 we found that *CSI* and other forensic police procedurals obscure the role of human judgement in detection, thus transforming police-work into a purely technical pursuit. Here humans don't solve cases through mental agility or deep insider knowledge of a social world; rather, machines do the work of detection, thus eliminating the apparent limitations of human perception and evaluation. This says more about our scepticism concerning human impartiality than actual police-work. I hope that this book has more generally demonstrated that crime stories tell us much about ourselves and very little about crime and the criminal justice system.

# Bibliography

Alexa Global News Traffic Rank (August 2012). Alexa, 1st August. Available at www.alexa.com/topsites/category/Top/News.

Alexa Global Traffic Rank (August 2012). *Alexa*, 1st August. Available at www.alexa.com/topsites/global.

Alexa UK Traffic Rank (August 2012). *Alexa*, 1st August. Available at www.alexa.com/topsites/countries/GB.

Alexander, J. (2004) 'Toward a Theory of Cultural Trauma', in J. Alexander, R. Eyerman, B. Giesen, N.J. Smelser, and P. Sztompka (eds.) *Cultural Trauma and Cultural Identity*. Berkeley: University of California Press, pp. 1–30.

Alexander, J., Eyerman, R., Giesen, B., Smelser, N.J., and Sztompka, P. (eds.) (2004) *Cultural Trauma and Collective Identity*. Berkeley: University of California Press.

Anderson, B. (1991) *Imagined Communities: Reflections on the Origin and Spread of Nationalism*. London: Verso.

Anderson, E. (1999) *Code of the Street: Decency, Violence, and the Moral Life of the Inner City*. New York: W.W. Norton.

Ariès, P. (1965) *Centuries of Childhood: A Social History of Family Life*. London: Vintage.

Auden, W.H. (1948) 'The Guilty Vicarage: Notes on the Detective Story, By An Addict', *Harper's*, May 1948, pp. 406–412.

Australian Bureau of Statistics (2004) 'Sexual Assault in Australia: A Statistical Overview'. Available at at www.abs.gov.au/ausstats/abs@.nsf/mf/4523.0.

Barker, M. (1992) 'Stuart Hall, Policing the Crisis', in M. Barker and A. Beezer (eds.) *Reading into Cultural Studies*. London: Routledge, pp. 81–100.

Barille, L. (1984) 'Television and Attitudes About Crime: Do Heavy Views Distort Criminality and Support Retributive Justice?', in R. Surette (ed.) *Justice and the Media: Issues and Research*. Springfield, IL: Charles C. Thomas.

Barnett, B. (2005) 'Perfect Mother or Artist of Obscenity? Narrative and Myth in a Qualitative Analysis of Press Coverage of the Andrea Yates Murders', *Journal of Communication Inquiry*, 29(1): 9–29.

Barr, T. (2000) *Newmedia.au: The Changing Face of Australia's Media and Communications*. St Leonards, New South Wales: Allen and Unwin.

Barthes, R. (1972) *Mythologies*. London: Cape.

Bazin, A. (1971a) 'The Western, or the American Film *par excellence*', in H. Gray (ed.), 2 vols., *What is Cinema?* Berkeley: University of California Press, pp. 140–148.

Bazin, A. (1971b) 'The Evolution of the Western', in H. Gray (ed.), 2 vols., *What is Cinema?* Berkeley: University of California Press, pp. 149–157.

Beck, U. (1992) *Risk Society: Towards a New Modernity.* London: Sage.

Becker, H. (1997 [originally 1963]) *Outsiders: Studies in Sociology of Deviance.* London: Simon and Schuster.

Becker, L., Lowrey, W., Claussen, D., and Anderson, W. (2000) 'Why Does the Beat go On? An Examination of the Role of Beat Structure in the Newsroom', *Newspaper Research Journal*, 21(4): 2–16.

Benedict, H. (1993) *Vamp or Virgin: How the Press Covers Sex Crime.* Oxford: Oxford University Press.

Best, J. (1990) *Threatened Children: Rhetoric and Concern about Child Victims.* Chicago: University of Chicago Press.

Best, J. (1999) *Random Violence: How We Talk About New Crimes and New Victims.* Berkeley, CA: University of California Press.

Best, J. and Horiuchi, G.T. (1985) 'The Razor Blade in the Apple: The Social Construction of Urban Legends', *Social Problems*, 32(5): 488–497.

Bickerton, I.J. (2009) *The Arab–Israeli Conflict: A History.* London: Reaktion Books.

Blumer, H. (1954) 'What is Wrong with Social Theory?', *American Journal of Sociology*, 19: 3–10.

Bonaparte, H. (1941) 'The Myth of the Corpse in the Car', *American Imago*, 2: 105–126.

Box, S. (1983) *Power, Crime, and Mystification.* London: Tavistock.

Brown, D. (1997) *The American West.* London: Simon and Schuster.

Brunt, M. (2007) 'The Crime Beat is Hard Labour Now', *British Journalism Review*, 18(4): 33–38.

Brunvand, J.H. (1983) *The Vanishing Hitch-Hiker: American Urban Legends and their Meanings.* London: W.W. Norton.

Brust, R. (2008) 'The 25 Greatest Legal Movies', *ABAJournal*, August, Cover Story.

Burgess, A., Donovan, P., and Moore, S.E.H. (2009) 'Embodying Uncertainty? Understanding Heightened Risk Perception of Drink "Spiking"', *British Journal of Criminology*, 49(6): 848–862.

Caputi, J. (1987) *The Age of Sex Crime.* Bowling Green, OH: Bowling Green University Popular Press.

Carringella-MacDonald, S. (1998) 'The Relative Visibility of Rape Cases in National Popular Magazines', *Violence Against Women*, 4(1): 62–80.

Carruthers, S. (2000) *The Media at War: Communication and Conflict in the Twentieth Century.* Basingstoke: Palgrave Macmillan.

Carter, C. (1998) 'When the "Extraordinary" Becomes "Ordinary": Everyday News of Sexual Violence', in C. Carter, G. Branston, and S. Allen (eds.) *News, Gender, and Power.* London: Routledge.

Cavender, G. and Deutsch, S.K. (2007) '*CSI* and Moral Authority: The Police and Science', *Crime, Media, Culture*, 3(1): 67–81.

Center for Media and Public Affairs (July/August 1997) 'Network News in the Nineties: The Top Topics and Trends of the Decade', *Media Monitor*, 9(3).

Chadee, D. and Ditton, J. (2005) 'Fear of Crime and the Media: Assessing the Lack of a Relationship', *Crime Media Culture*, 1(3): 322–332.

Chandler, R. (1988 [originally 1944]) 'The Simple Art of Murder', in R. Chandler *The Simple Art of Murder*. New York: Vintage, pp. 1–18.

Cheit, R.E. (2003) 'What Hysteria? A Systematic Study of Newspaper Coverage of Accused Child Molesters', *Child Abuse and Neglect*, 27(6): 607–623.

Chermak, S. (1995) 'Image Control: How Police Affect the Presentation of Crime News', *American Journal of Police*, 14(2): 21–43.

Chermak, S. (1997) 'The Presentation of Drugs in the News Media: News Sources Involved in the Production of Social Problems', *Justice Quarterly*, 14(4): 687–718.

Chermak, S. and Weiss, A. (2005) 'Maintaining Legitimacy using External Communication Strategies: An Analysis of Police–Media Relations', *Journal of Criminal Justice*, 33(5): 501–512.

Chibnall, S. (2005 [originally 1977]) *Law and Order News*. London: Routledge.

Chiricos, T., Eschholz, S., and Gertz, M. (1997) 'Crime, News and Fear of Crime: Toward an Identification of Audience Effects', *Social Problems*, 44(3): 342–357.

Chomsky, N. and Herman, E.S. (1979) *The Washington Connection and Third World Fascism: The Political Economy of Human Rights: Volume 1*. Cambridge, MA: South End Press.

Christie, N. (1986) 'The Ideal Victim', in E. Fattah (ed.) *From Crime Policy to Victim Policy*. Basingstoke: Macmillan, pp. 17–30.

Christie, N. (1998) 'Between Civility and State' in V. Ruggiero, N. South, and I. Taylor (eds.) *The New European Criminology: Crime and Social Order in Europe*. London: Routledge.

Christie, N. (2000) *Crime Control as Industry: Towards Gulags, Western Style*. London: Routledge.

Clegg, N. (20 May 2013) 'Deputy Prime Minister's Speech: The Rehabilitation Revolution' (delivered at Nacro, London). Transcript of speech available at www.gov.uk/government/speeches/deputy-prime-ministers-speech-the-rehabilitation-revolution.

Clover, C. (1998) 'God Bless Juries!', in N. Browne (ed.), *Refiguring Film Genres*. Berkeley: University of California Press, pp. 255–277.

Cohen, S. (ed.) (1975) *Images of Deviance*. London: Penguin.

Cohen, S. (1987) *Folk Devils and Moral Panics: The Creation of the Mods and the Rockers*. 2nd edition. Oxford: Wiley-Blackwell.

Compaine, B.M. and Gomery, D. (2000) *Who Owns the Media? Competition and Concentration in the Mass Media*. London: Routledge.

Corrigan, P. and Sayer, D. (1985) *The Great Arch: English State Formation as Cultural Revolution*. Oxford: Blackwell.

Critcher, C. (2002) 'Media, Government, and Moral Panic: The Politics of Paedophilia in Britain 2000–1', *Journalism Studies*, 3(4): 521–535.

Critcher, C. (2006) *Critical Readings: Moral Panics and the Media*. Maidenhead: Open University Press.

Critcher, C. (2009) 'Widening the Focus: Moral Panics as Moral Regulation', *British Journal of Criminology*, 49(1): 17–34.

Critcher, C., Hughes, J., Petley, J., and Rohloff, A. (eds.) (2013) *Moral Panics in the Contemporary World*. New York: Bloomsbury.

Cuklanz, L. (1996) *Rape on Trial: How the Mass Media Construct Legal Reform and Social Change*. Philadelphia: University of Pennsylvannia Press.

Curtis, L. (1984) *Nothing But The Same Old Story: The Roots of Anti-Irish Racism*. Belfast: Information on Ireland.

Curtis, L. and Jempson, M. (1993) *Interference on the Airwaves: Ireland, the Media, and the Broadcasting Ban*. 2nd edition. London: Campaign for Press and Broadcasting Freedom.

Cushion, S. (2010) 'Three Phases of 24-Hour News Television', in S. Cushion and J. Lewis (eds.) *The Rise of 24-Hour News Television: Global Perspectives*. New York: Peter Lang, pp. 15–30.

Davies, N. (2009) *Flat Earth News*. London: Chatto.

Davison, W.P. (1983) 'The Third Person Effect in Communication', *Public Opinion Quarterly*, 22: 91–106.

De Lauretis, T. (1987) 'The Violence of Rhetoric: Considerations on Representation and Gender', in T. De Lauretis *Technologies of Gender: Essays on Theory, Film, and Fiction*. Bloomington: Indiana University Press, pp. 31–50.

Devlin, W.J. (2010) 'No Country for Old Men: The Decline of Ethics and the West(ern)', in J.L. McMahon and B.S. Csaki (eds.) *The Philosophy of the Western*. Lexington: University of Kentucky Press, pp. 221–239.

Dexter, G. (2008) *Why Not Catch-21? The Stories Behind the Titles*. London: Frances Lincoln.

Ditton, J. and Duffy, J. (1983) 'Bias in Newspaper Reporting of Crime News', *British Journal of Criminology*, 23(2): 159–165.

Ditton, J., Chadee, D., Farrall, S., Gilchrist, E., and Bannister, J. (2004) 'From Imitation to Intimidation: A Note on the Curious and Changing Relationship Between the Media, Crime, and Fear of Crime', *British Journal of Criminology*, 44(4): 595–610.

Donovan, P. (2002) 'Crime Legends in a New Medium: Fact, Fiction, and Loss of Authority', *Theoretical Criminology*, 6(2): 189–215.

Donovan, P. (2004) *No Way of Knowing: Crime, Urban Legends, and the Internet*. London: Routledge.

Douglas, M. (1986) *Risk Acceptability According to the Social Sciences*. London: Routledge.

Dowler, K. (2003) 'Media Consumption and Public Attitudes Toward Crime and Justice: The Relationship Between Fear of Crime, Punitive Attitudes, and Perceived Police Effectiveness', *Journal of Criminal Justice and Popular Culture*, 10(2): 109–126.

Dowler, K. (2006) 'Sex, Lies, and Videotape: The Presentation of Sex Crime in Local Television News', *Journal of Criminal Justice*, 34(4): 383–392.

Dreher, T. (2007) 'News Media Responsibilities in Reporting on Terrorism', in A. Lynch (ed.) *Law and Liberty in the War on Terror*. Sydney: Federation Press, pp. 209–221.

Driscoll, P.D., Salwen, M.B., and Garrison, B. (2005) 'Public Fear of Terrorism and the News Media', in M.B. Salwen, B. Garrison, and P.D. Driscoll (eds.) *Online News and the Public*. New Jersey: Lawrence Erlbaum Press, pp. 165–184.

Dundes, A. (1968) 'Introduction', in V.A. Propp *Morphology of the Fairytale*. Edited by L.A. Wagner. Austin: University of Texas Press.

Durkheim, É. (2008 [originally 1917]) *The Elementary Forms of Religious Life*. Oxford: Oxford University Press.

Eades, C., Grimsham, R., Silvestri, A., and Solomon, E. (2007) 'Knife Crime: A Review of Evidence and Policy', King's College London: Centre for Crime and Justice Studies.

Eagleton, T. (2005) *Holy Terror*. Oxford: Oxford University Press.

Eilders, C. (2006) 'News Factors and News Decisions: Theoretical and Methodological Advances in Germany', *Communications*, 31: 5–24.

Eldridge, J. (ed.) (1995) *The Glasgow University Media Group Reader: News Content, Language, and Visuals*. London: Routledge.

Epstein, E.J. (1973) *News from Nowhere: Television and News*. Chicago: Ivan R. Dee.

Erikson, R.V. (1991) 'Mass Media, Crime, Law and Justice', *British Journal of Criminology*, 31(3): 219–249.

Estrich, S. (1987) *Real Rape*. Cambridge, MA: Harvard University Press.

Evans, M. (2009) *The Imagination of Evil: Detective Fiction and the Modern World*. London: Continuum.

Evenson, B.J. (2007) 'Reporting the Israeli–Palestinian Conflict: A Personal View', in Wm. David Sloan and Jenn Burleson MacKay (eds.) *Media Bias: Finding it, Fixing it*. Jefferson, NC: McFarland.

Eyerman, R. (2004) 'Cultural Trauma: Slavery and the Formation of African American Identity', in J. Alexander, R. Eyerman, B. Giesen, N.J. Smelser, and P. Sztompka (eds.) *Cultural Trauma and Cultural Identity*. Berkeley: University of California Press, pp. 60–111.

Eyerman, R. (2008) *The Assassination of Theo Van Gogh: From Social Drama to Cultural Trauma*. Durham, NC: Duke University Press.

Fairclough, N. (2003) *Analysing Discourse: Textual Analysis for Social Research*. London: Routledge.

Fairclough, N. (2010) *Critical Discourse Analysis: The Critical Study of Language*. London: Longman.

Federal Bureau of Investigation (2005) 'Terrorism 2002–2005', US Department of Justice. Available at www.fbi.gov/stats-services/publications/terrorism-2002-2005/terror02_05.pdf.

Fine, G.A. (2010) *The Global Grapevine: Why Rumors of Terrorism, Immigration, and Trade Matter*. Oxford: Oxford University Press.

Finkelhor, D. (1994) 'Current Information on the Scope and Nature of Child Sex Abuse', *Child Abuse and Neglect*, 4(2): 31–53.

Fishman, M. and Cavender, G. (1998) *Entertaining Crime: Television Reality Programs*. New York: Aldine de Gruyter.

Foss, S.K. (1989) *Rhetorical Criticism: Exploration and Practice*. Prospect Heights, IL: Waveland.

Foucault, M. (1988) 'Technologies of the Self', in L.H. Martin (ed.) *Technologies of the Self: A Seminar with Michel Foucault*. Amherst: University of Massachusetts Press, pp. 16–49.

Foucault, M. (1990) *The History of Sexuality: Volume One, an Introduction*. London: Vintage.

Foucault, M. (1995) *Discipline and Punish: The Birth of the Prison*. London: Vintage.

Fox, R.L, Van Sickel, R.W., and Steiger, T.L. (2007) *Tabloid Justice: Criminal Justice in an Age of Media Frenzy*. 2nd edition. Boulder, CO: Lynne Rienner.

Fried, A. (2005) 'Terrorism as a Context of Coverage Before the Iraq War', *The International Journal of Press/Politics*, 10(3): 125–132.

Friel, H. and Falk, R.A. (2007) *Israel–Palestine on Record: How the New York Times Mis-Reports Conflict in the Middle East*. London: Verso.

Gadarian, S.K. (2010) 'The Politics of Threat: How Terrorism News Shapes Foreign Policy Attitudes', *The Journal of Politics*, 72: 469–483.

Galtung, J. and Ruge, M.H. (1965) 'The Structure of Foreign News', *Journal of Peace Research*, 2(1): 64–91.

Gans, H. (1979) *Deciding What's News: A Study of CBS Evening News, NBC Nightly News, Newsweek and Time*. New York: Random House.

Garfinkel, H. (1956) 'Conditions of Successful Status Degradation Ceremonies', *American Journal of Sociology*, 61(5): 420–424.

Garland, D. (2001) *The Culture of Control: Crime and Social Order in Contemporary Society*. Chicago: University of Chicago Press.

Garland, D. (2008) 'On the Concept of Moral Panic', *Crime, Media, Culture*, 4(9): 9–30.

Garofalo, J. (1981) 'Crime and the Mass Media: A Selective Review of Research', *Journal of Research in Crime and Delinquency*, 18: 319–350.

Gee, J.P. (2010a) *An Introduction to Discourse Analysis: Theory and Method*. London: Routledge.

Gee, J.P. (2010b) *How to do Discourse Analysis: A Toolkit*. London: Routledge.

Gerbner, G., Gross, L., Morgan, M., and Signorielli, N. (1980) 'The Mainstreaming of America: Violence Profile No. 11', *Journal of Communications*, 30: 10–29.

Gershkoff, A. and Kushner, S. (2005) 'Shaping Public Opinion: The 9/11–Iraq Connection in the Bush Administration's Rhetoric', *Perspectives on Politics*, 3: 525–537.

Gever, M. (2005) 'The Spectacle of Crime, Digitalized: Crime Scene Investigation and Social Anatomy', *European Journal of Cultural Studies*, 8(4): 445–463.

Giesen, B. (2004) 'The Trauma of Perpetrators: The Holocaust as the Traumatic Reference of German National Identity', in J. Alexander, R. Eyerman, B. Giesen, N.J. Smelser, and P. Sztompka (eds.) *Cultural Trauma and Cultural Identity*. Berkeley: University of California Press, pp. 112–154.

Gillespie, M. and McLaughlin, E. (2002) 'Media and the Shaping of Public Attitudes', *Criminal Justice Matters*, 49(1).

Gilliam, F.D. and Iyengar, S. (2000) 'Prime Suspects: The Influence of Local Television News on the Viewing Public', *American Journal of Political Science*, 44(3): 560–573.

Global Media Monitoring Project (2010) 'Who Makes the News: Global Report'. Published by Creative Commons. Available at www.whomakesthenews.org/images/reports_2010/global/gmmp_global_report_en.pdf.

Goddard, C. and Saunders, B.J. (2001) 'Child Abuse and the Media', *Child Abuse Prevention Issues*, 14 (Winter). Online edition, available at www.aifs.gov.au/nch/pubs/issues/issues14/issues14.html.

Golding, P. and Elliott, P. (1979) *Making the News*. London: Longman in H. Tumber (ed.) (1999) *News: A Reader*. Oxford: Oxford University Press.

Goode, E. and Ben-Yehuda, N. (2009) *Moral Panics: The Social Construction of Deviance*. 2nd edition. Oxford: Blackwell.

Graber, D. (1980) *Crime News and the Public*. New York: Praeger.

Greer, C. (2003) *Sex Crime and the Media: Sex Offending and the Press in a Divided Society*. London: Willan.

Greer, C. (2004) 'Crime, Media, and Community: Grief and Virtual Engagement in Late Modernity', in J. Ferrell, K. Hayward, W. Morrison, and M. Presdee (eds.) *Cultural Criminology Unleashed*. London: Routledge, pp. 109–121.

Greer, C. (2007) 'News Media, Victims, and Crime', in P. Davies, P. Francis, and C. Greer (eds.) *Victims, Crime, and Society*. London: Sage, pp. 20–50.

Griffin, S. (1977 [originally 1971]) 'Rape: The All-American Crime', in D. Chappel, R. Geis, and G. Geis (eds.) *Forcible Rape: The Crime, The Victim, and the Offender*. New York: Columbia University Press, pp. 47–67.

Gross, K. (2008) 'Framing Persuasive Appeals: Episodic and Thematic Framing, Emotional Response, and Policy Opinion', *Political Psychology*, 29(2): 169–192.

Gunning, T. (1990) 'The Cinema of Attractions: Early Film, Its Spectator and the Avant-Garde', in T. Elsaesser (ed.) *Early Cinema: Space Frame Narrative*. London: British Film Institute, pp. 56–62.

Habermas, J. (1991) *The Structural Transformation of the Public Sphere: An Inquiry into a Category of Bourgeois Society*. Cambridge, MA: MIT Press.

Habermas, J. (1997) *Legitimation Crisis*. Cambridge: Polity Press.

Hackett, R.A., Gruneau, R. Gutstein, D., Gibson, T., and Newswatch Canada (2000) *The Missing News: Filters and Blind Spots in Canada's Press*. Toronto: Garamond Press.

Hall, S. (1973) 'The Determination of News Photographs', in S. Cohen and J. Young (eds.) *The Manufacture of News: A Reader*. London: Sage, pp. 176–190.

Hall, S., Critcher, C., Jefferson, T., Clarke, J.N., and Roberts, B. (2013) *Policing the Crisis: Mugging, the State, and Law and Order*. 35th anniversary edition. Basingstoke: Palgrave Macmillan.

Hark, I.R. (2012) *Deadwood*. Michigan: Wayne State University Press.

Hayes, M. (2003) 'Political Violence, Irish Republicanism and the British Media: Semantics, Symbiosis and the State', in P. Mason (ed.) *Criminal Visions: Media Representations of Crime and Justice*. London: Routledge, pp. 133–155.

Heath, L. (1984) 'Impact of Newspaper Crime Reports on Fear of Crime: Multimethodological Investigation', *Journal of Personality and Social Psychology*, 47(2): 263–276.

Henley, N.M., Miller, M., and Beazley, J.A. (1995) 'Syntax, Semantics, and Sexual Violence Agency and the Passive Voice', *Journal of Language and Social Psychology*, 14(1–2): 60–84.

Herman, E.S. and Chomsky, N. (1988) *Manufacturing Consent: The Political Economy of the Mass Media*. New York: Pantheon Books.

Heywood, K.J. (2007) 'Situational Crime Prevention and its Discontents: Rational Choice Theory Versus the "Culture of Now"', *Social Policy Administration*, 41(3): 232–250.

Hiebert, R.E. and Gibbons, S.J. (2000) *Exploring Mass Media for a Changing World*. London: Routledge.

Hier, S. (2002) 'Conceptualizing Moral Panic through a Moral Economy of Harm', *Critical Sociology*, 28: 311–334.

Hier, S. (2008) 'Thinking Beyond Moral Panic: Risk, Responsibility, and the Politics of Moralization', *Theoretical Criminology*, 12: 171–188.

Hill, E. (2006) '"What's Afflictin' You?" Corporeality, Body Crises, and the Body Politic in *Deadwood*', in D. Lavery (ed.) *Reading Deadwood: A Western to Swear By*. London: I.B. Tauris, pp. 171–184.

Hilton, J.T. (2006) *All the News that's Fit to Sell: How the Market Transforms Information into News*. Princeton, NJ: Princeton University Press.

Home Office (2000) 'Rape and Sexual Assault of Women: The Extent and Nature of the Problem', Home Office Research Study 237. Available at www.iiav.nl/epublications/2002/rape_and_sexual_assault_of_women.pdf.

Home Office (2009) 'Homicides, Firearm Offences, and Intimate Violence 2007/08', Statistical Bulletin for the Home Office. Available at http://webarchive.national archives.gov.uk/20110220105210/rds.homeoffice.gov.uk/rds/pdfs09/hosb0209.pdf.

Howitt, D. (1998) *Crime, the Media, and the Law*. New York: Wiley.

Hunt, A. (2003) 'Risk and Moralization in Everyday Life', in R.V. Ericson and A. Doyle (eds.) *Risk and Morality*. Toronto: Toronto University Press, pp. 165–193.

Innes, M. (2003) 'Signal Crimes, Detective-Work, Mass Media, and Constructing Collective Memory', in P. Mason (ed.) *Criminal Visions: Representations of Crime and Justice*. Collumpton: Willan.

Innes, M. (2004) 'Signal Crimes and Signal Disorders: Notes on Deviance as Communicative Action', *British Journal of Sociology*, 55(3): 335–355.

Innes, M. and Fielding, N. (2002) 'From Community to Communicative Policing: "Signal Crimes" and the Problem of Public Reassurance', *Sociological Research Online*, 7(2). Available at www.socresonline.org.uk/7/2/innes.html.

Iyengar, S. (1991) *Is Anyone Responsible? How Television Frames Political Issues*. Chicago: Chicago University Press.

Jacobs, J. (2012) *Deadwood*. London: BFI.

Jenkins, P. (1992) *Intimate Enemies: Moral Panics in Contemporary Great Britain*. New York: Aldine de Gruyter.

Jenkins, P. (1996) *Pedophiles and Priests: Anatomy of a Contemporary Crisis*. Oxford: Oxford University Press.

Jenkins, P. (1999) *Synthetic Panics: The Symbolic Politics of Designer Drugs*. New York: New York University Press.

Jermyn, D. (2007) *Crime Watching: Investigating Real Crime TV*. London: I.B. Tauris.

Jewkes, Y. (2011) *Media and Crime*. 2nd edition. London: Sage.

Katz, J. (1987) 'What Makes Crime "News"?' *Media Culture and Society*, 9.

Kitses, J. (2004) *Horizons West: Directing the Western from John Ford to Clint Eastwood*. London: BFI.

Kitzinger, J. (1996) 'Media Representation of Sexual Abuse Risks', *Child Abuse Review*, 5: 319–333.

Kitzinger, J. (1999) 'The Ultimate Neighbour from Hell? Stranger Danger and the Media Framing of Paedophilia', in C. Critcher (ed.) *Critical Readings: Moral Panics and the Media*. Maidenhead: Open University Press, pp. 135–147.

Kitzinger, J. (2004) 'Media Coverage of Sexual Violence Against Women and Children', in K. Ross and C.M. Byerly (eds.) *Women and Media: International Perspectives*. Oxford: Blackwell, pp. 13–38.

Kitzinger, J. and Skidmore, S. (1995) 'Playing Safe: Media Coverage of Child Sex Abuse Prevention Strategies', *Child Abuse Review*, 4(1): 47–56.

Korn, A. and Efrat, S. (2004) 'The Coverage of Rape in the Popular Israeli Press', *Violence Against Women*, 10(9): 1056–1074.

Krippendorff, K.H. (2012) *Content Analysis: An Introduction to Its Methodology*. London: Sage.

Krippendorff, K.H. and Bock, M.A. (eds.) (2009) *The Content Analysis Reader*. London: Sage.

Kubrin, C.E. (2005) 'Gangstas, Thugs, and Hustlas: Identity and the Code of the Street in Rap Music', *Social Problems*, 52(3): 360–378.

Lang, A., Newhagen, J., and Reeves, B. (1996) 'Negative Video as Structure: Emotion, Attention, Capacity, and Memory', *Journal of Broadcasting and Electronic Media*, 40(4): 460–477.

Larcombe, W. (2002) 'The Ideal Victim Vs Successful Rape Complainants: Not What You Might Expect', *Feminist Legal Studies*, 10: 131–148.

Lavery, D. (ed.) (2006) *Reading Deadwood: A Western to Swear By*. London: I.B. Tauris.

Lees, S. (1995) 'The Media Reporting of Rape: The 1993 British "Date Rape" Controversy', in D.D. Kidd-Hewitt and R. Osborne (eds.) *Crime and the Media: The Post-Modern Spectacle*. London: Pluto Press.

Lees, S. (2002) *Carnal Knowledge: Rape on Trial*. 2nd edition. London: The Women's Press Ltd.

Lenz, T.O. (2003) *Changing Images of Law in Film and Television Crime Stories*. New York: Peter Lang.

Levenson, J. (2004) 'The War on What, Exactly? Why the Press must be Precise', *Columbia Journalism Review*, 43(4): 9–11.

Levi, M. (2009) 'Suite Revenge? The Shaping of Folk Devils and Moral Panics about White-Collar Crime', *British Journal of Criminology*, 49(1): 48–67.

Lévi-Strauss, C. (2005 [original 1978]) *Myth and Meaning*. London: Routledge.

Liebes, T. and First, A. (2003) 'Framing the Israeli–Palestinian Conflict', in P. Norris, M. Kern, and M.R. Just (eds.) *Framing Terrorism: The News Media, the Government, and the Public*. London: Routledge, pp. 59–74.

Lieblich, A., Tuval-Mashiach, R., and Zilber, T. (1998) *Narrative Research: Reading, Analysis, and Interpretation*. Thousand Oaks: Sage.

Lloyd, A. (1995) *Doubly Deviant, Doubly Damned: Society's Treatment of Violent Women*. London: Penguin.

Lowney, K. and Best, J. (1995) 'Stalking Strangers and Lovers: Changing Media Typifications of a New Media Problem', in J. Best (ed.) *Images of Issues: Typifying Contemporary Social Issues*. New York: Aldine Transaction, pp. 33–59.

Lowry, D.T., Nio, J., and Leitner, D.W. (2003) 'Setting the Public Fear Agenda: A Longitudinal Analysis of Network TV Crime Reporting, Public Perceptions of Crime, and FBI Crime Statistics', *Journal of Communication*, 53(1): 61–73.

Lule, J. (2001) *Daily News, Eternal Stories: The Mythological Role of Journalism*. New York: Guildford Press.

Lynch, M. (2002) 'Pedophiles and Cyber-Predators as Contaminating Forces: The Language of Disgust, Pollution, and Boundary Invasions in Federal Debates on Sex Offender Legislation', *Law and Social Inquiry*, 27(3): 529–566.

Machin, D. and Mayr, A. (2012) *How To Do Critical Discourse Analysis: A Multimodal Introduction*. London: Sage.

Marsh, H.L. (1991) 'A Comparative Analysis of Crime Coverage in Newspapers in the United States and Other Countries from 1960–1989: A Review of the Literature', *Journal of Criminal Justice*, 19: 67–79.

Marx, K. and Engels, F. (2004) *The Communist Manifesto*. London: Penguin.

Mason, P. (2006) 'Prison Decayed: Cinematic Penal Discourse and Popularism 1995–2005', *Social Semiotics*, 16(4): 607–626.

Mathiesen, T. (2000) *Prisons on Trial*. London: Waterside.

Mawby, R.C. (2010) 'Chibnall Revisited: Crime Reporters, the Police and "Law-and-Order News"', *British Journal of Criminology*, 50(6): 1060–1076.

McChesney, R. (1999) *Rich Media, Poor Democracy: Communication Politics in Dubious Times*. London: New Press.

McCormick, C. (1995) *Constructing Danger: The Mis/Representation of Crime in the News*. Halifax, Nova Scotia: Fernwood Publishing.

McLuhan, M. (1964) *Understanding Media: The Extensions of Man*. New York: McGraw-Hill.

McRobbie, A. and Thornton, S. (1995) 'Rethinking "Moral Panic": The Construction of Deviance', *British Journal of Sociology*, 46(4): 559–574.

Mehrhof, B. and Kearon, P. (2005 [originally 1971]) 'Rape: An Act of Terror' in D. Keetley and J. Pettegrew (eds.) *Public Women, Public Words, Volume III: A Documentary History of American Feminism*. Oxford: Rowman & Littlefield.

Meyer, P. (2009) *The Vanishing Newspaper: Saving Journalism in the Information Age*. 2nd edition. Columbia, MI: University of Missouri Press.

Meyers, M. (1997) *News Coverage of Violence Against Women: Engendering Blame*. London: Sage.

Meyers, M. (2004a) 'African American Women and Violence: Gender, Race, and Class in the News', *Critical Studies in Mass Communication*, 21(2): 95–118.

Meyers, M. (2004b) 'Crack Mothers in the News: A Narrative of Paternalistic Racism', *Journal of Communication Inquiry*, 28(3): 194–216.

Michelle, C. and Weaver, K.C. (2003) 'Discursive Manoeuvres and Hegemonic Recuperations in New Zealand Documentary Representations of Domestic Violence', *Feminist Media Studies*, 3(3): 283–299.

Miller, D. (1994) *Don't Mention the War: Northern Ireland, Propaganda, and the Media*. London: Pluto Press.

Miller, W.I. (1998) 'Clint Eastwood and Equity: Popular Culture's Theory of Revenge', in A. Sarat and T.R. Kearns (eds.) *Law in the Domains of Culture*. Ann Arbor: University of Michigan Press, pp. 161–202.

Ministry of Justice (2009) *Statistical Bulletin: Story of the Prison Population 1995–2009*. London: Ministry of Justice.

Mitchell, L.C. (1996) *Westerns: Making the Man in Fiction and Film*. Chicago: University of Chicago Press.

Moeller, S.D. (2004) 'A Moral Imagination', in S. Allen and B. Zelizer (eds.) *Reporting War*. London: Routledge, pp. 59–76.

Moore, S.E.H. (2009) 'The Cautionary Tale: The British Media's Handling of Drug-Facilitated Sexual Assault', *Crime, Media, Culture*, 5(3).

Moore, S.E.H. (2011) 'Tracing the Life of a Crime Category: The Shifting Meaning of Date Rape', *Feminist Media Studies*, 11(4).

Moore, S.E.H. (2013) 'The Cautionary Tale: A New Paradigm for Studying Media Coverage of Crime', in C. Critcher, J. Hughes, and J. Petty (eds.) *Moral Panics*. London: Routledge, pp. 33–49.

Muravchik, J. (2003) *Covering the Intifada: How the Media Reported the Palestinian Uprising*. Washington, DC: Brookings Institution.

Nacos, B.L. (1996) *Terrorism and the Media: From the Iran Hostage Crisis to the Oklahoma City Bombing*. New York: Columbia University Press.

Nacos, B.L. (2002) *Mass-Mediated Terrorism: The Central Role of the Media in Terrorism and Counter-Terrorism*. Maryland: Rowman & Littlefield.

Nelmes, J. (2003) *An Introduction to Film Studies*. London: Routledge.

Nelson, B.J. (1984) *Making an Issue of Child Sex Abuse: Political Agenda-Setting for Social Problems*. Chicago: University of Chicago Press.

Neuendorf, K.A. (2002) *The Content Analysis Guidebook*. London: Sage.

'Newspaper Sites Across Europe Demonstrate Growth in the Past Year' (2011). *ComScore*, 18th August. Available at www.comscore.com/Press_Events/Press_Releases/2011/8/Newspaper_Sites_across_Europe_Demonstrate_Growth_in_the_Past_Year/.

Norris, P., Kern, M., and Just, M.R. (2003) 'Framing Terrorism', in P. Norris, M. Kern, and M.R. Just (eds.) *Framing Terrorism: The News Media, the Government, and the Public*. London: Routledge, pp. 3–26.

NSPCC (2010) 'Child Abuse and Neglect in the UK Today'. Available at www.nspcc.org.uk/Inform/research/findings/child_abuse_neglect_research_PDF_wdf84181.pdf.

Oakes, G. (1975) *Roscher and Knies: The Logical Problems of Historical Economics*. New York: Free Press.

O'Connell, M. and Whelan, A. (1996) 'The Public Perception of Crime Prevalence, Newspaper Readership, and "Mean World" Attitudes', *Legal and Criminological Psychology*, 1: 179–195.

Organisation for Economic Co-operation and Development (2010) 'The Evolution of News and the Internet'. Paris: Directorate for Science, Technology, and Industry.

O'Sullivan, S. (2001) 'Representations of Prison in Nineties Hollywood Cinema: From *Con Air* to *The Shawshank Redemption*', *The Howard Journal of Criminal Justice*, 40(4): 317–334.

Palmer, G. (2003) *Discipline and Liberty: Television and Governance*. Manchester: Manchester University Press.

Paltridge, B. (2012) *Discourse Analysis: An Introduction*. London: Continuum.

Papke, D.R. (1999) 'Conventional Wisdom: The Courtroom Trial in American Popular Culture', *Marquette Law Review, Faculty Publications*. Paper 61. Available at http://scholarship.law.marquette.edu/facpub/61.

Parisi, P. (1998) 'The *New York Times* Looks at One Block in Harlem: Narratives of Race in Journalism', *Critical Studies in Mass Communication*, 15(3): 236–254.

Park, R.E. (1999 [originally 1940]) 'News as a Form of Knowledge: A Chapter in the Sociology of Knowledge', in H. Tumber (ed.) *News: A Reader*. Oxford: Oxford University Press, pp. 11–15.

Pastor, J.F. (2009) *Terrorism and Public Safety Policing: Implications of the Obama Presidency*. New York: Taylor and Francis.

Peelo, M., Francis, B., Soothill, K., Pearson, J., and Ackerley, E. (2004) 'Newspaper Reporting and the Public Construction of Homicide', *British Journal of Criminology*, 44(2): 256–275.

Philo, G. and Berry, M. (2004) *Bad News From Israel*. London: Pluto Press.

Pippin, R.B. (2009) 'What is a Western? Politics and Self-Knowledge in John Ford's *The Searchers*', *Critical Inquiry*, 35(2): 223–253.

Pitts, G. (2002) *Kings of Convergence*. Toronto: Doubleday.

Propp, V.A. (1968) *Morphology of the Fairytale*. Edited by L.A. Wagner. Austin: University of Texas Press.

Prosise, T.O. and Johnson, A. (2004) 'Law Enforcement and Crime on *Cops* and *World's Wildest Police Videos*: Anecdotal Form and the Justification of Racial Profiling', *Western Journal of Communication*, 68(1): 72–91.

Reiner, R., Livingstone, S., and Allen, J. (2003) 'From Law and Order to Lynch Mobs: Crime News Since the Second World War', in P. Mason (ed.) *Criminal Visions: Media Representations of Crime and Justice*. Collumpton: Willan, pp. 13–32.

Richardson, J.E. (2004) *(Mis)representing Islam: The Racism and Rhetoric of British Broadsheet Newspapers*. Philadelphia: John Benjamins.

Riffe, D., Lacy, S., and Fico, F. (2005) *Analyzing Media Messages: Using Quantitative Content Analysis in Research*. London: Routledge.

Rohloff, A., Hughes, J., Petley, J., and Critcher, C. (2013) 'Moral Panics in the Contemporary World: Enduring Controversies and Future Directions', in C. Critcher, J. Hughes, J. Petley, and A. Rohloff (eds.) *Moral Panics in the Contemporary World*. New York: Bloomsbury Academic, pp. 1–32.

Rolston, B. (1996) 'Political Censorship', in B. Rolston and D. Miller (eds.) *War and Words: The Northern Ireland Media Reader*. Belfast: Beyond the Pale, pp. 235–243.

Rosnow, R.L. (1991) 'Inside Rumour: A Personal Journey', *American Psychologist*, 46: 484–496.

Rubin, A.M., Haridakis, P.M., Hullman, G.A., Sun, S., Chikombero, P.A., and Pornsakulvanich, V. (2003) 'Television Exposure not Predictive of Terrorism Fear', *Newspaper Research Journal*, 24.

Russell, D.E.H. (1982) *Rape in Marriage*. New York: Macmillan.

Russell, D.E.H. (1986) *The Secret Trauma: Incest in the Lives of Girls and Women*. New York: Perseus Press.

Ruthven, M. (2007 [originally 2001]) 'Cultural Schizophrenia', in F. Haulley (ed.) *Critical Perspectives on 9/11*. New York: The Rosen Publishing Group.

Sacco, V.F. (1995) 'Media Constructions of Crime', *The Annals of the American Academy of Political and Social Science*, 539: 141–154.

Sacco, V.F. and Fair, B.J. (1980) 'Images of Legal Control: Crime News and the Process of Organizational Legitimation', *Canadian Journal of Communication*, 13(3/4): 114–123.

Said, E. (1997) *Covering Islam: How the Media and Experts Determine How We See the Rest of the World*. New York: Vintage Books.

Saunders, D. and Vanstone, M. (2010) 'Rehabilitation as Presented in British Film: Shining a Light on Desistance from Crime?' *The Howard Journal of Criminal Justice*, 49(4): 375–393.

Schlesinger, P. and Tumber, H. (1994) *Reporting Crime: The Media Politics of Criminal Justice*. London: Clarendon Press.

Scraggs, J. (2005) *Crime Fiction*. London: Routledge.

Scribner, T. and Chapman, R. (2010) 'Wall Street Journal', in R. Chapman (ed.) *Culture Wars: An Encyclopaedia of Issues, Viewpoints, and Voices. Volume I*. Armonk, NY: M.E. Sharpe.

Shelton, D.E., Young, S.K., and Barak, G. (2006) 'A Study of Juror Expectations and Demands Concerning Scientific Evidence: Does the "*CSI* Effect" Exist?', *Vanderbilt Journal of Entertainment and Technology Law*, 9(2): 331–368.

Sherizen, S. (1978) 'Social Creation of Crime News', in C. Winick (ed.) *Deviance and Mass Media*. Beverly Hills: Sage.

Silbey, J. (2007) 'A History of Representations of Justice. Coincident Preoccupations of Law and Film', in A. Masson and K. O'Connor (eds.) *Representations of Justice*. New York: Peter Lang, pp. 131–154.

Silvestri, A., Oldfield, M., Squires, P., and Grimshaw, R. (2009) 'Young People, Knives and Guns: A Comprehensive Review, Analysis, and Critique of Gun and Knife Crime Strategies', King's College London: Centre for Crime and Justice Studies.

Smelser, N.J. (2004) 'Epilogue: September 11, 2001, as Cultural Trauma', in J. Alexander, R. Eyerman, B. Giesen, N.J. Smelser, and P. Sztompka (eds.) *Cultural Trauma and Cultural Identity*. Berkeley: University of California Press, pp. 264–282.

Soothill, K. (1991) 'The Changing Face of Rape?', *British Journal of Criminology*, 31(4): 383–392.

Soothill, K. and Walby, S. (1991) *Sex Crime in the News*. London: Routledge.

Sparks, R. (1992) *Television and the Drama of Crime: Moral Tales and the Place of Crime in Public Life*. Milton Keynes: Open University Press.

Stern, P.V.D. (1941) 'The Case of the Corpse in the Blind Alley', *The Virginia Quarterly Review*, Spring: 227–236.

Surette, R. (2010) *Media, Crime, and Criminal Justice: Images and Realities*. 2nd edition. Belmont, CA: Wadsworth Press.

Sutherland, E. (1940) 'White-Collar Criminality', *American Sociological Review*, 5(1): 2–10.

Sutton, R. and Farrall, S. (2005) 'Gender, Socially Responsible Reporting and the Fear of Crime: Are Women Really More Anxious About Crime?', *British Journal of Criminology*, 45(2): 212–224.

Sztompka, P. (2000) 'Cultural Trauma: The Other Face of Social Change', *European Journal of Social Theory*, 3: 449–466.

Taylor, P. (1996) 'The Semantics of Political Violence', in B. Rolston and D. Miller (eds.) *War and Words: The Northern Ireland Media Reader*. Belfast: Beyond the Pale, pp. 329–339.

Taylor, P.M. (1999) *British Propaganda in the Twentieth Century: Selling Democracy*. Edinburgh: Edinburgh University Press.

Teo, P. (2000) 'Racism in the News: A Critical Discourse Analysis of Reporting in Two Australian Newspapers', *Discourse and Society*, 11(1): 7–49.

TE-SAT (2011) 'EU Terrorism Situation and Trend Report', The Hague: Europol. Available at www.europol.europa.eu/sites/default/files/publications/te-sat2011_0.pdf.

Thatcher, M. 'Speech at Stormont Castle Lunch', 28 May 1981 (broadcast on BBC Radio News on the same day at 6pm, released as a Press Release by the NIO). Transcript of speech available at www.margaretthatcher.org/document/104657.

Thompson, K. (1998) *Moral Panics*. London: Routledge.

Thussu, D.K. (2006) 'Televising the "War on Terrorism": The Myths of Morality', in P. Anandam Kavoori and T. Fraley (eds.) *Media, Terrorism, and Theory: A Reader*. Maryland: Rowman & Littlefield.

Todorov, T. (1981) *Introduction to Poetics*. Minneapolis: University of Minnesota Press.

Tunstall, J. (1999) *The Anglo-American Media Connection*. Oxford: Oxford University Press.

Turner, F.J. (1921) *The Frontier in American History*. New York: Henry Holt and Co.

Turner, V. (1980) 'Social Dramas and Stories About Them', *Critical Inquiry*, 7(1): 141–168.

Ungar, S. (2001) 'Moral Panic Versus the Risk Society: The Implications of the Changing Sites of Social Anxiety', *British Journal of Sociology*, 52(2): 271–291.

US Department of Justice (2006) 'Extent, Nature, and Consequences of Rape Victimization: Findings from the National Violence Against Women Survey'. Available at www.ncjrs.gov/pdffiles1/nij/210346.pdf.

Valverde, M. (2008) 'From the Hard-Boiled Detective to the Pre-Crime Unit', in C. Greer (ed.) *Crime and the Media: A Reader*. London: Routledge, Chapter 24.

Voumvakis, S. and Ericson, R. (1984) *News Accounts of Attacks on Women: A Comparison of Three Toronto Newspapers*. Toronto: Toronto University Press.

Waiton, S. (2008) *The Politics of Antisocial Behavior: Amoral Panics*. New York and London: Routledge.

Wardlaw, G. (1989) *Political Terrorism: Theory, Tactics, and Counter-Measures*. 2nd edition. Cambridge: Cambridge University Press, pp. 76–86.

Wardle, C. (2008) 'Crime Reporting', in B. Franklin (ed.) *Pulling Newspapers Apart: Analysing Print Journalism*. London: Routledge, pp. 136–144.

Wardle, C. and Gans-Boriskin, R. (2004) 'Who Deserves to Die? Discussions of the Death Penalty on Primetime Television', *Journal for Crime, Conflict, and the Media*, 1(3): 68–88.

Warshow, R. (2002 [originally 1956]) 'Movie Chronicle: The Westerner', in R. Warshow *The Immediate Experience: Movies, Comics, Theatre, and Other Aspects of Popular Culture.* Cambridge, MA: Harvard University Press, pp. 105–124.

Weaver, D.H. and Wilhoit, G.C. (1991) *The American Journalist: A Portrait of US News People and Their Work.* 2nd edition. Bloomington: University of Indiana Press.

Welch, M., Weber, L., and Edwards, W. (2000) 'All the News that's Fit to Print: A Content Analysis of the Correctional Debate in the New York Times', *The Prison Journal,* 80(3): 245–264.

Westerfelhaus, R. and Lacroix, C. (2009) 'Waiting for the Barbarians: HBO's Deadwood as a Post-9/11 Ritual of Disquiet', *Southern Communication Journal,* 74(1): 18–39.

White, D.M. (1950) 'The Gatekeeper', *Journalism Quarterly,* 27: 383–390.

Wilczynski, A. and Sinclair, K. (1999) 'Moral Tales: Representations of Child Abuse in the Quality and Tabloid Media', *The Australian and New Zealand Journal of Criminology,* 32: 262–283.

Wilde, O. (2008 [originally 1891]) *The Soul of Man Under Socialism.* Hong Kong: Forgotten Books.

Wilkinson, P. (1997) 'The Media and Terrorism: A Reassessment', *Terrorism and Political Violence,* 9(2): 51–64.

Williams, P. and Dickinson, J. (1993) 'Fear of Crime: Read all about it? The Relationship between Newspaper Crime Reporting and Fear of Crime', *British Journal of Criminology,* 33(11): 33–56.

Wilson, B. (2010) *What Price Liberty? How Freedom Was Won and is Being Lost.* London: Faber and Faber.

Wilson, D. and O'Sullivan, S. (2004) *Images of Incarceration: Representations of Prison in Film and Television Drama.* London: Waterside.

Winkel, F.W. and Vrij, A. (1990) 'Fear of Crime and Media Crime Reports: Testing Similarity Hypotheses', *International Review of Victimology,* 1: 251–266.

Wooffitt, R. (2005) *Conversation Analysis and Discourse Analysis: A Comparative and Critical Introduction.* London: Sage.

Young, J. (1971) 'The Role of the Police as Amplifiers of Deviancy, Negotiators of Reality and Translators of Fantasy: Some Aspects of Our Present System of Drug Control as Seen in Notting Hill', in S. Cohen (ed.) *Images of Deviance.* Harmondsworth: Penguin.

Zelizer, B. (ed.) (2009) *The Changing Faces of Journalism: Tabloidization, Technology, and Truthiness.* London: Routledge.

Zelizer, V. (1994) *Pricing the Priceless Child: The Changing Social Value of Children.* Princeton, NJ: Princeton University Press.

Zillman, D. and Wakshlag, J. (1987) 'Fear of Victimisation and the Appeal of Crime Drama', in D. Zillman and J. Bryant (eds.) *Selective Exposure to Communication.* Hillsdale, NJ: Erlbaum.

## Filmography

Francis Ford Coppola (dir.) (1997) *The Rainmaker.* USA: Constellation Films.

Jonathan Demme (dir.) (1993) *Philadelphia.* USA: Tristar.

John Ford (dir.) (1939) *Stagecoach*. USA: United Artists.

John Ford (dir.) (1956) *The Searchers*. USA: United Artists.

John Ford (dir.) (1962) *The Man Who Shot Liberty Valence*. USA: United Artists.

Howard Hawks (dir.) (1946) *The Big Sleep*. USA: Warner Bros.

John Huston (dir.) (1941) *The Maltese Falcon*. USA: Warner Bros.

Stanley Kubrick (dir.) (1971 USA, 1972 UK) *A Clockwork Orange*. UK: Warner Bros.

Sergio Leone (dir.) (1964) *A Fistful of Dollars*. USA: United Artists.

Sergio Leone (dir.) (1965) *For a Few Dollars More*. USA: United Artists.

Sergio Leone (dir.) (1966) *The Good, The Bad, and The Ugly*. USA: United Artists.

Sidney Lumet (dir.) (1957) *12 Angry Men*. USA: MGM, United Artists.

Anthony Mann (dir.) (1950) *Winchester '73:* USA: Universal Pictures.

Anthony Mann (dir.) (1953) *The Man From Laramie*. USA: Columbia Pictures.

Robert Mulligan (dir.) (1962) *To Kill a Mockingbird*. USA: Universal Pictures.

Alan J. Pakula (dir.) (1993) *The Pelican Brief*. USA: Warner Bros.

Sam Peckinpah (dir.) (1969) *The Wild Bunch*. USA: Warner Bros.

Otto Preminger (dir.) (1959) *Anatomy of a Murder*. USA: Columbia Pictures.

Billy Wilder (dir.) (1957) *Witness for the Prosecution*. USA: Universal Artists.

## News

BBC News Online (2010) Bloody Sunday report published, 15 June.

*Daily Mail* (1993) 'Three Suspects Named in Race Murder Hunt', 22nd December.

*Daily Mail Online* (2008) 'The Five Troubled Victims of the Suffolk Prostitute Slayer', 16th January. Available at www.dailymail.co.uk/news/article-508727/The-troubled-victims-Suffolk-prostitute-slayer.html.

*Daily Mail Online* (2011) 'Jo's Last Night Out', 14th October. Available at www.daily-mail.co.uk/news/article-2048622/Vincent-Tabak-trial-Pictures-Joanna-Yeates-drinking-night-died.html.

Greenslade, R. (2011) 'Norway or Amy? How Editors Confront the Hierarchy of Death', The Greenslade Blog at *The Guardian Online*. Available at www.guardian.co.uk/media/greenslade/2011/jul/25/norway-amywinehouse.

Martinson, J. (2011) 'Rape is Rape, Ken Clarke', *The Guardian Online*, 18 May 2011, Comment is Free. Available at www.theguardian.com/commentisfree/2011/may/18/rape-ken-clarke-serious-5-live.

*New York Times* (1999) 'Ruling on Tight Jeans and Rape Sets Off Anger in Italy', 16th February: A6.

*Orlando Sentinel* (1996) 'Rape Victims Urge Harsh Penalties for Rohypnol', 17th July.

*Sunday Mirror* (2006) 'Knife Crime Soaring: 236 Stabbed to Death in Year; 5,784 Stopped with Weapons; 37 Pupils Stopped with Blades', 18th June 18: 2.

*Telegraph Herald* (2011) 'Police: Be Wary of Date-Rape Drugs', 2nd October: 12.

*The Times* (1993) 'Inquest Halted on Stabbed Schoolboy', 22nd December.

*Washington Post* (2001) 'America at War', 12 September: A22.

## Novels and short stories

Chandler, R. (2000 [originally 1939]) *The Big Sleep and Other Novels*. London: Penguin.

Chandler, R. (2005 [originally 1949]) *The Little Sister*. London: Penguin.

Christie, A. (1948 [originally 1926]) *The Murder of Roger Ackroyd*. London: Penguin.

Christie, A. (1948 [originally 1938]) *Appointment with Death*. London: Penguin.

Christie, A. (1985 [originally 1953]) *A Pocket Full of Rye*. London: Chivers.

Christie, A. (2007 [originally *Ten Little Niggers*, 1939]) *And Then There Were None*. London: Harper.

Christie, A. (2011 [originally 1952]) *They Do It With Mirrors*. London: Harper.

Collins, W. (1998 [originally 1868]) *The Moonstone*. London: Penguin.

Collins, W. (2007 [originally 1859]) *The Woman in White*. London: Penguin.

Doyle, A.C. (1999 [originally 1890]) 'The Sign of Four', in A.C. Doyle *The Original and Complete Illustrated 'Strand' Sherlock Holmes: Vol I*. London: Wordsworth, pp. 64–113.

Hammett, D. (1982 [originally 1930]) *The Maltese Falcon*, in D. Hammett *Dashiell Hammett: The Four Great Novels*. London: Picador.

Poe, E.A. (2009) *Edgar Allan Poe: The Complete Short Story Collection*. London: CreateSpace Publishing.

Sayers, D.L. (2003 [originally published in 1931]) *Five Red Herrings*. London: Hodder and Stoughton.

## Television

*Cops*, Season 20. USA: Fox.

*CSI: Crime Scene Investigates*, Season One (first aired 2000). USA: CBS.

*Deadwood*, 'Deadwood' (first aired 2004). USA: HBO.

## Websites

Hoax-slayer (www.hoax-slayer.com)

Snopes (www.snopes.com)

# Index

9/11 40–41, 88, 90, 143–144, 149–150
12 Angry Men (film) 263–265, 271–273, 292

A Clockwork Orange (film) 229, 233–239, 292
action film, rise and influence of 270
America's Most Wanted (television) 276
Anatomy of a Murder (film) 265–267, 271–273, 292
Auden, W.H. 177, 246–247

Bazin, André 217, 218, 220
Becker, Howard 107
blame 10, 42–43, 70–71, 118, 124, 145, 148, 190, 205, 291, **292–294**

cautionary tale 100, 101, **123–132**, 290–291, 294
  audience 125
  crime legends, comparison to 124, 133
  gender 123, 129–130, 131
  interest groups, role of 128
  media formats 124–125
  moral panics, comparison to 100, 123–124, 131, 294
  moral regulation 125
  perpetrator, depiction of 124, 126
  rape 126–127
  risk 125–126, 128–129
celebrity trials 261
centralisation of media ownership 18–19

Chandler, Raymond 241, 249–251
child sex abuse in the news **73–80**, 81, 294–295
  child-victim, construction of 76, 77, 82, 294–295
  historical changes in reporting 73–74
  moral panic 76, 113
  official statistics, compared to 75–76, 81
  Sarah's Law campaign 74
  stranger-perpetrated abuse 79, 80, 81
Christie, Agatha 244–248
citizen journalism 58, 289–290
Cohen, Stanley 104–108, 175–176, 236–237, 292
Collins, Wilkie 242
comic-books
  see 'Superman'
content analysis 50–51, **163–176**
  coding 172
  counting schedule 164
  gun crime, sample analysis 164–166
  limitations 163–164, 172–173, 174
  measurement 163, 172, 173
  qualitative analysis 166–167, 171
  quantitative analysis 164–166, 168–169, 170
  themes for analysis 170–171
  see 'inter-rater reliability'
  see 'murder'
  see 'rap music'

*Cops* (television) **275–288**, 295
  conventions 277–280, 284
  crime, depiction of 284–285
  police, depiction of 284, 285–287,
    295
  surveillance 280–284
  suspects/offenders, depiction of 284,
    285–286
courtroom, media representations of
  261–262
'crack mothers' in the news 186–188
crime categories, construction of
  *see* 'date rape'
  *see* 'knife crime'
  *see* 'mugging'
  *see* 'paedophilia'
  *see* 'stalking'
crime legends 99–100, 101, **133–142**,
  143, 289–290
  cars, as a setting/prop 138, 139, 141
  cautionary tales, comparison to 124,
    133, 141
  'corpse in the car' legend 135, 139
  criminal gangs, as a theme in 136,
    137, 138
  drugging, as a theme in 138, 141
  fears about modern life 136, 138
  hitchhiker, characterisation 135, 137,
    139, 141
  Internet as a method of circulation
    134, 138, 141
  malleability of 136, 141
  moral panics, comparison to 100, 133,
    141, 143
  organ theft legends 136, 139–140
  'razor blade in the apple' legend 135
  strangers, fear of 139–140, 141, 142
  uncertainty 134, 135, 139–140
  urban legend, sub-category of 134
  victim, representation of 137
  violence 138, 291–292
*Crimewatch UK* (television) 276
criminal law 264, 266–267, 271, 272
  *see* 'legal drama (genre)'

*CSI* (television) **252–257**, 291, 295, 296
  *see* '*CSI* Effect'
'*CSI* Effect' 2, 93–94, 253
cultural trauma 100–102, **143–152**, 294
  9/11 143–144, 149–150
  collective identity 143, 144, 145, 146,
    148–149, 294
  definition 144, 151
  institutional arena 145
  media, role in 145–146, 147, 151
  media as a spectator to 146–147
  moral panics, compared to 142
  social drama 144–145
  *see* 'Theo van Gogh, assassination of'

date rape 7, 109, 124
*Deadwood* (television) 215, 218–219,
  **221–227**, 292
detective fiction (genre) **241–258**, 295,
  296
  criminals, depiction of 247, 248, 251
  deductive vs inductive detection
    242–244
  detective, depiction of 245, 249, 250,
    256–257
  golden age 245–248, 254–257, 296
  hard-boiled fiction 249–252, 254–257
  police procedurals 253–254
  science 252, 254, 257
  *see* 'Chandler, Raymond'
  *see* 'Christie, Agatha'
  *see* 'Collins, Wilkie'
  *see* '*CSI*'
  see 'Hammett, Dashiell'
  *see* 'Poe, Edgar Allan'
  *see* 'Sherlock Holmes'
Dickens, Charles 230
discourse analysis 193–210
  critical discourse analysis 197,
    199–201, 205–207
  deductive vs inductive approach 198
  discourse, definition 193–195
  discursive practices 194
  experts 196

Foucauldian analysis 195–196,
198–199
limitations 208
prison films, analysis of 202–204
see 'domestic violence'
see 'gangs'
see 'paratactic vs hypotactic syntax
structure'
documentary programmes about crime
see '"real crime" television'
domestic violence 204–205
double trial structure 260–261
drug-facilitated sexual assault 126–127
drugs 186–188, 205–207, 284
Durkheimian approach to crime news
32–33, 48–49, 78, 82, 294–295

effects of crime news **84–96**, 157, 290
cause and effect 88–89, 93–94, 94–95,
157
criminal justice policy 85, 94
deceptive reporting 89
media effects debate across disciplines
85–86
memory 87, 95
modulator model of media effects 89
public attitudes to crime 90, 95
public attitudes to foreign policy 90,
95
see 'fear of crime, media influence on'

fear of crime, media influence on
91–92
see 'crime legends'
see 'moral panics'
female offenders 186–190
female victims of crime 123–132
see 'cautionary tale'
folk devils 105, 112, 114, 115–116, 119,
121, 126, 289, 293
Foucault, Michel 195–196, 213–214, 234,
282–283
framing
see 'news frames'

gangs 205–207
Garland, David 93, 273, 276–277
gatekeepers 33
gender 62–63, 66–73, 80, 81, 123,
129–130, 131, 186–188, 188–190,
204–205, 224–225, 292, 293–294
global crime news stories
see '9/11'
see 'Madeleine McCann'
Global Media Monitoring Project
62–63
Grisham, John 268, 269–270, 271
gun crime 164–166
guns 215

Hammett, Dashiell 249, 251
homicide
see 'murder'
'hoodie' 111

infanticide 188–190
infotainment 261
Internet, impact on crime stories 146
see 'citizen journalism'
see 'crime legends'
see 'online news'
inter-rater reliability 171–172
intimization 205
Islamic fundamentalism 41–42, 59
Israel–Arab conflict **49–53**, 60
Glasgow University Media Group
study of 50–52, 55
history of 49–50
Israeli vs Palestinians, depiction of
51–52
pro-Palestinian reporting 52
in US news 52–53

jury, 262
see '12 Angry Men'

Katz, Jack 16, 31–33, 294
knife crime 4–7

Larsson, Stieg (Millennium trilogy) 241, 244, 247–248
lawyers 267, 269, 271–272
see 'legal drama (genre)'
legal drama (genre) 259–274, 292–293, 295, 296
1990s legal drama 267–271, 295, 296
adversarial system 259–260
conventions 261–262, 267, 270–271
early legal drama 262
Golden Age 260, 263–267, 292, 296
legal thriller 270
pre-trial process 269–270
television legal dramas 268
see '12 Angry Men'
see 'Anatomy of a Murder'
see 'courtroom'
see 'criminal law'
see 'double trial structure'
see 'Grisham, John'
see 'jury'
see 'lawyers'
see 'The Pelican Brief'
see 'Philadelphia'
see 'The Rainmaker'
see 'witness coaching'
Leveson Inquiry 23, 289

Madeleine McCann 8–10
Manufacturing Consent 53–54
media effects
see 'effects of crime news'
medium specificity 27, 145, 172–173, 217, 253–254
modernity 213–214
moral panics 76, 99–101, 103–122, 123–124, 128, 131, 133, 292, 293, 294
amoral panics 116
British vs US approaches 111–112, 113
cautionary tales, comparison to 100, 123–124, 131, 294
child sex abuse 76, 113

crime legends, comparison to 100, 133
definition 105, 112–113, 119, 120
deviance amplification spiral 106–107, 120
drugs 114
interest groups, role of 113
'law and order' agenda 111
Mods and Rockers 104–108, 119–120, 121, 292
moral regulation 117–118, 121
news 99, 114–115
online news, impact on 115, 121
origin of the concept 104
problem convergence 113
relevance 120–121
risk 116
signification spiral 110–111
symbolic politics 114
see 'folk devils'
see 'mugging'
mugging 108–110, 122
murder 168–169

narrative analysis 177–192
counter-narratives 179, 183, 189
holistic vs categorical approach 181–183
limitations 191
Stephen Lawrence case, sample analysis 179–181
structuralism 178–179
see '"crack mothers", news reporting on'
see 'infanticide, news reporting on'
see 'Superman'
news beat system 21–22
news frames 42, 43–44, 78, 87, 114, 146, 151
news values 26–31, 36
Chibnall 29–30
Galtung and Ruge 27–29
Jewkes 30–31
novelty 30

sexual violence 66
terrorism 55
violence 26
newspapers
  crime-related campaigns 74
  crime reporting, proportion given to
    15–16
  financial constraints on 19–20, 36
  moral panics, role in 99, 114–115
  proprietarial bias 19
  *see* 'news beat system'
  *see* 'news values'
  *see* 'newsworthiness'
  *see* 'sources of crime news'
newsworthiness 26, 36
Nexis® 158–161
Northern Irish 'Troubles' **44–49**, 60
  broadcasting ban 47
  history of 44–45
  hunger strikes 48
  media censorship 46–48, 60
  Northern Ireland Information Service
    47–48
  Prevention of Terrorism Act 1974
    46–47
  reference upwards system 46

online news 34–35, 36–37, 115
over-lexicalisation 206

paedophilia 74, 79
paratactic vs hypotactic syntax structure
  200–201, 207
*The Pelican Brief* (film) 268–273
penal populism 202, 231
*Philadelphia* (film) 261
Poe, Edgar Allan 242
police 5, 22–23, 109–110, 148, 295
  historical changes in representation
    295
  news organisations, relationship to
    22–23
  primary definers of crime 5, 109–110,
    148

*see* '*Cops*'
*see* '"real crime" television'
press agencies 24–25
primary definers of crime 5, 22–23, 47,
  109–110, 148
prison film (genre) 202–204, 230–231,
  233–239, 295
propaganda model of news production
  53–54, 60
Propp, fairytale analysis 178
punishment
  functions of 232–233
  *see* 'prison film (genre)'

race and ethnicity 205–207
*The Rainmaker* (film) 268–269, 271–273
rap music 170–173
rape in the news **64–73**, 81, 292
  ethnicity 68–69
  feminist approaches 66–73, 81
  'hierarchy of victimisation' 68–71
  historical changes in reporting 64, 81
  ideal victim, construction of 70, 81
  sex 67–68, 81
  stranger-perpetrated assaults 64, 66–67
  verb voice in reporting 71–72
'real crime' television
  history of 276–277
  police, depiction of 286–287
  violence 291–292
  *see* '*America's Most Wanted*'
  *see* '*Cops*'
  *see* '*Crimewatch UK*'
  *see* 'stop and search'
rehabilitation 236–239
research question 157–158
revenge vs retribution 215, 220, 222–225
risk discourse 116, 118, 125–126,
  128–129

sampling 161–162
sampling frame 161
Sherlock Holmes 242, 243, 244
shrinkage 63–64, 73, 80, 169

signal crimes 74–75
'Soham Murders' 146
sources of crime news 21–25, 36, 54
spectacle 270
stalking 7
status degradation ceremony 293
stranger-perpetrated crime 64, 66–67, 79, 80, 135, 139, 256, 289, 291–292
Stephen Lawrence 179–181
stop and search 286
*Superman* (comic-book) 183–185
surveillance 280–284

tabloidisation 68, 261
terrorism 39–61, 88, 90–91, 143, 148, 151, 292
  in the news **39–61**, 88, 90–91, 143, 148, 151, 292
    crime 44, 48, 59, 292
    decontextualisation 49, 50–51, 60, 292
    fear of terrorism, impact on 88
    foreign policy, impact on 90–91
    initiator–retaliator relationship, construction of 43, 44–45, 59
    Marxist approaches 53–54, 60
    media censorship 46–48, 53, 60
    nation-state, depiction of 43, 45–46, 48, 56–57, 59
    'them' versus 'us' 42, 55–56, 148, 151
    'war on terror' 43–44, 60, 143
  mass media, symbiosis with 40–41, 59
  origin of the term 43
  *see* '9/11'
  *see* 'Islamic fundamentalism'
  *see* 'Israel–Arab conflict'
  *see* 'Northern Irish "Troubles"'
Theo van Gogh, assassination of 147–149, 151
third person effects 84, 85, 94
Todorov, T. 178–179, 189
trial by media 90
trials
  *see* 'legal drama (genre)'

victims of crime 62–63, 70, 76, 77, 80, 82, 293–295
  child-victim, construction of 76, 77, 82, 294–295
  global news reports 62–63
  idealised representation of 70, 80
  prominence in cautionary tales 123
  *see* 'female victims of crime'
violence 16, 26, 138, 214, 222–225, 233, 235, 237, 239 255, 266, **291–292**
  in *A Clockwork Orange* 233, 235, 236, 237, 239
  in crime fiction 214, 255
  in crime legends 138, 291–292
  in legal drama 266
  in 'real crime' television 291–292
  in Westerns 215, 222–225
  news value 26
  over-reporting in the news 16
  *see* 'child sex abuse in the news'
  *see* 'rape in the news'
  *see* 'stranger-perpetrated crime'
  *see* 'terrorism in the news'

Watergate 144
Western (genre) 215–220
witness coaching 266